HISTORY OF THE GARDEN

HISTORY OF THE GARDEN
Its Evolution & Design

Edited by Howard Loxton

Bounty
BOOKS

This book is not the work of a single author but of many authors, each of whom is credited at the end of sections which they wrote by their initials, and of contributions from some of the world's best garden photographers. A key to authors' names is given below.

Dr. Christopher Grey-Wilson, Sarah Guest and Carole Ottesen were consultants for the entire book.

M. B. Matthew Biggs
R. C. Rosalind Creasy
S. G. Sarah Guest
P. K. Peter King
M. L. Marilyn Light
H. L. Howard Loxton
M. M. Michael Maunder
J. M. John Medhurst
C. O. Carole Ottesen
A. P. Allen Paterson
G. P. Graham Pattison
A. S. Tony Schilling
D. S. David Squire
C. S. Charles Stirton

First published in Great Britain in 1996

This edition published 2005 by Bounty Books,
a division of Octopus Publishing Group Ltd
2–4 Heron Quays, London E14 4JP

Copyright © David Bateman Ltd 1996

ISBN 0 7537 1107 9
ISBN13 9780753711071

A CIP catalogue record for this book is available from the British Library

Printed and bound in China

Design: Errol McLeary
Picture research: Jan Croot
Copy editing and index: Margaret Forde
Production: Paul Bateman
Typesetting: Typocrafters, Auckland

CONTENTS

FOREWORD

Buried deep in this fascinating series of essays on garden history and practice is the observation, "Digging is both an art and a science." So also, of course, is gardening, and in this single wide-ranging volume the topic of gardening is approached from many directions: From the main directions of botany and horticulture. From history and garden history. From the direction of aesthetics and garden art, to research into plants that might cure diseases. From the chemistry of soils to how to survey and analyze your own garden site. Even how to dig!

And of course it has taken a distinguished group of horticulturists, scientists, artists, writers, photographers, historians, and editors to assemble such a set of essays. This is a major compendium of garden information, almost encyclopedic in its intention, but it is also, I am here to tell you, a good read for a rainy weekend.

Readers who are above all plant lovers will turn immediately to "Plants of the Garden." Those who like gardening's literary associations will read happily of Prince Genji's damming a stream in the garden of his palace to make a new lake in "The History of Gardens." In "Garden Design" those of us who are students of gardens as designed places will appreciate the observation that, "The form of a garden is hewn from the space it occupies." For city gardeners wondering what to advise their apartment-dwelling friends about making roof gardens (always a difficult subject!), a beautiful series of photographs of various rooftop places in "Gardens Worldwide" provides useful reference. And everyone concerned with conservation will be gratified to read of the existence of The Center of Plant Conservation in the "Botanical Gardens" chapter.

The very existence of this book for American readers is heartening. The broad range of this book echoes my belief that as Americans become more interested in domestic gardening, in perennials and shrubs and trees for their own gardens, in organic gardening methods, and in the history of horticulture and garden design, they will become truer and more passionate lovers of nature, and therefore conservationists. The rapid loss of species of plants and animals we are today experiencing is perhaps the most serious of our environmental crises. This loss of "biological diversity" is proceeding at such a fast pace that we now know 25–50 percent of all species on earth might be lost in the next 50 years. Unlike other major environmental issues we face (global warming, ozone depletion, toxic wastes), the extinction of species is irreversible — the very genetic material needed by both society and nature for the engineering of adaptation is fading away.

Sargon of Mesopotamia (born in 2334 B.C.) was a gardener, and such a good one that he was made king, as all readers of this book will learn. Modern Sargons are at work today in America creating wildflower gardens in their own backyards, teaching community volunteers to garden in new programs such as "Bronx Green-Up" in New York City, and collecting and studying the plants of Latin America just ahead of the bulldozers.

Here at the New York Botanical Garden (top right) we are part of an international network of research institutions and museums devoted to the study and appreciation of plants. At the professional level the study of plants is essentially linked to the creation of conservation programs, and public policy we hope will mitigate the crisis in biological diversity internationally. By the same token, the knowledge that will be gained by the educated amateur as he or she studies the spectrum of information about the plant world and gardening available in this book will make thousands of Americans better environmental thinkers. From my office here in the middle of this precious 250-acre collection of plants, I wish you a most pleasant and rewarding stroll through THE GARDEN.

Gregory Long
President
The New York Botanical Garden

INTRODUCTION

"mais il faut cultiver notre jardin."
Voltaire: *Candide*

" . . . but we must cultivate our garden" says Candide at the end of Voltaire's moral tale. Whether we interpret that to mean that human beings have made such a mess of everything else that they had better stick to growing vegetables or see it as a challenge to make a little beginning on turning the world into a better, happier and more just place we must decide for ourselves, but the making of gardens and the enjoyment of them must rank among the most satisfying of human pleasures.

To the city dweller, especially, a garden may seem a tiny piece of nature among the concrete but gardens are as much a human creation as a skyscraper. They have been created to satisfy a range of needs, from growing food to providing a symbol of power and control. For some they have been a way of demonstrating power and wealth, for others a place of escape from the pressures of their lives.

A large garden may encompass several smaller ones, often in different styles, including perhaps a *giardino segreto*, a "secret," or more properly perhaps, secluded garden, since, though it might be a place for secrets, it would not really be one itself. The secret garden seems to answer a need in the human imagination, offering a garden of surprise and delight, of magic, a setting for Beauty and the Beast, a place which novelists have used to link past and present or as a symbol of regeneration as well as a place of assignation.

For some it can still be a place to recall lost innocence and recapture the past — even the deserted tennis court behind the roses can seem to echo with forgotten calls. For many others it is a place of activity and fun.

The splashing of a fountain and the scent of herbs and flowers filling the night air can hardly fail to create an atmosphere of romance, so thrillingly caught in music such as Manuel de Falla's *Nights in the Gardens of Spain*. Sometimes the atmosphere is not just romance but erotic adventure. In the late Middle Ages and early Renaissance the garden provided an escape from the prying eyes that saw every moment of a life lived in court or in a large household. Here, in the shadow of an arbor, England's Henry VIII might make an assignation with Ann Bullen, as a surviving letter to her shows, and gardens became an obvious place for clandestine meetings. The evidence in fiction is considerable, from Boccaccio's bawdy *Decameron* to the stratagems of the last act of *The Marriage of Figaro* for which Mozart and da Ponte chose the concealing *allées* and arbors of a garden as an ideal location.

Gardens have often been chosen as settings for plays, operas and ballets, even when they are not specifically required by the story. In Anton Chekhov's *The Seagull* the garden highlights the contrast between country and cosmopolitan metropolitan life; a garden is often chosen for the "country" scene of *La Traviata*, and although there is no reason why tea should not be drunk indoors, a garden makes a perfect background for the town and country competition of Gwendolen and Cecily in Oscar Wilde's *The Importance of being Earnest*. Beatrice and Benedict in *Much Ado About Nothing*, Malvolio's gulling in *Twelfth Night*, and scenes in many other Shakespearean plays, suggest a garden setting. In *Richard II* when the Queen talks with a gardener Shakespeare uses the cultivation of a garden as a parallel for the care of the kingdom, while Michael Tippett's *The Knot Garden* matches the complexity of its patterns to the knotted relationships of the opera's characters.

Sometimes a lovely garden can hide something evil — in Igor Stravinsky's *The Firebird*, for instance, it is the evil magician Kolchak, and in Richard Wagner's *Parsifal*, Klingsor conjures magic gardens and beautiful women to seduce the knights from the quest for the Holy Grail until Parsifal makes them all disappear. As in life, however, a garden usually creates a sense of restfulness and tranquility, qualities captured in Frederick Delius's rhapsody *In a Summer Garden*, a tone poem inspired by his own garden at Grez.

Gardens not only appear in theatrical and musical works; they are often often chosen for their performance. The "green theater" became a regular feature in many Renaissance villa gardens and has frequently been imitated with hedges usually forming a backcloth and wings. The Boboli Gardens still house spectacular productions during the Florence *Maggio Musicale*, the fine gardens of Prague resound with music during the annual "Prague Spring," and all over the world orchestras and ensembles give outdoor concerts.

Painters and engravers have left us topographic records of the famous princely villas and great estates of their time. The house and park land is often shown as background in portraits of the owner or his family, but these are usually displays of wealth and status, with little emphasis on the garden. Although artists, in the Low Countries especially, developed a fine school of flower painting in formal arrangements, the flower garden did not really come into its own among the upper classes until the nineteenth century. Only then did gardens begin to appear as a subject in themselves.

Few writers, except, of course, those whose books have been about gardens, have felt the need to describe a garden setting fully, a mere suggestion being enough to fuel the reader's imagination. This book rarely attempts to describe gardens either, for it uses many photographs and other images to show them to the reader. While the painters, poets and composers present the garden through art the object here has been to show the art of the garden, an art which paints in three dimensions, using touch, scent and sound as well as form and color. Since to create and maintain a garden requires some understanding of botany and horticulture they too feature in these pages, and readers will find advice and information that will help them in their own gardening endeavors, but essentially this book sets out to celebrate the delightful diversity of gardens both in the past and in the present day.

H. L.

THE HISTORY OF GARDENS

EARLY GARDENS

Life began in a garden, at least according to the Hebrew poet who wrote the book of Genesis in the Judaic Bible. The biblical Garden of Eden is described as a garden which provides "every tree that is pleasant to the sight and good for food." There is no reference to flowers where Adam was set to "dress it and keep it," though "tree" might perhaps be understood to stand for all kinds of vegetation. Certainly, when Neolithic peoples, who had previously gathered food from the wild, began to develop cultivation it was food crops that they grew.

Above and opposite *An eighteenth-century carpet from Persia. A formalized representation of a garden was a popular design for Persian rugs long before the Arab conquest. One made for the ruler Chosroes I in the sixth century was said to cover 10,000 sq ft (900 sq m). It had a gold background worked to* look like yellow earth and colored gems to represent flowers and fruits; tree trunks and branches were worked in gold and silver thread and the leaves and plants in colored silks. The conquerors were so impressed by it that they cut it into pieces to divide between them!

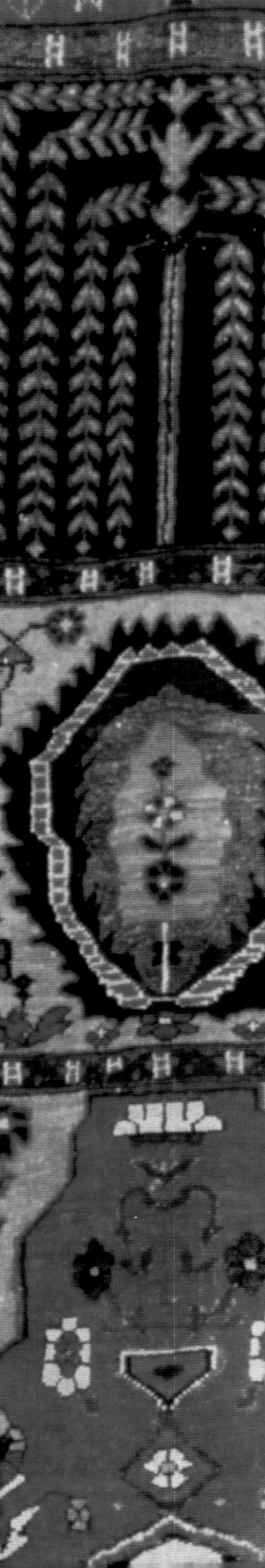

PARADISI IN SOLE.
Paradiſus Terreſtris.
or
A Garden of all ſorts of pleaſant flowers which our
Engliſh ayre will permitt to be nourſed vp:
with
A Kitchen garden of all manner of herbes, rootes, & fruites
for meate or ſauſe vſed with vs,
and
An Orchard of all ſorte of fruitbearing Trees
and Shrubbes fit for our Land
together
With the right ordering planting & preſeruing
of them and their vſes & vertues
Collected by John Parkinſon
Apothecary of London
1656

Qui veut parangonner l'artifice a Nature   Le pas de l'elephant parle pas du ciron,
Et nos fleurs à l'Eden, mais ſeroit il meſure.   Et de l'aigle le vol pareil du mouſcheron.

The Garden of Eden. The title page from John Parkinson's Paradisi in Sole Paradisus Terrestris, as published in 1656. Exotic plants shown and already introduced in Britain and Europe include tulips, pineapples and cacti.

The earliest known indications of agriculture date back only ten thousand years but an enjoyment of the beauty of flowers almost certainly goes back much further. The placing of bouquets of cornflowers, yarrow, grape hyacinths and other flowers around the corpse at a Neanderthal burial of sixty thousand years ago shows that they had an aesthetic and possibly ritual role. Early men and women must also have taken pleasure in the natural "gardens" that they found, enjoying a flower-dotted forest clearing or the shade of palms on a river's banks, for such places often became closely associated with the gods and spirits of the natural world. Later, when permanent settlements developed, the food crops growing near an individual habitation, the shade of a tree and the flowers and fruits of climbers such as vines around the portal would have formed a more personal garden. Shelter from the sun

and water for the plants and to cool the air were the ingredients of a miniature oasis — a microcosm of Eden.

Enclosure might be necessary to protect a settlement or keep animals from crops, and the elements of a garden could seem to be without plan, but the urge to specially create a pleasure garden apparently did not develop until larger settlements or palace complexes began to cut people off from easy access to such natural havens. Societies in direct touch with the natural world felt less need to make gardens, which also required a society able to spare the resources to create them and people with the time to enjoy them.

The first gardens

Cultivation and the beginning of civilization is generally agreed to have first occurred in the "fertile crescent" of the Middle East between the valleys of the rivers Tigris and Euphrates, the Mediterranean Sea and the Persian Gulf. It was probably here that the first gardens appeared. Excavations at Mohenjo-daro and other Indus valley sites from the third millennium B.C. suggest that they did not have gardens, although they may have grown plants in pots. China has a very ancient gardening tradition which goes back to 2000 B.C., and almost certainly much earlier, but firm evidence is lacking.

King Sargon (2334–2279 B.C.), ruler of Akkad in Mesopotamia, was said to have been the son of a priestess and abandoned, Moses-like. He floated in a reed basket on the Euphrates until found by a gardener who brought him up to be one too. An inscription recording the king's achievements declares "My service as a gardener was pleasing to the goddess Ishtar and I became king."

The Sumerians, who had become established in southern Mesopotamia by about 3000 B.C., are believed to have come from the forests of the mountains of Armenia to the north, where the Tigris and Euphrates have their sources. They built mounds or platforms which they planted with trees, supposedly to provide new homes for their forest gods. These mounds, layer by layer, eventually rose up to the sky to form stepped pyramids or *ziggurats*, man-made mountains. Excavations of the ziggurat at Ur revealed a complex irrigation and drainage system in the mud core. Mounds were a feature of early Chinese gardens and stepped pyramids appear in American cultures too — but not necessarily for the same reasons.

Apart from the venerated trees, whose shade would have been most welcome, we know little of what Sumerian or Assyrian gardens were like. A carving from the palace of Ashurbanipal shows him celebrating a victory by feasting with his queen beneath a vine. It shows several kinds of tree but no flowers, and this is as late as 660 B.C.

The earliest evidence of what an actual garden was like, appears in Egyptian tomb paintings which show garden scenes much older than Ashurbanipal's feast. These were

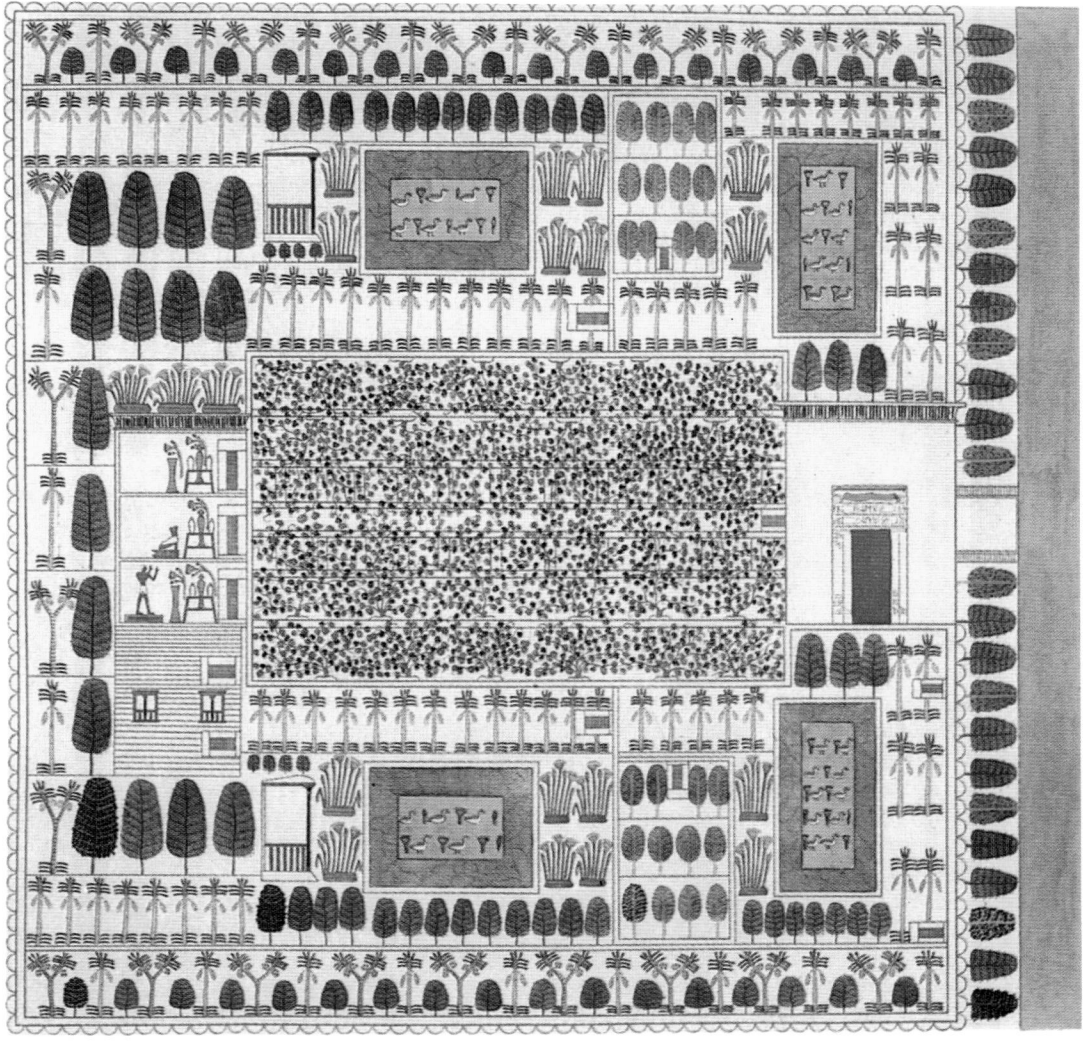

Ashurbanipal feasting in his garden to celebrate a victory c.660 B.C. The head of one of his vanquished enemies is hanging from a tree. From a carved relief in his palace at Nineveh.

The large garden of an Egyptian high official of about 1400 B.C. is shown on the walls of his tomb at Thebes. A large gateway (shown turned 90 degrees by the artist, for the convention is to show individual frontal images) leads from a tree-lined canal to a series of symmetrically arranged walled gardens (the walls shown in plan form as double red lines). In the center is a vineyard, with the owner's house to the left. There are date palms and doum palms (with forked trunks) and various other trees. Four ornamental ponds, with waterfowl and lilies have papyrus beds beside them and two have garden pavilions. (From Rossellini: Monumenti dell' Egitto e' della Nubia).

Below right A pond in the garden of Nebuman, a Theban scribe who kept the corn accounts at the temple of Amun, from his tomb. Fringed by papyrus, the pond is surrounded by date palms, pomegranates, figs and sycamore figs with grapevines beyond on the left.

not entirely pleasure gardens. Figs, dates and grapes and other useful crops are cultivated in them but they are clearly intended to be enjoyed. They show all the elements which most people now associate with a garden: an enclosed space, usually adjacent to a dwelling place, where selected plants are grown and tended, consciously ordered to create a pleasant ambience.

The mud walls around these Egyptian gardens absorbed some of the sun's heat, trees gave shade, and water further refreshed the air. In the simplest gardens there would be irrigation channels which divided up the ground, imposing a formal, geometrical pattern, but in larger gardens these became more elaborate pools which might have fish in them.

Temple gardens and royal gardens were the largest. For over two miles (3 km) the sphinx-lined avenue between the temples of Luxor and

The Hanging Gardens of Babylon may not have been quite like this artist's representation of them but their green terraces so impressed contemporaries that a thousand years later the Greeks and Romans still accounted them one of the Seven Wonders of the World.

Karnak was edged with trees and flowers. About 1540 B.C. Queen Hatshepsut sent an expedition to the land of Punt (usually identified as Somalia) to bring back incense trees. These were destined for the terraced gardens of the mortuary temple which she built for herself at the foot of the cliffs at Deir-el-Bahri outside Thebes. Egyptian gardeners had the skill to dig them up, preserving a ball of soil around the roots to prevent them from drying out during transit, to transport them over hundreds of miles and to plant them into large holes cut out of the rock of the hillside. All but one survived and flourished.

We know that the Egyptians grew culinary and medicinal herbs. Paintings and surviving wreaths and garlands found in mummy wrappings show that flowers included cornflowers, mallow, corn poppies and convolvulus and many others were introduced during the Graeco-Roman period.

Most famous of all the ancient gardens were those which became known as the Hanging Gardens of Babylon, ranked among the Seven

Wonders of the World. Excavations early in the twentieth century revealed a stone-built, vaulted structure which appeared to confirm the essential points of the descriptions given by the Greek historians Strabo and Diodorus Siculus, who both wrote in the first century A.D.

These hanging gardens were said to have been built by Nebuchadnezzar (although they date from earlier than his time) to please a Persian wife who was homesick for her native hills — or according to Diodorus by Cyrus to please a Persian courtesan. One hundred feet (30 m) square and 75 ft (22.5 m) high, level with the city walls, they consisted of vaults built upon vaults in tiers with the main garden on the top where a roof of stone beams 16 ft (5 m) long was covered with a layer of reeds set in tar. Over this were two courses of brick, above them a layer of lead to make it waterproof, and then a depth of topsoil sufficient to allow large trees to root which was irrigated by a system of conduits. Diodorus says water was pumped up, by means that could not be seen. Strabo reported that slaves drew water direct from the Euphrates by wheels of buckets or Archimedean screws — but the archaeologists found a well with three shafts to carry buckets up and down.

Terraced gardens were a feature of other palaces and there were extensive parks for hunting game, including lions which were captured in the wild and released for royal sport. An Assyrian king, another Sargon, ruling in the eighth century B.C., created a park outside Nineveh "like the Amanus mountains, where all flowers from the Hittite land and herbs from the hill are planted together" and his son Sennacherib made great claims for the gardens he created, including one carved from rock around a temple, cut with water channels and holes for planting trees as at Queen Hatshepsut's temple in Egypt.

The Israelites, whose ancestors had come from Ur and who had lived in Egypt and been enslaved in Babylon, also made gardens. The historian Josephus describes gardens where Solomon used to ride and the *Song of Songs* uses a garden as a metaphor.

When the Persians conquered Assyria, Babylon and Egypt they developed and adapted the garden styles they found: the parks which they called *pairidaeza* (paradise), the terraces and the private enclosures of the Egyptians. The Persian gardens made a great impression upon the Greeks and later re-established a pattern for gardens throughout the Arab world.

Gardens of the Greeks and Romans

The Greeks of archaic times were shepherds and farmers, rarely flower gardeners. In spring, Greek mountainsides were brightly decked with flowers and the garlands in evidence at celebrations and religious festivals were collected from the countryside or, later, grown by professional garland suppliers and perfumers.

Below The peristyle of a house in Pompeii.

Greek gardens were practical places, with fruit trees and vines. It is possible that Minoan palaces had gardens. Their terraces offered natural sites and close links with Egypt would have made Cretans aware of Egyptian gardens, but it was not until the conquests of Alexander the Great took Greeks to Persia, Egypt and beyond that they saw and adopted the idea of the pleasure garden. The garden of Alcinous described in Homer's *Odyssey* is practical rather than ornamental. There are fountains and ponds for irrigation purposes, vegetables, fruit trees and useful herbs — but no flowers are mentioned.

Like their eastern neighbors, the Greeks attached significance to trees; young men in both Greece and Persia were made to plant trees — Odysseus identifies himself on his return from his travels after the Trojan War by pointing out the 13 pear, 10 apple and 40 fig trees which had been given to him when a child — and a particular grove of trees was often considered sacred. Some such sacred spots and their temples became the center of a complex of gymnasia, baths and other social buildings. Elsewhere, in the rapidly developing cities of fifth-century Greece, trees were planted to give shade in public places where people of leisure met to gossip and debate and teachers disputed with their students. A short distance outside Athens there was a grove which was dedicated to an obscure hero called Academus, giving us the word academy for a school, a place where a philosopher came to converse with his pupils. Later, large Roman and Renaissance gardens often included a cool and shady Academy or sacred grove as a fashionable feature in the antique manner.

Greek city homes were usually closely set within the walls and there was little space for a garden, except in the central court, where flowers might be grown in pots. For the festival of Adonis every year, Greek women would plant the seeds of lettuce, fennel and other fast-growing plants. The briefness of their maturing and rapid withering symbolized the short life of Aphrodite's lover, killed in a boar hunt.

When Alexander's conquests took Greek armies into Persia and Egypt they were amazed at the richness of the gardens. In the Greek colonies, gardens were created which became increasingly extravagant, especially at Alexandria, where one quarter of the city consisted of hanging terraces and flower-filled patios complete with statues, fountains and hydraulic toys which animated figures or sprayed water on the unsuspecting as their passing set off hidden mechanisms.

Alexander had been taught by Aristotle and from all parts of his empire the king had information and specimens sent back to the philosopher in Athens. Here, at Aristotle's Lyceum, the first known botanical garden was established and another pupil, Theophrastus, who later took over the Lyceum, began the first classification of plants. From the books on gardening that Theophrastus wrote we know that, by the third century B.C., the gardens of Athens included roses, lilies, violets, anemones and poppies, all plants which grow wild in the region.

Roman gardens were modeled at first on the Greek design. Excavations at Pompeii and Herculaneum, in an area which had earlier been a Greek colony, uncovered houses much like those of Greece, built around small peristyle courtyards where a small plot, tubs or an earth-filled trough like a deep window box were planted for the pleasure of the inhabitants. Wall paintings of flowers and garden scenes were used to give the illusion of greater garden space. When there was no other space rooftops were utilized as gardens and pots placed on window ledges of apartment blocks. Larger houses might have a series of courtyards and the Romans also began to develop gardens as an extension of their homes.

At their country villas the wealthy Romans were able to make elaborate gardens. They echoed the concept of the Greek gardens which had developed from the sacred groves, but might feature fish ponds and lakes, aviaries, hillside terraces, a hippodrome for exercise on horseback, natural-looking glades and stylized formal beds and plantings. Even in the heart of Rome the wealthy, including the emperors, created large pleasure gardens. After the fire in A.D. 64, Nero demolished houses to create a private pleasure park of 125 acres (50 ha) for a new palace — the Golden House. Its woodlands were stocked with game and some idea of its scale can be gained from its fish pond which later became the site of the Colosseum.

With the decline of Roman power the great pleasure gardens disappeared from Europe but gardens must have survived to provide herbs and vegetables for the kitchen and, with the development of monastic life, the peristyle garden which the Romans had adopted from the Greeks, was continued in the cloisters of the new foundations.

The villas of Pliny the Younger

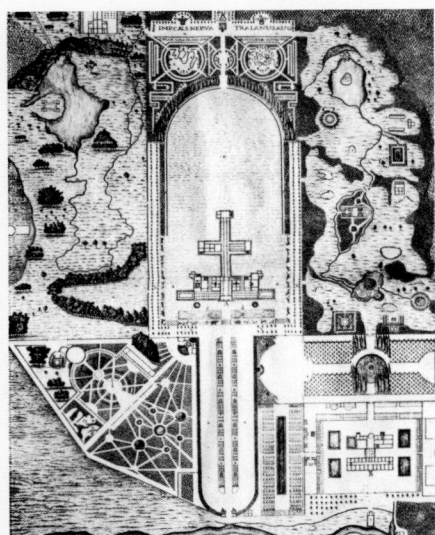

Hypothetical plans of Pliny's villas as envisaged by Robert Castell and drawn by T. Wilson in The Villas of the Ancients Illustrated. **Above** in Tuscany; **below** Laurentium by the sea.

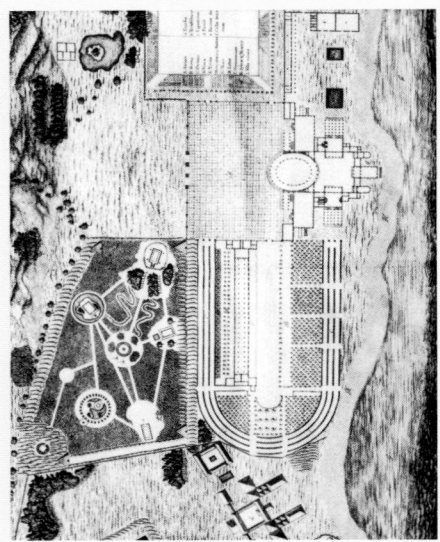

The Younger Pliny, so called to distinguish him from his uncle who wrote a *Natural History*, had two country villas. One was by the sea at Laurentium, near Ostia, 17 miles (27 km) from Rome. Farm land and buildings were to landward, the house by the sea, though sheltered from storms. The summer dining room overlooked the sea, a winter dining room looked out onto a garden edged with box where it was sheltered by the buildings, or with rosemary where exposure to sea wind and salt spray made box wither. There were mulberry and fig trees, a flower terrace with scented violets, and a vine arbor shading an exercise area around the garden. A pillared walk offered shade in summer and shelter in winter. A small pavilion provided a retreat from the household, especially from the noise of merrymaking when they celebrated the winter Saturnalia.

His Tuscan estate was a much grander place with extensive pleasure gardens. Set on a gradual, almost imperceptible slope, it commanded fine views all around and was cooled by gentle breezes on even the calmest days. The main facade, with its fine portico, looked south to the sun over a terrace embellished with figures and bounded by a box hedge. Animals cut in box decorated a slope down to the lawn of *Acanthus* (though it cannot have been the plant we now give that name), surrounded by a walk again enclosed by clipped evergreens. Next, was the *gestatio*, an area for exercise, ornamented with many more topiary figures and trimmed shrubs, the whole shut in by a wall of layered box. Beyond, lay a meadow, which Pliny said "owes as many beauties to nature as . . . within does to art, then fields interspersed with thickets."

At one end of the portico he describes a grand dining room opening onto the terrace and with a view of meadows, woods and garden and, almost opposite the center of the portico, four plane trees surrounding a fountain that spilled into a marble basin. Then to the front:

"a very spacious hippodrome, entirely open in the middle, by which means the eye, upon your first entrance, takes in its whole extent . . . It is encompassed on every side with plane trees . . . ivy twining round the trunk and branches, spreads from tree to tree and connects them . . . Between each plane tree and the next are planted box trees and behind these bay trees . . . This plantation . . . bends at the further end into a semi-circle which, being set round and sheltered with cypress trees, varies the prospect and casts a deeper gloom; while the inward circular walks (for there are several), enjoying an open exposure, are perfumed with roses and correct, by a very pleasing contrast, the coolness of the shade with the warmth of the sun.

"Having passed through these winding alleys, you enter a straight walk, which breaks out into a variety of others, divided by box hedges. In one place you have a little meadow, in another the box is cut into a thousand different forms: sometimes into letters expressing the name of the master; sometimes that of the artificer; whilst here and there little obelisks rise, intermixed alternately with fruit trees: when, on a sudden, in the midst of this elegant regularity, you are surprised with an imitation of the negligent beauties of rural nature: in the centre of which lies a spot surrounded with a knot of dwarf plane trees.

"Beyond these is a walk planted with the smooth and twining Acanthus, where the trees are also cut into a variety of names and shapes. At the upper end is an alcove of white marble, shaded by vines, supported by four small Carystian pillars. From this bench the water, gushing through several little pipes, as if it were pressed out by the weight of the persons who repose themselves upon it, falls into a stone cistern underneath, from whence it is received into a fine polished marble basin, so artfully contrived that it is always full without ever overflowing. When I sup here this basin serves as a table, the larger sort of dishes being placed around the margin, while the smaller ones swim about in the form of little vessels and waterfowl."

Linked to this was a fountain with a high jet and opposite was a marble summer house with a pleasant green view. There were many other marble seats on which to rest from walking, each with a little fountain, and throughout the hippodrome "small rills run murmuring along."

The emphasis is on shade and cooling fountains and topiary, which Pliny says was the invention of one Gaius Matius, a friend of the Emperor Augustus. By Pliny's time it had become very elaborate with whole hunting scenes and naval battles clipped out of the foliage. Note that the slave who was *toparius* (the ornamental gardener; early use of this word does not seem to have been connected with tree shaping) was allowed to record his own name as well as that of his master. Another specialist, the *aquarius*, was in charge of all the fountains. Pliny had 500 slaves working at his house in Rome and on his country estates in Tuscany.

El Patio de los Naranjos, *Cordoba, is divided into three plots, each with a central fountain and palm trees at the corners of the design. Irrigation channels run from tree to tree.*

Below *A Persian carpet, woven about 1700, the pattern depicts a garden of* chahar bagh *type: the four rivers of paradise are clearly seen. In the center a pavilion is represented by its floral canopy and surrounding platform. Alternate flower panels include chenar trees (most noticeable against the lighter center panels). Around the inner border stand evergreen cypress trees, symbols of eternity.*

ISLAMIC GARDENS

When Arab armies carried Islam east and west from the seventh century A.D. they encountered the gardens of Persia, which centuries before had themselves borrowed from the enclosed Egyptian garden style to produce a simple form of shallow crossing water channels. These were usually supplied from underground *quanats,* huge subterranean tunnels, which brought water from the mountains many miles away. The rectangular enclosure of larger gardens might have a central pool, sometimes with a pavilion set over it and tree-lined canals instead of shallow channels, while a further enclosed area of park might lie beyond the garden wall. On a hillside the slope would probably be terraced but the basic layout remained the same. Against the formal geometry of these shapes flowers flourished freely, those with rich scents being much favored. Among them were narcissi, tulips, lilac, jasmine, orange trees — which had been introduced from China in exchange for grapes and horses as early as the second century B.C. — and, last and longest blooming, roses, probably including the Chinese perpetually-flowering form as well as indigenous Persian types.

The Arabs found the Persian gardens very similar to the paradise which was promised to the faithful in the Koran, a state of blessedness conceived as an ideal garden with cool pavilions and fountains of running water with fruit and flowers and trees with spreading shade where birdsong and black-eyed houris completed the beauty of the scene. The classic arrangement, the *chahar bagh* (four gardens), itself matched the Koranic descriptions. In the centuries that followed, this Persian garden became the basic form for Islamic gardens from Spain to India.

Westward, the Moors brought the Persian garden to Andalusia where, in the eighth century, the conquerors began a garden at Cordoba, modeled on one in Damascus, the first of 50,000 gardens in the city. Today they are gone, although the Spanish courtyard houses still echo the enclosed Islamic garden, and beside Cordoba's Mosque (now the Cathedral) the *Patio de los Naranjos* (Court of the Oranges) still survives, its rows of orange trees continuing the rows of columns inside the mosque as they did when it was laid out in A.D. 976.

In Seville the Alcázar have been changed many times over the centuries but excavations have revealed gardens of the *chahar bagh* type, one of which had beds sunk far below the surrounding level. At Granada, too, excavation in the famous *Patio de la Acequia* in the Generalife has shown that the flower beds were formerly below the level of the paths (looking down on them made the garden like one of the carpets which in turn represented gardens). The Generalife and the Alhambra, lower down the hill at Granada still preserve much of the feel of the original Moorish gardens, although many of the details have been changed.

The Saracen conquest of Sicily in the ninth century brought Persian-style gardens to that island and when the Normans in turn took over the island, despite destroying what was already there, they too built gardens, including cloister gardens, in a similar style.

To the east the Persian and Turkish garden was taken by Mogul conquerors to northern India where garden art reached a peak in the sixteenth century.

The Alhambra and the Generalife

The Alhambra — *Al Qual'a al-Hambra*, the Red Castle, is the proper Arabic name — was built as a fortress on the hill above Granada. The red walls of the original Alcazaba, raised in the eleventh century, formed the defenses for the palace which Ibn Ahmar created when he made this the capital of his kingdom in the early thirteenth century. To feed its pools and fountains with running water he diverted the river Darro for nearly five miles.

There have been many changes made by his successors since, especially by Mohammed V; by Ferdinand and Isabella when they drove out the Moors; and by Emperor Charles V who demolished whole wings to build his Renaissance palace. However, its deeply shadowed halls, opening onto patios and gardens, still capture the essence of the Moorish style, and the gentle sound of fountains and cooling channels of water continue to refresh the senses.

The Generalife (meaning "garden of the architect"), set higher up the hill, was the summer garden and palace of the sultans. Those parts of comparatively recent date still exploit the hillside to use water to the full. It even flows down the balustrades of a staircase and beneath the feet as it descends from one level to another.

Right The Patio de la Riadh *is typically Moorish, although the arching water jets over the central canal are a later addition. The lotus-flower-shaped basins at each end and where the transverse path divides the canal are a reminder of the eastern sources for the style. Excavations after a fire in 1958 revealed that here too the original planting was well below the present level so that blossoms would probably have been level with the paths. Bases of columns at the central crossing suggest that there was originally a canopy or a pavilion there.*

Above *The* Patio de Daraxa, (or Patio de Lindaraja, *Court of the Sultana's Boudoir) can be entered from the Patio de los Leones. Cypress and orange trees are typical Moorish planting but the box edging is a later addition. The central fountain was moved here from another court but is typically Arab. The outer basin, combining square and circle forms to provide eight projections (like the designs repeated in the Persian carpet on page 19), eight being important to Moslems as one more than the seven spheres or the seven stories of Hell.*

The fountain which gives its name to the Patio de los Leones, Court of the Lions, forms the center of a chahar bagh. The narrow water channels flowing from it divide the garden into four as they lead outward to low fountain basins beneath the delicate arcades. To recreate the original scene the areas between the stone channels and the paving below the arcades which now present a level gravel surface must be imagined as a meter lower and planted with orange trees and flowers. The lions are probably eleventh century, 300 years older than their surroundings.

MEDIEVAL EUROPEAN GARDENS

"Hoe your ground, set out cabbages, convey water to the conduits," was the injunction of St. Jerome (A.D. 342–420) to a young man about to adopt his hermit style of life. Earlier, St. Antony had also kept a garden and when he founded the first Christian monastery, in Egypt in A.D. 305, gardening was an important feature of monastic life. The monastic movement spread to Europe and when St. Benedict, who wrote the first monastic Rule, became a monk at Subiaco in Italy, he is said to have planted the rose garden which still survives today. Later, he founded the monastery at Monte Cassino within the remains of a Roman villa. Many early monasteries made use of such locations or were built along similar lines and the influence of the peristyle of Roman houses on later monastic cloisters is obvious.

It used to be generally considered that these cloisters, where monks came to meditate and study, would have been planted as ornamental gardens. It now seems more likely that, in the early Middle Ages at least, this was only greensward with such flowers as might grow in it uncultivated and perhaps a tree. The "little cloister," the yard around which the infirmary and its chapel were grouped, was often used for growing medicinal herbs and sometimes the sacristan had his own plot for growing flowers for the altar. Other spaces within the monastic complex might be utilized for planting, and both vegetable and pleasure gardens, sometimes edged with their own cloister-like walks, might be established on the outer land of the monastery.

Members of the Carthusian order, who lived a solitary life, each had their own cell set in a separate garden and enclosed by a high wall, although grouped around a central cloister. These monks must have tended their own plots but elsewhere servants may have been responsible for the manual labor. The low number assigned to the garden — for instance only three, plus five in the vineyard out of a total of sixty servants employed in Evesham in the twelfth century — may indicate the comparatively low priority which gardens had even by this date.

Plan of an ideal monastery drawn about 825 by the Benedictines at St. Gall. At the center is the cloister garth, divided into four plots with a holy water basin in the center and planted with grass and flowers. The school, hospital and guest house also have cloisters but there is no indication whether they were to be planted or with what. There is a physic garden (top left) next to the doctor's quarters, for raising medicinal and culinary herbs, including lilies and roses, and a larger garden (top right) marked out into 18 parallel beds for vegetables. To its left is the monks' cemetery, the graves set between fruit and blossom trees including apple, pear, plum, peach, fig, quince, hazel, almond, mulberry, walnut and chestnut. At both ends of the church is a semicircle labeled "Paradise" — a link with the gardens of the east — which was an enclosed area for meditation and prayer. Although a paradise at the altar end was common to many churches, it is unusual to have one at the west end too.

At the monastery of St. Gall, in Switzerland, a ninth-century plan for an ideal monastery has been preserved which shows how important horticulture was. As monasteries grew with the benefactions of the faithful they often gained extra land for vineyards and field crops. Most had a fish pond, which might also be ornamental and sometimes, as at Clairvaux and later at St. Germain-des-Pres, there was a garden beyond the abbey buildings.

The library at the monastery of St. Gall preserves a long poem by Abbot Walafrid Strabo (809-49) of Reichenau Abbey, not far distant on an island in Lake Constance: his *Liber de cultura hortorum* (usually known as *Hortulus*, the little garden). It consists mainly of details of the plants he grows and their qualities but first there is some guidance about the making of a garden and begins:

Though a life of retreat offers various
    joys,
None, I think, will compare with the
    time one employs
In the study of herbs, or in striving to
    gain
Some practical knowledge of nature's
    domain.
Get a garden! What kind you may get
    matters not.

Right *A "paradise garden" painted c. 1410 by the Master of the Upper Rhineland. Lily of the valley, periwinkle, peony, hollyhock, violet, rose, strawberry, cowslip, wallflower, daisy, borage, iris and a cherry tree are among the plants that can be identified. The demon in this paradise has presumably been rendered harmless and the dragon rolls over to have its belly tickled. In early Christian times growing flowers was discouraged — roses and lilies especially were associated with pagan cults. By the seventh century attitudes changed. Flowers were grown in monasteries to deck the church and on feast days monks might wear wreaths of blossoms. The small enclosed garden, the hortus conclusus, was often associated with the Virgin Mary and known sometimes as a "Mary garden." The Madonna lily and the rosebud became a symbol of purity. Late medieval paintings often show Madonna and Child in a garden, surrounded by symbols which would be understood by contemporaries, such as the fountain, source of the rivers of the Garden of Eden, the four streams representing the Gospels, daisies innocence, dandelions bitterness and grief (and by implication the Passion of Christ), and plantain, the path taking the faithful to Christ.*

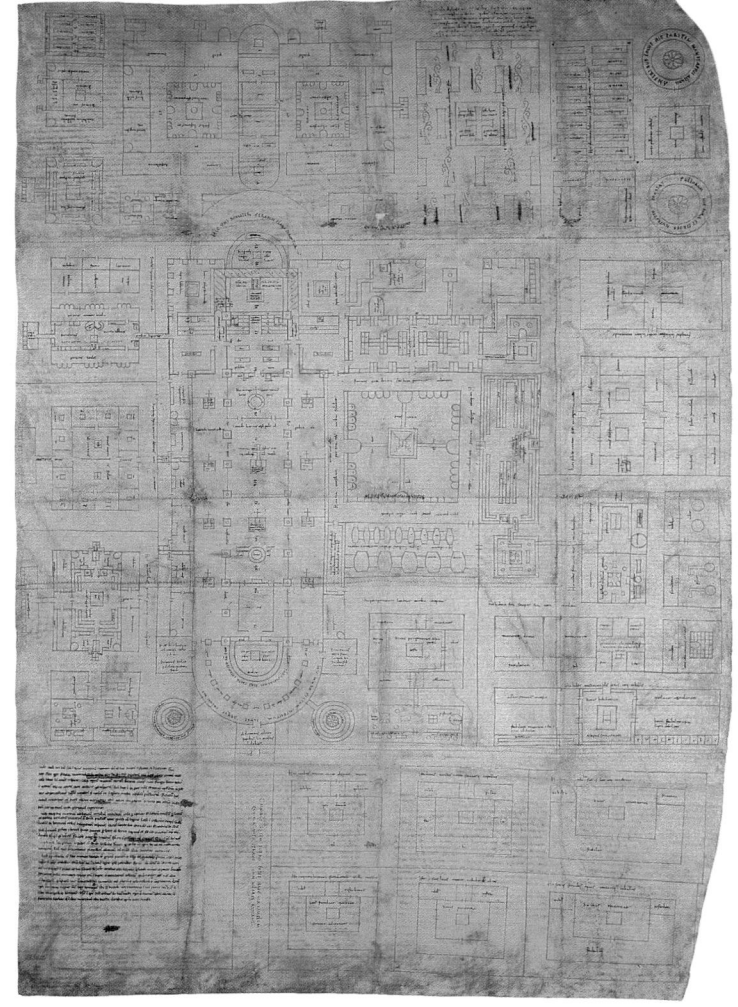

The cloister at Arles has the quadripartite division of the Islamic garden but its central planting is anachronistic. Probably most cloisters were grass with natural wild flowers occurring in it, though a tree, well or fountain may have been a feature in some cases.

A little earlier than the St. Gall plan, the Emperor Charlemagne issued regulations for the administration of towns which included a list of 89 plants to be grown. As well as fruit- and nut-bearing trees and 73 varieties of medicinal and culinary herbs, it includes lilies and roses. Most medieval herbals give us little real information about current horticulture for, like the bestiaries, they are based upon classical originals and the monkish authors often had no personal knowledge of the plants that they described. More reliable evidence is often to be found in plants that have survived on monastic sites, plants such as birthwort, which nuns gave to women to relieve labor pains, alexanders, which grows on several monastic sites, and wild peony which was valued as an herb for depression, jaundice and a number of other conditions. By the fourteenth century, when the first gardening book in English appeared, John Gardener's *The Feate of Gardening*, daffodil, daisy, catmint, cowslip, primrose, violet, periwinkle, gentian, foxglove, hollyhock, iris, lily, lavender, water lily and red and white roses are all listed, while earlier Latin and French sources also mention heliotrope, peony, gillyflower (probably the clove pink, although the name was used for several flowers) and marigold (*Calendula*).

The castles of the nobility were, like the monasteries, complete communities. Main produce would be grown outside the castle walls but within the space would be found for a small garden, probably near the castle well or with one of its own, where physic and culinary herbs would be cultivated under the charge of the mistress or chatelaine of the castle. It would be a place of refuge from the bustle of the bailey, and a place with greater privacy than

A small private garden from a
manuscript c.1465 of Livre du Cuer
d'Amours. *Both lawn and seats are
turf, not the usual medieval "flowery
mead." Vines and roses grow on the
trellis and tunnel; other plants
include carnations, pinks, columbine,
mallow, stocks and rosemary.*

was possible in the great hall or the solarium.
Larger castles, especially those which doubled
as palaces and were not planned entirely for
defense, would have been, like monasteries, a
collection of buildings within the ramparts —
almost a small town — and there would have
been space for gardens on the ground between
them.

Knowledge of Moorish Spain and diplomatic
contacts, such as that of the Court of Charlemagne with Caliph Harun al-Rashid in Bagh-
dad, gave some awareness of eastern gardening
tradition. With the conquest of Sicily by the
Normans and the journeying of crusading
knights to lands where they saw Arab gardens,
Europeans began to rediscover the delights of
the pleasure garden. They took home both
ideas and plants from their travels, including
flowers new to most of Europe, introducing
them to the gardens of palaces and chateaus
and the fortified manor houses which developed
with more settled times. Emperor Frederick II
spent much of his youth in Sicily and his
familiarity with Arab styles influenced gardens
in Apulia and Naples as early as the thirteenth
century. A French crusader, returning home in
1270, introduced hydraulic automata and water
tricks to his garden at Hesdin in Picardy which
made it famous throughout France.

There is no visual or documentary evidence
to tell us exactly what a castle garden of the
early Middle Ages would have been like. In the
twelfth century the troubadours of the cult of
courtly love began to use the garden as a setting
for their romances and later the miniature

painters of the fourteenth century provided
garden scenes. By then there were many garden
features which seem to have been common, but
we do not know when they came into use in
western Europe.

As times became more settled orchards (*hort-
yard*, the word did not then imply only fruit
trees) and pleasure gardens were established
outside the main castle, though often still
behind protective battlements. Even in more
settled times gardens would still be walled to
give privacy, keep out animals and provide
shelter for plants. The orchard or "pleasaunce"
offered shade beneath the trees and the turf
beneath the grass would have been patterned
with wild flowers in season.

Peasants would have had little time to enjoy
a garden and any plants they grew are likely to
have been strictly practical — after all, there
were wild flowers for the picking when in
season. As people moved into towns the pot
herb on the windowsill would have been
common but the surrounding countryside was
usually still within easy reach. Even within the
cities there was often space to grow food crops
and keep animals. Larger cities provided public
gardens for the recreation of their citizens —
meadows planted with trees as at Saint-
Germain-des-Prés in Paris, the Prater in Vienna
and the Prado in Madrid, while London, as
described by William FitzStephen in the twelfth
century, had tree-shaded gardens around
several of the city wells. Towns which developed
on rocky eminences or which clustered at the
foot of castle walls might lack soil or space to

*The rose bush in the cloister of the
Dom at Hildesheim, in Lower
Saxony, on which it is said, in 815,
Ludwig, son of the Emperor
Charlemagne, hung relics of the
Virgin while he went off hunting. On
his return they could not be removed
so he endowed a new church to house
them. There is some dispute as to
whether this rose is quite so old, but
it does go back centuries and, when
bombs destroyed much of the Dom in
World War II it burst into flower
soon after the raid.*

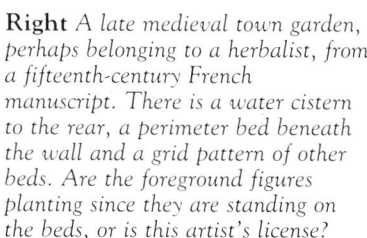

The lover plucks the rose. A woodcut from an early printed version of the Roman de la Rose *shows a small garden fenced with wattle.*

A maze from Thomas Hill's The Profitable Arte of Gardening, *1586.*

create gardens but many of their inhabitants, as workers or landowners, would be involved in agriculture in surrounding fields or the valley below.

London houses were built with gardens until late in the Middle Ages when a few sets of "chambers," four- or five-story apartment blocks, were built, usually for sale, not rent. In some European cities apartment dwelling was much more usual, but if there were no individual gardens in the town there were often garden plots on the outskirts, for the idea of an "allotment" of land worked on the edge of town goes back at least to the Middle Ages.

The nobility and richer merchants who had land available with city houses began to create pleasure gardens as well as kitchen gardens (from which they often sold surplus produce). The pleasure gardens of the nobility became a setting for the chivalric cult of courtly love, a romantic idealization in which a lover (not her husband) dedicated himself to his chosen lady and sought to serve her and defend her honor. Supposedly a pure love with no expectation of physical consummation, it was celebrated, and ridiculed, in medieval poems such as the *Roman de la Rose*, the assignations of which are often set in gardens — frequently a secret garden, a *hortus conclusus*, a garden within a garden, a "Mary" garden because of the association with the Virgin and in part inspired by the *Song of Solomon*.

Late in the Middle Ages the building of mounts or artificial hills returned to the garden. Sometimes a simple *herbier*, a bank of grass against a wall (from which the word arbor eventually came), sometimes free-standing and

perhaps with the core hollow and used for storage. They may have been intended simply to provide a slope for exposing herbs to the sun or shelter for plants beyond them but it is often suggested that they were intended to provide a vantage point, while the name is also used of a raised walk at the end of a garden. Later they became the location for gazebos or outdoor banqueting houses.

Fish ponds, well stocked to supply the kitchen, were a feature of monastic, palace and castle grounds, often becoming decorative as well as useful, although a moat might also perform this function. Another occasional feature was a maze. Most famous perhaps was the labyrinth designed for Henry II at his Palace of Woodstock. Here in an enclosed park which had formerly been stocked with exotic beasts such as lions, lynxes and camels from the royal menagerie, a maze was constructed. There the king could meet his mistress, "the fair Rosamund." This may have been a building, not a garden feature, and it was destroyed by the queen, Eleanor of Aquitaine, when she penetrated its mysteries. However, the idea of a garden labyrinth gained popularity. Hedge mazes became a common feature in sixteenth- and seventeenth-century Europe and new ones are still being made today.

The idea of the labyrinth goes far back into antiquity to the legend of the minotaur and beyond. A maze design was sometimes marked on the pavement of churches, or cut in the turf outside. Penitents could follow its configurations on their knees, a symbolic journey made by those who could not make the pilgrimage to Jerusalem, especially at the time of the Crusades.

GARDENS OF THE EAST

China

The garden tradition of China is probably the oldest in the world. The essential elements of Taoist and Buddhist philosophy — oneness with and the contemplation of nature — are always reflected in Chinese gardening styles. Garden and house are conceived as separate entities. The house, usually a succession of courtyards each with their role, reflects the Confucian principles of order in human life, while the garden represents the natural world, although it will have its own buildings and pavilions, carefully placed to enhance the contemplation of a particular view.

At first, gardens were no more than nature enclosed, and even when they were carefully planned and meticulously constructed they eschewed the straight lines and formalism which developed in the western world. They could, however, be very contrived and huge in their scale. Marco Polo described how, near the winter palace of the Great Khan at what is now Beijing, Kublai Khan had ordered the creation of a huge artificial mount, a hundred paces high and a mile around. It was densely planted with evergreen trees, to which new specimens were often added. Whenever the emperor heard of a particularly interesting specimen he had it uprooted and brought there by elephant. The pits from which the soil was excavated for the mount were turned into lakes fed by a stream and stocked with fish. Paths were raised high above the ground so that they were

always clear of mud and puddles did not settle on them. The raising of great mounds was already a thousand-year-old custom in China; the Han Emperors had raised them as part of a traditional reverence for mountains.

Gardens formed a retreat from the worldliness of life and even the most elaborately created were usually intended for private contemplation and not for show, although around 2000 B.C. sumptuous show gardens were reported to have been made for the Emperor Chou, which were sometimes seen as an example of excess. Under some rulers they were open to the public. However, nothing is really known about these gardens from the days long before Confucius and Tao.

By the end of the third century B.C. the Emperor Qin Shi Huang was already forming a collection of rare animals and plants. It became a microcosm of the world he ruled, and this formed another element of the Chinese garden concept. The garden could become both a retreat from the world and a symbolic representation of the countryside, combining the essential elements of water, rocks and trees. To this was added another element, the symbolism of the islands of the *hsien*, the immortals. These beings were thought to live either in the mountains of the west or on a group of islands in the Pacific which moved from place to place and became shrouded in mist and disappeared whenever humans came near. An emperor of the Ch'in dynasty (third century B.C.) sent out expeditions to find them, but they were unsuccessful. One of his Han successors tried a different approach: he built a new set of islands in the lake of his park, in the hope that the immortals, who flew through the air on the backs of cranes, would visit them and share their knowledge with him. The immortals never arrived but the islands became a frequent feature of Chinese garden plans.

Chinese philosophy is based on balance, an equilibrium between *yin* (the dark and feminine) and *yang* (the bright and masculine). In the landscape the mountains form the hard yang and the water the soft, reflective yin. High and low, shade and sunshine alike form a balance of opposites. Garden mountains might be built of rocks to a height of a hundred feet (30 m) but individual stones could equally be symbolic mountains. Rocks with twisted shapes and interesting textures were particularly sought after for gardens. Mount Tai Shan in Shantung province was for centuries a holy place where pilgrims climbed thousands of steps up to the top. At its foot a group of large, strangely-shaped rocks stood in a temple garden and were thought to have the same sacred virtues as the mountain. Such stones became very desirable, especially ones found close to the shore of Lake Tai-hu, near Suzhou. They were limestone, worn by the water into fantastic shapes. They fetched high prices and when the supply became exhausted rocks were carved in imitation or placed in the lake for the water to

The Summer Palace, Beijing, a painting on silk. Bridges link the separate pavilions with the main buildings. Pavilions were placed for enjoying particular views, sometimes of a moonlight scene. A great many groups of stones are erected at locations all round the lake shore. Twisted and gnarled trees were also favored.

shape them. The most valued stones were some 15 ft (4.5 m) high, overhanging with the top wider than the bottom, with furrows gouged out of the surface and irregularly-shaped holes. Single rocks could be erected in a garden, or an asymmetrical group arranged. Small stones with the base cut flat to stand upon a table, were even displayed indoors.

Paths, fences and walls in Chinese gardens were never planned in straight lines but meandered so that they would offer ever-changing views. Like the scrolls on which artists drew and painted landscapes they were not intended to be viewed in total, or even at one time, but "unrolled," revealing a sequence of individual scenes for contemplation, though their sequence would also be intended as a further element. The architecture of the garden, with its pavilions and bridges, was a yang element, the free shapes of the garden yin. A favorite feature was the circular moon gate — often an ungated opening — which was a symbol of heaven.

Almost everything in Chinese gardens had a symbolic role, even the plants. The chrysanthemum, which flowers later in the year than most other plants, is the symbol of longevity. The flowering plum, which blossoms early, became a symbol of hope and courage; the pine, of venerable age, the lotus, of purity and perfection; the bamboo, dependability and an upright character; the tree peony was associated with elevation in rank or the acquisition of riches. This last plant went through a period when it was so fashionable that enormously high prices were offered for rare or particularly beautiful plants like the "tulip mania" which gripped the Netherlands many centuries later.

Orchid, bamboo, chrysanthemum and flowering plum were linked with the four seasons and together were considered to represent the ideal human qualities: grace, dependability and resilience, nobility, courage and endurance.

Chinese gardens came and went, with new gardens built by conquerors on the same site as the old, but the style remained consistently the same until very recent times when late nineteenth-century western ideas began to be copied. There was one exception. In the eight-

A zigzag bridge in the Garden of the Lotus Root links paths contained within rock walls that direct the visitor from one viewing point to another, giving a succession of visual experiences. This is one of several beautiful gardens surviving in Suzhou.

Below *Chinese gardens were separate from the houses of the great, although pavilions were contained within them. But lesser houses, at least when William Chambers reported on them in his* Designs of Chinese Buildings *in 1757, were frequently a succession of different apartments for the divisions within the extended family, each with its own garden patios linked to a particular set of living quarters. At the far end of each little court was "generally a pool, or cistern of water, with an artificial rock placed therein, on which grow some bamboo trees, and shrubs of different sorts; the whole forming a little landscape pretty enough: the cistern or pool is stocked with goldfish, some of which are so tame that they will come to the surface of the water and feed out of one's hand. The sides of the court are sometimes adorned with flower-pots, and sometimes with general shrubs, or vines, and bamboos, that form arbors. In the middle is generally placed, on a pedestal, a large porcelain vase, in which grow those beautiful flowers called Lien-Hoa; and in these courts they frequently keep pheasants, bantam, fowls and other curious birds." The essays in this book, especially "Of the art of laying out gardens among the Chinese," helped popularize Chinoiserie in western gardens.*

eenth century the Emperor Chi'en Lung asked Jesuit missionaries at his court to demonstrate fountains, which he had seen in drawings by one of the priests, and then to create buildings of European style set in a European garden. For a time the Chinese had what they saw as an amusing curiosity — a garden like a miniature Versailles — but they were not copied and had no effect on Chinese garden style.

The gardens of Japan

The Japanese religion of Shinto — the Way of the Gods — sees man, animals, plants and natural things as all equal parts of creation, and nature is respected. The rare and the exotic, the new variety or the bigger blossom have no place in traditional Japanese gardening. Beauty lies in the natural form and this is what the gardener seeks to achieve. Paradoxically this can also mean the most careful and meticulous placing of every garden feature and the rigorous control of plant forms through pruning. This is seen at its most extreme in *bonsai*, the art of producing miniature trees by potting and careful pruning of both roots and branches; but at the same time *bonsai* exemplifies the respect for nature, for the forms which it seeks to create are precisely those which occur in nature: a windswept pine upon a mountain crag for instance, lovingly recreated in small scale in a bowl.

A garden in the Chinese style with a lake and island was built for the Empress Suiko at Nama in 612 by a Korean gardener and was probably influenced by the first known embassy from Japan to China led by one of her kinsmen. What earlier gardens were like we do not know and none survive from this period either, but the pool and island garden became a well-established form. *Shima*, Japanese for island, was for centuries also used as the word for garden.

The famous novel *The Tale of Genji*, written by a court lady at the beginning of the eleventh century, describes how, at his palace, the prince (according to Arthur Waley's translation):

"effected great improvement in the appearance of the grounds by a judicious handling of knoll and lake, for though such features were already there in abundance, he found it necessary here to cut away a slope, there to dam a stream, that each occupant of the various quarters might look out of her windows upon such a prospect as pleased her best. To the southeast he raised the level of the ground, and on this bank planted a profusion of flowering trees and in the foreground, just beneath the windows, he planted borders of cinquefoil, of red plum, cherry, wisteria, kerria, rock azalea, and other such plants as are at their best in springtime."

Prince Genji's pavilions were occupied by his several ladies but it was usual for courtiers to live in separate pavilions, all facing south and linked by covered walkways. The main pavilion would be by a lake with a beach of silver sand used as a location for entertainments.

Rules for garden making

During the Heian period (781–1185), when the court moved to Heian-Kyo (modern Kyoto), strict rules developed for the design of gardens. They were set out in the *Sakuteiki*, a treatise probably written in the eleventh century by Tachibana no Toshitsuna, and elaborated by later garden experts. To practical and aesthetic considerations are added elements that are propitious or contrary in effect. It recommends visits to study famous scenic spots so that the elements that make up their beauty can be reproduced in modified form in the garden. It concentrates in great detail on the recreation of mountain streams in gardens.

While a pond only requires a depression which can be filled with water to look natural and a waterfall only requires a rock to fall over, a stream should attempt to reproduce all the stages of its course in miniature: first a racing rivulet cutting through a mountain cleft, then either a gently moving or eddying stretch and then a wider stream before it enters a lake or pond. Instructions for cascades specify different types and appropriate scale and suggest that their source should sometimes be hidden. Stones have to be carefully matched, water-worn stones used in water features, craggy ones in mountain-inspired scenes. Sometimes their use is practical, to prevent erosion of the banks of a lake or stream for instance, but those at the base of a fall need to be selected for their acoustic as well as other qualities, and instructions for the arrangement of rocks are frequently based on religious considerations and taboos. However, modern designers find that their aesthetic considerations are still of great value.

The *Sakuteiki* also describes *kare sansui* — "dry gardens." These gardens, developed when Zen Buddhism was growing in influence in Japan, were plantless, except perhaps for moss, and formed of rocks and raked sand. They are intended for contemplation and spiritual exercise.

Prince Genji's garden was designed for enjoyment from the lake and for viewing from its many pavilions, but a new style now appeared. Generally known as "stroll" or "tour" gardens they reveal a succession of different aspects as a path is followed through them. They also began to feature the use of the *shakkei* or "borrowed view," a concept already known in China as *jie jing* by which a feature outside the garden, from a tree to a distant panorama, is made part of the composition of a view.

The gardens of Muso Soseki

The still-surviving garden of the temple of Saiho-ji, west of Kyoto, shows the lake "paradise garden" and the dry landscape side by side. It was made by the Zen priest Muso Soseki (1275–1351). The area around the Golden Pond originally boasted a boathouse and a number of pavilions linked with twisting covered corridors, including the Ruri-den, on the

Five main shapes are recognized as most suitable for Japanese gardens: 1 flat; 2 arching; 3 recumbent; 4 low vertical; and 5 statue. They are usually used singly or combined in groups of three or five. Stones are chosen to match the size of the garden and placed to look as though they had arrived by natural means. Some groupings are considered particularly suited to certain locations: a vertical stone with a flat stone by a stream, two vertical stones with a flat stone to screen the outlet of a waterfall.

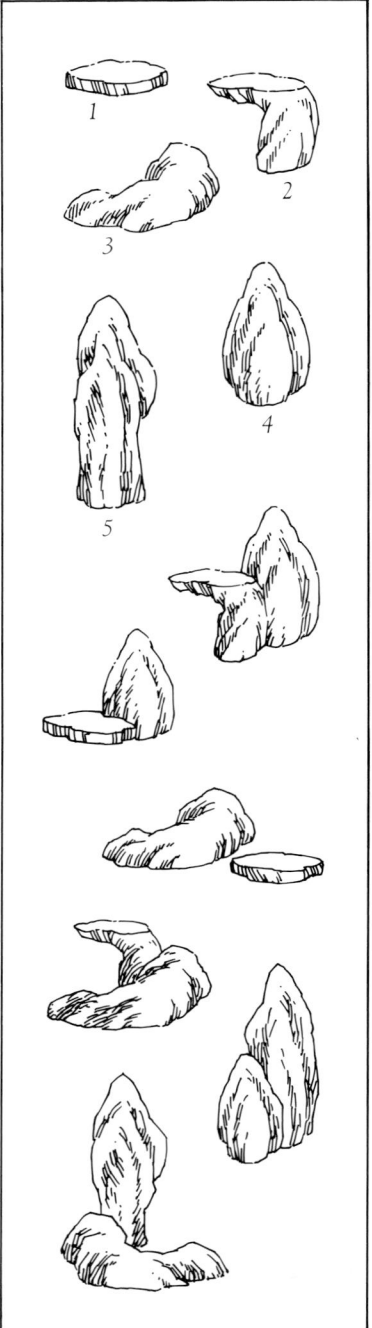

design of which the famous Golden and Silver Pavilions of later Kyoto gardens were based. The paths around the pond affording the stroller a sequence of changing views were possibly an innovation of this designer. It has been suggested that this concept was linked with the development of the tea ceremony, offering a suitable approach to the tea house. The lake garden at Saiho-ji is formed of trees and mosses — more than forty different kinds — but was once bright with flowers and famous for its cherry trees.

A path from this lower garden passes through a gate and up a rough stone stair, leading past a group of stones representing a huge tortoise, floating on a sea of moss, then past a group of a form known as *shuminsen* because they symbolize Mount Sumeru, the center of the universe in Buddhist cosmology. Another group of stones near a spring is said to prefigure the washing basin of later tea gardens. At last a group of stones is revealed down the central slope of the hill arranged as a waterfall and stream, but, whereas earlier gardens carefully

The Golden Pond of the moss garden at the temple of Saiho-ji, Kyoto. Yodomari ishi, "night mooring stones," suggest a line of anchored boats. First created in the seventh century, Muso Soseki was commissioned to convert this into a Zen garden in 1339. A "stroll" garden, designed to be enjoyed from the paths around the pond which offer continually changing views, it was originally much more ostentatious than its present serenity suggests.

Kinkaku-ji, The Golden Pavilion, at Rokuon-ji garden, Kyoto, was based on one in Muso's Saiho-ji garden. Built at the end of the fourteenth century, the garden used many features similar to Muso's, making much use of reflection in the Kyoko or Mirror Lake. The pavilion was destroyed by fire in 1950 but has since been rebuilt in exact facsimile.

followed the *Sakuteiki* in imitating nature, this does more, for there is no stream, yet the arrangement of rocks gives the impression of the tumult of a waterfall and the swirling currents at its base. Two pools, encircled with smaller stones and filled with moss, complete the picture, in a powerful symbolic capturing of the essence of a violent cascade, not a literal representation.

This upper garden may have originally been reserved for the use of the Zen priests but the lower garden was seen and admired by many and its ideas were copied in other gardens. The Saiho-ji garden (popularly known as the Moss Temple Garden because of its many mosses) was commissioned in 1339. Only three years later Muso Soseki was given the task of converting a garden formerly belonging to the emperor Godaigo into a Zen temple garden and adopted a very different approach. Again a dry waterfall is featured, but set on the far side of a pool too small for boating and planned as a scene to be viewed from the abbot's quarters, not as a strolling garden. This Tenryu-ji garden is in no way designed for amusement and entertaining. It offers a static picture for appreciation.

Raked gravel

Zen teaching prohibits the copying of the work of others but waterfall and river form the theme of many later *kare sansui* gardens. The Daisen-in, a subtemple of the Kyoto temple Daitoku-ji, made early in the sixteenth century, occupies a space only 10 ft (3 m) deep adjacent to the abbot's quarters. Here upright stones represent a waterfall from which the river bed traverses a narrow valley until it opens out into a raked gravel space past islands and a boat-shaped rock. Halfway, a scaled-down bridge crosses the stream, one side of it walled with a window and a narrow bench which separates the scene in two.

In contrast to this tightly enclosed scene the Ryoan-ji garden, also in Kyoto, and made perhaps a few years earlier, uses a much larger enclosure by the abbot's quarters. This is surfaced with a level layer of white gravel, raked into regular lines and circles around the perimeter of carefully placed rocks. The rocks, fifteen in all, are arranged in groups of twos, threes and five. It is sometimes called the Garden of Crossing Tiger Cubs and the stones interpreted as tigers and their young swimming across a river, or the rocks are simply seen as islands. Such a literal meaning is unlikely to have been the Zen artist's intention, the abstract forms being rather a starting point for meditation. This temple was once famous for its cherry trees — viewing the cherry blossoms in the spring is still an occasion for alfresco parties in Japan — and it is only in the seventeenth century that attention is drawn to the

The abbot's dry landscape garden at Daisen-in, a subtemple of Daitoku-ji, Kyoto. The foreground represents the lower reaches of a river which has its source among the rocks seen through the "window" of the bridge — a later addition which now bisects the kare sansui scene.

The Ryoan-ji temple garden, Kyoto. A more abstract use of rocks and raked gravel than those which show waterfalls and streams, although it has been given literal interpretations.

stones. Architect and garden authority Masao Hayakawa has suggested that it was after the trees died that someone erected the enclosing walls and removed all plants from the garden.

Tea ceremony gardens

The origins of the tea ceremony stretch back to Chinese monks drinking tea before meditating to ensure they stayed awake. In Japan, as *cha-no-yu*, it was developed in the fifteenth century as a ritual for the contemplation of something of beauty — a flower, a painting, a piece of porcelain — and philosophical discussion. As conceived by teamaster Murata Juko (1423–1502) there should be a special garden leading to the tea room in a garden pavilion — or later to a special very simple tea room the size of only four tatami mats each about 3 ft x 6 ft (1 m x 2 m) approached through a garden containing only a single tree.

Teamaster Sen no Rikyu (1522–91) developed this further so that it took place in a tea house with a single window to admit light, but affording no outward view, with only a small entrance doorway and attended by no more than five people. Outside, the tea garden (*cha-niwa*) was a preparation for the event. Those taking part would assemble on a bench where they would cast off the cares of the outer world as they waited to be called to take the *roji*, or "dewy path" (the name comes from a Bhuddist sutra referring to a place of rebirth without worldliness), which itself became a form of preparation. Stepping stones, initially a measure to prevent erosion of the moss, guided their feet along the path, their spacing imposing a certain pace as well as direction, by their size and arrangement. Here, they concentrated attention on the stones themselves, there they guided the participant to contemplate a particular view or feature. Plantings were devoid of flowers; trees, ferns and moss created a feeling of serenity and timelessness.

Rikyu's garden was near the sea but this was screened from view until, on reaching a stone with a basin, where each participant would perform a ritual cleansing, they would bend to wash their faces and catch sight of the sea through a gap in the leaves, the water in the bowl linked with the vastness of the ocean.

Since the tea ceremony was often held at night, stone lanterns of a type originally found in Korean monasteries were introduced. These then became a traditional feature of the Japanese garden.

Later gardens

Variations on the garden forms described continued right up to modern times when western influence saw gardens of European type appearing in Japan. In the Edo period (1603–1867) the influence of the *cha-niwa* was seen in even the grandest gardens where the emphasis (cherry blossom apart) was usually on form, it being important that a garden should preserve its beauty the year round and not depend on flowers. Azaleas were heavily pruned to rounded shapes. Even chrysanthemums, although identified as the imperial flower, were not grown in the garden but raised in pots to be placed in position when in flower. In the internal courts of merchants' houses carefully contrived arrangements for viewing from indoors, often designed to make them appear more spacious than they were, reflected the concept of the abbots' gardens.

If there is not even that amount of space available, a miniature garden in a box or tray (the *hako-niwi* or *bon-kai*) will reproduce the larger garden that they cannot have.

The careful combination of water, rock, trees and plants so typical of Japan and even the aestheticism of the dry gardens have been imitated in many countries, sometimes being authentically created by gardeners from Japan.

The art of bonsai, *miniaturizing shrubs and carefully shaping them, has flourished in Japan for centuries and is gaining many adherents in the West.*

Rocks, mosses and carefully shaped trees in a garden at Chiran, Kyushu.

RENAISSANCE ITALY

Right *The Villa Medici, Fiesole. The property was bought by Cosimo de Medici the Elder in 1458 and the villa built about 1460 for his son Giovanni. The house was built into the hillside and the intimate terraced garden exploits fine views over the Arno valley and Florence.*

The reawakening to classical ideas, which we know as the Renaissance, brought a renewed interest in the garden concepts of ancient Rome. The peristyle had survived in courtyard gardens and the Arab influence, but now the country villa with its formal garden returned to favor with the wealthy. Medieval horticultural writing frequently owed much to Roman originals. We know that the poet Plutarch closely followed classical texts in the cultivation of his small garden but it was a treatise by the Italian humanist and architect Leon Battista Alberti (1404–72), *De re aedificatoria*, written in 1452 and published just over 30 years later, which established the new style, especially around Florence. The sections which deal with gardens are directly based on classical writings. Alberti gives no precise instruction on either layout or architectural elements but he recommends that villas and their gardens be sited on hillsides both for exposure to sun and wind and to provide a view, though the climb through the garden should be gradual. Visitors should scarcely notice the ascent until they see the view when they reach the house — a direct echo of Pliny the Younger. He also places an emphasis on the use of topiary of box and scented evergreens, grottos, stone vases, fountains and flowing water and statuary "if not indecent."

Alberti is thought to have designed a garden at the Villa Quaracchi for the wealthy Giovanni Rucellai, whose diary describes it as having the recommended features, including box topiary in the shapes of giants and centaurs, though retaining its pre-existing simple axial plan which was extended across a road and down to the Arno by an avenue of trees. There were still such medieval features as arbors, a mount and pergolas, one of which connected the house with a private garden or *giardino segreto* where there were scented herbs and flowers which included violets, marjoram and basil grown in terracotta vases. The garden was a place where Rucellai could sit and conduct business on one of the many seats and there was a sheltered area suitable for playing ball games — a garden to be used by the family and into parts of which the local peasants were allowed.

It was a garden such as this, in imitation of a Roman villa garden, which Cosimo de Medico (1389–1464) and his architect Michelozzo Michelozzi created at Careggi, where he held gatherings of his Platonic Academy, the meetings of artists and intellectuals which gave much of the impetus to the new thinking of the Renaissance. Later the Academy moved to a newer villa at Fiesole, also designed by Michelozzi, with two terraces laid out to command fine views and a delightful *giardino segreto*. Access between the parts of the garden was by simple cypress walks, the lower terrace being reached through underground rooms or

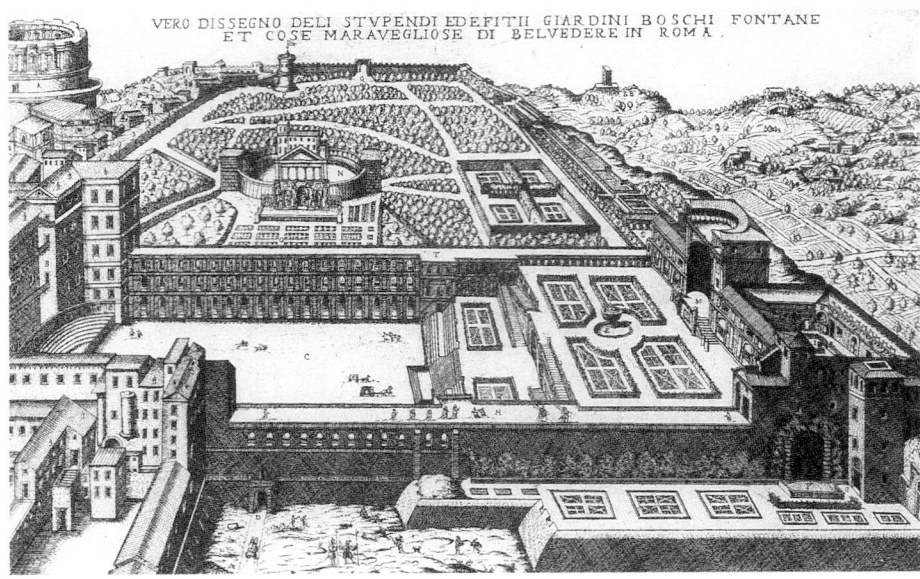

Bramante's Court of the Belvedere at the Vatican in an engraving made in 1571 by C. Duchetti.

Below *The Villa Medici, Rome. It was laid out originally in 1544 and in 1580 purchased by Cardinal Ferdinand de Medici who installed his collection of classical sculpture in the gardens, in the facade of the house and along the side of the loggia on the left. Above the loggia a terrace provides a view over the formal beds. Behind it, though set back much deeper in the woods than shown here, rises a mount with a pavilion at the top which still gives a fine view over Rome. Beyond this was probably a lemon orchard and the vegetable garden. Behind the gallery which is at right angles to the main palazzo was a small walled knot garden, a giardino segreto. Despite the obelisk and the abundance of statuary this garden still retains more of the character of a late medieval garden than of the more theatrical Renaissance style.*

via an awkward indirect path. The idea of connecting the parts of the garden with grand flights of steps or imposing ramps which characterizes the fully developed Italian Renaissance style was introduced not in Florence but in Rome.

Pope Julius II (pontiff 1503–13) had assembled a considerable collection of classical statuary, originally displayed in a garden he had created at his palace attached to the church of St. Peter in Vincola. In 1503 he decided to move this collection to the Vatican and commissioned Donato Bramante (1444–1514) to design a link between the Vatican palace and the old Villa Belvedere which lies on a slope above it. Bramante created a huge courtyard divided into three levels. Lowest was an area for pageants and jousting, arcaded along the sides and with an arc of steps providing seating at the Vatican end. Across the far end, steps rose to a level terrace providing space for more spectators, with a grand stair at the center. Above this, double flights carried one to the upper level at the height of the roofs of the porticos where a formal garden provided a setting for the statuary. The change in level was dramatically exploited and hillsides rather than level terrain now became the fashion for grand gardens. Bramante not only provided an out-

door sculpture gallery, he turned statues into fountains, including enormous figures of the Tiber and the Nile. Architectural and sculptural embellishment, terraces connected by grand flights of steps and the lavish use of water in pools and fountains became characteristic of the Italian style.

When Raphael and other artists created the Villa Madama on the slopes of Mount Mario outside Rome for Cardinal Giulio dé Medici between 1516 and 1520, the axis was a building with a central court around which were, to the north, formal terraces leading to a *giardino segreto*, to the west a classical amphitheater excavated from the hillside, to the south a courtyard with monumental stairs up the slope and to the east a hippodrome, with stabling for 250 horses, over which could be seen a spectacular view toward Rome. Although burned when Rome was sacked in 1527, it set a pattern for grand villas in the countryside like those of ancient times.

It was in the years following the sack of Rome that the style now known as Mannerist became prominent in Italian art. The name derives from the word *maniera* which Gorgio Vasari (1511–74), the artist and architect whose history of art is an important source of information on his contemporaries, used to describe the schematic quality of much of the work then produced which was based on intellectual ideas rather than what the artist saw. The first major garden in which this was apparent was probably the Villa Medici at Castello which Niccolo Tribolo (1500–50) designed from 1538 (though it was not completed until after his death) to a concept worked out by the scholar Benedetto Varchi (1503–65). It celebrated the greatness of the Medici family, and featured the rivers Arno and Mugnone both as sources of fertility and as symbols of the power of the Medici.

What is now known as the Villa Medici in Rome was laid out in the 1540s, then bought by Cardinal Ferdinand de Medici in 1580. His large collection of sculpture was set up around the gardens or into the garden facade of the villa, but the garden is not very different from the medieval type.

This is certainly not the case with the Boboli Gardens, behind the Pitti Palace in Florence, begun in 1549 by Tribolo for Eleanora de Medici. They are the grandest in scale of the Medici gardens, although originally very simple in concept. Tribolo enlarged the natural amphitheater behind the house into a horseshoe and planted dense woodland, laying out a garden of formal beds in different geometrical patterns to the side of the palace. In 1583 a group of three grottos, incorporating statues by Michelangelo, were erected beside the palace. In 1618 the Ocean fountain was taken from the front of the palace and relocated on an island in the middle of a pool set at the end of the avenue which leads westward, and a fountain with a figure of Neptune replaced a previous formal water tank. Also in the seventeenth century, the amphitheater was cleared of trees, ranks of seating built around it, and the slope of the central path replaced by a series of steps

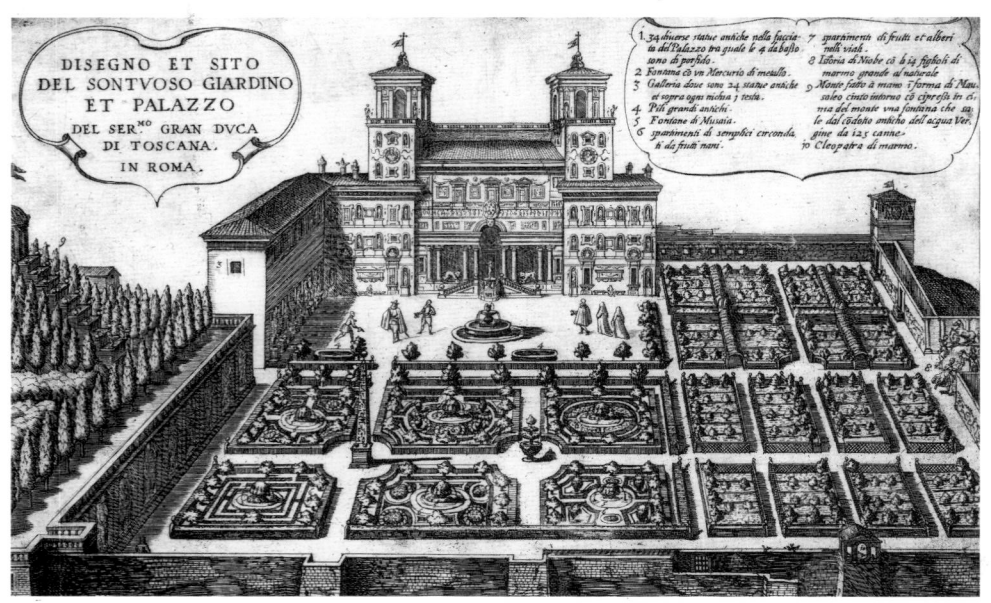

Between 1599 and 1602 Giusto Utens, a Flemish-born artist, painted a series of 18 lunettes for the Villa di Atimino which all showed gardens in Tuscany. All were painted from life but to enable more features to be included they sometimes use a very free perspective.

Right The Villa Medici, Castello. An avenue of trees stretched from the Arno to the bridged fish pond which fronts the house and this axis is continued up the hillside. Small private gardens flank the house. Behind on the first raised terrace stands a fountain (now transferred to the Villa Petraia, nearby) capped by a figure variously described as Venus or as representing Florence, and above this, where at first there was a labyrinth of myrtle and bay within the cypress grove, is a fountain in the form of Hercules overcoming Anteus with the water gushing from Anteus' mouth. Beyond this garden is a lemon terrace in the further wall of which is a central grotto sculpted with animals and with surprise fountains to catch the unwary. Steps at the sides lead on to a wooded area where the pool with a fountain in the form of a male figure represents the Apennines. Further gardens extend on both sides with orchards, a herb garden, more water tanks and pavilions.

Center Villa Medici, Pratolini, created for Francesco Medici between 1569 and 1581. Utens shows only the front part of the gardens. The slope was not terraced, apart from a platform for the house, beneath which were a number of grottos. The gardens were full of waterworks, including automata and musical fountains, fish tanks, aviaries and statues. There is a tree house reached by a spiral stair in the right foreground and near it a fountain of Perseus and Andromeda with the dragon, though this was actually placed higher up the slope beyond the house. The garden was remodeled in 1819 as what was thought to be an "English garden."

Below The Pitti Palace, Florence, with the Boboli Gardens behind and Fort Belvedere on rear left. Shown before the clearing of the amphitheater.

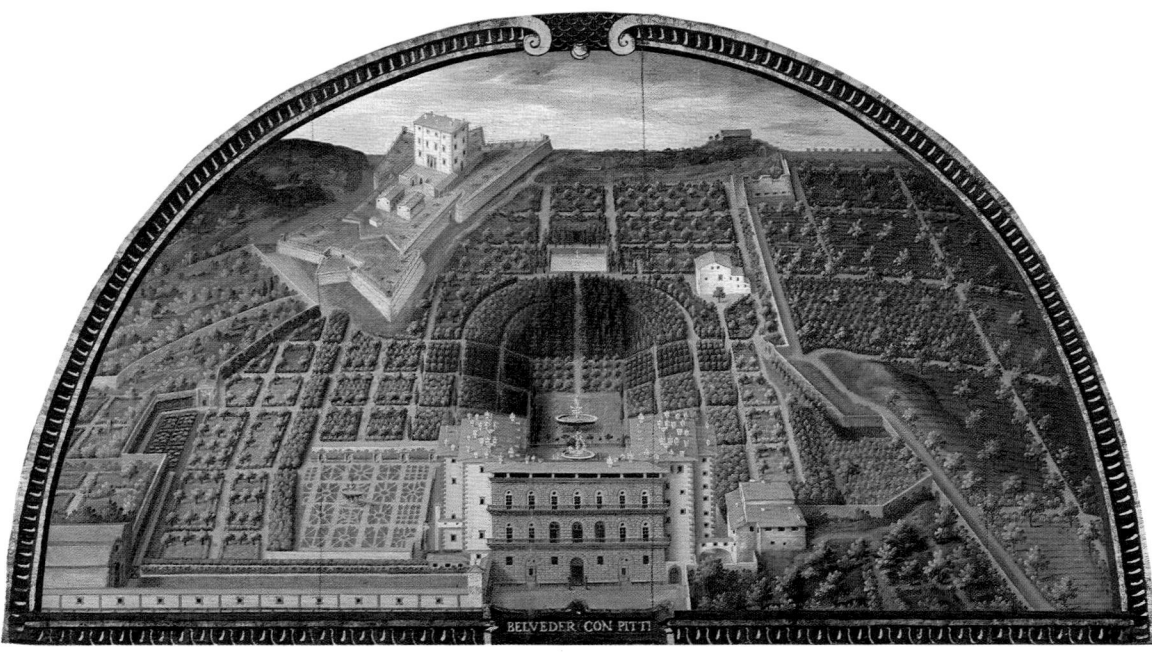

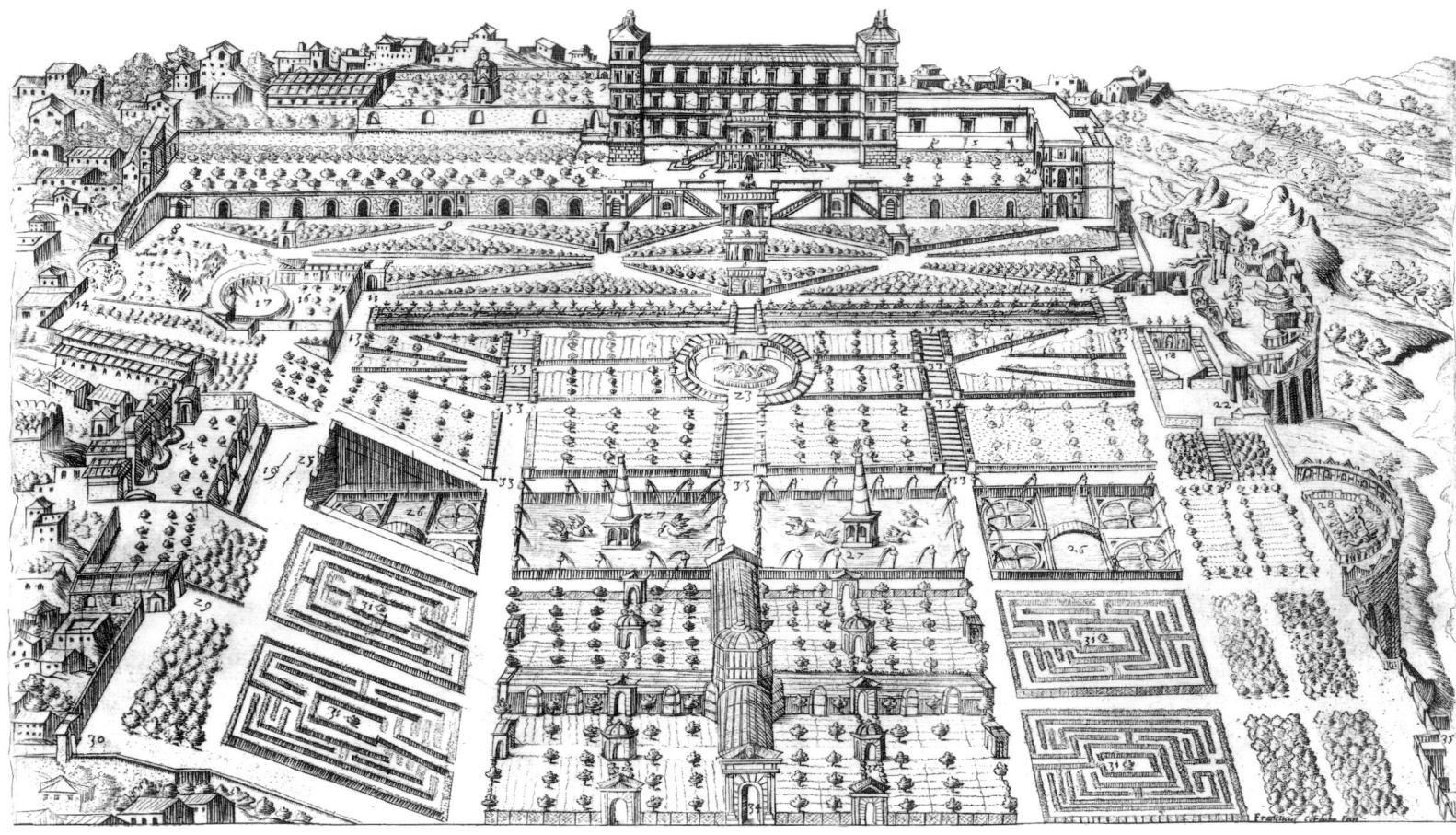

An early engraving of the Villa d'Este at Tivoli; not all the features shown here were actually completed. The visitor originally entered the gardens at the lower gate and progressed through pergolas among herb gardens flanked by mazes, between fish ponds and up past more plantations to the Dragon Fountain (23) where ramped staircases circle up to the path of One Hundred Fountains. At this level, to the visitor's left is the Fountain of the Oval (17) and the Grotto of Venus, to the right the Rometta (21). A series of ramps then link terraced paths until the palace of the cardinal is reached with its own private garden (3) set on one side and a tennis court on the other (5).

Right A terrace near the Venus fountain at the Villa d'Este. This 1675 engraving by Venturini shows a number of giochi d'acqua (water jokes) in action. As a stroller flees from one water jet he or she is drenched by another.

Far right The terrace of One Hundred Fountains at the Villa d'Este.

and terraces. This now became the setting for grand spectacles, which were performed there rather than in the palace courtyard.

In 1550 at Tivoli, not far from the site of the Villa Adriana, about 20 miles (30 km) from Rome, Cardinal Ippolito II d'Este (1509–72) began the creation of a new villa and gardens, though work on the garden was mainly between 1560 and 1575, competing with the development of the Farnese Palace at Caprarola. At Tivoli, on a steep slope, the Villa d'Este became one of the most imaginative of Renaissance gardens. It was built around the symbolism of Hercules, from whom the d'Estes fancifully claimed descent, as a symbol of strength, and Hippolytus, the cardinal's namesake, a symbol of chastity. The placing of

statues (originally including many removed from Hadrian's Villa) and fountains offered visitors a symbolic choice between, for instance, virtue if they chose a path to the Grotto of chaste Diana, or sensual pleasure if they took the alternative path to the Grotto of Venus.

The gardens at Caprarola, near Viterbo, were simpler than those at the Villa d'Este. Cardinal Alessandro Farnese concentrated both the Mannerist ideas and the emphasis on the palace itself. Two walled gardens, both divided into four square plots or parterres, adjoin the house, one designed for summer, the other for winter use. From the summer garden a path leads through a wood to a casino below which is a parterre from which steps descend to a fountain flanked by giants from which the

water flows down a dolphin-edged cascade to a shell fountain and then a circular basin with a central jet. The effect is elegant but modest compared with the theatrical displays at Tivoli where a diversion of water from the River Aniene provided ample supplies for the innumerable fountains.

Real competition for the Villa d'Este came some years later with another Villa of the Medici family, at Pratolino, near Florence, completed by 1580, where the garden was full of water tricks and automata. The house is set halfway up the hillside. The main garden was below; above it an amphitheater was surmounted by a fountain in the form of a huge figure representing the Apennines and above that a round maze. Sadly, most was destroyed to make a new garden in the English style in 1819, leaving only a retaining wall and the Apennine statue as a reminder of past glories.

A relative of the Farnese, Cardinal Gambara, built another villa near Viterbo, the Villa Lante, which uses water as the axis of its main garden, descending through a series of fountains. This is one of the least altered of Italian Renaissance gardens and has been recently restored.

Philosopher and garden architect Giacomo Barozzi da Vignola (1507–73) was probably involved in the design of the Villa d'Este, the Villa Orsini and both the Farnese gardens. In Rome in 1551 he was commissioned to design the Villa Giulia for Pope Julius III (1551–5) on the Via Flaminia. The heavily wooded grounds extended to the Tiber with fountains, grottos and statuary but the central feature is a vertical semicircular court with a view through to a further small garden, enclosed within the building.

Even the smallest gardens would feature statuary. English diarist John Evelyn, himself an active gardener, while traveling in Italy in 1645, saw a small garden behind the palace of Hieronymo del Negroes in Genoa which was

Left *The dragon fountain at the Villa d'Este, Tivoli. This great upward jet forms the heart of this great Renaissance garden.*

Opposite *The Palazzo Farnese at Caprarola. There are two formal terraced gardens at the fortified palazzo with a smaller garden set between them. Across the park moat is a casino, now used as a summer residence for the President of Italy, from which this dolphin-edged cascade descends, completed c. 1620.*

Below *An engraving of the Villa Lante, Bagnaia, created between 1564 and 1580, from Antique Urbis Splendor, 1612, clearly shows the descent of water from terrace to terrace through a succession of fountains and pools between the two pavilions of the villa. In the adjoining woodland with its shady walks are set a maze, a reservoir dominated by the Pegasus fountain of Giambologna (the final destination of the water in the garden) and other fountains which were later altered or destroyed by Cardinal Montalto who took over the villa in 1590.*

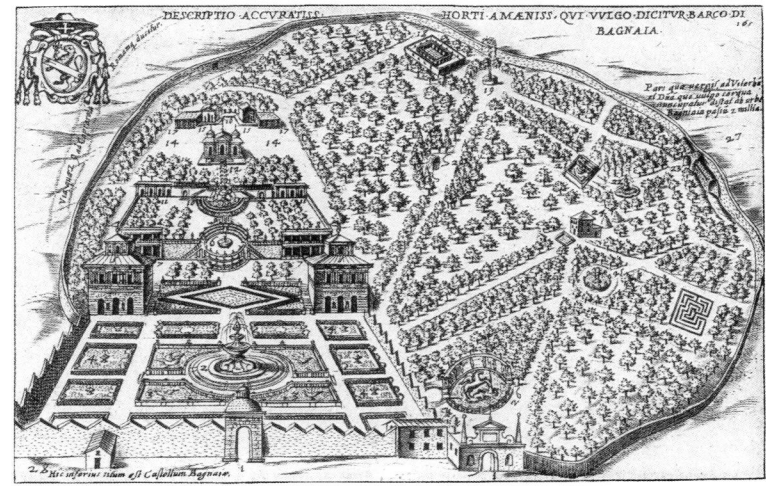

Left *The lower terrace of the Villa Lante. The central fountain of four Moors holding high the mount and star emblem of the Montaltos was installed by the cardinal to replace one which Montaigne described as "a pyramid which spouts water in many different ways: one rises another falls." The boats in each quadrant originally held archers who shot "arrow" jets of water to the center.*

The fountain of lamps, at the Villa Lante, on the terrace above the fountain of the Moors.

"furnished with artificial Sheepe, Shepheards, & Wild beasts, so naturally cut in a grey-stone, fountaines, rocks, & Piscinas . . . all within one Aker of ground."

By the time of Evelyn's visit a highlight of the Italian tour was a visit to Frascati on the steep slopes of the Alban Hills southeast of Rome, where a group of villas was built in the Baroque style which succeeded Mannerism. They exploit the different levels, fountains, cascades, water jokes, parterres, private enclosed gardens and

woodland planting (a *bosco*) and most use a semicircular declivity cut into the hillside as the setting for the main water features.

At Collodi, in Tuscany, the Villa Garzoni rivals the Frascati villas in its baroque grandeur, with a garden dating from 1652 which displays many of the same features, and there are a number of other lesser villas in the region. Further north at Genoa the Palazzo Podesta offers a combination of terraces, fountains and a grotto on a steep hill, though sadly the magnifi-

The gardens of the Villa Torlonia, Frascati, were created in the 1630s. From a fountain in a clearing on the hilltop, there are fine views across the Roman campagna. A cascade descends through oval basins to crash into the pool set in a dense ilex wood, through which straight paths lead to the unpretentious villa.

This yawning mouth, like the entrance to hell in a medieval mystery play, is in the Sacra Bosco at Villa Orsini, Bomarzo. It houses a seat and table and bears the inscription "Every thought flies." The Sacred Wood is full of strange, huge sculptures, many taking their theme from Ariosto's Orlando Furioso. An inscription tells the visitor "You who wander through the world to see its stupendous marvels, come here, where there are horrible faces, elephants, lions, monsters and dragons." The gardens were created between 1552 and 1580 by the Duke of Bomarzo on the rocky hillside below his castle. Fountains, through which water once flowed from level to level, no longer survive.

The Villa Garzoni, Collodi, created in the mid-seventeenth century. This baroque stairway forms the centerpiece of the gardens. Above it a water cascade falls from a reservoir, and below are a sloping parterre with heraldic plantings (here being set out) and round lily ponds with high fountain jets.

Below *The Isola Bella, in Lake Maggiore. An engraving of 1726 in M. A. Dal Re's Ville di delizia. The pointed "prow" of the boatlike design was never built, though the gardens, begun in 1630, were otherwise complete by 1671. The terraces rise to a statue-pinnacled "water theater" on the side facing toward the palace.*

Bottom *Isola Bella, looking out to "stern" from the platform behind the "water theater."*

cent garden of Admiral Andrea Doria's palace just outside the city was obliterated by Genoa's expansion in the nineteenth century.

On the opposite coast, most Venetian gardens were small courtyard gardens, although there were larger ones on the edges of the city, and the villas built inland along the banks of the Brenta, though often true farmstead villas, had mainly rectangular, rather old-fashioned walled gardens.

One of the most florid of seventeenth-century Italian gardens was begun about 1630 on Isola Bella in Lake Maggiore. Legend says that the ladies of the Borromeo family who built it were disturbed by the cries of prisoners in the dungeons of their mainland castle so this island palace was created for them. It is not designed as a retreat but was intended for recreation and lavish entertainment to match its theatricality. The original idea was to extend the island to a point and model it like a ship and although this prow was never created the garden does appear to sail upon the water, though perhaps more barge than galleon. The flat part of the island, with the villa to the west, was laid out with parterres, to the east ten terraces are built over natural rock prominences to culminate in a flat-topped pyramid. Obelisks and statues on plinths rise like masts into the air and cool grottos and arcades give shelter from the sun while lake breezes and views toward the shore add to the garden's attractions.

Visits to Italian gardens led other Europeans to emulate them and their influence can still be seen in many countries. However, while in Italy itself some similar gardens were still created in succeeding years, the much more rigid style which had been developing in France began to replace them in influence during the seventeenth century.

THE RENAISSANCE IN THE NORTH

Garden concepts, like other artistic and intellectual ideas, spread through Europe, but the proposals put forward by Alberti were not always so suited to northern locations. Medieval features persisted during the sixteenth century, especially in smaller gardens, but more and more the garden became a place for pleasure and entertainment and an opportunity to display taste and wealth. The Dutch humanist philosopher Desiderius Erasmus, in *The Godly Feast* (1522) outlined the concept of an enclosed square pleasure garden planned on Mannerist lines — though using Christian rather than classical symbolism — with a gallery raised on marble pillars around three sides which housed a library and an aviary and had trompe-l'oeil paintings of plants and animals along its walls.

A combination of medieval enclosed gardens and Mannerist style is shown later in the designs of Hans Vredeman de Vries (1527–1606), engravings of whose designs had wide influence toward the end of the century. In his work a succession of individual compartments, formed by hedges or trelliswork, displaying fountains and intricate parterres, often planted with exotic species, reflected the skill of Dutch gardeners in rearing rare plants.

The Netherlands was under Spanish control, so Spanish influence was present in Holland. Both Holland and England were affected by their contacts with Burgundy (which was annexed by France in 1482) and the tastes of the Burgundian court, but France itself was the channel through which many ideas traveled north.

French military campaigns laying claim to Naples and Milan gave her nobility an opportunity to see what was happening in Italy and on their return to France they began to intro-

The modern arrangement at the Chateau de Langeais in the Loire, recalls the geometrical beds, topiary and the enclosing trelliswork within an outer hedge or fence which appears in sixteenth-century engravings of northern European gardens.

duce citrus fruits, grown under protection in the winter. François I was captured by the Emperor Charles V and held prisoner in Italy. Released in 1527, he returned with a knowledge of Italian styles, invited Italian gardeners to France and put in hand a number of garden projects.

The idea of an overall design incorporating gardens and chateau had begun to appear in France from the late fifteenth century. But French nobles retained the defensive moats around their chateaus and integrated gardens were not easily created. At Ancy-le-France, in Burgundy, an Italian designer in the service of François I designed a formal rectangular plan surrounded by a raised viewing terrace, an idea also followed by French architect Philibert de l'Orme in a design for Diane de Poitiers at Anet, further north. At Fontainbleau, François I created new gardens around the chateau with no moat but with canals and a lake and a grotto, though there was little overall unity to the plan. At Chantilly, built on marshy ground

for the Constable of France c. 1530, water naturally features but although there is a raised terrace the plan is again irregular. The gardens of the small chateau at Dampierre, laid out about 1560–70 for the Cardinal of Lorraine, Charles de Guise, appears to be the first to be planned with canals, ponds, flower beds and orchards all arranged to a formal plan. The changes effected during the sixteenth century are recorded in the engravings of architect Jacques Androuet du Cerceau, especially in his *Les plus excellents bâtiments de France* (1576 and 1579).

Despite the civil wars of the mid-sixteenth century the Italian-born Queen, Catherine de Medici, familiar with the gardens of her homeland, had elaborate additions made to the gardens at Fontainbleau, the Tuileries and other palaces. High churchmen and nobles also followed Italianate ideas. In the northern plains of France, however, few garden sites were on the steep slopes favored in Italy. The enclosed garden was opened out for greater display,

Below *Anet, laid out by Philibert de l'Orme for Diane de Poitiers c. 1550, had a small garden on either side of the entrance gate and a large formal garden at the rear viewed from a terrace (hidden by the building in this view by du Cerceau).*

Bottom *Cerceau's drawing of Montargis which his chief patron, the Duchess of Ferrara, made a refuge for Huguenots such as he during the French wars of religion. There is a medieval-style garden on a small terrace within the castle yard. Outside the moat is a raised arc of ornamental gardens, including mazes, tunneled paths and a complex of elaborate pergolas, beyond which are vegetable gardens, orchards and a cemetery.*

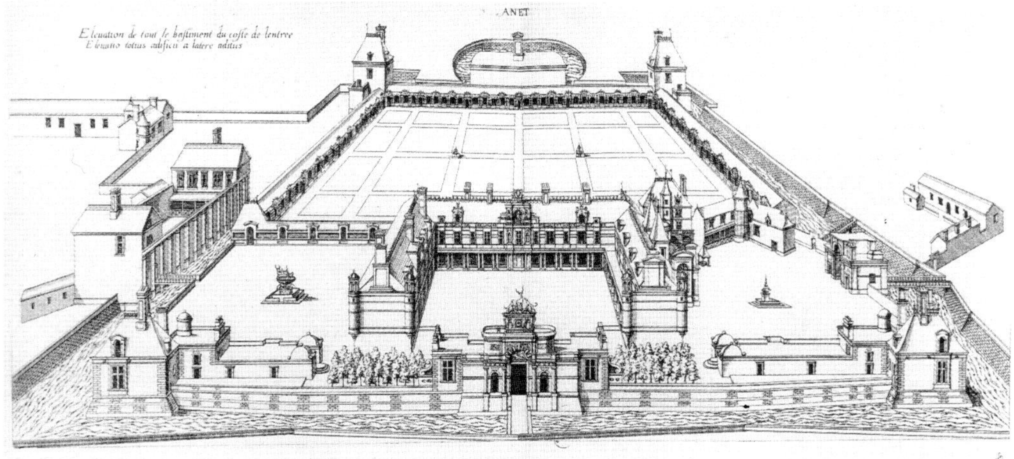

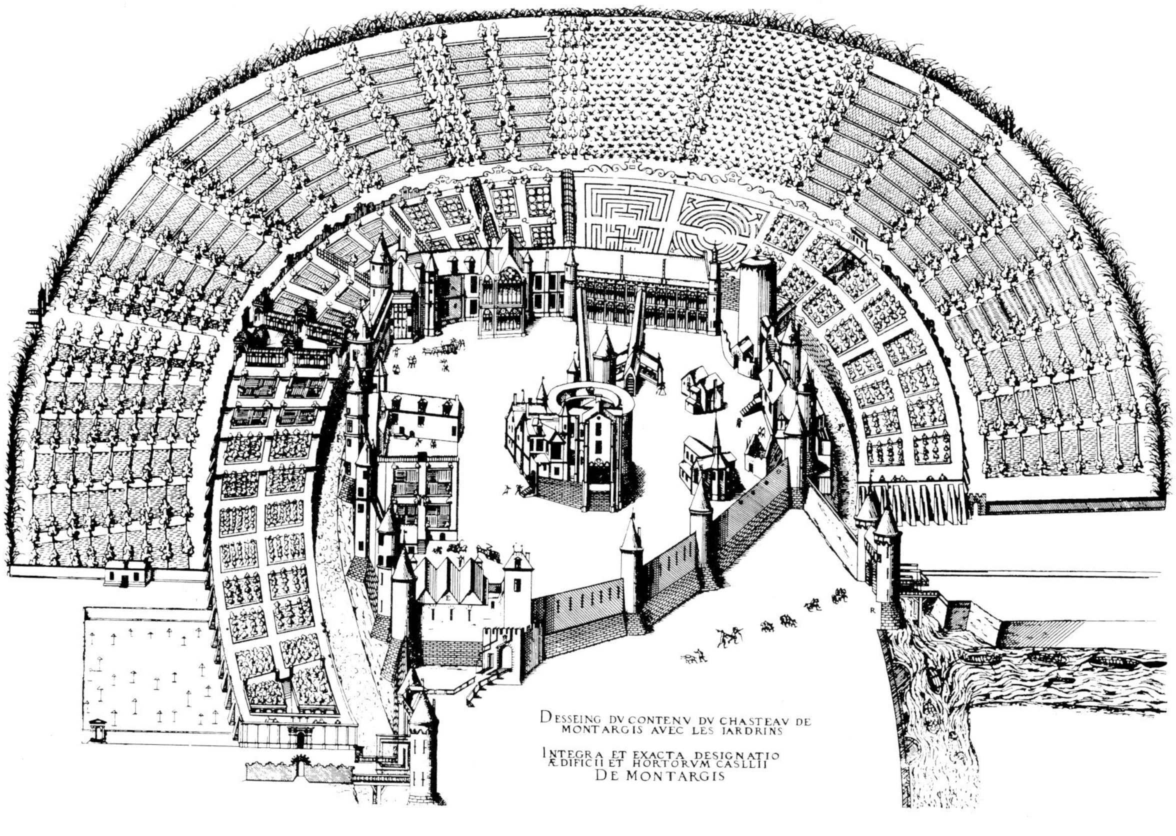

A tapestry in the Uffici Gallery, one of a series celebrating the Medicis, shows Catherine de Medici receiving Polish ambassadors at a ballet given in their honor at the Louvre. The performance, with its elaborate floats, took place inside the palace but has been given the garden as a backdrop. Although the plantings still recall the medieval gardens of northern Europe, fountains and statues are given considerable importance though some of them may have been temporary features erected for the celebrations. To the sides are raised terraces with carved and painted figures.

providing its own vistas, but the successive terracing so common in Italy appears only rarely — most notably at Saint-Germain-en-Laye, where elaborate terraces, replete with waterworks, grottos and automata were created for Henri IV at the very end of the sixteenth century.

In England elaboration of garden design did not develop until after the disruption of the Wars of the Roses, when the accession of Henry VII brought relative peace. At the beginning of the sixteenth century the new king's palace at Richmond had a series of small enclosed gardens linked by covered walks, with plantings and patterns in colored sand in intricate shapes including lions and dragons; in Britain these versions of the parterre were known as knots. In 1515 Cardinal Wolsey, Lord Chancellor to Henry VIII, began building his palace at Hampton Court. Here again there was a series of enclosed gardens with arbors, turf seats and knots, still inward looking, but

much more elaborate than medieval forerunners had been.

Wolsey took great pleasure in his gardens but when he fell from favor after failing to procure the king's divorce, he was pressured into making a present of his grandiose palace to the king. Henry began new construction at Hampton Court, adding tilting grounds and a private garden with a mount, climbed by a spiral path which led to a summer house that looked down on the River Thames and the gardens in which carved and gilded heraldic animals were raised on posts and pedestals among the flowers. At this time Italian workmen were employed at Hampton Court and some Italian influence was to be expected, but the spur to Henry VIII's ostentation was competition with François I of France, whom he met at the Field of Cloth of Gold in 1520, and in general Italian style arrived via France.

In 1538 Henry began building a great new palace at Nonsuch, south of London, which

Sir Thomas More, Wolsey's successor as Lord Chancellor, until he too crossed the King's wishes, laid out a garden at his riverside home in the village of Chelsea a few miles upstream from London. Contemporaries said it "was crowned with almost perpetual verdure; it had flowering shrubs, and the branches of fruit trees . . . appeared like a tapestry woven by nature itself." Here, like Cosimo de Medici at his villas, he entertained friends and scholars, such as Erasmus, in a way reminiscent of the ancient Academies. A century later, when Beaufort House was built on the site, fine gardens were retained, for the Duchess of Beaufort was a keen botanist.

In *Utopia*, his humanist blue print for an ideal state, More made the inhabitants "set great store by their gardens . . . [with] study and diligence [that] cometh not only of pleasure, but also of certain strife and contention that is between street and street, concerning the trimming, husbanding and furnishing . . . "

may have been influenced by François's palace at Fontainbleau and offered a similar halfway stage between the medieval and the fully Italianate garden.

The English nobility began to follow the fashion for more elaborate gardens and though smaller homes clung longer to the older styles, gardens still had an important place in towns and cities. By the end of the sixteenth century historian John Stow was complaining, in his

Survey of London, that land was being enclosed "not so much for use or profit as for show and leisure, betraying the vanity of men's minds."

The trading contacts of the Netherlanders led to the introduction of many new plants in Holland and when Protestant refugees fled to England from the Low Countries and France the gardeners among them brought their horticultural skills. English trade and exploration were also growing ever wider and an increasing interest in plants was developing. The reign of Elizabeth I saw the publication of a number of popular books on gardening. Thomas Hill, was the first in 1558, the year of her accession, with what its title page described as:

"A most briefe and pleasante treatise, teaching how to dresse, sow and set a Garden, and what properties also these few herbs here spoken of, have to our commodity; with the remedies that may be used against such beasts, worms, flies and such like that commonly annoy gardens, gathered out of the principallest Authors . . . and now Englished by Thomas Hill, Londoner."

This book was expanded in 1563 as *The Profitable Arte of Gardening* and a third version, further enlarged in 1577, was retitled *The Gardener's Labyrinth*.

As an illustration from Hill's book shows, small gardens remained enclosed and quadrilinear, closer to those of the Moors than the gardens of the great Italian villas.

Among large gardens the most sumptuous of Elizabeth's reign were probably those made for the Earl of Leicester at Kenilworth castle and for Lord Burleigh at Theobalds but, although they featured statuary and fountains, it was not until the next reign that the continental style

An illustration from the title page of Thomas Hill's A most briefe and pleasante treatise, teaching how to dresse, sow and set a Garden, *published in 1563, shows formal beds and an inner fence of lattice work.*

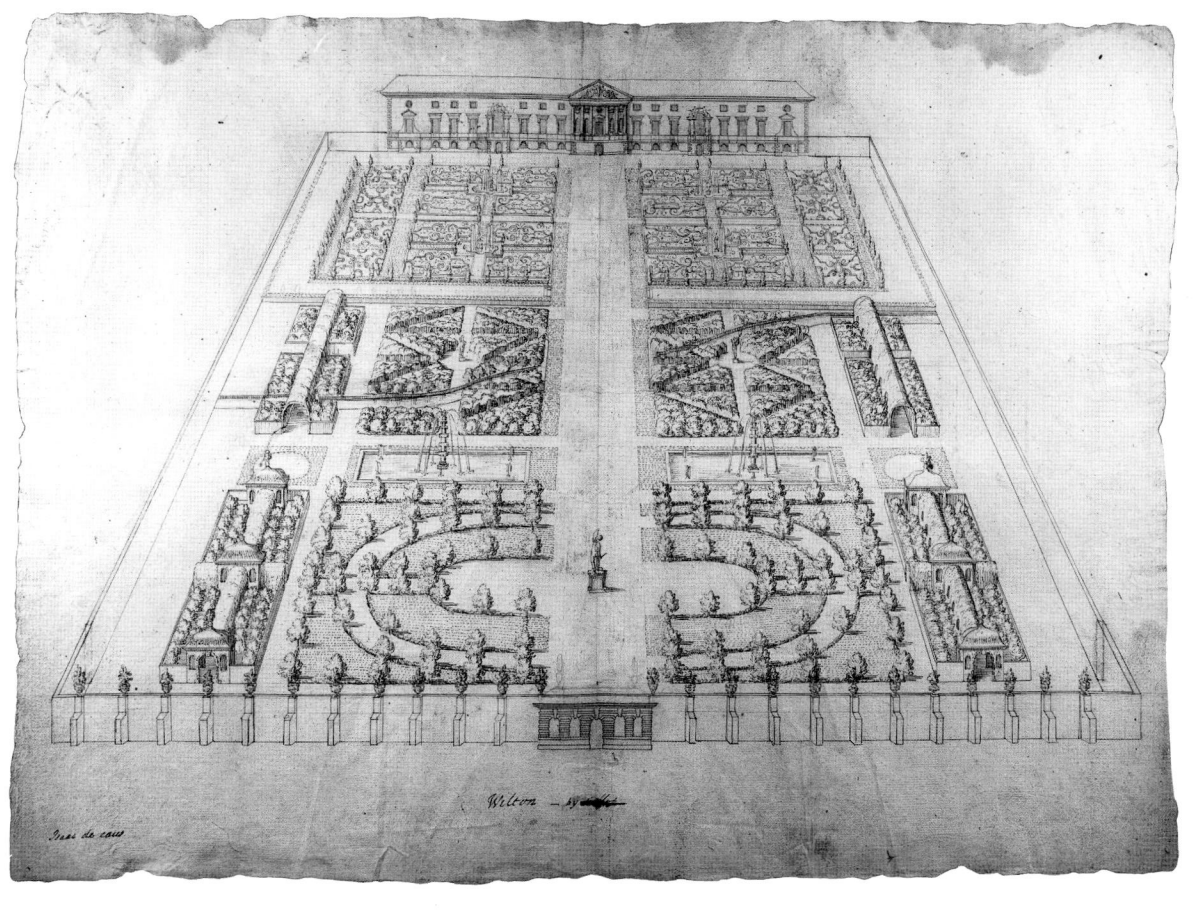

Left *The gardens at Wilton House, as laid out by Isaac de Caus for the fourth Earl of Pembroke c. 1632. More than 1000 yds (900 m) long, 350 (315) broad and symmetrical, except for the irregular course of the river Nadder, the garden is in three clear sections. Nearest the house are formal beds set with knots and four elaborate fountains. They can be viewed both from the house and from the raised terrace which runs along the sides and then encloses this garden. Next is a woodland section, with statues of Flora and Bacchus in the central clearings, flanked by covered walks, then two large basins around columns which spout water. The end section offers walks among grass and cherry trees around a central statue of a gladiator, with more covered walks at the sides. The main axis ends in a grotto with more water effects set under a final terrace which looks back on the garden. Major alterations were made in the first half of the eighteenth century and additions by James Wyatt in 1801 and as recently as 1971 have produced a very different scene today.*

began to dominate with the gardens created by Isaac de Caus for the Earl of Pembroke at Wilton from 1632.

Caus was probably the son of Salomon de Caus, a French Huguenot expert in fountains and waterworks, who after installing Italian-style grottos, fountains and water automata in the gardens of the Brussels Court, undertook a number of royal commissions in England. When James I's daughter Elizabeth married the Elector Palatine in 1613 he went to Heidelberg to create an elaborate garden for her, which he illustrated in his *Hortus Palatinus*. (He also published books on perspective and hydraulics.) The terrain at Heidelberg precluded an Italian-style linking of house and garden but the garden contained many Renaissance features. Both German princes and rich commoners such as the Fugger banking family had begun to adopt the Italian style but the outbreak of the Thirty Years' War in 1618 delayed the further development of garden design in the German principalities.

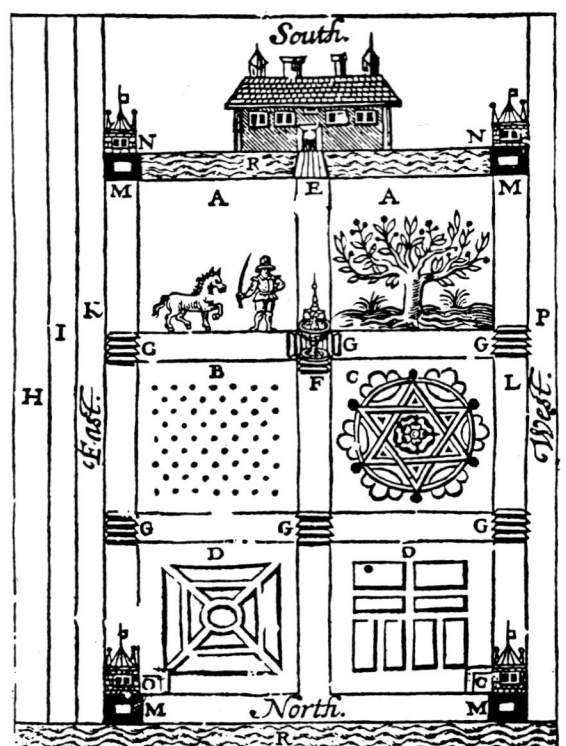

A garden plan from William Lawson's A New Orchard and Garden, first published 1616. The figures of a horse and a man are probably meant to suggest topiary work rather than statues. Lawson's key:
A. All these square must be set with Trees, the Garden and other Ornaments must stand in spaces betwixt the trees, and in the borders and fences. B. Trees twenty yards asunder. C. Garden Knopts. D. Kitching Garden. E. Bridge. F. Conduit. G. Staires. H. Walks set with great wood thick. I. Walks set with great wood round about your Orchard. K. The Out fence. L. The Out fence set with stone-fruit. M. Mount. To force Earth for a Mount or such like, set it round with quick, and lay boughes of Trees strangely intermingled, the tops inward with the Earth in the middle.
N. Still house. O. Good standing for Bees, if you have an house. P. If the River run by your door, and under your mount, it will be pleasant.

Left *The garden outside Heidelberg castle designed by Salomon de Caus, as illustrated by Mattaeus Marian in 1645. At right angles to the castle and on a steep slope it was a difficult commission. It included mazes, grottos, fountains and automata and Caus even composed the tunes to be played by his water organs.*

Francis Bacon: Of Gardens

English philosopher and essayist Francis Bacon — and another Lord Chancellor from 1618 — wrote an essay entitled *Of Gardens*, which appears in the second edition of his collected Essays, published in 1625. It expresses his opinion of what a garden should be like rather than describing contemporary gardens of the late Elizabethan and early Jacobean period, and his ideas look both back and forward in time and taste. He disliked elaborate topiary — "images cut out in juniper or other garden stuff; they be for children" he declared, but "little low hedges, round, like welts, with some pretty pyramids, I like well." Knots with patterns of colored earth he also thought "but toys, you may see as good sights many times in tarts," and he considered that "pools mar all and make the garden unwholesome and full of flies and frogs," though he liked fountains and bathing pools and even found water jokes acceptable although "nothing to health and sweetness." His own pools at Gorhambury were presumably of moving water. They had colored pebbles set into the bottom in patterns of fishes and other figures clearly visible through the clear water. He liked lawns, declaring "nothing more pleasant to the eye than green grass closely shorn," and recommends planting alleys with burnet, wild thyme and water mints which smell delightful when crushed underfoot. Mounts also have his approval — a "princely garden" should have "in the very middle, a fair mount, with three ascents, and alleys, enough for foure to walk abreast; which I would have to be perfect circles, without any bulwarkes or embossements; and the whole mount to be thirty foot high; and some fine banquetting house, with some chimneys neatly cast, and without too much glass."

Bacon thought 30 acres quite enough for the grandest garden — a green approach of four acres, a main garden of twelve and beyond that a further six acres of "natural wilderness," dotted with thyme, pinks, daisies, periwinkles, cowslips and other flowers in clumps "in the nature of molehills" with some taller bushes, kept well trimmed.

Entertaining in a garden, from an early seventeenth-century engraving.

MOGUL GARDENS

The Mongol conquerors who swept westward in the thirteenth and fourteenth centuries overran Persia and brought destruction with them. Later, especially under Timur (Marlowe's Tamberlaine) they adopted Persian ways, and art, including garden art, again began to flourish. At Bokhara and Samarkand extensive irrigation works fed many gardens and Timur himself had a number of magnificent palaces with fine gardens. In one of them, the *Bagh-i-Blisht*, or Paradise Garden, palatial apartments were set on an artificial hill, like that of Kublai Khan at Beijing. The garden was full of fruit trees, and fountains with six large rectangular pools were linked by water channels and raised paths lined by avenues of trees.

After Timur's death, his empire disintegrated as contenders struggled for power but from them emerged the Emperor Babur ("The Tiger") — Zahir ud din Mohammed (1483–1530). He grew up in Ferghana, an oasis of fruit and flowers in what is now Uzbekistan, which he inherited at the age of 12. At 14 he briefly captured Samarkand and eventually, in 1508, emerged as conqueror of Kabul in Afghanistan and began to build an empire, driving into India and making a new capital, first in Delhi, then at Agra. At Kabul and Agra, Babur and his court created many gardens. Even city streets and squares were planted with trees and flowers. After temporary burial in one of his Agra gardens his body was taken to Kabul and, as he wished, buried in the Bagh-i Babur Shah, overlooking one of his favorite views.

A feature of the Mogul gardens is the chadar *(shawl), a form of water chute used instead of a cascade to take water from one level to another. Set at an angle so that it will always catch the sun, whatever its position, its surface is carved with patterns, usually fish scales or shells, offering many facets to increase both the glittering refraction and the sound made by the water as it flows. Here, devoid of water, the patterning is clearly seen.*

Babur's successor was Hamayun, an insignificant ruler by comparison. The garden around his tomb, south of Delhi, is interesting in that it shows the narrowness of the watercourses of early Mogul gardens more suited to Kabul than to the hot flat lands of India where Babur at first thought it impossible to make successful gardens.

The Garden of Fidelity

Four years after his conquest of Kabul, the Emperor Babur created the *Bagh-i-Wafa*, the Garden of Fidelity. He describes it in his memoirs recorded in the *Babur-nama* as:

"opposite the fort of Adinaphur, to the south on rising ground . . . It overlooks the river which flows between the fort and the palace . . . I brought plantains and planted them here. They grew and thrived. The year before I had planted sugar cane in it, which throve remarkably well, and the climate in the winter season is temperate. In the garden there is a small hillock, from which a stream of water, sufficient to drive a mill, incessantly flows into the garden below. The fourfold field plot of the garden is situated on this eminence. On the southwest part of this garden is a reservoir of water . . . .which is wholly planted round with orange trees; there are likewise pomegranates. All round the piece of water the ground is quite covered with clover. This spot is the very eye of beauty of the garden. At the time when the oranges become yellow the prospect is delightful."

The Emperor
Babur directing
his gardeners
in the making of
the Bagh-i-Wafa
(Garden of
Fidelity) near
Kabul.

The next Emperor, Akbar, another great warrior, extended his power to Kashmir and, though not a passionate gardener, made the first of many fine Mogul gardens there. His son and grandson, Jahangir and Shah Jahan, were garden enthusiasts. During the former's reign no less than 77 gardens were laid out around Lake Dal in the center of the Vale of Kashmir. Shah Jahan was responsible for the spectacular *Shalamar Bagh* at Lahore, a celebration of a new canal which brought plentiful water to the city, but his greatest garden, made as a memorial to Mumtaz Mahal, his favorite wife, is that around her tomb, the Taj Mahal at Agra.

The Abode of Love

The Shalamar Bagh (Garden of the Abode of Love), Srinagar, Kashmir, was one of the finest of Mogul gardens and enough remains to give an impression of its former glory. Originally it was approached from Lake Dal by boat up a canal lined with poplars which led to a pavilion, the *Diwan-i-Am* (Hall of Public Audience), where the emperor would take his seat on a black marble throne placed above a waterfall and approached by stepping stones. Beyond that a further canal with fountains spaced down its length led to the emperor's private garden with a hall of audience set across a cascade (of which only the throne remains), and then to the zenana garden for the women where a large square pool studded with 140 fountains surrounds a black marble pavilion built by Shah Jahan. The cascade behind it was embellished with *chini-kanas*, niches where lights could be put at night to glimmer through the water. A stream at the head of the garden supplied water to flow through the canal and gravity-fed fountains everywhere sent up great plumes of water, not the fine sprays of the fountains there today.

The Taj Mahal

The Taj Mahal, though a classic, four-part *chahar-bagh* or paradise garden divided by canals, has the tomb of Mumtaz placed on a raised terrace at the end of the garden instead of at its center where there is a raised tank which reflects the white marble mausoleum. The central avenue was higher than the surrounding garden, aiding irrigation and giving the carpet effect seen in Moorish gardens. Star-shaped parterres, outlined in stone, line the main canals but these are now planted with single trees and, like the lawns and open treatment of the garden today, must be replaced in

The Diwan-i-Am *or Hall of Public Audience at Shalamar Garden in Kashmir was the place where Mogul emperors conducted court business in water-cooled comfort. The great tree is a chenar,* Platanus orientalis, *a species which forms an important element of the garden.*

the mind's eye by the abundance of flowers and fruit trees, with shade trees along the walks, which would originally have added color, scent and shelter from the sun. Shah Jahan himself was deposed by his son and imprisoned in Agra's Red Fort, where for the six years until his death he looked out at the memorial he had raised to his beloved Mumtaz.

Shah Jahan was the last of the garden-building emperors. though a fine garden was made at Pinjaur, near Simla, during the reign of Aurungzebe, his usurping son. Built by Aurungzebe's foster brother, Fadai Khan, it has a series of seven terraces with a central channel of water flowing through them with *chini-khanas* behind the cascades which can still give a magical effect at night.

Below *The Taj Mahal in the evening.*

Bottom *From the sixteenth to the eighteenth century, model gardens made of wax or of cake decorated with marzipan and icing were carried in procession at Turkish festivals and given as presents on special occasions. This illumination comes from a sixteenth-century manuscript in the Topkapi Museum.*

Persia and Turkey

While the Mogul tradition was growing there had been a revival of garden-making in Persia after Shah Abbas defeated the Uzbeks and the Ottomans and established a new capital at Isfahan, though little remains of the gardens he created there. Later Shahs made gardens at Shiraz and Persian gardens maintained their traditional style.

In Turkey, too, gardens follow Persian style, though not their fourfold division. Fountains and pools, rectangular flowerbeds and scented plants, especially roses and tulips, were the main features plus the kiosk, or small pavilion, from which the garden would be enjoyed rather than by walking through it. Along the coast a kiosk would often be placed to look out to sea or even be sited above the water. By the seventeenth century western influence was already leading to the introduction of terraces and parterres.

FRENCH FORMALITY

Opposite *The gardens of the Chateau du Vaux-le-Vicomte were reconstructed toward the end of the nineteenth century and restored almost to their original condition, though lacking some of their water features. The main building of the house is raised on a platform and surrounded by a moat. A bridge links it to the main parterre where compartiments de broderie lead down to lower levels. There, fountains and basins of water are interrupted by the line of the Grotte, a wall with niched cascades, faced by another row of cascades hidden from an approach from the chateau side. Beyond, the vista continues into the distance, broken by a huge statue of Hercules. This main axis is crossed at right angles by a long canal basin, hidden from view by the woods on either side. Vaux has its great fountains and cascades but unlike most Italian gardens exploits its level planes and the reflective surfaces of the water rather than its movement.*

Following pages *The view from the end of the canal, down the tapis vert of the allée royale, back to the Palace of Versailles at ground level, the Apollo Fountain in the foreground. This was a view which the Sun King himself particularly recommended in his instructions for visiting the gardens.*

Below *The great vista from the first terrace at Versailles, past the Fountain of Latona and the water parterre, down to the Apollo fountain where the canal stretches into the distance before the ground begins to rise. An engraving by Gabriel Perelle in* Recueil des plus belles maisons royales de France. *This view is similar to that seen from the king's bedchamber at the center of the palace facade.*

By the beginning of the seventeenth century French gardens were beginning to develop a style of their own. In *Théâtre d'Agriculture*, published in 1600, Olivier de Serres claimed that "our own France has won the prize from all other nations." His book emphasizes balance in design and is the first to point out the need for design to compensate for the distortion of perspective from particular viewpoints.

Etienne du Perac (appointed *architecte du roi* by Henri IV in 1595) is credited by his pupil Claude Mollet with the introduction of the idea of creating the whole parterre as a single unit. He may have picked up the idea on his travels in Italy but it was a concept more suited to the flat French gardens than the multilevel terraces of Italy. He devised the first elaborate parterre patterns known as *compartiments de broderie* for the chateau at Anet in 1582, where Mollet was responsible for their making. On a much larger scale than earlier parterre patterns, they were appropriately named, for the same designs were often used for embroidery. They employed colored earth, not flowers, between the box-hedge patterns and sometimes incorporated bands of turf. Later, Mollet's own sons — they became a dynasty of gardeners — produced broderie designs in flowing plant-like forms, a style also produced by Jacques Boyceau de la Barauderie, author of the first French text devoted to pleasure gardens and their ornament, *Traité du Jardinage*, published posthumously in 1638.

In 1651 Mollet's son André, who after working for the French king had become head gardener to Sweden's Queen Christina, published *Jardin de Plaisir*, in which he detailed the concept of a garden which set a pattern for the kind of formal garden which was soon being widely copied in England and other parts of Europe. From the main rooms of the house there was an uncluttered view of the *parterres de broderie* beyond which were parterres of turf and *bosquets* (formal woods). A statue or a fountain was placed at the end of most of the walks and there would be grottos, aviaries, canals and other waterworks. André Mollet even suggested that painted scenes should be set up at the end of walks (removable in bad weather) to provide a more effective vista. The whole garden, especially in France, was designed to be viewed from the house and its ordered forms reflected man's control and the authority of the owner.

The garden as aggrandisement appeared on a magnificent scale when Louis XIV's Superintendent of Finances, Nicolas Fouquet, engaged the architect Louis le Vau and the painter Charles le Brun to create a magnificent new chateau at Vaux-le-Vicomte. Fouquet was confident of becoming France's next Chief Minister and wanted a setting to match his expectations. It was probably Le Brun who recommended André le Nôtre as garden designer. He had been a fellow art student when both were young and had then been trained by his father who was in charge of the gardens of the Tuileries.

Begun from scratch in 1656, with three villages being demolished to clear the space, this was to be a place for extravagant entertaining. It cost more than 16 million *livres* and at times up to 18,000 laborers were at work. After five years all was complete and a great entertainment planned to which the royal family were invited. Cardinal Mazarin had recently died but Louis, taking power into his own hands at last, decided he would be his own First Minister. Fouquet had overreached himself; he was not to have as much power as he thought. The king refused a first invitation to Vaux but then his curiosity got the better of him and he accepted.

On their arrival on August 17, 1661, Fouquet's guests were first encouraged to view the gardens and their fountains. Then, after a fine dinner, there was an outdoor performance of Molière's comedy *Les Fâcheux*, a ballet and a magnificent firework display. It seemed a great success, everyone was most impressed — but Fouquet had miscalculated. The king was furious at this ostentatious display. The subject seemed to be competing with his monarch (and was he perhaps also competing for the attentions of the beautiful Louise de la Vallière?). Within three weeks Fouquet had been arrested, charged with embezzlement and treason. How could he possibly afford such extravagance if he had not been defrauding the exchequer? He spent the rest of his life in prison.

Louis had been impressed by Vaux-le-Vicomte and set Le Brun and Le Nôtre to create a garden for himself which would top it, and indeed has had no equal since. He decided to make it at Versailles, not far from Paris, where there was a small hunting lodge built by Louis XIII. It was to be an embodiment of Louis' own ideas of the monarchy, taking as its central emblem the sun, embracing the idea of the sun god Apollo, together with his sister

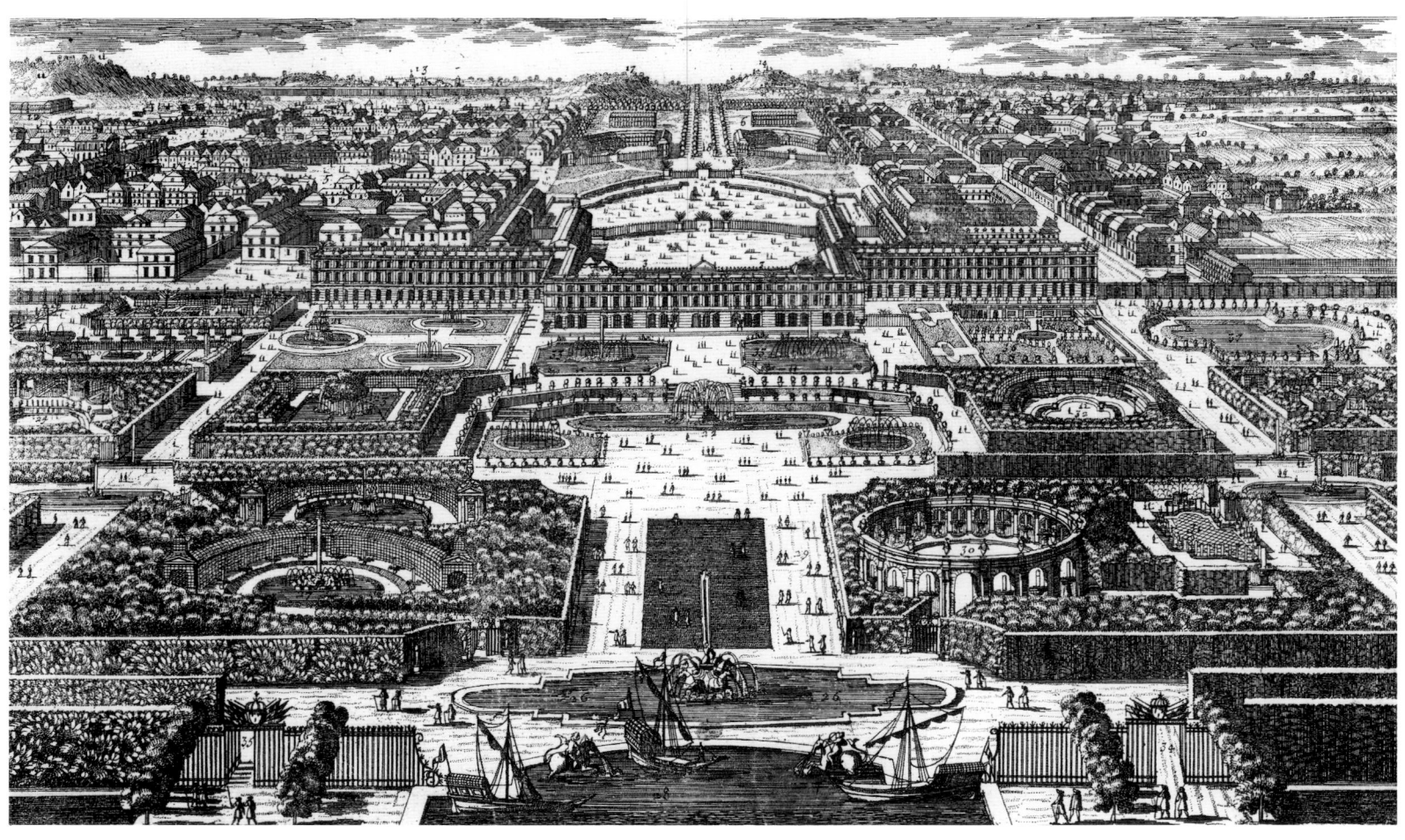

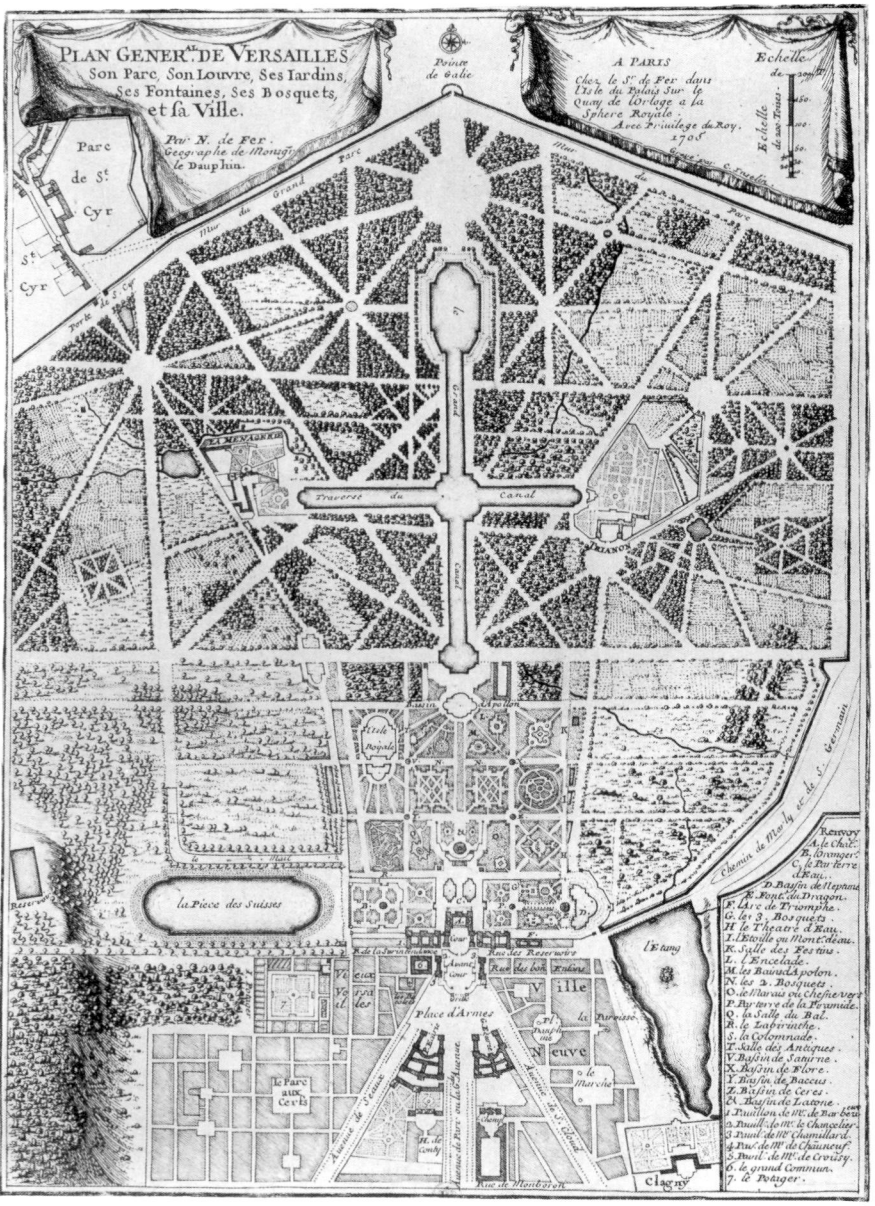

Diana, and thus allowing for a presentation of everything from the hours of the day to the seasons of the year. Le Brun was in charge of the iconography and sculpture, Le Nôtre the landscape and gardens. The site was poor, lacking views, water or woodland but Le Nôtre transformed it.

Louis involved himself closely in the whole undertaking, approving every design and asking for new versions when dissatisfied. He made additions and changes during the whole of his long reign. The gardens were worked on for five years before the building of the palace began and quite literally armies of workmen were employed: the largest of the lakes (not begun until 1678) is called the *Pièce de l'Eau des Suisses* after the regiment of Swiss Guards which made it.

The main axis of Le Nôtre's plan is from the royal apartments at the center of the palace — making Louis the pivot of the whole design — westward to the setting sun. Leading past fountains and *compartiments de broderie* and around a long lawn or *tapis vert* (green carpet) and edged by regimented woodland, the main path gives place to the mile-long stretch of the canal beyond which the ground rises steeply and the path cuts its way to the horizon through more massed woodland. Parallel paths and cross routes led between formal thickets, carefully planted woodland surrounding groves with fountains and water features. The canal was crossed by another north-south channel linking the sites of a menagerie and the Trianon, a supplementary palace built to provide a greater degree of privacy. It was originally built in 1669 for the king's mistress, Madame de Maintenon, in a supposedly "Chinese" style as the *Trianon de Porcelaine* (it was covered with Delft tiles) but, disused after a few years, it was replaced in 1687 by the Grand Trianon.

Louis XIV himself wrote a guide to the gardens, autocratically instructing visitors where to go and what to observe and admire. There are several versions, updated as the gardens were changed and new fountains and other features added. Louis was continually encouraging his designers to create bigger and grander fountains and as his guide directs visitors from one fountain to another it is clear how important they are to his concept of the gardens. But Versailles had poor supplies of water. A network of reservoirs was created west of Saint-Cyr, a huge machine at Marly raised water from the Seine with 14 enormous water-wheels and it was brought by aqueduct to Versailles. Another plan was to bring water from the Eure at Pontgoin via nearly 70 miles (110 km) of canal and aqueduct. Although the aqueduct was built, and 30,000 soldiers were employed on it, work was abandoned when they were needed at Neustadt in 1688. Despite all these provisions there was still insufficient water to keep more than those fountains closest to the palace playing all day long. When Louis went out into the *Parc* an elaborate system of observers and runners communicating by whistles and signal flags gave warning to the mechanics when the king was coming within

sight of fountains. They would then turn the fountains on, turning them off again when the royal party had passed. Today's visitors can only imagine the effect of seeing the thousands of spurting jets in action through a complete circuit at Versailles.

Although the main impression of Versailles today is of grass, trees and water there was a flower parterre near the original chateau. It was lost with the expansion of the palace, but at the Trianon flowers in vast numbers were again to be seen, even in the winter, when plants might be set out and even replaced while the king dined so that there would still be a fine display in the afternoon. Michelle Bouteau, who was married to Le Nôtre's niece, was in charge of plants and kept nearly two million flower pots ready planted, frequently setting out huge displays of potted plants to fill the parterres.

In time Louis decided he needed a more distant setting for his private entertaining and began building at nearby Marly, in a valley closed in on three sides by hills and with a magnificent view to St. Germain. A raised terrace preserved privacy by blocking any view of the garden from outside. This new "retreat" was no small love nest; in addition to the royal chateau it included a group of palatial pavilions set around a great terraced rectangle of pools and fountains. Despite the grand scale a feeling of exclusiveness and intimacy was maintained. On the hillside above the chateau was built a cascade of 53 stages known as the *Rivière* which discharged into three stepped basins. For the amusement of guests there was a switchback railway, a huge swing and a course laid out for an early form of golf, called *mail*.

The chateau at Marly has now gone, demolished during the rule of Bonaparte, and only the outline of the gardens remains. Versailles however, despite the changes over the years, retains the essence of Le Nôtre and Louis' vision intact. It can still lay claim to being the world's largest and grandest garden. It was much copied, though never on quite the

Opposite above *A view from the end of the Grand Canal looking back to the palace and town of Versailles. As well as the fountains and parterre of the terraces near the palace, the fountains and areas for dancing and entertainment within the bosquets can be seen. The aqueduct bringing water from Marly is visible on the left just below the horizon.*

Opposite below left *A plan of Versailles and its park in 1705.*

Opposite below right *View from the terrace above the Orangery to the Pièce de l'Eau des Suisses.*

Below *An early eighteenth-century engraving of the chateau and its visitors' pavilions at Marly.*

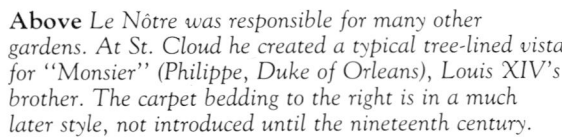

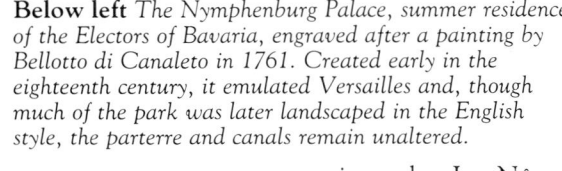

same extravagant egocentric scale. Le Nôtre worked on other royal gardens and for some of the nobility, including a remodeling of the Grande Condé chateau at Chantilly. His imitators created gardens following the formal French style all over Europe and even, though on a very much simpler scale, in America. In the German principalities the most important examples are at Herrenhausen, in Hanover, and Nymphenburg and Schleissheim, in Bavaria. The resources of the Austrian and Russian crowns enabled both Schönbrunn in Vienna and Peterhof near Leningrad to rival Versailles in grandeur. In Holland Het Loo was remodeled in the French manner and at Hampton Court under William and Mary a grand new scheme was effected much influenced by the Le Nôtre style.

The Parc de Sceaux, laid out by Le Nôtre for Colbert, Louis XIV's chief minister, in the 1670s. Massive earthworks were required to create his design of two axes, radiating at right angles from the chateau.

Below *Petervorets (Peterhof) Palace was Peter the Great's summer palace, 19 miles (30 km) outside Leningrad (St. Petersburg) created in the first two decades of the eighteenth century. Its magnificent fountains and cascades (and some water tricks) and the grand overall plan make a challenging comparison with Versailles.*

NEW WORLD GARDENS

Opposite At Historic St. Mary's City, Maryland, seventeenth-century homesteads and gardens have been reconstructed.

Below De Bry's engraving of the village of Secota as seen by Captain John White, leader of the first expeditions to what he called New England. The ordered plantings of sunflowers, pumpkins and tobacco do not appear in White's original sketch.

When Europeans first reached the Americas they found elaborate gardens around the Aztec palaces of Mexico with terraces, cascades fed with water brought by aqueducts, woodland areas, scented flowers and aviaries. At Iztapalapan gardens were laid out in regular squares with trellis bordering the paths between them. When the Aztecs conquered the lands westward they brought back plants for the emperor's own garden, long before the botanic gardens of the European Renaissance. The great city of Tenochtitlan, where Mexico City now stands, had planted terraces between the buildings and gardens on the roofs. In the surrounding lake were artificial islands, floating rafts loaded with earth and planted as nursery gardens.

In Peru the Inca civilization also had its parks and gardens, served by elaborate irrigation systems. The Inca's favorite palace at Yucay, according to the contemporary Spanish report of Garcilasso de la Vega, had spacious gardens and groves with a great variety of flowers and scented plants. Among them there were also beautifully modeled plant forms in silver and gold, and corn shown with the golden ear half enwrapped by silver leaves.

All this was swept away by the conquistadors and their successors. Only a few vestiges remain, some of the irrigation systems in Ecuador, ruins of some of the garden structure at Tezcotzinco and a reminder of Tenochtitlan in the *Chinampas*, or floating gardens, which can still be seen at Xochimilco, all that survives of the once great lake.

Further north there is no evidence of elaborate early gardening. The first English expeditions under the command of Captain John White found agriculture well established by the east coast Amerindians. They had no pleasure gardens although the apparent fertility and carefully tended, well-ordered plantings led the new arrivals to call them gardens. White's own paintings show only corn, at three consecutive growing stages, but when the German engraver Theodor de Bry came to engrave the scenes for publication he added tobacco plants, pumpkins and sunflowers, perhaps on the basis of further information because the indigenous peoples are known to have cultivated a variety of fruit and vegetables.

The early European settlers in North America were far too busy growing food crops and maintaining and protecting their settlements to bother with flower gardens. The colonists took seeds, plants and books on European gardening practice with them. It is said that the 90 women who arrived at Jamestown in 1619 as wives for the earlier male settlers brought daffodil bulbs, but at first the emphasis was on the herbs they needed as medicines and salves, and for flavoring food, repelling moths and vermin, dyeing cloth and sweetening the air. Later, as settlements became more established, the garden plot within each home's simple wooden fence began to include some flowers from Europe and from the countryside around. By the mid-seventeenth century, with prosperity increasing, Edward Johnson, in his

The reconstructed settlement of the Pilgrim Fathers at Plimouth Plantation, Massachusetts, shows the small enclosures in which housewives might grow their herbs and necessary plants.

Opposite and below
Since 1926 the gardens and old houses of Williamsburg, Virginia, have been restored and maintained in their original colonial style — the formal box hedges and geometrical beds of late seventeenth-century England and the Netherlands. The fine display of springtime tulips is a reminder of the great vogue for them in Holland in the first half of the seventeenth century.

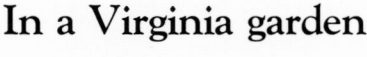

Wonder Working Providence of Sions Saviour, is describing the gardens of New England as "bright with a variety of flowers." Gardens had to be fenced to keep out livestock. Where houses were strung out along main streets they had gardens on one side and orchards on the other but when set around a green, like that of an English village, they had gardens and orchards to the rear.

Further north, in the Dutch settlements around New Amsterdam, on Long Island and along the Hudson River gardening was probably more formal and sophisticated and they imported a great many ornamental plants as well as growing native flowers. New Englanders made their gardens with raised geometrical beds and trimmed hedges in the English style and kept to this kind of simple formality much longer than in Europe.

When the city of Philadelphia was laid out in 1682, William Penn and his commissioners adopted a gridiron plan. There were two main streets, each 100 ft (30 m) wide, with a ten-acre (4 ha) public square or park at the intersection, and twenty-eight cross streets of half the width with four smaller parks, one for each quarter of the town. His recommendation was that each house should be placed in the center of its plot with gardens, orchards or fields on all sides so that it should be a country town that could never be destroyed by a widespread fire. At Pennsbury Manor, the house which Penn planned for himself, there were terraces down to the river and an upper and a lower garden. An avenue of poplars lined a broad graveled path from the landing stage on the river to the front door of the house. Penn commented on the variety and bright colors of the native flowers and instructed his gardeners to transplant them from the woods.

In a Virginia garden

Have you pleasure in a garden? All things thrive in it, most surprisingly; you can't walk by a Bed of Flowers, but besides the entertainment of their Beauty, your Eyes will be saluted by the charming colors of the Humming Bird, which revels among the Flowers and licks off the Dew and Honey from their tender Leaves on which it only feeds. Its size is not half so large as an English Wren, and its color is a glorious shining mixture of Scarlet, Green and Gold. Colonel Byrd in his garden which is the finest in that Country has a Summer House set round with the Indian Honey-Suckle which all the summer is continually full of sweet Flowers, in which these Birds delight exceedingly.

Robert Beverly: *The History and Present State of Virginia*, 1705.

Williamsburg, capital of Virginia, was named for William III, Britain's Dutch king, and its formal gardens reflect English and Dutch style of the period, soon to be outmoded in most of Europe, but remaining popular in America. In the grounds of the Governor's "palace" there was a mound, a feature by then out of fashion in England, and a maze in American holly. The townhouses of the wealthy were built on acre plots (0.4 h) and featured box edgings and topiary. Summers were hotter and winters colder than in the old countries and box managed to survive both. Arbors, covered walks and leafy trees provided summer shade and dogwood and box hedges some winter color.

ENGLISH LANDSKIP

A bird's eye view of Hampton Court Palace and its park, engraved by Johannes Kip from a drawing by Leonard Knyff. The patte-d'oie, or "goose-foot" pattern of avenues radiating out into the deer park was made for Charles II — the central element here formed by a canal. There is also a small canal between the arcs of lime trees from which the avenues lead. The elaborate broderie parterre with its many fountains was designed for the taste of William of Orange and the parterre on the river side of the palace for his wife Mary II, but their successor, Mary's sister Anne, disliking the smell of box and anything pertaining to her late brother-in-law, uprooted the box, grassed over the parterre and removed most of the fountains. However she was responsible for having the famous maze built on the north side of the palace.

Following the defeat of the Royal party in the English Civil War and the execution of King Charles I, his son fled to France. There he would have been well aware of the developing French garden style and after his return to England in 1660 as Charles II, it is thought that Le Nôtre may have been involved (although he did not actually cross the Channel) in the new plans for St. James's Park in London, which was developed with a straight canal and wooded walks. André and Gabriel Mollet were already in England and became royal gardeners — André had already made two previous visits to England. At St. James's the *patte-d'oie* (goose-foot) pattern of three to five paths radiating at acute angles was adopted and later used at Hampton Court, a long canal forming the central "toe," though full developments at Hampton Court had to wait until 1689 when the new king, Dutchman William of Orange, joint monarch with his wife, Queen Mary, added a parterre, fountains and statues.

In 1664 John Evelyn published *Sylva, or a Discourse of Forest Trees*, prompted partly by the need to grow timber for shipbuilding. A later edition included a plan for a garden with fountain gardens near the house and geometrically ranged trees and with areas marked for timber

trees, meadows and corn beyond. Two years later Samuel Pepys recorded in his diary a conversation with Hugh May, Comptroller of the Works to Charles II, during which they

"discussed of the present fashion of gardens to make them plain that we have the best walks of gravel in the world, France having none, nor Italy; and the green of our bowling alleys is better than any they have. So our business here being air, this is the best way, only with a little mixture of statues, or pots, which may be handsome, and so filled with another pot of such or such a flower or green, as the season of the year will bear. And then for flowers, they are best seen in a little plot by themselves: besides, their borders spoil the walks of another garden: and then for fruit, the best way is to have walls built circularly one within another, to the south, on purpose for fruit, and leave the walking garden only for that use."

However, if flowers were out of place among the lawns and wooded walks there was a growing interest in horticulture, especially in the exotics then being introduced from other countries, and nurserymen began to function on a major scale. The Brompton Nursery (later

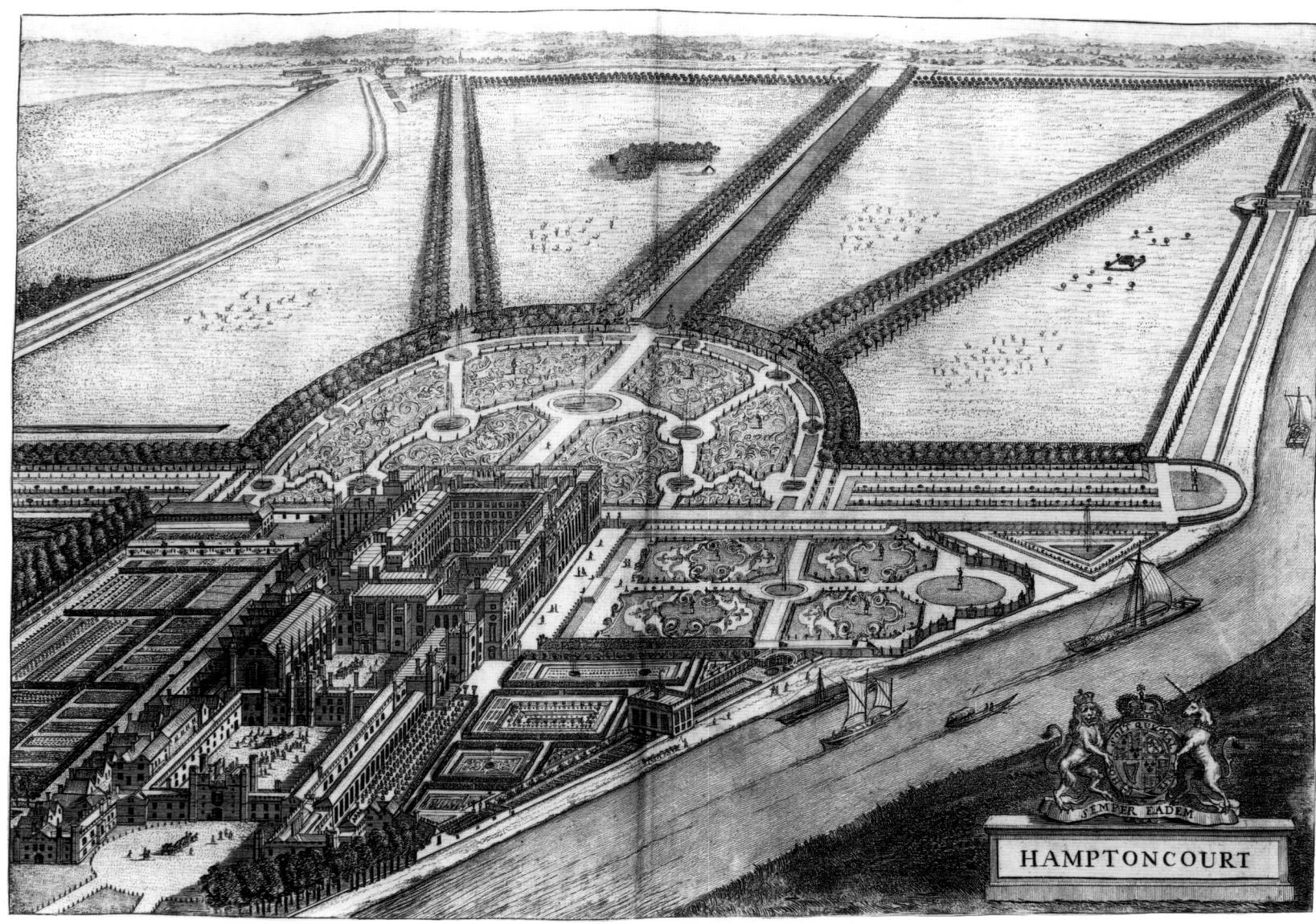

HAMPTONCOURT

London and Wise), established in 1681, became dominant not only as plant suppliers but as garden designers.

Evergreens were particularly fashionable: holly, box and yew clipped into formal shapes and citrus trees, which had to be protected in winter so that orangeries became a feature of grand houses. Although the British landscape is not so flat as Holland, Dutch influence was strong. Via Holland also came news of Chinese style, following a Dutch mission to Beijing reported, with illustrations, in a book published in 1665 and later translated into English. The Porcelain Trianon at Versailles shows this influence and in England as in France, it affected decoration rather than garden design with pagodas and screens and bridges in "Chinese" style. However, in 1685 Sir William Temple, a former envoy to the Hague who created a Dutch-style garden in Hertfordshire, wrote an essay which made the first English reference to Chinese landscape design. Called *Upon the Gardens of Epicurus* it contrasts the formal symmetry and ruled lines of European taste with the Chinese taste for irregular forms or *Sharawadgi*, though the word has no Chinese roots and it is possible that Temple made it up.

"The Chinese scorn this [formal] way of planting," he wrote, "and say, a boy, that can tell a hundred, may plant walks of trees in straight lines ... But their greatest reach of the imagination is employed in contriving Figures, where the Beauty shall be great and strike the Eye, but without any Order or Disposition of Parts, that shall be commonly or easily observed."

It was to be many years before the first "Chinese" buildings appeared in England but the idea of a break with formalism was beginning to take shape. In 1710 the Earl of Shaftesbury, Ashley Cooper, declared in *The Moralists* that he would

"no longer resist the passion for Things of a natural kind: where neither Art, nor the Conceit or Caprice of Man has spoiled their genuine order ... Even the rude Rocks, the Mossy Caverns, the irregular unwrought Grottos and broken Falls of Waters, with all the horrid Graces of the Wilderness itself, as representing nature more, will be the more engaging, and appear with a Magnificence beyond the formal Mockery of Princely Gardens."

He was not alone. In the *Spectator* in 1711 Joseph Addison is describing the perfect garden as one in which Nature and Reason go hand in hand with "rocks shaped into grottos covered with woodbines and jessamines ... springs made to run among pebbles." In the following June he is suggesting that "if the natural Embroidery of the Meadows were helpt and improved by some small Additions of Art and the several Rows of Hedges set off by Trees and Flowers ... a Man might make a pretty landskip [Landscape] of his own Possessions." He attacks the way in which "British gardeners

... love to deviate from [nature] ... Our trees rise in Cones, Globes and Pyramids. We see the marks of the Scissars on every Plant and Bush."

The poet Alexander Pope also attacked topiary the following year in an article in the *Guardian*, offering a satirical "Catalogue of Greens" for sale, including:

Adam and Eve in Yew; Adam a little shattered by the fall of the tree of knowledge in the great storm; Eve and the Serpent very flourishing.
The Tower of Babel, not yet finished.
Noah's ark in holly, standing on the mount; the ribs a little damaged for want of water.
A Pair of Giants, stunted, to be sold cheap.
A Queen Elizabeth in Phylyraea, a little inclining to the Green Sickness, but of full growth.
Another Queen Elizabeth in Myrtle, which was very forward, but Miscarries by being too near a Savine.

Neither Pope nor Addison, in retrospect, were as radical in their ideas as may appear. Pope's own garden, for instance, would probably have looked very formal to modern eyes. But the reaction against formality was already beginning to show in the garden designs of Charles Bridgeman and Stephen Switzer and during the eighteenth century there was a rapid evolution of garden style in England.

Meanwhile, in Europe dating from about 1715, the year of Louis XIV's death, the baroque lines of the formal garden began to give way to a lighter and more light-hearted style of rococo decoration. Italian and French styles were not abandoned but in the eighteenth century it was England that took the lead in innovative garden design which began to be copied on the Continent.

The landscape garden

The change in English attitudes was partly due to changing circumstances. Reclamation of wasteland, swamp and scrub brought more of the countryside under human control, more scientific methods were being applied in agriculture to increase fertility and yield and a succession of political measures enabled the nobles and larger landowners to extend their holdings, to take over areas which had formerly been available for common grazing and to reallocate landholdings so that the small strips separately farmed within a common field were replaced by larger blocks. This "rationalization" had already deprived many peasants of their livelihood under Elizabeth but throughout the eighteenth century it grew in pace, especially after 1740.

Whereas former English gardens had tended to be enclosed — "on ev'ry side you look, behold the Wall," Pope said — there was now more inclination to look out and survey the new parkland. The new fashion for Palladian architecture, and for building and remodeling country mansions in the style, demanded a different setting for their pillared porticoes and classical proportions.

Following pages The garden at Stourhead, Wiltshire, was designed and developed in the English landscape style of grass, woods and water by the owner, Henry Hoare II, in the mid-eighteenth century. There are temples, a grotto, and springs utilized to form cascades but the design is dominated by the lake and its elegant bridge around which the other elements are ranged.

In 1715 Switzer published his *Nobleman's Gentleman's and Gardener's Recreation* in which he advocated the treatment of the whole of an estate as a unity with one or two main axes to hold the design together and dispensing with the parterre beside the house. Queen Anne, who succeeded to the throne in 1702, helped influence opinion against the box parterre, statues and fountains of the Dutch style, partly by insisting on the eradication of all the additions which her predecessor had made at Hampton Court, and partly by giving Henry Wise, now royal gardener, a reduced budget for managing the same amount of garden!

According to Horace Walpole, writing toward the end of the century, Bridgeman still made considerable use of "straight walks with high clipped hedges" but was responsible for the move to opening up the landscape by his use of the ha-ha. Walpole thought he may have invented this device, but it had in fact been used much earlier in France — where it was

Right *A ha-ha effectively keeps deer or domestic animals from crossing into the garden, but its height and width must be matched to those of the species grazing in adjoining fields. The same principle is often employed today in zoos so that there is no visual barrier between visitors and animals.*

Below *Even at close quarters a ha-ha can be used without attracting attention. Here it separates the lawn from the field beyond.*

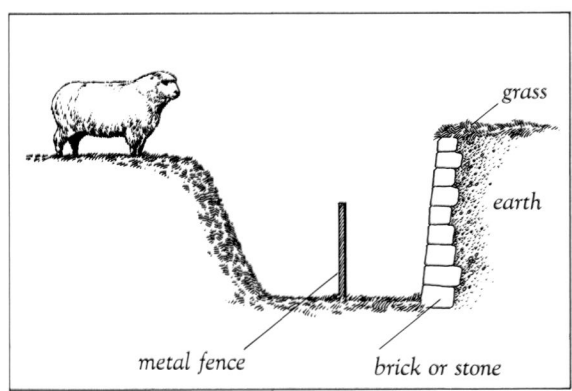

grass

earth

metal fence

brick or stone

A guide to garden design

In 1731 Alexander Pope published a poem under the title *Of Taste* which celebrates Bridgeman and encapsulates the new approach to garden design. In slightly amended form — and with Bridgeman's name replaced by that of Lord Cobham — it appears under *An Epistle to Richard Boyle, Earl of Burlington.*

To build, to plant, whatever you intend,
To rear the Column, or the Arch to
   bend,
To swell the Terrace, or to sink the
   Grot;
In all, let Nature never be forgot . . .
Consult the Genius of the Place in all;
That tells the Waters or to rise, or fall;

Or helps th' ambitious Hill the Heav'ns
   to scale,
Or scoops in circling theatres the Vale;
Calls in the Country, catches op'ning
   glades,
Joins willing woods, and varies shades
   from shades;
Now breaks, or now directs, th'
   intending Lines;
Paints as you plant, and as you work,
   designs . . .

Begin with sense, of ev'ry Art the soul,
Parts answering parts, shall slide into a
   whole,
Spontaneous beauties all around
   advance,
Start, ev'n from difficulty, strike from
   Chance;
Nature shall join you; Time shall make it
   grow
A Work to wonder at — perhaps a
   Stowe.

Without it, proud Versailles! thy glory
   falls;
And Nero's Terraces desert their walls:
The vast Parterres a thousand hands
   shall make,
Lo! Bridgeman comes, and floats them
   with a Lake;
Or cut wide views thro' Mountains to
   the Plain,
You'll wish your hill or shelter'd seat,
   again.

known as an ah-ah — and introduced to England by a French gardener in the 1690s. A ha-ha is a dry ditch, deep and wide enough to prevent cattle or other animals crossing it and used to stop them encroaching on a garden, but not visible from the higher side except when very close to it, so that the eye is carried beyond the enclosed garden into the landscape without interruption.

Though his early work remained formal, Bridgeman began to introduce winding walks and natural groves instead of regimented "wildernesses" and at Richmond even included a cultivated field within the garden plan.

His lead, however, was overtaken by the designs of William Kent, a northern England coach painter whose talent led a group of local landowners to sponsor an extended visit to Italy to study painting. There he met the Earl of Burlington who brought him back to England in 1719 and became his principal patron. He became first an interior designer, then an architect and, from 1730, a landscape designer.

In Italy he had been impressed by the paintings of Claude Lorrain (Claude Gellée) and Gaspard Dughet (who later adopted the surname of his father-in-law, Nicholas Poussin). One of his patrons had specifically asked him to acquire work in these styles, which depicted idealized scenes, many based on the countryside around Tivoli, and often with classical temples. It was these landscapes which he sought to reproduce when he turned his hand to designing gardens. They formed a perfect foil to the Palladian architecture which Lord Burlington and his circle were establishing as the new style for the country house. At Chiswick, near London, Burlington's own Palladian-inspired villa begun in 1725, Kent, working with Bridgeman, produced an asymmetrical layout with vistas leading to columns and temples.

At Rousham, in the county of Oxfordshire, he followed on from Bridgeman to create a carefully planned series of scenes and vistas which could be enjoyed if a precise route was followed. Here and at Chiswick the garden

The garden of Chiswick House, London, was designed by Charles Bridgeman and William Kent. There are temples, rustic buildings, a river with a cascade, avenues, and clipped hedge allées to create vistas. This pool and temple is lowest of a number of levels and the orange trees in tubs maintain the original design.

buildings include gothic as well as classical structures while, on a hilltop a mile distant is a triple arch — what became known as an "eye-catcher" carefully sited to give the impression of picturesque ruins in the distance.

In 1728 Robert Castell, another protégé of Lord Burlington, published his *The Villas of the Ancients Illustrated* (see page 18) and the "land-skip" style echoed some of Pliny's concepts in seeing the house open to the countryside. Kent decorated his landscapes with carefully placed classical buildings and ornament but, although there was some degree of intellectual purpose in the temples and statuary, Kent himself is said to have spent a whole night meditating beside his domed temple at Chiswick. It was imbued with a romanticism drawn from the ruins and ruined gardens which he had seen in Italy and in the paintings which formed his inspiration.

At the same time as Kent was becoming established as a garden designer Philip South-cote, newly married to the wealthy Duchess of Cleveland began the creation of a garden at Woburn Farm in Surrey. He took the "scene painting" beyond the garden and planted his hedgerows with ornamental shrubs and climbers. The sanded paths between his garden temples and buildings and around the fields of the farm itself were planted on one side with an herbaceous border, giving him both a pleasant walk and a convenient way of seeing what was happening on the farm.

Switzer had already suggested the mixing of the practical and ornamental in his first book and by 1733 he was using the term "ornamental farm" or later "*ferme ornée*," an indication that it was already an established form in France although it was several decades before the term was used there.

Most well known of the gardens imitating Southcote's work was Leasowes, at Halesowen near Birmingham, where the poet William Shenstone spent almost all his resources in creating an Arcadian sequence of lawns, streams, pools, grottos, cascades, woodland and outward views — some carefully scaled to present magnificence in miniature — to be viewed from a serpentine route along which seats, stone plaques and urns presented verses, quotations from classical texts and memorials to friends.

Top left *William Kent's own sketch for the Venus Vale at Rousham House, Oxfordshire, c.1738. Kent was more artist than practical gardener and the finer details of architecture and planting were probably left to the builders and gardeners, but the original planting at Rousham showed the quite separate use of open groves of trees, whose bare trunks helped to emphasize perspective — like the stage sets designed by Inigo Jones which seem to have been one of his inspirations — and of screens of woodland, especially of evergreens thickly underplanted with blossom trees, climbing roses and honeysuckle.*

Center *The Venus Vale, Rousham, as it looks today.*

Left *Philip Southcote's ferme ornée at Woburn.*

"Capability" Brown

Lancelot Brown (1716–83), who took the landscape style one stage further, spent his youth as a gardener in Northumberland where he was soon entrusted with the laying out of gardens. Early in his twenties he moved south and by 1741 was engaged to work at Stowe, Lord Cobham's Buckinghamshire estate, where he was responsible for carrying out Kent's designs and absorbed the elements of his style. Recommended by Lord Cobham to his friends, Brown soon became the leading landscape designer, sometimes drawing up designs to be

executed by estate workmen, sometimes contracting to carry out the work under his own supervision.

Brown's approach differed from Kent's in that, rather than creating a landscape to reflect a painting style, he thought in terms of the natural forms in the landscape, organizing and orchestrating them to create a unified but multidimensional scheme. The effect is what a great many people today consider the typical English landscape. He adopted the use of an encircling belt of woodland from Southcote's *ferme ornée*, useful for concealing boundaries and unwelcome sights but broken for fine views

The Queen's Theatre at Stowe from the rotunda, by Jacques Rigaud, in 1739. Lord and Lady Cobham are being pushed around the grounds in wheelchairs accompanied by garden designer Bridgeman. The formal pool, geometric vistas, trimmed hedges and general formality, still seem very close to the French style.

Below *Stowe, today, is the work of "Capability" Brown, imposed on that of Bridgeman and of Kent, who reshaped the lake. Most of the architectural elements remain but, although skilfully contrived, the formality is now contained within an apparently natural landscape.*

The gothic "temple" at Stowe in its bucolic setting.

Lancelot "Capability" Brown, engraved after a painting by N. Dance.

or decorative features. He made great use of water, usually in the middle distance of the major views, damming a stream to form a lake, or even two, with the dams usually carefully hidden and the extent of the lake often made to look greater by the placing of a bridge or other feature. Banks were left unplanted, with turf sweeping down to the water and ha-has were used to link the garden with the countryside beyond. He summed up his approach in 1775 in a letter giving advice on what he called good "place-making." The essentials, he said, were

" . . . a good plan, good execution, a perfect knowledge of the country and the objects in it, whether natural or artificial, and infinite delicacy in the planting, etc., so much Beauty depending in the the size of the trees and the color of the leaves to produce the effect of light and shade so very essential . . . as also hiding what is disagreeable and showing what is beautiful; getting shade from the large trees and sweets from the smaller sorts of shrubs, etc."

Brown earned the nickname "Capability" from his habit of saying, when asked to advise on the development of a property, that the estate had "capabilities" which he would be able to bring out if he were given the commission. Brown's work does indeed seem to grow out of the countryside but, in the massive changes that he sometimes made, he swept away much that had gone before, and for this his work has often been castigated by his critics.

While Brown's landscapes became the predominant style in England, it was Kent's

gardens with their temples and the *ferme ornée* which were more copied on the Continent. To this was added the idea that English style had its basis in ancient Chinese gardens. This was a misunderstanding which arose from the English translation of a letter from a French Jesuit priest in China which referred to turning and winding walks, serpentine waterways and the use of pavilions and grottos. It had certainly given some authority to the already evolving style and launched a fashion for "Chinese" buildings in gardens, most famously perhaps the pagoda which Sir William Chambers included in his designs for Princess Augusta's garden at Kew, where there were also Moorish, Roman and Gothic structures. Upstream, at Richmond, Kent had already furnished Queen Caroline's garden with a hermitage and a Merlin's Cave, complete with an appropriate tenant, a poet called Stephen Duck!

The fashion for the *jardin anglais* or the *Englischer garten* spread across Europe and included the Marquis de Girardin's estate at Ermenonville, the Little Trianon where Marie Antoinette played shepherdess at Versailles, and the summer residence of the Elector Palatine. At Rosswald, in Silesia, Count Holditz had a plethora of garden buildings erected, including pagodas, Druid caves, a hermitage, Chinese temple, and even a town for dwarves, peopled by genuine dwarves and some small children to increase their numbers.

Christian Hirschfeld, Danish Professor of Aesthetics at the University of Kiel, was an enthusiast for English landscape styles and author of a number of books on "garden art" which had a considerable influence in Scan-

Stowe

The house and garden at Stowe in Buckinghamshire went through many changes and additions from 1680 when Sir Richard Temple built a new house in Wren style to replace the old family home and its walled garden. He laid out formal parterres to the south and planted an avenue across the park towards Buckingham. They crossed the old gardens at an awkward angle and lacked the fashionable symmetry of the times, a situation which Temple aggravated rather than improved by planting an avenue of limes to the west of the house.

His successor, who became the 1st Lord Cobham, brought Vanbrugh in to expand and redesign the house and Charles Bridgeman to rework the garden.

Bridgeman made the awkward diagonals a feature of his design, which was deliberately asymmetrical, with slanted views and a few winding walks and natural groves, creating a garden halfway between the formal seventeenth-century style and the landscape gardens which were to follow. He introduced both a formal octagonal lake and a ha-ha, which made the surrounding countryside appear part of the park, and added temples designed by James Gibbs and William Kent to the classical garden buildings, tower and fake castle (actually two cottages) with which Vanbrugh enhanced his vistas. Kent continued to develop the gardens, changing the lake to a more informal shape and creating areas of more intimate landscaping, blurring or removing some of the straight lines of planting.

In 1740 Lancelot "Capability" Brown joined the staff to run the kitchen garden and, after working under Kent, by whom he was considerably influenced, and executing his designs, was himself put in charge and increased the scale of the park and opened up wide vistas. The results were not to everybody's taste: in *Planting and Rural Ornament* (1796) William Marshall commented, "Art has evidently done too much at Stowe. It is over wooded and over built: everything appears to be sacrificed to temples . . ."

By the end of the eighteenth century the development of the gardens was almost complete and the woodlands maturing. Less enthusiasm for gardens

and a bankruptcy in 1848 ended further development, and although trees and plantings may be taller and denser and more floral color can be seen today, most of the character of the eighteenth-century landscape is retained. The house was turned into a public school in 1923 and several rather undistinguished buildings have been added to it, but the gardens are frequently open to the public.

The Temple of the Worthies, commemorating poets, scientists and philosophers.

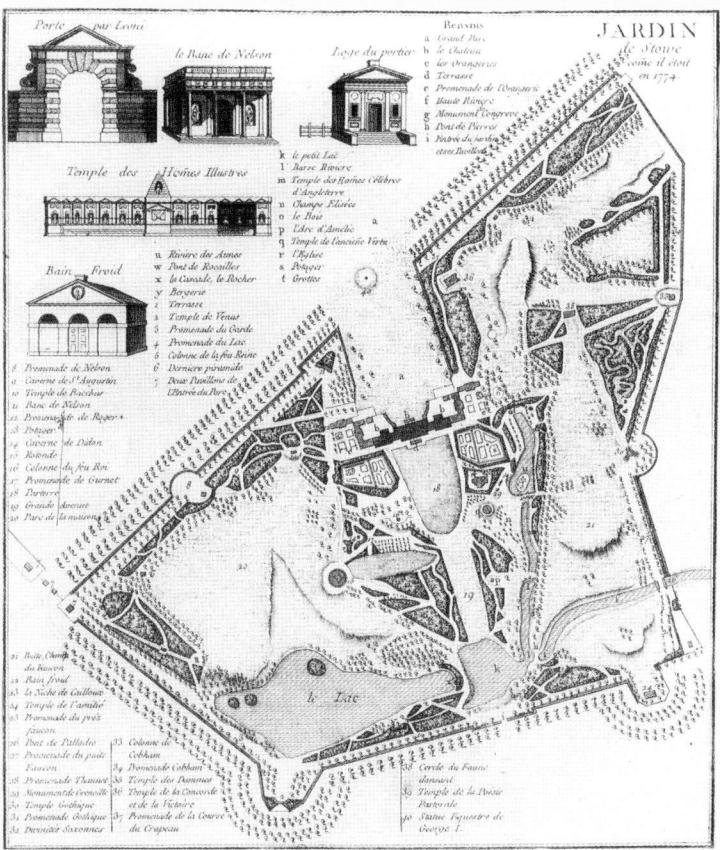

Plan of the gardens of Stowe Park.

Right *At Blenheim, "Capability" Brown raised the level of the lake, improving the proportions of Vanbrugh's bridge. The scene remains much as he intended.*

The French writer and philosopher Jean Jacques Rousseau (1712–78), with his romantic idealization of nature and rural simplicity was another spokesman for the "natural" garden — especially in his description of Julie's garden in the novel La Nouvelle Hèloïse, *part of which he wrote in a garden hermitage. By the end of his life Rousseau was against all kinds of gardens, considering them a disfigurement of nature. The Bocage, part of the garden at Ermenonville, was one of several inspired by his description of a garden concealed from passers-by by thick bushes and trees. It was on the Ile des Poupliers at the end of the Ermenonville lake that he was laid to rest in this simple tomb. Later his body was removed to the Pantheon but the tomb, copied in several other gardens, remains.*

dinavia and in Germany, where Goethe and Schiller followed his enthusiasm. Schiller commented

"Nature which we find in the English gardens is no longer the same as the one we had left outside. It is a nature enlivened by a soul, a nature exalted by art, which delights not only the simple man, but the man of education and culture; the one she teaches to think, the other to feel."

Swedish designer Frederick Magnus Pioer, who had studied painting and architecture in France, Germany and especially in England, was another enthusiast for the English landscape style and when commissioned by the Swedish king, Gustavus III to design parks at Drottningholm, Haga and Stockholm was responsible for introducing it to Scandinavia.

Brown's successor

It was not until after Brown's death that a designer of comparable stature appeared. Humphry Repton (1752–1818) had a better education and a more comfortable background than his predecessors. When a young man he returned from a rather unsuccessful period in business in Holland to a gentlemanly life in Norfolk where he bought an estate and gained practical experience in managing his land. He made drawings of local country houses and estates for a *History of Norfolk* and for a time '

became assistant to the Chief Secretary of the Lord Lieutenant of Ireland. It was not until 1788, after business failures and the loss of a great deal of his capital, that he made the decision to become a designer of gardens. Through his connections in society he soon gained commissions which he executed so successfully that "Capability's" son Lancelot gave him access to his late father's papers.

Repton's style did not, at first, differ greatly from that of "Capability" Brown, though his plantings were somewhat denser and his buildings were more frequently of a rustic character. Later, instead of bringing sweeping lawns right up to the house he began to reintroduce some of the formal features of earlier styles: terraces, balustrades, steps, trelliswork and fountains. He introduced exotic species in his woodlands and made a much greater use of flowers. What he is best known for, however, is the way in which he presented proposals to his clients.

In a series of what are now known as his "Red Books" (they were bound in red) he showed a painting of each vista as it was and then, revealed by the lifting of a flap, which he called a "slide," the same scene as he proposed to modify it. His paintings contrive to emphasize the contrast, exaggerating the severity of the initial scene and somewhat prettifying the effect of his proposals. Often working within an existing Brownian landscape Repton was catering for and often leading a change in taste.

In the nineteenth century interest began to move from landscape to the flower garden and

the many new and colorful plants, recently introduced from overseas, that could be grown in it. While Repton, like Brown, modeled the landscape, he also leads the way to new, more floriferous styles.

Town gardens

While the fashionable landscape style was changing on the large estates of the wealthy, the increasingly affluent middle classes of eighteenth-century England were also becoming enthusiastic about gardening. Stimulated by the publication of Thomas Fairchild's *The City Gardener* in 1722 and encouraged by the growing number of nurserymen and jobbing gardeners, people who had until then been content with the use of a city square now sought the privacy of their own gardens.

Although the idea of a garden was attractive, the work of creating and tending it was often left to the professionals. The "instant garden" — not a twentieth-century invention as might be

thought — was available pot by pot from the nurseryman, to be replenished when the blossoms faded or the plants gave up in the smoky air of the city. Flowers and shrubs were even available on hire, either as long-term displays which would be tended and replaced as necessary, or for a special occasion. Fashionable entertainment in Regency London saw the interiors of houses turned into garden settings with potted plants and cut shrubs and creepers, until such conceits were taken up by the middle classes and consequently lost their appeal to the *beau monde*.

By the end of the eighteenth century not only new city developments boasted flower gardens. New middle-class suburbs were developing with individual gardens an essential feature behind the rows of terraced houses.

Above *The frontispiece to Thomas Fairchild's* The City Gardener *suggests a garden of considerable size and a very formal layout.*

Above left *About a century later, when Mr Upcott's garden in Upper Street, Islington, was painted, a much more informal look includes typical cottage plants such as hollyhocks and sunflowers. Despite the comparatively small scale of his garden, Upcott was well known as a collector of plants who grew a great number of varieties.*

Left *Vauxhall Gardens, London, in the early nineteenth century. By the mid-eighteenth century there were several well-established public gardens in London. At Vauxhall, and others like it, music and dancing might be climaxed with a firework display. The wooded walks were the home of lakes and nightingales and helped provide an Arcadian quality as well as a setting for romantic adventures. Tivoli Gardens in Copenhagen did not open until 1843 but still survive in the heart of the city.*

AMERICAN STYLE

Although there was a busy traffic in plants between Britain and her American colonies, the landscape style that became fashionable in England was only loosely interpreted on the other side of the Atlantic. George Washington's library contained Batty Langley's *New Principles of Gardening* (1758), which decried stiff, formal layouts, and Washington planted groves of trees, wildernesses and shrubberies in "natural seeming groups and thickly" as Langley suggested. These prompted a Polish visitor to comment that, although "the General has never left America" the garden is "quite in the English style." However, in plan, the symmetry of the serpentine drive and the geometric garden shapes flanking the bowling green at his property at Mount Vernon, on the Potomac River, reveal Washington's seventeenth-century love of order and formality.

Away from his plantation during the War of Independence and his years of political service, Washington remained in constant contact with Mount Vernon's overseers. A large amount of correspondence survives, detailing innovative methods such as crop rotation, grafting experiments and plans for the design and development of the garden.

Washington took great interest in the native flowering trees and shrubs and, although he had a botanical garden for exotics which people sent him, he says little about flowerbeds in his letters. His wife, Martha Custis, may have taken responsibility for the extensive flower garden at the side of the house. Washington comments that there were so many roses that it took "Old Sal" two days to pick them. Martha's father-in-law in her first marriage was John Custis, a considerable gardener in Williamsburg. Although he died the year she married his son it is possible she gained much from Custis's knowledge and enthusiasm.

For many years John Custis corresponded and exchanged plants with Peter Collinson, an English plant enthusiast with a garden in Peckham, south of London, who also kept in active contact with John Bartram, plant hunter and nurseryman of Philadelphia. Bartram ran a subscription service for a number of English clients, annually sending them seeds of about a hundred different species, and occasionally plants. Washington, Thomas Jefferson and Benjamin Franklin were all clients of Bartram Nurseries at Kingsessing, which had begun as a private botanical garden.

A flower-lined path with pruned crab apples at Mount Vernon leads to one of four pepper-pot garden houses.

Mount Vernon, George Washington's
Virginia home, from the entrance
gates.

The English landscape style and *ferme ornée*
was not unknown to American landowners;
some had seen them for themselves. Thomas
Jefferson and John Adams, both future Presidents of the United States, together made a
tour of English gardens in 1786. Adams was
then the new nation's First Minister to the
Court of St. James and Jefferson Minister in
Paris (which gave him the chance to see some
grand French gardens too). They saw Chiswick
and Hampton Court, Hagley and Leasowes,
Stowe and many others. Leasowes was already
starting to decay and though Jefferson found
the cascades beautiful thought it "only a grazing
farm with a path around it, here and there a
seat of board . . . Architecture has contributed

nothing. The obelisk is of brick . . ." At Chiswick he thought "the garden still shows too
much of art. An obelisk of very ill effect;
another in the middle of the pond useless."
Hampton Court he found "old fashioned." His
notes on every garden are equally critical.

Adams it seems was more easily pleased. He
thought "Stowe, Hagley and Blenheim are
superb," found "grandeur and beauty" at
Hagley, and at Leasowes reported, "I saw no
spot so small that exhibited such a variety of
beauties."

But Adams, the Yankee farmer, was not
going to be overimpressed: he noted manure
heaps along the Edgware Road and considered
it "may be good manure, but it is not equal to
mine" and, patriotically declared:

"It will be long, I hope, before Ridings, Parks,
Pleasure Grounds, Gardens and ornamented
Farms grow so much in fashion in America.
But nature has done greater Things and
furnished nobler Materials there."

Jefferson, his comments notwithstanding,
preferred the "landskip" to the parterres and
box trees of the old formal gardens. It was, after
all, designed to accompany the Palladian style
of architecture which he admired and its
influence can be seen at Monticello, his house
built on a hill west of Charlottesville, Virginia.

Right *The west font at Monticello
from the "roundabout border" which
edges the oval lawn.*

Opposite below *A spring display of
tulips along the "roundabout walk."
Jefferson used the pond to keep fish
fresh until they were needed for the
table.*

Jefferson studied botany as a young man and his interests were centered on indigenous flowers. He leveled off the top of the hill to make an oval platform for the house and an extensive lawn, roughly oval in shape but with a bulge inward on each side, surrounded by a walk which he wanted bordered with flowers. His several designs all feature the same form but sometimes with four oval shrubberies — two making the bulges, two cut into the lawn — sometimes with six. Other beds near the house were colorful with pinks, sweet william, carnations, poppies, hyacinths and tulips in their season. There are mounts on each side of the house, built over utilities beneath, one topped with a small office and the other furnished with seats.

Terraces on the slopes of the hill to the front and sides of the Palladian house accommodate vineyard, vegetable garden, flowering trees and shrubs, over which are wide views to the Blue Ridge Mountains, 47 miles (75 km) away, and the University of Virginia. Jefferson designed the grounds of the University too, though there the influence is more of France and Marly than of the landskip and the *ferme ornée*.

More modest homes might still have lawns, some terracing, trelliswork and arbors, a vegetable garden, orchard and beds of flowers in season in rectilinear beds.

No occupation is so delightful to me as the culture of the earth, and no culture comparable to that of the garden. I am still devoted to the garden. But though an old man, I am but a young gardener.

Thomas Jefferson.

Above *In 1763 William Paca, later to be a signatory of the Declaration of Independence, built a fine townhouse in Annapolis, Maryland, and began a garden which has now been carefully recreated. Terraced lawns lead down from the house to a pond with a wilderness garden beyond and, in Paca's day, a vista to the River Severn.*

In the south the plantations along the coast and rivers of Maryland and the Carolinas centered on the waterways, not on any road system, and presented an impressive display of terracing rising from the riverside to the owner's house. Known as falls, they were usually simply turfed, kept well cut, and not decorated with flower beds, forming an architectural podium for the house. Ornamental ponds, included as a practical means of dealing with drainage, were squarely cut with no planting at the edges, though elsewhere beds of bright flowers pleased the eye, trellises and climbing plants gave shade and high walls provided privacy.

Along the Mississippi, owners did not live on the plantation, though they stayed nearby all the year living in townships of elegant houses with formal gardens.

Middleton Place, on the Ashley River near Charleston, South Carolina, boasts the oldest landscaped garden in America, laid out by Henry Middleton in 1741. Another first at Middleton Place are camellias, planted by André Michaux. When it was a working plantation, Middleton Place, like Mount Vernon and Monticello, housed dozens of people, both slave and free. Plantation outbuildings often included carpenters' shops, dairies, stables, liveries, storehouses and kitchens.

At nearby Magnolia Plantation, purchased around 1671 by the first of nine generations of the same family to own it, gardens were undertaken and by 1717 the first part of the garden, Flowerdale, was well established. After the American Civil War, the Reverend John Grimke Drayton laid out a portion of the garden in the "new" English style. "Dr Drayton's Garden" was listed in the European edition of Baedecker's travel guide to the United States, along with the Grand Canyon and Niagara Falls.

THE NINETEENTH

While the gardens of late eighteenth-century Europe — or at least those of wealthy landowners — placed their emphasis on landscape, the nineteenth century saw a growing interest in flowers, especially the exotics that were brought from overseas by the plant hunters sent out by nurseries and botanic gardens. Humphry Repton had already reintroduced the flower bed near the house and, as the century progressed, great glasshouses were built to house the specimens from warmer lands, and formal beds were laid out with massed displays of blossoms. Half-hardy exotics could now be raised under glass and then "bedded out" when summer approached. Later in the century "bedding-out" became a seasonal affair, one set of plants being replaced by another as a new group came into season in a way reminiscent of the instant parterres of potted plants which ensured that the beds at the Petite Trianon were always full of flowers.

Formal terraces, balustrades and fountains also made a comeback and although the sweeping greensward no longer dominated the prospect near the house the invention of the lawn mower made it possible to have smooth carpets of turf in which to set the new decorative beds

Carpet bedding in the Royal Horticultural Society's garden at Wisley.

In 1804 the Horticultural Society of London was founded (it became "Royal" in 1861) by a number of amateur and professional gardeners, but a wider influence was probably the development of popular gardening magazines. There had been earlier botanical journals aimed at the gentry but in 1826 John Claudius Loudon launched his *Gardener's Magazine*, followed a few years later by a number of others. The swelling numbers of the middle classes with their suburban villas and smaller terraced houses were eager for advice on the development of their lawns and shrubberies and the planting of their flower beds. The better-off workers, the skilled artisans, when they had a patch of garden, became enthusiastic about flower-growing too and formed "florists' clubs" which sometimes concentrated on the raising of a particular flower. Yorkshire and Derbyshire miners favored the pansy, the knife-makers of Sheffield the polyanthus and cotton workers in Lancashire the auricula. Nottingham lace-makers excelled with roses, while weavers in Paisley, Scottish home of the famous Paisley pattern fabrics (who formed a club as early as 1782), specialized in pinks and developed the laced pink.

Loudon, the son of a Scottish farmer, established himself in London as a landscape gardener at the beginning of the century, publishing his first article, "Laying out the Ground in Public Squares," in 1803 and producing books, magazines and an *Encyclopedia of Gardening* that ran into numerous editions over the next four decades. He began as an exponent of the "picturesque," the romanticizing of the landscape in the manner of paintings and the addition of "mouldering abbies and the anti-quated cottage with its chimney covered in ivy" as Repton characterized the look when defending his own work against attack by proponents of the picturesque. Loudon built himself a *ferme ornée* but by the publication of the first edition of his *Encyclopedia* in 1822 was already acknowledging the attractions of earlier more formal styles, influenced no doubt by gardens he had seen on several tours in Europe.

Writing in the *Gardener's Magazine* in 1832, he proposed a style, which he called "gardenesque," because it could only appear in gardens, which would be clearly distinguished from nature, rather than blending with it as the English landskip style and even the "picturesque" had done. Part of the effect was to be achieved by including exotics, even species of grasses being carefully selected to differ from those in surrounding fields, so that a garden would be instantly recognizable as a work of art, not nature.

The term was taken over by others to mean an eclecticism of style, rather than just eclectic planting, and a mixture of formal and informal became a characteristic of many Victorian gardens, as indeed it must have been of many earlier gardens which had not been entirely "done over" in a particular style.

American Andrew Jackson Downing, who became the best-known and most influential American arbiter of garden design and architecture of his day, introduced Loudon's works to his countrymen. In Downing's contribution to the magazine *The Horticulturalist* and in his books, he established the notion of garden design and strove to establish culture and "correct taste" for the aspiring middle class. He wrote, "So long as men are forced to live in log huts and follow the hunter's life, we must not be surprised at lynch laws and the use of the bowie knife. But, when smiling lawns and tasteful cottages begin to embellish a country, we know that order and culture are established."

Downing drowned at the age of 36 in a Hudson River boating accident while trying to save friends. His protégé Calvert Vaux, whom he had brought over from Europe after a visit to England in 1850, stepped into his shoes and later collaborated in the design and execution of Central Park in New York City.

Loudon was an advocate of public parks as amenities for the expanding cities of the nineteenth century. He even made proposals for a preserved band of countryside around each urban area to prevent the development of continuous conurbations, a proposal taken up in the British "green-belt" concept a century later. The Royal Parks in London had been

The opening of Birkenhead Park, Liverpool, in 1847.

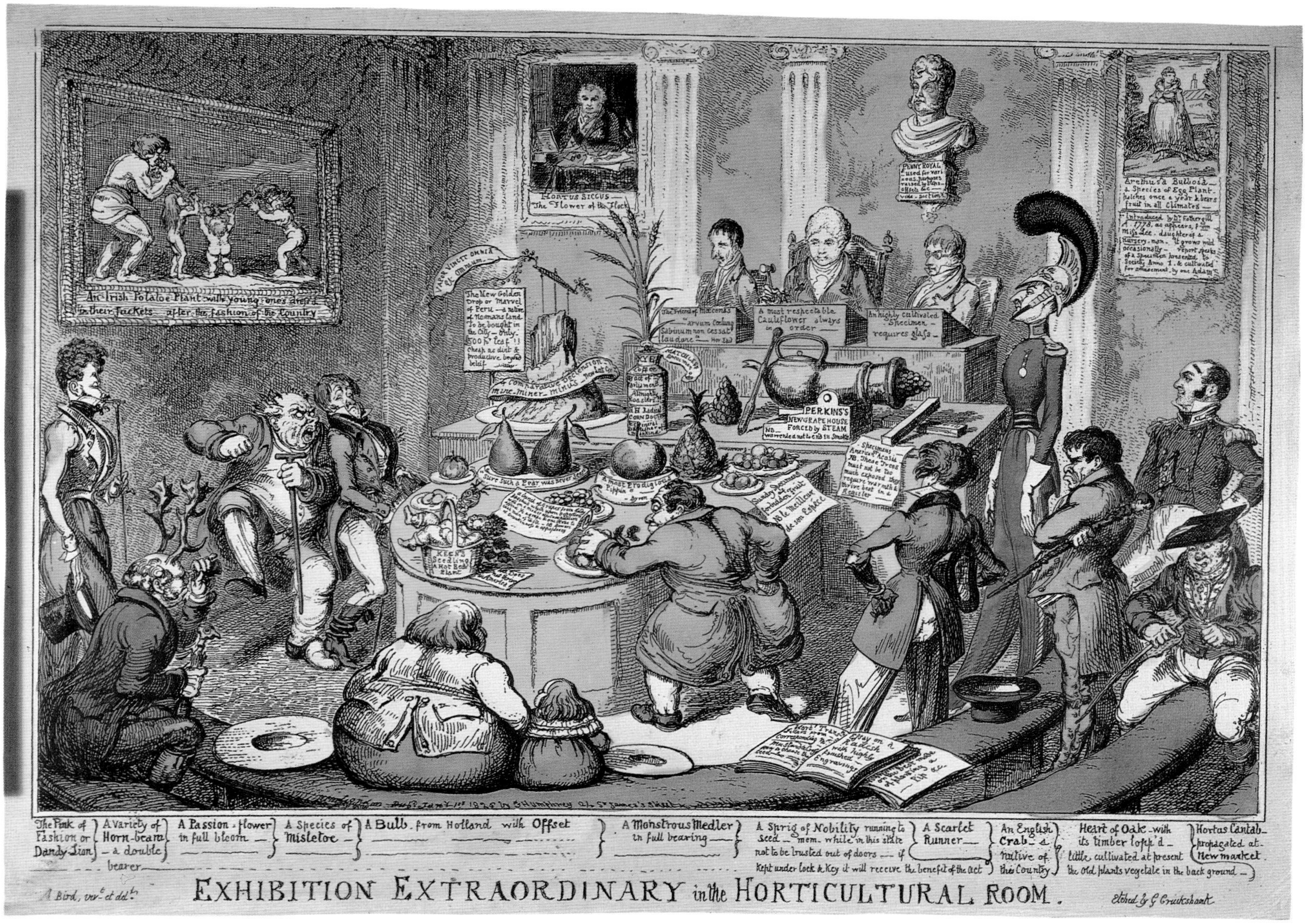

opened to public use for some years (Hyde Park since the 1630s) and there were public promenades in many European cities, but Loudon proposed somewhere not only where people could get fresh air, but which would also help to "raise the intellectual character of the lowest classes of society." In 1835 he was responsible for the design of the first British public open space created with both promenades and a public botanical collection — the Terrace Garden at Gravesend, but it was the Birkenhead Park in Liverpool, designed by Joseph

A cartoon by George Cruikshank showing a meeting of the Horticultural Society in 1824.

EXHIBITION EXTRAORDINARY in the HORTICULTURAL ROOM.

The garden of Mrs. William Lawrence at Drayton Green, illustrated by J. C. Loudon in The Villa Gardener. He described this medium-sized middle-class garden, created by a surgeon's wife about 1838, as "a perfect bijou of floricultural beauty . . . All the most rare and beautiful hardy flowers and peat shrubs are here . . ." Shrubberies, statues and vases are placed around the extensive lawn; the garden is about 150 x 280 ft (45 x 84 m) overall. To the left of the house is a "French" parterre, a greenhouse behind it. From this an "Italian" walk extends along the side of the garden, on the left by a herbaceous border with standard roses set into it, backed by fruit, roses and other climbers on the wall, and lined on the right by statues on plinths. Just over halfway along the lawn side is an arch of rockwork, topped by a cupid. At the end is a rustic arch over a large vase to complete the vista while a simple fence separates the garden from the paddock where cows graze. There is a circular fountain basin in the lawn and small fountains flank the rock arch nearby. There was a quite separate kitchen and reserve garden. Mrs. Lawrence was quite a gardener: in 1838 she was growing 3,266 different species or varieties — and that after losing many in a hard winter, including 500 roses.

Paxton in 1843 and opened in 1847, which became the first large public park in Britain. It made a great impression on Frederick Law Olmsted, who with Calvert Vaux, was responsible for the design of Central Park. A few years later the Bois de Boulogne was given to the people of Paris by Napoleon III and public open spaces became a feature of George Haussman's designs for the restructuring of that city.

In many cities part of the function of cemeteries was to serve as public pleasure-parks and, in the United States especially, the design of both public and private cemeteries has made an important contribution to landscape art.

Among the grand gardens that were created in mid-century and later, special areas were often devoted to gardens within gardens which, in some features at least, sought to reproduce Chinese style, or Japanese toward the end of the century after that country had opened up to the West at the end of the Edo period. From the mid-1830s, the architect Sir Charles Barry

(best known for his design of the gothic Houses of Parliament) was responsible for the design of a number of large country houses in an Italianate style, complete with Italian style gardens which brought staircases, balustraded terraces, fountains and urns back into fashion — a style which was often followed by the new industrial magnates of North America when they built palatial homes and developed estates in emulation of European aristocracy.

It was not only flowers from abroad which brightened European gardens. Among the species which plant hunter David Douglas took back to Kew was the conifer *Pseudotsuga menziesii*, which commemorates him in its common name, the Douglas fir. Conifers became extremely fashionable, often forming the centerpiece to an elaborately planted bed as well as encouraging the development of private arboretum collections. Another new species which was to find a place in many suburban gardens and radically to alter the appearance of

The language of flowers

Most flowers are liked for their scent, attractive color or size and shape, but in the seventeenth century many became popular because of the messages they were understood to convey. In Turkey flowers gained meanings which enabled lovers to communicate with one another without having to write or talk. The "language of flowers" was spread by Lady Mary Wortley Montagu, an English society poet and friend of Alexander Pope, who accompanied her husband to the Turkish Court in Constantinople. She sent a letter to England which interpreted the meanings of some plants, flowers and spices. The wonder of flowers, she proposed, was that words and messages of love — even altercations — would be conveyed in a refined and subtle manner, without "inking the fingers."

The passing of such messages was taken up by the French, and the convention later aroused new interest in England in Queen Victoria's time through the book *Le Langage des Fleurs* by Madame de la Tour. Many of the meanings were risqué and too lusty for Victorian tastes, however, and English flower language books were therefore tempered and less robust. Nowadays more direct ways are usually employed in wooing a prospective partner, although for many people saying it with flowers still holds romance and enchantment.

More than 800 flowers have special meanings associated with them. Indeed, there are over 30 for roses. Messages could become quite complex when several flowers were offered in a bouquet. For instance, a sheaf of oak-leaved geraniums, gillyflowers and heliotropes with a leaf of virginia creeper means "I offer true friendship, affection and devotion," while a bouquet of monkshood, mountain ash and blue violets suggests "Danger is near, be prudent and faithful." A bouquet of red poppies, clematis and harebells, bound with virginia creeper means "I offer consolation. You have mental beauty. I submit to you." One consisting of mistletoe, hawthorn and heliotrope turned to the right would mean "I surmount difficulties. I hope. I turn to thee."

In addition to the flower and its meaning, the way in which it was presented and worn also contributed to the language of flowers. A flower bent toward the right signifies "I," while one to the left means "You." Therefore a red rosebud bent toward the left means "You are pure and lovely."

The foliage also has a significance. Leaves mean "hope" and thorns "danger." Therefore a rose with the thorns plucked off, and the leaves left on, implies "hopeful love and confidence."

The language of flowers is further enriched by the hand that gives the flower, as well as the one that receives it. An affirmative is suggested by the right hand, while the left one indicates a negative. Thus a Provence rose offered by the right hand firmly confirms the sentiment "My heart is in flames," and if received by the right hand would give encouragement to the giver.

If flowers could not be presented personally, they were sent in boxes tied with ribbons, and this too held a message, depending on where the knot was tied.

D.S.

Illustration from Amateur Cultivator's Guide, *1869.*

Central Park, a green lung in the heart of New York City, was designed by Calvert Vaux and Frederick Law Olmsted to a plan that set out to translate democratic ideas into trees and dirt! Ponds, lake and a great reservoir are set amid meadows and green hills with rocky outcrops.

many of the landscapes designed in the previous century, was the rhododendron. Introduced from Asia in mid-century by Joseph Hooker, it was first grown in the southwest of England and areas touched by the warm Atlantic Drift, and later found everywhere as hardy strains were developed.

Prince Herman von Pückler-Muskau (1785–1871), after visiting England and seeing the new style in gardens there, began a park at Muskau which was very influenced by Humphry Repton. In later years, however, especially as the author of *Hints on Landscape Gardening* in

1834, and through his follower Eduard Petzold (1815–91), court gardener at Weimar from 1848, the Prince was responsible for spreading the picturesque style on the Continent and encouraging the use of carpet bedding.

Some attempts were also made in Italy to create English landscape gardens, but it was mainly foreign residents, later in the nineteenth century, who designed new Italian gardens — and they looked back to traditional Italian style with an added interest in individual plants which clearly distinguished them from Renaissance gardens.

THE NATURAL GARDEN

Victorian carpet bedding was not to everybody's taste. William Robinson (1838–1935), an Irish gardener who moved to the Royal Botanic Garden at Regent's Park in London when he was 23 and began writing for the *Gardeners Chronicle*, was the leading proponent of a different approach. In 1871 he started a magazine called *The Garden* and set out to wean people away from the bedding system and persuade them to return to growing flowers such as carnations, roses and the many herbaceous plants which were being neglected. He proposed the naturalizing of plants, infiltrating the garden into the countryside rather than trying to shape the garden as a piece of classic landscape as Brown and Repton had done, or border an estate with flowers as had the creators of the *ferme ornée*.

Instead of formal lawns and tonsured topiary he suggested letting the grass grow, along with the wild flowers in it, returning to the medieval flowery mead. He advocated allowing climbers to grow over trees rather than building pergolas and metal frames to support them.

It was not Robinson's idea to attempt to reproduce the wild, however; it took the ecological awareness and conservation movement of nearly a century later to produce that kind of habitat recreation. He was opposed to serried rows of pelargoniums but had no objection to exotics; indeed in *The Wild Garden*, published in 1870, he positively encouraged "the placing of perfectly hardy exotic plants under conditions where they will thrive without further care" and in the same year his *Alpine Flowers for Gardens* set out "to dispel a general but erroneous idea, that the plants of alpine regions cannot be grown in gardens."

There had been a rockery at the Chelsea Physic Garden in the 1780s, though it was used more to display geological specimens than for alpine plants, and William Beckwith's gardeners made him an alpine garden in a quarry at Fonthill. In the 1830s Lady Broughton had constructed a model imitation of the mountains of Chamonix in her Cheshire garden, set around three sides of a large lawn and designed as a striking contrast to its smooth surface and formal flower beds. Such rockeries had more relation to grottos than habitats for plants, but at the Surrey garden of a William Wells a natural ridge of rock above a lawn was turned into a rock garden and complementary rocky beds made on the lawn below it.

Late in the 1840s cement manufacturer James Pulham developed artificial rockwork molded into natural-looking shapes, but it was not until the 1880s that solid rocks and boulders representing craggy mountainsides became a common feature. Alpines were more usually grown in Britain among rock debris suggesting moraine or scree, though on the Continent soil in pockets among rocks was already an established technique, one which was used at Back-

Lady Broughton's rock garden at Hoole House, illustrated in Loudon's The Villa Gardener.

house Nursery in York and later by Sir Charles Isham at Lamport Hall, planted with dwarfed trees.

In 1875 Gertrude Jekyll, a middle-class woman from a comfortable background who had trained as a watercolor artist, met William Robinson and became a contributor to *The Garden*. The following year, after the death of her father, she began making a garden at her family's new home at Munstead. Commissions to design for others followed.

Miss Jekyll shared many of Robinson's convictions and was to become an even greater influence as gardening writer and designer. In 1891, suffering from severe progressive myopia she was told that she should give up painting, if she was to preserve her sight, and by then she had already met young Edwin Lutyens, an architect less than half her age. Their collaboration was to prove a much greater achievement than her painting had ever been.

Left *Gertrude Jekyll's own garden at Munstead Wood.*

Below *A Gertrude Jekyll garden on the island of Lindisfarne.*

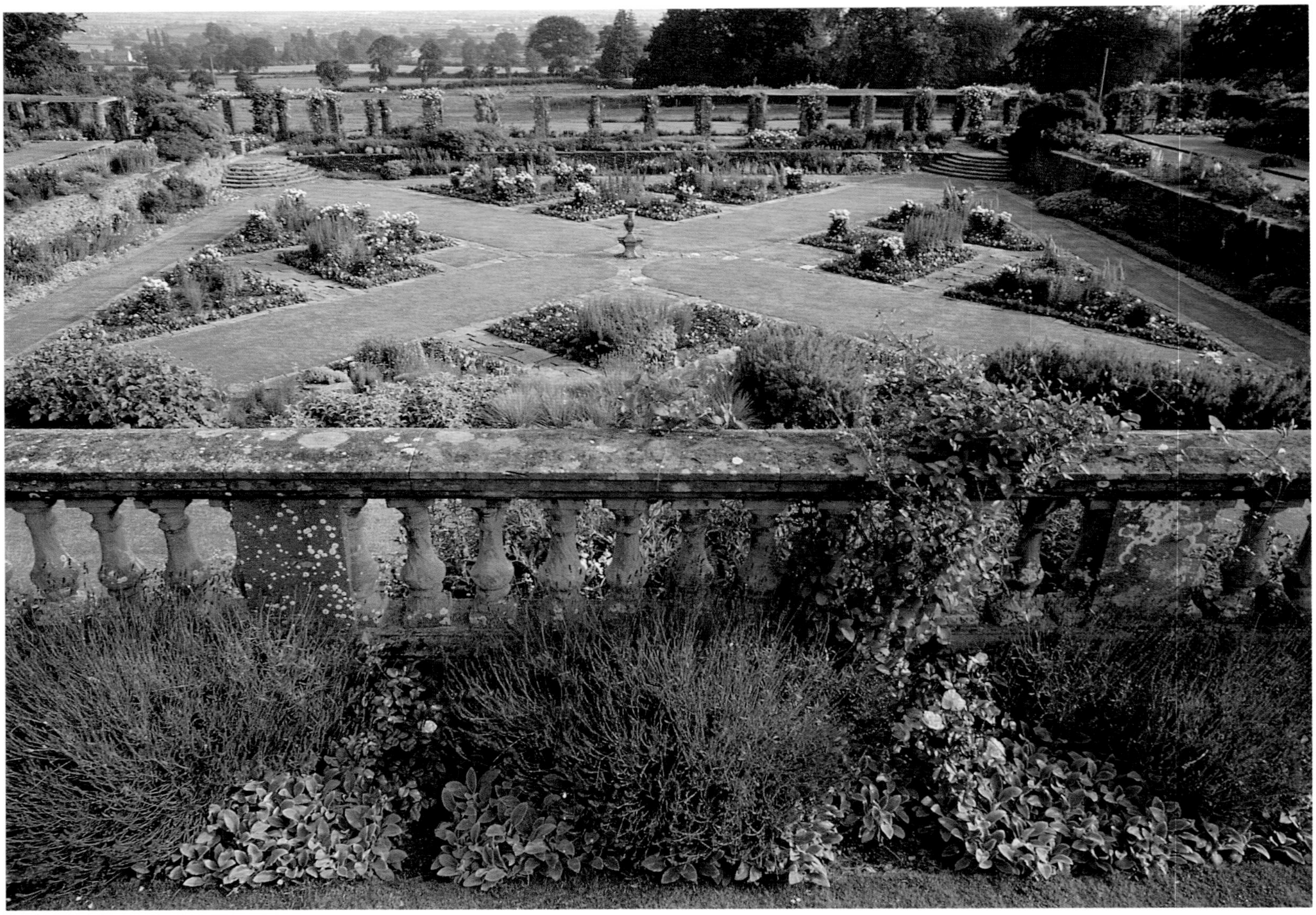

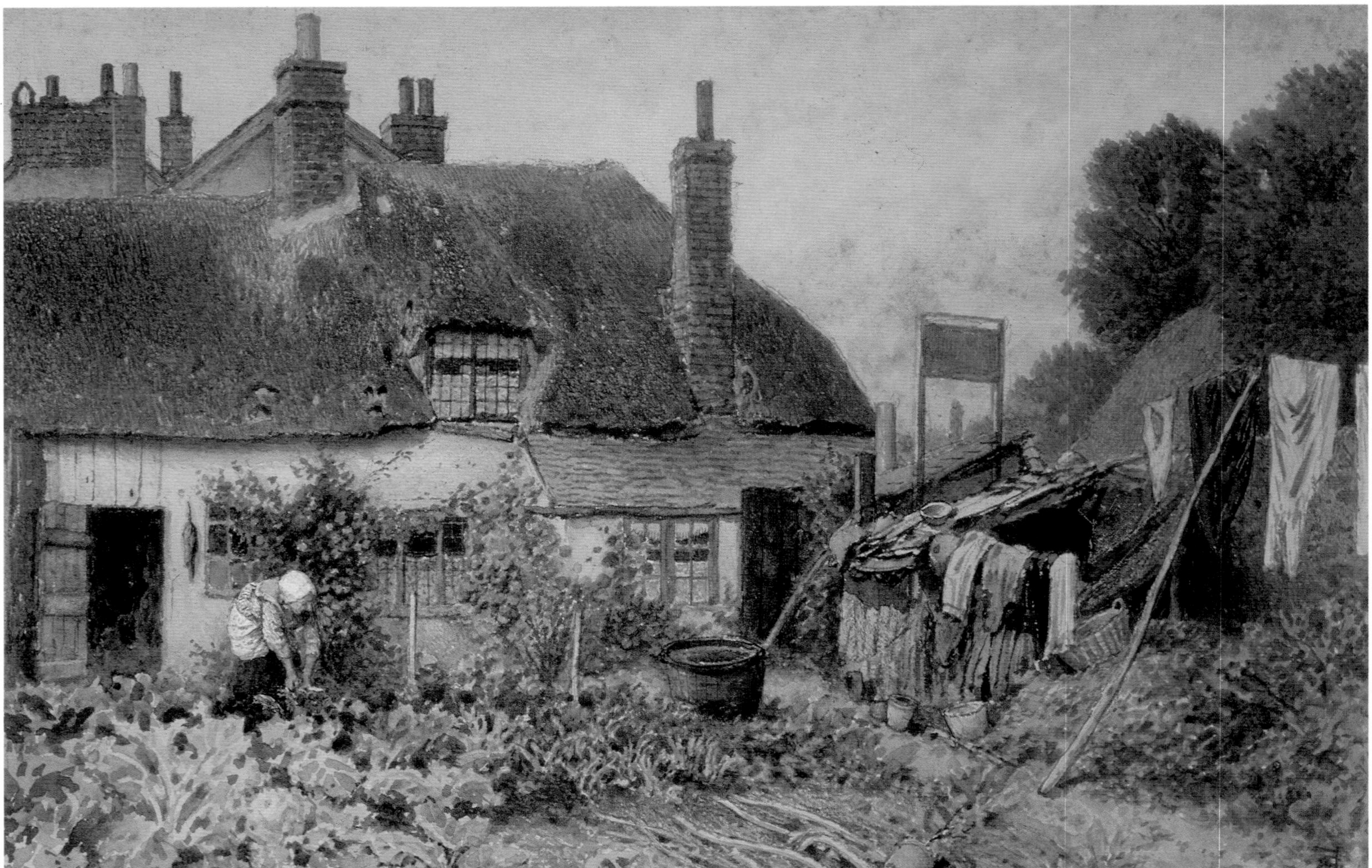

There is no such thing as a style fitted for every situation. Only one who knows and studies the ground well will ever make the best of a garden. Any "style" may be right if the site fits it. I never see a house the ground around which does not invite plans for itself only. A garden on the slopes of Naples is impossible without much stonework to support the earth. In the neighbourhood of London or Paris such necessity seldom exists. But these considerations never enter into the minds of men who plant an Italian garden in one of our river valleys, where in nine cases out of ten an open lawn is often the best thing before the house.

William Robinson in
The English Flower Garden.

That same year *Garden Craft*, by J. D. Sedding, followed by Reginald Blomfield and F. Inigo Thomas's *The Formal Garden in England* led the argument against Robinson's naturalism. The latter book proposed that the architect should be responsible for garden design, the horticulturalist for planting, and argued that Robinson's gardens were no more natural than formal gardens and that it was wrong to give plants so much importance at the expense of the unity between house and garden which had prevailed in the Renaissance. The contention between the two sides was great, though with hindsight it is difficult to see why there should not be room for both types of garden. The created naturalness of Robinson never pretended to be nature, although it espoused the idea that plants looked best where they grew best. Near the house his plans were still comparatively formal and at his own home, Gravetye Manor, the sloping site was terraced and in places he actually moved earth to make a more "natural" scene before giving it a "natural" planting.

Miss Jekyll was more than just a horticulturalist choosing plants, although increasingly as her sight deteriorated it was Lutyens who not only related the building to the site but planned the dominant garden features, though always in consultation with her. Often they divided the garden space into separate "rooms," making it possible to create a number of different, contained, effects rather than aiming at a grander vista. Together, Gertrude Jekyll and Edwin Lutyens created 70 gardens in the 20 years from their meeting; then Lutyens became increasingly involved with public projects — New Delhi from 1912, the War Graves Commission after World War I — and his work more classical in style. Jekyll's worsening sight made design work increasingly difficult but, though she did not personally design them all, she is credited with advising on the design or planting of some 300 gardens.

Both she and Lutyens were influenced by the Arts and Crafts movement and traditional English architecture and it was from "cottage"

gardens that she gained much of her inspiration. "They have a simple and tender charm," she wrote, "that one may look for in vain in gardens of greater pretension. And the old garden flowers seem to know that there they are seen at their best."

Gertrude Jekyll considered that flowers which bloom at the same time should be grouped together and she often placed plants in horizontal drifts of color, one shade merging with another from silver at the ends of a border, through blue, pink, white and pale yellow to strong oranges and reds in the central section of the flower bed.

Lutyens believed in a firm structure. "Every garden scheme," he declared, "should have a backbone, a central idea beautifully phrased. Every wall, path, stone and flower should have its relationship to the central idea."

The cottage gardens which Gertrude Jekyll acknowledged as such an influence are rather more difficult to define. Topographic paintings and drawings from earlier times do not offer a record of farm workers' cottage gardens burgeoning with flowers. Country life was hard. Gardens were for raising a few vegetables to feed the family and though space might be found for a few flowers that grew themselves the horticulturalists at the village show were more likely to be the village postman and the local craftspeople, to whom gardening would

Old Sally's

Old Sally's was a long, low, thatched cottage with diamond-paned windows winking under eaves and a rustic porch smothered in honeysuckle. Excepting the inn, it was the largest house in the hamlet.

The garden was a large one, tailing off at the bottom into a little field where Dick grew his corn crop. Nearer the cottage were fruit trees, then the yew hedge, close and solid as a wall, which sheltered the beehives and enclosed the flower garden. Sally had such flowers, and so many of them, and nearly all of them sweet-scented! Wallflowers and tulips, lavender and sweet william, and pinks and old-world roses with enchanting names — Seven Sisters, Maiden's Blush, moss rose, monthly rose, cabbage rose, blood rose, and, most thrilling of all to the children, a big bush of the York and Lancaster rose, in the blooms of which the rival roses mingled in a pied white and red. It seemed as though all the roses in Lark Rise had gathered together in that one garden. Most of the gardens had only one poor starveling bush or none; but, then, nobody else had so much of anything as Sally.

Flora Thompson: *Lark Rise.*

Opposite above *Hestercombe, Somerset, on which Edwin Lutyens and Gertrude Jekyll collaborated in 1906. This sunken parterre — the "Grat Plat" — is flanked by narrow water gardens, each with a central rill. A pergola separates the garden from the countryside beyond. A rotunda with a pool at one corner forms the approach to the rest of the gardens. The gardens have been planted in accordance with the original plans.*

Opposite below *A Cottage Garden by Myles Birket. Perhaps rather more typical of the nineteenth-century English cottage than the romanticized image suggested by Miss Jekyll.*

A desirable suburban home from Frank J. Scott's The Art of Beautifying Suburban Home Grounds of Small Extent, 1870.

Opposite *Vizcaya Villa, James Deering's Italianate winter home in Florida.*

Randolph Hearst's Californian mansion adopts an aggressive classicism.

be recreation, than the hard-pressed farm worker. To Miss Jekyll, perhaps, the well-built yeoman's house, if thatched, half-timbered or built of Cotswold stone, might already be called a cottage as so many city people visiting the country consider it today.

Yet there is evidence of decorative as well as useful gardens in earlier times and the country-man always had a love of flowers, even if no time to grow them. When the eighteenth- and nineteenth-century Enclosure Acts reshaped the English countryside into large hedged fields, animals were less likely to wander right up to the cottage door, and loss of grazing rights on common ground to the big land-owners made it necessary to exploit what land was available. Villagers would then make the most of what little land they had. When better roads replaced wide muddy tracts it was easier to fence off front gardens and here the flower-ing plants (not bought but exchanged, flowers were not something to spend money on) could make a show among the cabbages.

The formal style continued in parallel with the "wild garden" and even topiary had a revival in the middle of the century, including a representation of the Sermon on the Mount at Packwood in Warwickshire in 1850, the famous topiary at Compton Wynyates created in the 1870s and an Egyptian temple at Biddulph Grange. One of the most fantastic creations was in the United States at Green Animals, on Long Island, where the carefully trimmed menagerie included bears, elephants, camels and giraffes.

In America the marketing of many brightly-colored annuals from Texas and Mexico had given great impetus to the development of carpet bedding early in the century and Frank P. Scott's *The Art of Beautifying Suburban Home Grounds of Small Extent*, published in 1870, offered some particularly American ideas on garden design. While Europeans had preferred the garden square, Scott sought the collabor-ation of town and city dwellers in leaving their front gardens as an uninterrupted sweep of green lawns, with individual private gardens being kept to the back of the property. It was an expression of American egalitarianism, for Scott felt that hedges and fences used to hide from others "the beauties of nature which it has been our good fortune to create or secure" were an indication only of "how unchristian and unneighborly we can be."

Writing in 1927, Frank Waugh, Professor of Agriculture at the University of Massachusetts in Amherst, regarded this hedgeless, fenceless style as patriotic:

"Everyone who is patriotic and wants to do something for his country will promote to the utmost of his ability the development of ideal American homes. In the Old Country the primary planting is a hedge along the street front. The American home is open to the street. The plantings instead of forming a hedge are pushed back against the foundations of the house. They are foundation plantings. This type of planting is fundamental to the whole of domestic landscape architecture. It is well and sadly known that tens of thousands of individual homes have not been planted. We may all accept the patriotic duty of promoting this campaign of planting."

The Jekyll style had a wide and lasting influence, affecting even gardens on the great estates, such as at Shelburne in Burling, Ver-mont, where Lila Vanderbilt laid out a "Grand Allée" with two long perennial borders. Most great country houses, however, tended to look backwards to historic styles for inspiration. This was especially so in the United States in the country homes of the millionaire industri-alists and financiers who, sometimes actually importing European bricks and mortar and transporting buildings and architectural features across the Atlantic, sought to recreate the grandeur of the European princes on American soil.

Biltmore, North Carolina, built for the Vanderbilts in the style of a François I chateau, has a formal garden designed by Frederick Law Olmsted and patterned after the style of Le Nôtre with large plantings of trees, to which a walled English garden with espaliered trees, a rose garden and an Italianate water garden have been added. More common, however, were gardens with an Italian Renaissance inspiration, such as that created during World War I as a winter home for James Deering, at Vizcaya Villa, Florida.

Colonial styles

The British and other Europeans took their home country styles of gardening with them out to the colonies. Like the early settlers in America they took plants they thought they would need for immediate survival, but some also added a few acorns of European oaks, or may, on their travels, have taken a cutting from the great willow which hangs over the Emperor Napoleon's temporary grave on the island of St. Helena. Some of these sentimental imports thrived in their new lands and pro-vided welcome shade and a tangible reminder

of faraway landscapes. The residences of governors and administrators often emulated the formal gardens or the Brownian landscapes of Europe and the British lawn was sometimes attempted in places where it was totally inappropriate. While plant hunters brought back new plants for British gardens from the Himalayas, the tea planters of Darjeeling sought to recreate a tiny patch of the Home Counties, with indigenous rhododendrons contributing to the Englishness!

IF I SHOULD PLANT A TINY SEED OF LOVE (No. 1).

Busy little honey bees were buzzing to and fro,
Humming in the summer air,
Gathering the honey and the little drops of dew
Th... within the blossoms fair.
A yo... ...arden strayed,
An...
So...
"

IF I SHOULD PLANT A TINY SEED OF LOVE (No. 2).

If I should plant a tiny seed of love
In the garden of your heart,
Would it grow to be a great big love some day,
Or would it die and fade away?
Would you care for it and tend it every day
Till the time when all must part,
If I should plant a tiny seed of love
In the garden of your heart?

BY ARRANGEMENT WITH B. MACDOUGAL, J. W. TATE & B. FELDMAN & CO.

Native palm trees were used to enhance the environs of important public buildings and in Australia the Moreton Bay fig, *Ficus macrophylla*, was widely planted in parks and gardens from the early days of settlement but, though colorful native plants did find a place, there was often a nostalgic emphasis on familiar plants from the mother country. Sometimes colonial gardens were totally enclosed, keeping out the supposed dangers of the outside world or hiding the "ugliness" of an unfamiliar landscape. As the surroundings became less alien and the view of the new land part of the settler's emotional inheritance, native plants were added to the ornamental plants from Europe and European styles were modified to suit a new way of living. From time to time, styles evolved, such as bush gardens or tropical rainforest gardens, which owed little or nothing in either design or plant material to a European cultural inheritance. Today, there is a much stronger emphasis on growing indigenous plants.

Merely having plants or having them planted unassorted in garden spaces, is only like having a box of paints from the best colour man; or, to go one step farther, it is like having portions of these paints set out upon a palette. This does not constitute a picture; and it seems to me that the duty we owe to our gardens and to our own bettering of our gardens is so to use the plants that they shall form beautiful pictures; and that, while delighting our eyes, they should be always training those eyes to a more exalted criticism; to a state of mind and artistic conscience that will not tolerate bad or careless combination or any sort of mis-use of plants, but in which it becomes a point of honour to be always striving for the best.

It is just in the way it is done that lies the whole difference between commonplace gardening and gardening that may rightly claim to rank as a fine art.

Gertrude Jekyll.

An early twentieth-century New Zealand garden tries to impose some formal order within the natural landscape.

Above left *St. Peter's parsonage in an Indian hill station captures the mood of an English country garden.*

Below left *A set of postcards and a popular lyric from the beginning of the century take the garden as a romantic metaphor.*

GARDENS FOR ALL

A popular image of a suburban garden in the 1930s.

The disruption and change brought by World War I and the years of the Depression did not entirely stop the creation of grand gardens, especially in the United States, but the twentieth century saw a shift of emphasis in garden design from the large scale to the modest suburban garden and increasingly in the latter part of the century to the small garden. Even on the great estates of Britain, with the introduction of more equitable taxation and the drop in income from the land when agriculture was hit by depression and cheap imports, it became increasingly difficult to keep up the expensive maintenance which formal styles of gardening and bedding out demand.

World War II saw flower gardens given over to vegetables and even public parks plowed up to help Britain feed itself. America too had her Victory Gardens. In the postwar years the low paid workforce which had mowed the lawns and tended the flower beds could find more lucrative employment and "gardeners" who had relied upon much outside help to mow the lawns, trim the hedges and tend the flower beds now began to undertake these chores themselves. New mechanized equipment and a plethora of chemical aids arrived on the market to ease their tasks but many people began to look for garden designs that were, as far as pos-

sible, maintenance free. With the development of garden centers, linked to increasing car ownership, and the introduction of container-growing, a garden could be established much more rapidly or, as demonstration gardens at increasingly popular garden shows and festivals exhibit, an almost instant garden became a possibility.

Paralleling these changes has been a reappraisal of garden usage, especially by the owners of small gardens. The large Renaissance garden, an emblem of status and a spectacular setting for entertaining and impressing others, might serve as sculpture gallery or theater, entertain with practical jokes or offer areas of privacy for diplomacy or dalliance, but its many uses were accommodated within the grander plan. Now small garden owners wanted to find space for a variety of leisure activities.

The Edwardians might indulge in croquet on the lawn or mark out the space for a tennis court, but in general the garden remained a tranquil place for taking tea in the shade or a gentle walk to admire the flowers. Even in the terraced houses of the less affluent cricket or football was more likely to be played in the street; the garden was for a deckchair on the path, the rope swing strung beneath the branches of a tree. But now people began to

Right A garden set on top of a garage, designed by Pietro Porcinai.

emerge from beneath their parasols and lie out in the sun. Removed from inner cities to the suburbs they centered life on the home, rather than in the community. Even in the brief northern summers there was an increasing vogue for outdoor living.

While the first part of the century was still dominated by an eclectic range of influences from the past and the styles of the Jekyll school, tending either to the formal axial design or extreme informality, a new style began to emerge in the 1930s to complement the new styles in art and architecture.

California led the way, its life-styles carried around the world by Hollywood movies. The garden became an area to live and play in, a place for active leisure rather than just relaxation and contemplation. The swimming pool, the barbecue, the place for dining out and perhaps the sandpit for the children have joined, or ousted the rockery and vegetable garden. Even the lawn is no longer ubiquitous, paving requiring much less attention and being more suited to an area of heavy usage, though there are still many, even in areas where climate is entirely unsuitable for lawnmaking. This is a garden where the plants are subordinate to the activity to which they form a backdrop, but the plants are still the pride of those who tend them.

San Francisco designer Thomas Church and a slightly younger group of students from the Harvard School of Design, James Rose, Daniel Urban Kiley and Garrett Eckbo, helped to establish a new attitude to garden design without the preconceptions of previous historic styles, responding to site and circumstance and by the third quarter of the century their refreshingly modern approach was having a wide influence.

Even where garden living is limited to the summer months, the link between house and garden has become increasingly strong. Large picture windows bring the garden close with indoor plants leaping the barrier of the glass. The Victorian conservatory has returned in popularity, though often now as a glazed garden room which brings the garden into the house. In shopping malls and offices great garden atria offer a controlled environment often as lushly planted as the nineteenth-century winter garden.

As city real estate has soared in value gardens have become smaller, and great ingenuity has been exercised in making tiny courtyards into patios and creating rooftop and balcony gardens for the city-dweller.

A unique style of garden has been developed by the Brazilian Roberto Burle Marx whose

Landscape architects

Although the Company of Gardeners was formed in London in 1605, it was not until the last year of the nineteenth century that the first professional body for garden designers was formed — the American Society of Landscape Architects. Among the eleven founder members were Frederick Law Olmsted, junior, John Charles Olmsted and Beatrix Farrand, designer of the gardens at Dumbarton Oaks.

The term "landscape architecture" was used by Gilbert Meason in his book *On the Landscape Architecture of the Great Painters of Italy* in 1828, and by Olmsted and Vaux in referring to their designs for Central Park, but it was well into the twentieth century before British designers called themselves garden or landscape architects. At the end of 1929 they formed the British Association of Garden Architects, changing the name to the Institute of Landscape Architects early in 1930.

The modern landscape architect is as likely to be involved in the landscaping of a factory development or a shopping mall, or the planting of a highway as creating a private garden. Their training in botany and horticulture as well as in design awakened in many an awareness of ecological concerns, earlier perhaps than among the general public, and this has been reflected both in their contribution to environmental planning and in the creation of small-scale designs related to the environment, to human scale and to local habitat.

The garden hill at Shute House, Wiltshire, gardens designed by Sir Geoffrey Jellicoe.

work is often characterized by the use of native plants in sculptural groups and swirling patterns in colorful ground-cover plants. Burle Marx belonged to the group of architects who were associated with Le Corbusier in the building of the Ministry of Education in Rio in 1938 and subsequently in the creation of Brazilia. His work makes use of water matched with strong architectural forms in concrete, while his planting often favors the heliconias, relatives of the banana family.

It was not, of course, only the New World which produced modern designers. In Europe the designer would generally be working within a wider range of reference, although more often constrained by designing to match an existing older house or to fit within a well-established environment. Sir Geoffrey Jellicoe, co-author of a study of Italian Renaissance gardens, could equally well produce a classically formal garden at Ditchley Park or a modernist water garden for the roof of a department store, or another with a glass-bottomed pool at the Caveman Restaurant, Cheddar Gorge. His sometime partner Russell Page, though following in the tradition of Gertrude Jekyll in his planting and expert at achieving a completely natural look, collaborated with him at Cheddar and in building up a wide international reputation showed an ability both to handle modern forms and to meet the low-maintenance requirements of his clients.

In Italy Page has influenced Pietro Porcinai, who sensitively reinterprets the traditional Italian materials of stone and greenery, whether roofing an underground garage as part of a terraced garden outside Florence, or producing an elegant swimming pool design. In Germany modernism in the garden was frowned on under the Third Reich, despite its aggressive architectural style, though Hermann Mattern's postwar designs showed increasingly abstract forms linked with naturalistic plantings.

Plantings outside the National Theater in Brazilia. Roberto Burle Marx was responsible for the landscaping and gardens of Brazil's capital.

Gardening has now become a popular participatory pursuit. The barrage of books and television programs, to which this volume adds, provides unlimited advice on horticultural techniques. Garden festivals and events such as the annual Chelsea Flower Show attract enormous crowds. Visitors to historic and other gardens open to the public and to the design projects created for exhibition at the flower shows are able to see a wide range of styles and plantings.

Each year the exhibitions tend to feature a particular trend — this year more formality, topiary perhaps, next an emphasis on the indigenous flowers of the countryside — but no prevailing fashion now predominates. Yet that might well have been said by commentators often in the past for in looking back it is the impact of comparatively few gardens, surviving in fact or in description, that have formed our understanding of their history. As deepening interest leads garden enthusiasts to look more closely at the past, some received ideas about the extent of a particular fashion or the introduction of a particular style come into dispute. It would be fascinating to know what future generations will make of the gardens of our own time and what then will be considered the late twentieth-century style!

H.L.

A design by Thomas Church.

PLANTS OF THE GARDEN

THE DIVERSITY OF PLANTS

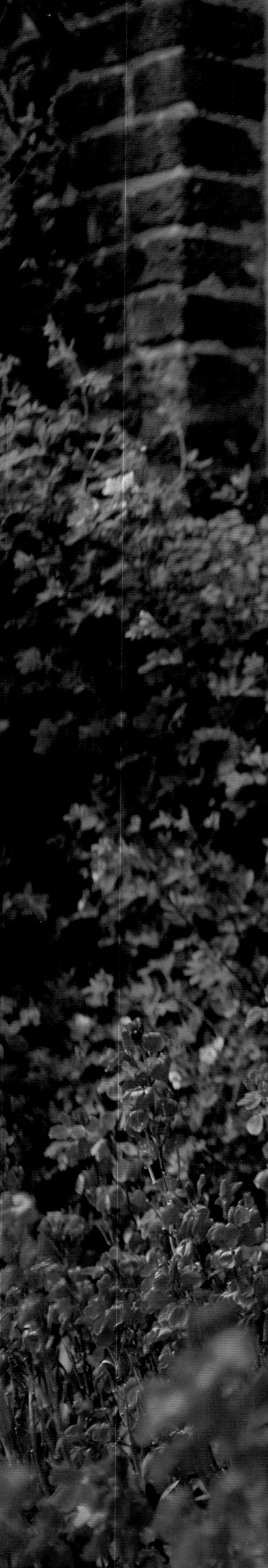

One of the outstanding features of the average garden is the diversity of its plants. Even the smallest suburban garden usually contains species representative of most groups in the plant kingdom. Some, like the green algae which cloak sheds, walls and damp places, are microscopic plants and usually ignored or go unnoticed. Others, such as ferns, arrive uninvited and cling to walls and secluded corners. If they look attractive or fill gaps unobtrusively they may be left to fend for themselves. The majority of plants in our garden are the showy flowering seed plants.

Above and right *Rock cress (Aubretia), seen here on a wall, is popular for rockeries and borders. Wallflowers (Cheiranthus) will grow in walls, but are widely used as bedding plants. There are more* *than 500,000 known plant species in the world, and many more that have never been recorded. Not all would be welcome in your garden but for each that is, there may be many different forms.*

Seed plants belong to two major groups: angiosperms, or flowering plants with their seeds enclosed in a protective cover, and gymnosperms, the conifers and their allies whose seeds have no enclosing structure. Angiosperms include annuals (which germinate, grow, flower, produce seed and die in one year); perennial herbs (which are long-lived and have variable life spans); and biennial herbs (whose life cycle takes two years, producing leaves and storing nutrients in the first year and producing leaves, flowers and seeds in the second), and shrubs and trees. Gymnosperms are more commonly seen in parks and botanical gardens than in private gardens but most gardeners will know gymnosperms as dwarf conifers, pine trees, ginkgoes (the Maidenhair Tree) or the palm-like cycads.

Seed plants are remarkably diverse in form, structure, color, smell and usefulness to mankind. They may be slow- or fast-growing, salt tolerant, liking limestone/chalk, neutral or acid soil, requiring free drainage or waterlogging, and may need full sun or be shade tolerant. Their variation accounts for the many different ways in which we use them.

Our ancestors were primarily interested in plants as providers of shelter, food and clothing. They supply grains, fruits, nuts, beverages, spices, herbs, medicines, fabrics, rubber, resins, glues, gums, turpentine, oils, perfumes and drugs such as tobacco, opium, cocaine and alcohol. In many parts of the world plants are still the cornerstone of local economies. Some peoples have a deep understanding of them. A supreme example is the remarkable ability of the Koi-San (Bushmen) to master an extremely inhospitable arid environment in southern Africa by exploiting the plants that grow there. It is ironic that the more complex the society,

the more knowledge that society has about plants but the less the individual in that society knows of them.

People first learned to domesticate plants as a matter of survival. Perhaps the gardener's urge to "tame wild plants" goes back to the same instincts; but nowadays most of us grow them for pleasure, except perhaps for those organic gardeners who want their food unpolluted by chemicals and the determined competitors in village horticultural shows who vie with each other to produce the largest or best quality vegetables. We chose our plants more for their ornamental than their useful value and have developed whole new ranges that do not appear in nature. However, the characteristics which have led gardeners and horticulturalists to select particular species over the years have, for the most part, been the very features that have made those plants so evolutionarily successful.

Plant evolution

To understand the evolution of plant life we need to look far back in geological time. The land area of our planet has changed its form many times during geological history. The impact of human beings, slowly but surely altering their surroundings, has greatly affected the diversity of life it supports. Many of the organisms that live on it have evolved only recently in its long history. Although in the distant past there have been major cycles of extinctions of both animals and plants, we are living today in one of the most cataclysmic periods of extinction of all time — one caused by us, by men and women. The rate of habitat destruction in tropical forests, wetlands, natural grasslands and Mediterranean shrublands is stunning. You have only to consider how much the places you know well have changed in your own lifetime to realize its pace, and changes in some areas of the globe are even more accelerated and drastic. We are living through and have to deal with a period of great loss in biotic diversity, but only now are we beginning to really understand something about the great sweep of evolution that brought us to this point.

Life has progressed a long way since primitive green algae, the ancestors of modern garden plants, washed about in primeval seas. These algae could only survive in water and had a very simple structure, but even at that stage they contained the green chlorophyll pigmentation found in nearly all modern land plants. They stored their reserves as starch, had cell walls composed of cellulose and reproduced by motile sperm and spores. From these primitive plants arose two great evolutionary lines: non-seedbearing plants which lack water and food-conducting tissue, and plants with conducting tissue, some producing seeds, others not. The great stride forward was the movement of plants from water onto the land.

The availability of water, and the ability to make use of it, were probably the most important factors in enabling plants to transfer from

The "Trail of Evolution" in the Brooklyn Botanic Garden uses extant species and models to trace the way in which the plant kingdom has developed.

water to land. Plants growing in the sea enjoyed a stable environment of temperature and moisture, a constant nutrient supply and a supporting medium with light intensity dependent on their depth below the water surface. In contrast, early land surfaces were precarious habitats. Water availability and temperature were unpredictable, soil was absent, surfaces were unstable and nutrients variable or absent. To avoid desiccation plants evolved less complex forms, developed shorter life cycles and began to survive hostile conditions via dormant life stages. To regulate water loss they evolved protective skins called cuticles, breathing pores, called stomata, and mucilage secretions. They also enclosed their reproductive parts in protective structures.

As plants spread out onto exposed amphibious landscapes they grew along the ground with some parts exposed and others lying in damp substrates. This reduced water loss but increased the need to conduct the water and the food manufactured by the action of sunlight on their chlorophyll (photosynthesis). As competition became intense, with plants scrambling over and shading each other, the erect habit developed and some began to grow upwards. This increased light availability and allowed their reproductive organs to be borne on the tips of shoots and branches, making it possible for spores to be dispersed by the wind rather than by water. An erect habit required the development of special conducting tissues, xylem, to take water and dissolved minerals from the roots to the leaves, and phloem, which transports synthesized food. These physiological, anatomical and morphological changes were accompanied by changes in the reproductive organs of the plants. The most significant was a shift from one spore type in a species to the segregation of spores into two types alongside a drastic modification of the respective spore-bearing structures.

Three main features appeared in the development of seed plants: the reduction in the number, shape, size and function of spores; the formation of pollen, with its distribution and receiving mechanisms; and the establishment of protective covers around the developing seed. During the Carboniferous age, over 300 million years ago, Europe was covered by the great coal forests. Landscapes were dominated by seed ferns, tree ferns, species of giant horsetails, clubmosses and early relatives of the gymnosperms. By 130 million years ago the Wealdon region of southeastern England was a landscape of swamps containing ferns, cycad-like trees, tree ferns, cycads and early conifers. As climates became colder and drier the conifers, cycads and ginkgoes developed new forms which were adapted to become less reliant upon water.

The success of the angiosperms, or flowering plants, was closely linked with the rise and fall of the dinosaurs. Dinosaurs dominated the world's landscape for over 130 million years. Our own period seems paltry by comparison. Dinosaurs must be the number one success story in the history of life. But what was their crucial role in botanical evolution?

In the age of dinosaurs, gymnosperms were one of the main plant forms on Earth. Why were they eclipsed by the angiosperms? Until recently evolutionists tended to study the plant and animal kingdoms independently and most modern textbooks still give only a cursory consideration of the interaction between dinosaurs and plants. Yet the evidence is clear. The fossil record suggests that there were several periods of extinction and reappearance of dinosaurs.

The cone of the cycad Encephalartos ferox. The seed form shows its kinship with the firs which are the better known gymnosperms in modern gardens.

The Maidenhair Tree (Ginkgo biloba), a deciduous gymnosperm that has existed for 280 million years, is a popular street, park and garden tree. Male and female flowers are produced on separate trees. Males are generally preferred because the fruit releases an acid as it rots that smells like a strong parmesan cheese.

The angiosperms sprouted up in a landscape grazed by gymnosperm-eating dinosaurs.

Plants have evolved all sorts of devices to foil plant eaters (herbivores): they include poisonous alkaloids, thorns, prickles, spines, unchewable tissue and phasing of leaf production to when herbivore populations are at their lowest. Many gardeners will have observed that the new shoots of many garden plants are tinged reddish or brownish-purple as they emerge, becoming harder and more green as they mature. These colors are usually caused by chemicals which give protection against the ultra-violet radiation in sunlight and may also be toxic to herbivores.

Herbivorous dinosaurs seem to have responded to the defenses of plants by developing bigger and better teeth for crushing, larger shoulders and longer necks to reach into trees, or lower heads and squarer muzzles to crop lower leaves. This struggle between plants and animals began when herbivorous arthropods grazed on algae in the Silurian age, 400 million years ago, and still continues.

There is an interesting transition of dinosaur types from the tall archisaurs which fed on ancient conifers and cycads in the late Triassic Period to diverse high-browsing brontosaurs and stegosaurs which fed on taller, more modern relatives of cycads and conifers, and latterly the age of low-browsing Cretaceous nodosaurs, iguanodonts and horned dinosaurs. The grazing dinosaurs ranged from broad-snouted edmontosaurs to narrow-beaked parksosaurs. Many of these large, squat, low grazers evolved massive plate-like armor to protect themselves from carnivores, while the plants in turn had to evolve means to protect themselves.

The Cretaceous dinosaurs which fed at ground level decimated many of the non-flowering ferns, cycads and conifers. Such plants were either prevented from, or were less successful in completing their life cycles than the flowering plants which could often produce their seed between the grazers' visits. They evolved with mammals, birds and flying insects and have been the dominant plants for 250 million years. Gymnosperms of ancient origin can still be found in gardens, however, including the Maidenhair Tree *Ginkgo biloba*, the Monkey-puzzle Tree *Araucaria araucana* and the Common Yew *Taxus baccata*.

Plant relationships

The scientific discipline concerned with identification and classification is called taxonomy. Plants are classified in a hierarchy of relationships which places together in groups those plants which have similar evolutionary characteristics.

Plants with a greater number of similarities are grouped together to form a species, the species are grouped to form a genus, similar genera to form a family and similar families to form an order. This continues until finally they all become part of the largest grouping — the plant kingdom.

Taking the Common Primrose *Primula vulgaris* as an example, these are the major taxonomic divisions of the plant kingdom:

Kingdom — Plantae (plants)
Division — Magnoliophyta (flowering plants or angiosperms)
Class — Magnoliatae
Order — Primulalaes
Family — Primulaceae (a group also containing *Cyclamen*, *Soldanella* and *Lysimachia*)
Genus — *Primula* (a group of some 400 species including *P. obconica* (Drumstick Primula) and *P. elatior* (Oxlip))
Species — *Primula vulgaris* (English Primrose)

Plant adaptation

The way in which the flowering plants survived, despite their importance as food for dinosaurs, is an example of the way in which accidental mutations can increase a plant's chances of survival, and how nature "selects" that particular form as the basis of new populations. The study of fossils shows that there have been tremendous extinctions and dispersals of new forms in the past which still continue.

There are some quite remarkable adaptations to be found in the plant world. This can per-

haps be most clearly seen in closely related species where selection for survival in different habitats has produced wide variation of form. Hebes belong to a genus which is native to temperate Australasia and South America. A large number of different species occur in New Zealand. In the relatively warmer North Island and on its offshore islands we find the tree hebe *Hebe parviflora* var. *arborea*, which can grow up to 26 ft (8 m) tall in the moderate maritime climate. South Island has a shrub form *Hebe salicifolia* which likes damp places and stream-sides and grows to 10 ft (3 m).

There are attractively flowering forms, found on the coasts, which have glossy leaves with a waxy layer to prevent the salt in the battering sea winds from coming into contact with living cells, leathery enough to provide protection and fleshy inside to store water when salt levels become too high for water intake, and guard against water loss.

High altitudes create adverse conditions for plants which must develop ways to protect dormant parts in winter, to prevent water loss and freezing, to produce rapid growth in the short periods when the weather is suitable and to bind scarce nutrients within the plant for as long as possible. The screes of New Zealand provide good protection for the overwintering buds of alpine forms of hebe and these species have adapted to solve the problem of being constantly covered by rock debris by branching from below the surface. Though available as snows melt, water is scarce in summer and frozen during winter when atmospheric humidity is also low, but hebes have developed ways of overcoming this too. A group known as the whipcords have cord-like stems and closely overlapping scale leaves to conserve water. Their reduced foliage and whip-like branches are ideal for blustery mountain-top conditions. *Hebe gibbsii* which lives on dry, rocky ridges has evolved tough, fringed leaves which condense water from mountain mists. The hebes on the mountain crag or towering to 26 ft (8 m) tall come from the same stock as the hebe in your garden.

Another example of this wide adaptation is in *Lobelia*, which in temperate climates is used by gardeners as an edging for flower borders, or in windowboxes and hanging baskets. Most people think of it as a low-growing or trailing plant with small leaves and small blue flowers,

but in the mountains of East Africa there are giant lobelias that grow upright with large leaves all pointing skyward, and circlets of flowers that can rise in a spire 6 ft (2 m) tall. This species seems to contradict the general rule that the higher up a mountainside a plant is found, the smaller it becomes in stature and leaf size, and the more compact and diverse its leaf structure, increasingly branching from the base rather than higher up the stem.

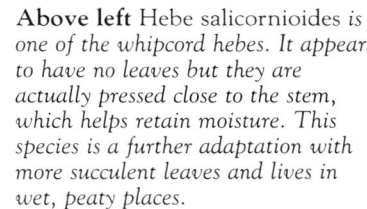

Above left Hebe salicornioides *is one of the whipcord hebes. It appears to have no leaves but they are actually pressed close to the stem, which helps retain moisture. This species is a further adaptation with more succulent leaves and lives in wet, peaty places.*

Above right H. odora *is a form adapted to alpine habitat.*

Above Lobelia telekii *grows to 13 ft (4 m) tall in the high mountains of Kenya. Its hairy, almost feathery bracts, hang down, hiding its small white and purple flowers. It makes a startling contrast to the familiar garden edging plant* (**left**).

Proteas and banksias

Pattern and diversity is manifested in many ways in plants. Consider the essentially Australian genus *Banksia*, named after Sir Joseph Banks who accompanied James Cook on his first voyage around the world, and its African relative, *Protea*, both members of the family Proteaceae.

Nearly all 75 species of banksia are found in Australia and are often known as Australian honeysuckles. They vary in size from tall trees to erect shrubs and squat species which are sometimes stemless. Proteas are found mainly in southern Africa, though now grown extensively as garden plants in other similar climates. In both groups many species have adapted to survive in an arid Mediterranean-type climate, sometimes in zones where bush fires are a frequent hazard. Some have fire-resistant bark, others have underground stems which regenerate from dormant buds a few months after aerial parts have been burned off. In others, the seeds are protected in a capsule containing a resinous layer which has to be burned away before germination can begin. Both genera have large, showy flowerheads

composed of many beautiful colored flowers arranged in various ways to attract their pollinators — bees, beetles, mice, small marsupials and birds. They also show tremendous variation in size, shape, texture, color, thickness and hairiness of leaves. Although found in different continents these plants have undergone similar adaptations to the hostile environments in which they occur.

Left *The King Protea (Protea cynaroides) has the largest flowers of any Protea, up to 1 ft (30 cm) across. It has subterranean rootstock which withstands fires on the South African veldt. It produces great quantities of nectar which attracts pollinators. The blooms of the Small Green Protea (P. scolymocephala)* **(below)** *are less than one-sixth the size. The Queen Protea (P. magnifica)* **(bottom)** *has flowers up to 6 in (15 cm) across when fully opened. Its forms range from prostrate to small trees. The Scarlet Banksia (Banksia coccinea)* **(below left)** *is an Australian member of the same Family. Banksias have stunning spikes of tubular flowers and range from shrubs under 3 ft (1 m) high to trees 16 ft (5 m) tall. Small marsupials, such as Honey and Pygmy possums which feed on nectar and pollen, act as pollinators.*

Convergent evolution

Many quite unrelated plant groups produce very similar features in response to comparable environmental or biotic pressures. These features may be modifications of the same or of different organs, but they have evolved to look like each other. Thorns, for instance, may have developed from different parts of the plant in different species. They may be remnants of flower stalks which harden, stipules, bracts or modified leaves. Other species have developed similar ways of attracting insects or other animals as pollinators, or adopted techniques for seed dispersal, such as seeds that blow away on downy parachutes or use burrs to hook onto passing animals.

Variation exists in nature because it is important for survival. Some species are better adapted to the environmental pressures of their habitat and will flourish, where others fail. Some may be able to cope with different conditions and be able to colonize new territory or to survive when their habitats undergo climatic or other changes. Many variants are not successful and disappear, but if they attract the interest of gardeners they may be nurtured as a garden plant and survive.

Further selection by the gardener for hardy strains that can withstand disease, drought or other harsh conditions can give the variant a chance to mutate further until it becomes a totally viable form.

Variations can be selected directly from the wild, and introduced unmodified into gardens. They can then be manipulated to produce new forms, including modifications to make a plant disease- and predator-resistant or give it a better chance of survival in a new habitat or different climate. It also allows the gardener to select for color variation, leaf pattern and other aesthetic considerations irrespective of their advantage to the plant. By deliberate and controlled crossbreeding — and now by genetic manipulation — it is possible to produce new color forms, changes in shape or growth and to attempt to produce a plant which meets some predetermined variation.

Although some plants have evolved to tolerate, or even thrive in, a wide range of conditions, there are many in our gardens which are restricted to very specific habitats and require conditions which are similar to those in which they grow in nature. It is a gardener's ability to be sensitive to the precise balance of water, light and nutrients required by a particular species or cultivar, coupled with a flair for design and balance in a garden, that makes

Top *Globe artichokes produce tufts of down to carry seeds on the breeze.*

Right *The Foxglove (Digitalis sp.) has developed a pattern of spots which guide insects to a landing pad and into the flower tube to pollinate the plant. Some orchids attract male bees by mimicking a female, smothering the bee with pollen when he attempts to mate.*

It is not only bees and other insects that carry pollen from flower to flower. Hummingbirds, such as this one taking nectar from a Columbine (Aquilegia alexandri), honey-creepers and other nectar-drinking-birds — and even small mammals — also do the job.

for "green fingers." The range of pests, specific or omnivorous, that need to be contended with complete the equation. Being a successful gardener means being flexible in response to your garden as an artificial environment containing many plants with specific needs. Most people learn by trial and error what they can grow in their garden — and, more often than not, at considerable expense — but the best gardeners are those who use a knowledge of the life histories of the plants they cultivate to place them in the best positions to resist the impulse to grow species unsuitable for the conditions which they can offer.

The naming of plants

We tend to take it for granted that everything has a name and that everyone will know what is meant by it, but someone has to give it that name in the first place. Things are known by different names in different languages and, even in the same country, different words are sometimes used for the same thing. This is especially true of plants. When explorers and emigrants to new lands found a plant that reminded them of something similar back home they often gave it that name. When a new plant was introduced from abroad, a new name might be given to it. It is easy to see how "daisy" could come to mean a whole range of plants.

To overcome the problems of different names and different languages, scientists give all living things a scientific name, based on Latin, the language used by the Christian church which once controlled almost all European teaching, and which became an international language for scholars and scientists.

Botanists do not now usually converse in Latin but they still give plants Latin botanical names which they all understand. In theory, using Latin as a universal language would avoid confusion, but many of the problems con-

cerned with vernacular, or common names, could still occur.

The solution was to name plants by a system which would make sure that only one name could be correct, a system which was based on the classification of each plant (or animal) by its relationship to others.

The modern system of classification was established by the Swedish scientist Carl Linné (or Linnaeus in Latin) in 1753 with the publication of *Species Plantarum*. Linnaeus was a taxonomist — a specialist in the study and description of variation in nature and its classification into groups with similar characteristics. Previously most botanists had referred to plants by a diagnostic phrase name covering a number of characteristics that seemed to circumscribe a species, such as the long-winded name for the European dog rose — *Rosa caule xuleato petiolis intermibus calycibus semipinnatis* (rose with a thorny stem, petioles without thorns and half pinnate sepals) or *Rosa sylvestris vulgaris flore odorato incarnato* (rose wild and common with a scented pink flower).

Such phrase names served as a means by which species could be recognized. They gave the characters essential for distinguishing one from another. The problem was that as the number of species increased so the names became longer to distinguish new species from those already known.

From 1753 on Linnaeus used two systems: a descriptive phrase name for use by the learned (which was not easily memorized) and a two-word name or "binomial," such as *Rosa canina*, which would have uncertain meaning unless linked to a descriptive name. As the phrase name became too lengthy the binomial became the standard.

The binomial is Latinized and consists of two parts, plus an abbreviation of the name of the person who originally described the plant. The first word (always written with a capital letter) is the name of the genus, the second is the species, of which there may be many in a genus or just one. The species name generally refers to some characteristic of the species, such as prickly thorns, or may commemorate a person and is written without a capital, even if formed from a person's name. For scientific purposes the Latin names are followed by the name of the person who published the first scientific description of the plant. The name of this "author" or describer is often abbreviated — L. for Linnaeus, for example, and L.f. for his son. Though of botanical importance, especially in unraveling the problems of a species which may have been described independently by different people, these details are rarely of importance to the gardener. Sometimes, however, you will find a third name, the subspecies, a further division to account for significant differences which occur between different plant forms in the same species.

Changes in scientific names

New discoveries which prove a different plant relationship, or the realization that a plant had in fact been given an earlier name, can mean that a name in regular use has to be changed. This can cause problems, especially when seed and nursery catalogs do not make the change or you know only the old name, but it is necessary to ensure that a name is not scientifically misleading.

Problems of nomenclature are sorted out by reference to an International Code of Botanical Nomenclature which lays down strict criteria for determining priority and valid scientific publication. These are based on the principle that plant names are irrevocably tied to preserved plant specimens, or, exceptionally, to paintings or original descriptions at the time of publication. It has nothing to do with the plant being a "typical" specimen. Often, indeed, the type specimen was quite atypical of the full variation of the species concerned.

Varieties, cultivars and hybrids

The subdivision of plants does not end with the species and subspecies. The smaller variations are often those which interest gardeners because the small botanical differences can make big differences in appeal to individual taste.

The differences that occur in nature due to a small mutation and become established, perhaps as a local variation, are known as varieties or forms; when they occur under cultivation and are preserved by human selection they are known as cultivars. Unless the same mutation occurs in a number of individuals — which may take longer than plant breeders are prepared to wait — reproduction has to be by vegetative means; cuttings or layering. These are forms of cloning since the cell reproduces identically and does not involve the combining of two sets of genes as in sexual reproduction. Varieties are identified by the word var. after the specific

Gregor Mendel.

Left *A portrait of Linnaeus in Wedgwood porcelain, based on a medallion by Carl Fredrik Inlander, 1773.*

name followed by a third Latin name; cultivars by cv. and a third name, not in Latin and written between quotation marks.

There is another possibility for the production of new forms: cross-pollination between different flowers — hybridization. It was Linnaeus who, in 1757, produced the first scientifically accepted cross between two kinds of toadflax. He found that the offspring displayed some of the character of each parent — they were hybrids.

No one knew why this happened until 1866, when Gregor Mendel, an Austrian monk, found through experiments with peas that some characteristics were dominant and others recessive. It followed that by selecting plants with the characters a breeder wants and continually breeding them it is possible to end up with groups of plants all with the same predictable characters (strains). Hybrids are identified by inserting x between the generic and specific names in the case of hybridization between two species, the hybrid being given a new specific name. When plants of the same species are involved, this is known as "crossing," and the x is placed after the specific name and before the new subspecific. In cases where plants of different genera have successfully been hybridized, the x is placed before the generic name of the new plant.

Some hybrids are sterile and so, lacking fertile seed, propagation has to be vegetative. Even when fertile they do not necessarily breed true. The first generation, known as F_1, is usually vigorous and produces more of the new type; the second generation F_2, is likely to produce more throwbacks to original unwanted characteristics.

Sometimes a plant develops, either by mutation or as a result of grafting, which exhibits the separate characteristics of both the original plants. For example, it might have flowers of two different colors. Such plants are called chimera (a name originally given to a mythical animal that was part lion, part serpent and part goat). In this case the name is given with a + instead of the x symbol of the hybrids.

With recent developments in genetic engineering (interfering with the genes to create mutations), it is possible to create totally new plants in the laboratory, which may give future gardens forms and color that previous methods have been unable to produce. C. S.

Breeding a champion rose: *Aotearoa–New Zealand*

It is commonly said that a good plant breeder always has a long term objective in mind when he cross-pollinates his flowers. I work in a rather different manner, taking each generation as it comes.

For example, when I started breeding roses in 1952, the Floribundas were at the peak of their popularity. The Americans had taken the old-fashioned polyanthas with large clusters of rather shapeless flowers, and by crossing them with Hybrid Tea types had produced rather shy-flowering cluster-flowered varieties of beautiful form.

Nobody had used the modern miniature hybrids of Ralph Moore, so I decided to use his pink *New Penny* to bring back floriferousness. The resulting orange *Anytime* and deep pink *Moana* were just that. *Anytime* was semi-double and *Moana* had good miniature HT form. Both carried large heads of small blooms on biggish plants. Cross-fertilizing them gave me the soft pink *Seaspray*, which still had enormous heads of bloom and a bigger plant yet again, but the blooms were somewhat shapeless.

I used the pollen of several well-formed Hybrid Teas on *Seaspray*, knowing that *Seaspray* gave me lots of seed which germinated freely. One of these pollen parents was *Traumereii*, an orange salmon Hybrid Tea from Kordes of Germany. I knew it gave seedlings of excellent form. I raised thousands of seedlings. The best was to be *Sexy Rexy*. I could still walk to the exact spot in the field in Lincoln Road, Henderson, where I first saw it. It seemed to have almost everything, except fragrance.

On I went again, this time crossing *Sexy Rexy* with fragrant Hybrid Teas, to get it still bigger and more fragrant. This time, the pink colouring had almost gone, but the creamy-white *Auckland Metro* was fragrant and the flowers were big.

But I still needed more fragrance. *Harmonie* had it in abundance. It was but a short step to *Aotearoa–New Zealand*. It is big and lusty, very free-flowering, of beautiful form and ultra-fragrant — a far cry from the little pink mini *New Penny*.

It only took about forty years of my life!

S. McG

Internationally renowned rose breeder Sam McGredy has won top awards for his roses worldwide.

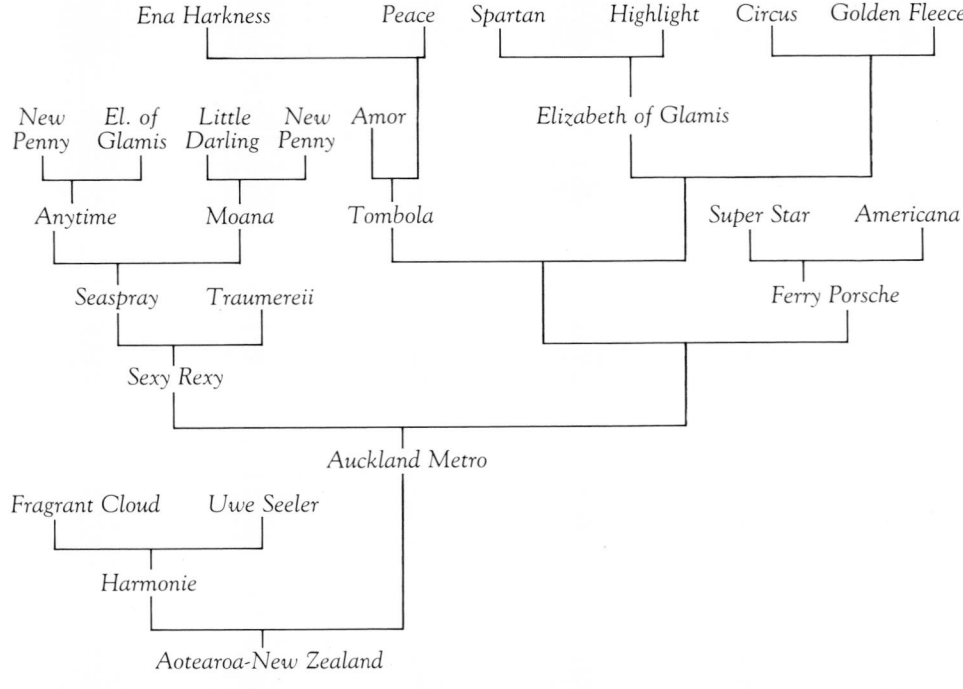

The Parentage of Aotearoa-New Zealand

Sexy Rexy

Auckland Metro

Aotearoa-New Zealand

PLANTS FROM AROUND THE WORLD

Some of the plants we grow are forms of indigenous species found in the wild in our own neighborhoods, but many of them have been introduced — sometimes from the other side of the world — and often carefully developed by plant nurseries until the strain we know is not immediately recognizable as the plant seen in the wild. Explorers, traders and travelers collected not only medical and economic plants, but many attractive new forms for the flower garden, and in recent centuries this trade has been increasingly important.

Exchanges were taking place between Asia and Europe many centuries ago; the Egyptians sent out expeditions to bring back exotics which we can now see carved on the walls of the temple at Karnak, Alexander the Great had specimens and descriptions of plants sent back from the lands he conquered to Aristotle in Greece. As empires waxed and waned, colonists took plants out with them, as well as sending exotics home. Some of the early discoveries resulted from the need for food, but later were widely grown as highly attractive ornamentals. Early colonists in New Zealand — as well as Captain Cook and his crew — ate blanched leaves and hearts of Ti Kouka (*Cordyline australis*), now better known as the Cabbage

Tree and widely grown as a beautiful house plant in cool countries.

Lilies were being cultivated more than 5,000 years ago: the Madonna Lily (*Lilium candidum*) is depicted on Cretan vases and other objects of the middle Minoan period, about 1750 to 1600 B.C. This lily was also known to the Assyrians and said to have been carried west by the Phoenicians. It is thought to have been planted near the permanent camps of the Roman legions, perhaps because an ointment made from its bulbs removes corns and takes away pain and inflammation from burns and scalds.

The Romans probably took rosemary, the grapevine and other herbs and flowers with them to countries they conquered, though many of the plants with which they were familiar in Mediterranean lands would not easily succeed in cold northern climes.

After the Romans, monks preserved much of the knowledge of horticulture and were probably responsible for introducing new plants from other parts of Europe, especially medicinal herbs, while in the south the spread of Islam carried plants from one end of the Mediterranean to the other. Roses that graced gardens in Persia began to scent the courtyards of

Rosemary (Rosmarinus officinalis) (left center) was originally a Mediterranean plant of southern Europe and Asia Minor. The Romans carried it to all parts of their Empire because of its medicinal and culinary uses. It is equally at home in this American garden. The bush against the wall behind it, the Blue Hibiscus (Alyogyne huegelii) is native to southwest Australia.

Spanish palaces. Crusaders, discovering the delights of gardens as they traveled south and journeyed to the Holy Land, added roses and other plants to the things they eventually took back to northern Europe.

Botanizing herbalists

In the century following the invention of printing by movable type in Germany in 1440, a number of herbals were published by men who were sometimes also plant explorers. Jules Charles de L'Ecluse (or Carolus Clusius, as he is often known, 1526–1609) was a Flemish doctor who traveled through southern France and Iberia, where he also saw some of the new plants arriving from North America, and east to Hungary. For a time he held a post at the Imperial Gardens in Vienna and through contacts in the Turkish Court at Constantinople received seeds and bulbs from western Asia. Clusius, and other plantsmen and herbalists, including Rembert Dodoens from the Netherlands, the Frenchman Mathias de l'Obel, Peirandrea Mattioli in Italy, William Turner in England, and Otto Brunfels, Jerome Bock and Leonhard Fuchs in Germany described more than 6,000 plants in books they published between 1530 and 1610.

Clusius is particularly linked with tubers and bulbs from Asia, including tulips, hyacinths, the Crown Imperial (*Fritillaria imperialis*), irises and narcissus. Tulips and hyacinths especially captured the attention of gardeners, as well as financial speculators. He was also instrumental in creating the passion for auricula, which lasted nearly four hundred years.

He supervised the planting of the botanic garden at Leiden, where ornamental plants became a feature, rather than purely medicinal ones, and his study of bulbs may be considered the starting point of the modern Dutch bulb industry.

Nurserymen and plant hunters

By 1600 nurseries were already well established. In France, Jean Robin, a botanist and apothecary who had the direction of the gardens of the Louvre under three kings and ran his own garden on the Ile de la Cité, issued catalogs of plants in 1601 and 1609, some of the species native to North America. He made the Tuberose (*Polianthes tuberosa*) fashionable, and the North American False Acacia (*Robinia pseudacacia*) is named after him — he grew the first in Europe from Virginian seeds. Later in the century, seedsman and nurseryman Le Febvre set up business in Paris. The company eventually became world famous as the nursery Vilmorin-Andrieux and is still thriving.

In England in 1605 James I granted a Royal Charter to the Company of Gardeners which banned the sale of poor-quality plants and seeds. Its members in and around the city of London had a flourishing trade and provided a

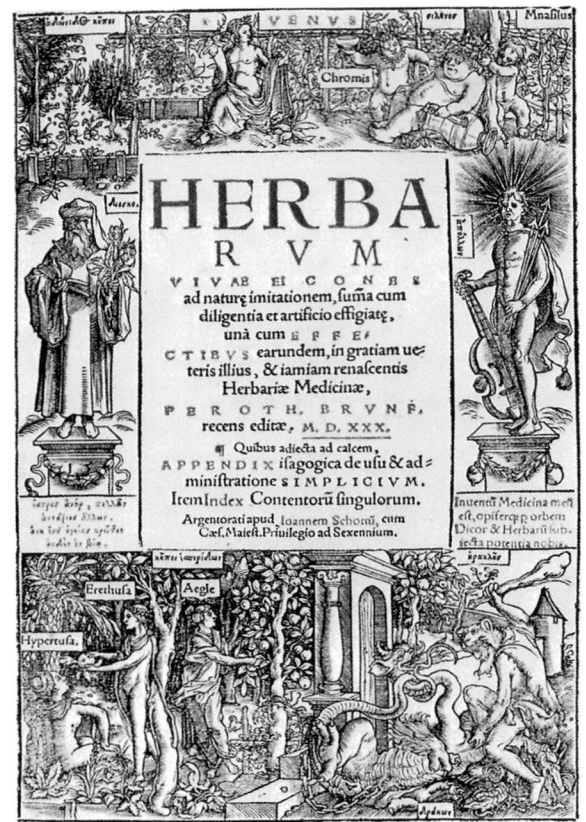

Left *The title page of Otto Brunfel's* Herbarum Vivae Eicones, *published 1630. The invention of movable type in 1440 made it possible to publish books and illustrate them with wood engravings.*

Opposite *Rhododendrons, azaleas and maples bring vivid color to the gardens of Compton Acres. Rhododendrons and azaleas thrive on very acid soil and in the wild, where there are over 800 species, usually grow on cool and rainy mountainsides. The first to be introduced to Europe came from North America, then from the mountains of Asia Minor, but it was only when seeds from Kashmir were raised in England that they began to become so popular. Originally they flowered too early for British winters but breeders produced hybrids that suited their new conditions and there are now vast numbers to choose from.*

channel through which new plants could be distributed. John Tradescant, the Elder (1570–1638), for instance, gardener to a succession of important patrons and eventually to Charles I, raised plants at his garden in Lambeth and himself went on plant-collecting expeditions to western Europe, Russia and North Africa. In 1617 he became a member of the Virginia Company which brought him such plants as the Spiderwort (*Tradescantia virginiana*), which Linnaeus named after him, and the Virginia Creeper (*Parthenocissus quinquefolia*).

Above *The Crown Imperial (*Fritillaria imperialis*) was discovered by the Mogul Emperor Jahangir and was carved into the walls of the Taj Mahal on the instructions of his successor Shah Jehan.*

Left *Crown Imperials rise above the tulips in the gardens of Monticello.*

John Tradescant the Elder, a portrait by Emanuel de Critz.

The title page of the 1633 edition of Gerarde's Herball, when it was revised by Thomas Johnson. Much of its content was freely taken from a book by Flemish herbalist Rembert Dodoens. As well as being a barber-surgeon and herbalist Gerarde was curator of the garden of the College of Physicians. His herbal is known for its "inaccuracies and blunders" but Gerarde's enthusiasm for plants is obvious and he makes the first printed reference to the potato.

The Tradescants

The Tradescants, father and son, were English plant collectors. John the Elder (1570–1638) was gardener to the Earl of Salisbury, Lord Wootton and the Duke of Buckingham before becoming royal gardener to Charles I. In 1609 and 1611 he visited the Low Countries collecting trees and flowers, and in 1618 he accompanied Sir Dudley Digges to Russia, botanizing around Archangel. He also traveled to North Africa, especially Morocco, where he is said to have acquired a variety of apricot prohibited to be exported. In 1617 he became a member of the Virginia Company, through which he gained many North American plants and, in 1626, his son John the Younger became his assistant. The younger Tradescant became a freeman of the Gardeners' Company in 1638 and visited America in 1637, 1642 and 1654. He returned with many plants which are now widely grown in gardens, including the superb American Cowslip (*Dodecatheon meadia*), Swamp Cypress (*Taxodium distichum*) and Tulip Tree (*Liriodendron tulipifera*).

The dazzling dahlia

The brightly-colored, frost-tender dahlia comes from Mexico and was first described by Francisco Hernandez (1515–78), botanist and physician to Philip II of Spain. In 1789 Vincent Cervantes of the Botanic Gardens in Mexico City sent dahlia seeds to the Royal Gardens at Madrid. The first seedling to germinate and bloom produced semi-double flowers and was called *Dahlia pinnata*, while later two others were named *D. rosea* and *D. coccinea*. At the time, botanists thought that their tubers, like those of the potato, might prove edible!

Plants sent to Kew in the 1790s failed to establish themselves but seed from Madrid planted at Kew flowered and seeded in 1804. At the same time, Empress Josephine's garden at Malmaison grew dahlias and after the exile of Napoleon in 1814 many of these varieties were introduced to England. In 1804 seeds had been sent to Berlin, where the botanist Carl Ludwig Willdenow named the variety after the Russian botanist Georgi of Petersburg. Since then, in parts of Europe east of the Rhine the dahlia has been known as

When the Conquistadors arrived in Central and South America they were interested in gold and silver, not in plants, and early settlers in North America were more interested in getting the seed they took with them to grow than in investigating indigenous plants. In about 1571 the Spanish physician Nicholas Monardes — who was the first European to receive seeds of nasturtiums from South America — wrote a book about American plants and Thomas Hariot, one of the colonists involved in Sir Francis Drake's unsuccessful attempt at settlement in Virginia, brought back plants which were described in Gerarde's *Herball* in 1597. Cannas and dahlias are other South and Central American plants, known in the 1500s, but which did not arrive in Europe until much later.

In 1556 the Spanish authorities promulgated a law that prevented publication of any information about their colonies. In theory, licenses could be obtained to allow publication, but none were forthcoming. Francisco Hernandez in the 1570s and Barnabos Cobo in the early 1600s both produced detailed studies of plants and flowers that were suppressed. However, from the third decade of the seventeenth century a considerable number of species from Virginia and Canada began to appear in European gardens.

As early as 1534 the French navigator and explorer Jacques Cartier sailed into the St. Lawrence river and the following year took

A modern hybrid dahlia, one of many different forms available.

Georgine. In Berlin, Christoph Friedrich Otto, the Curator of the Berlin Botanic Garden, was the central grower of dahlias, from there spreading them throughout Europe. Within 15 years, dahlias were fashionable in Germany, France and Britain.

conifers back to France. When settlements were established by Samuel de Champlain the following century on the sites of present-day Montreal and Quebec, plants were certainly collected. Around 1635, about forty plants of Canadian origin were known in the Jardin du Roi in Paris.

Henry Compton, Bishop of London from 1675 to 1713, was an enthusiastic gardener who grew over a thousand exotics in the gardens at Fulham Palace. He corresponded and exchanged seeds with botanists in Europe and North America, specializing in American trees. His particular supplier in America was a missionary, John Banister, for whose appointment he was responsible. Among the seeds sent back to England after his arrival in 1685 were many now widely grown in gardens, including the Sweet Gum (*Liquidambar styraciflua*), Box Elder (*Acer negundo*), Scarlet Oak (*Quercus coccinea*) and the beautiful Honey Locust (*Gleditsia triacanthos*).

In 1690 the curator of the Chelsea Physic Garden sent James Harlow on a plant-hunting expedition to Jamaica and he returned after two years with a large number of living plants, as well as herbarium specimens. Hans Sloane, the Irish physician and naturalist who later gave the Chelsea Physic Garden its new site, also visited Jamaica, accompanying the Governor, the Duke of Albemarle. He traveled via Madeira and Barbados, recording plants on the way and collecting 800 plants in Jamaica. In 1707 he published the first volume of his *Natural History of Jamaica*.

While the French and British were returning with plants from North America, the Dutch were bringing back plants from their colony at the Cape of Good Hope in South Africa. Many were introduced into England via Holland, but unfortunately the vast majority were not fully hardy in either country and had to be overwintered indoors. Nevertheless, in 1629 John Parkinson, the English gardener and garden writer, is said to have grown the splendid bulbous *Haemanthus coccineus*, one of the African Blood Lilies. Agapanthus, widely known as African Lilies, and *Pelargonium zonale* and *P. inquinans* were also found about that time.

The systematic exploration of plants in India began in 1600 when the East India Company gained a charter from Queen Elizabeth I, granting a monopoly of trade between England and the East. The Dutch East India Company was chartered two years later and its governor sent back material to the botanist J. Commelin in Amsterdam from which *Hortus Indicus Malabaricus* was compiled and published in 1703. Dr. Samuel Browne, a surgeon engaged

Above right Agapanthus *was introduced from Africa in the first half of the seventeenth century.*

Right *The Zonal Pelargonium is another African species which was known in Europe early in the seventeenth century.*

Chrysanthemums

Chrysanthemums have a long history and can be traced to 500 B.C. They were mainly yellow and probably forms of *Chrysanthemum indicum*. In the T'ang dynasty in China, A.D. 618–902, white-flowered forms were known and considered as *C. morifolium*. These two species must have hybridized and produced several different hybrids, creating *Chrysanthemum x hortorum*. Chrysanthemums became closely associated with Japan; in 1797 they were adopted as the personal emblem of the Emperor and later a chrysanthemum appeared on the Japanese flag as 16 petals around a central disc. This image is often thought to be the rising sun, because on the modern flag it has been simplified to a simple disc.

In 1689 chrysanthemums were recorded in Holland and in 1764 in the Chelsea Physic Garden. Unfortunately, none survived and it was not until 1789, when specimens reached France (and Kew Gardens a year later), that their introduction into Europe really began. Plants and seeds reached the nursery of Colville of Chelsea, London, from James Reeves who was employed as a tea buyer by the East India Company in Canton.

Between 1820 and 1830, nearly 70 varieties were introduced, and the first

English flower show where chrysanthemums were displayed was held in 1843.

Many countries avidly grew these flowers, especially France and the Channel Island of Jersey, where it is said 4,000 varieties have been cultivated. Nurseries specialized in growing them, with many different types such as Pompoms (said to be named after the pompoms on the hats of French sailors), Cascades, Charms, Decoratives, Reflexed Decoratives, Incurved Decoratives, Koreans, Spoons, and Rayonnantes.

During the 1900s many nurseries grew them for sale as cut flowers in fall, and especially at Christmas in the Northern Hemisphere. Chrysanthemums are "short-day" plants: they initiate flower buds when the period of darkness is longer than that of light. Flowering can be delayed by manipulating the disbudding and "crowns" on which they bear flowers, and during the 1950s commercial nurseries started to control periods of darkness — combined with specified temperatures — to make chrysanthemums flower throughout the year. At first cut flowers were grown, and then the blooms were grown for sale in pots. Chemicals are also used to decrease the height of tall varieties, making them more suitable for pot growing.

Chrysanthemums were recorded in Holland in 1689 and in Chelsea Physic Garden in 1764 but in neither case survived. It was another quarter of a century before their European introduction really began with nearly 70 varieties appearing in the next decade. In China they can be traced back to at least 500 B.C., when they were mainly yellow. White forms were known in the T'ang dynasty. Chrysanthemums became the emblem of the Japanese Imperial family and it is a 16-petalled chrysanthemum which is the origin of the disc which now appears on the Japanese flag, not the rising sun. There are now many forms, from the dainty white Chrysanthemum hosmariense (top) to the tricolored C. carinatum — the "Painted Daisy" from Morocco (above left) and the spherical incurving forms (above).

by the hospital in Madras in 1688, established a garden that included medicinal and economic plants. He sent seeds of these back to the Oxford Botanical Garden and the Chelsea Physic Garden.

Contact with China had brought eastern plants to Europe many centuries earlier, but the first western botanist to collect plants in Japan was another employee of the Dutch East India Company, Engelbert Kaempfer, a German working from their trading station on the island of Deshima, just off the port of Nagasaki, in the early 1690s. He recorded and wrote about numerous indigenous species, including many that today are widely grown in gardens, including hydrangea, skimmia, aucuba, ginkgo, camellia and lilies, many being named in recognition of his services to botany. He is well remembered in the naming of the outstandingly attractive beardless iris, *Iris kaempferi*.

The search for new plants

During the eighteenth century the search for new plants intensified. Mark Catesby (1683–1749) was probably the first fully professional plant hunter to be sent to North America. He was engaged by four botanist-gardeners — Dr. Hans Sloane, the Duke of Chandos, Dr. Richard Mead and William Sherard — and landed at Williamsburg, a town on the James River which runs into Chesapeake Bay. He visited the West Indies and the Bahamas, but much of his time was spent in North Carolina where he made two trips between 1722 and 1725. Plants he sent back to London included Indian Bean Tree (*Catalpa bignonioides*), the Bull Bay or Southern Magnolia (*Magnolia grandiflora*), Carolina Allspice (*Calycanthus floridus*), Pasture Rose (*Rosa carolina*) and herbaceous Summer or Fall Phlox (*Phlox paniculata*).

The first American-born plant hunter was the Quaker John Bartram, born in 1699 in

Above *John Bartram's home was set in the middle of his botanical garden, near Philadelphia. The influence of his English correspondent Peter Collinson secured him the appointment of King's Botanist and a pension of $50 per year. His house survives, together with part of his garden which is now a public park.*

Top and left center *Camellias were among the many plants recorded by Englebert Kaempfer, the first western botanist to collect plants in Japan.*

Left Iris kaempferi *is named after the German botanist.*

Above *The Southern Magnolia (Magnolia grandiflora) was sent to Europe by Mark Catesby.*

Right *Sweet Bergamot (Monarda didyma) was one plant John Bartram introduced to cultivation. Others include the Cucumber Tree (Magnolia cuminata), Fringe Tree (Chionanthus virginicus), Black Snake Root (Cimicifuga racemosa), American Turk's-cap Lily (Lily-royal) (Lilium superba), Dutchman's Pipe (Aristolochia macrophylla) and Ostrich Fern (Onoclea struthiopteris) — out of a total of more than 200 plants.*

Pennsylvania to a Derbyshire family who had emigrated about 1682. He was a self-taught botanist who in 1728 settled on the Schuylkill River, where he had a farm which he planted as a botanic garden. He started collecting seeds and plants, which he sent to Peter Collinson in England, a plant enthusiast who was in contact with many foreign scientists and botanists. Collinson received seeds and plants from many collectors, as well as Bartram, forming a "settled trade and business." Collinson, among his many other activities, was instrumental in founding the British Museum and the Cambridge Botanic Garden. During Bartram's 30 years of plant hunting in North America he explored vast areas, from the eastern states of Maryland, Georgia, the Carolinas and Virginia, south to Florida and north to New Jersey. He also ventured to Ohio and the Mississippi.

Botanists from many parts of Europe went to North America to hunt plants. Pedr Kalm was the son of a Finnish pastor and a pupil of Carl Linnaeus. Funded by three Swedish Universities and the Swedish Academy, and accompanied by Lars Yungstroem, a gardener, he arrived in Philadelphia in 1748. He was amazed at the range of new plants and soon visited John Bartram. On the encouragement and urging of Linnaeus, Kalm traveled north to Hudson Bay and Canada, the Governor of Quebec receiving and helping him. He returned to Sweden with a herbarium collection of about 325 plants, many later described by Linnaeus.

Collectors continued to arrive in the eastern states of North America, and included William Young, best known for his introduction of the Venus Flytrap (*Dionaea muscipula*) from the swamps of North Carolina and Florida. John Fraser, of Scottish descent, and André Michaux, a Frenchman, were others and although there was rivalry between them they collaborated on some expeditions. Among the now widely-grown plants introduced by Fraser are the Bottlebrush Buckeye (*Aesculus parviflora*), Silverberry (*Elaeagnus parviflora*), *Hydrangea quercifolia*, several *Vaccinium* spp., Early-leaved Umbrella Tree (*Magnolia fraseri*), Mountain Camellia (*Stewartia ovata*), *Zenobia speciosa* and the Flame Azalea (*Rhododendron calendulaceum*).

In South America it was the Andes region that was first botanized. In 1709 Father Louis Feuillée visited Peru and Chile, primarily for scientific purposes but also to survey the natural history and plant life. He recorded alstroemerias, a fuchsia, tropaeolum and mimulus, as well as many medicinal plants. A scientific expedition was engaged by the French Academy of Science, in collaboration with the Spanish Government, to test one of Sir Isaac Newton's theories and the best place for this was in Ecuador. Joseph de Jussieu was engaged as botanist, and they left France in 1735. One of the best-known plants he discovered was Heliotrope (*Heliotropium peruvianum* — now known as *H. arborescens*).

Spanish and Portuguese officials were always suspicious of other Europeans visiting South America and usually either refused permission or introduced problems. For example, Joseph Dombey arrived in South America in the mid-1770s and became burdened by restrictions imposed by the Spanish authorities. He had to submit two specimens of every plant he found,

so that the best could be selected by the Madrid Botanic Garden. He was further aggravated by having two Spanish assistants imposed on him, with drastically inferior knowledge but higher pay. He had to buy much of his own equipment and was, without doubt, shabbily treated by Spanish officials.

Charles III of Spain, more enlightened than his predecessors, commissioned a survey of the natural resources of Mexico. Headed by Dr. Martin Sessé y Lacosta and assisted by the Mexican José Mariano Mociño, a gifted botanist and physician, they began work in 1788, but by then the king had died and his successor stopped the survey.

Plant hunters in Asia

James Cunninghame (c.1698–1709), a Scottish doctor with the East India Company, left London in 1689 for Amoy, off the coast of China, collecting nearly 800 specimens there and at his other ports of call. After a year back in Britain he went to Chusan and then Cambodia, where he was the sole survivor of a massacre and kept prisoner for two years, but not before he had sent seeds and 600 dried specimens home, including a species of camellia, though few were of importance to gardeners.

The Chinese flora, nevertheless, is rich, with many of the same genera that also occur in North America, such as *Wisteria* and the Wych hazels, *Hamamelis*. China has probably yielded nearly as many garden plants as North

Below *The Golden Rain Tree* (Koelreuteria paniculata) *was one of the species which Pierre Nicholas le Chéron d'Incarville sent back to Paris.*

America, and no doubt would have provided even more if its extensive population had not, in earlier years, destroyed vast areas of plants to grow food crops.

The Jesuit missionary, Pierre Nicholas le Chéron d'Incarville, studied in Paris and Quebec before traveling in 1740 to Macao and eventually to Peking. His name is remembered in *Incarvillea*, a genus of beautiful herbaceous perennials. He introduced some magnificent plants, including the Chinese Tree of Heaven (*Ailanthus altissima*), known to the Germans as The Tree of the Gods, but to the French as the Stinking Ash because the greenish flowers have a disagreeable odor. Others included the Japanese Pagoda Tree (*Sophora japonica*), the Golden Rain Tree (*Koelreuteria paniculata*), the Chinese Arbor-vitae (*Thuja orientalis*), the Silk Tree (*Albizia julibrissin*), one of the Pea Trees (*Caragana sinica*), and the Paper Mulberry or Tapa-cloth Tree (*Broussonetia papyrifera*). It is unfortunate that he sent most of his seeds back to Bernard de Jussieu in Paris, as more than a century later packets of seeds d'Incarville had returned were found unopened.

In 1755 China was closed to foreigners, although some Jesuit priests who were scientific advisers to the court at Beijing were allowed to remain, but with restrictions. There were two loopholes, at Canton (but only when the merchant fleet was in residence) and the island of Macao, a Portuguese preserve which offered practically no access to other nationals. However, in 1770 Benjamin Torin, an employee of the East India Company, is recorded as sending a collection of plants to Kew. These included the highly scented Winter Daphne (*Daphne odora*), *Osmanthus fragrans*, a purple-leaved form of *Cordyline terminalis* variously known as the Good-luck Plant, Hawaiian Good-luck Plant and Tree-of-Kings, and *Saxifraga stolonifera*, also now rich in amusing common names such as Strawberry Geranium, Beefsteak Geranium, Strawberry Begonia, Creeping Sailor and Mother of Thousands.

About the same time other plants reaching Kew included the Tree Peony (*Paeonia suffruticosa*) and the superb and now widely-grown Japonica (*Chaenomeles japonica*), also known as Japanese Quince and Flowering Quince. The Chinese Flowering Apple (*Malus spectabilis*) appeared about the same time.

Britain decided to improve relations with China and Lord Macartney was appointed Ambassador, with Sir George Staunton, a botanist, his second-in-command, assisted in the field by two gardeners, Stronach and John Haxton. They departed Portsmouth in 1792, soon to present themselves as supplicants before the Emperor. This was more than just a token "bending the knee," but rather a matter of "licking boots." They refused to prostrate themselves nine times before the Emperor, or any article said to represent his majesty. They did, however, agree to kneel in the same manner as when addressing their own King. Honor was satisfied and they set out for Canton, thence to Macao, and after botanizing arrived back in Portsmouth in 1794. Their endeavors were greatly rewarded and included the Plume Poppy or Tree Celandine (*Macleaya cordata*), and Macartney's Rose (*Rosa bracteata*).

Sir Joseph Banks and the Kew hunters

Joseph Banks was an English naturalist chosen to travel with Captain Cook on H.M.S. *Endeavour* on its circumnavigatory voyage of exploration from 1776 to 1781. With him went Linnaeus's favorite pupil, Dr. Daniel Solander, and draftsman Sydney Parkinson, who died on the way home but whose color drawings of over 700 plants provide a detailed record of their discoveries. They visited South Africa, Brazil, Tahiti, New Zealand, Australia — where their botanizing gave the name to Botany Bay — and the East Indies, returning with seeds and 3,000 dried specimens, of which 1,000 were new to science. Among the plants he brought back were members of the genus later named *Banksia* in his honor.

On his return, as botanical adviser and virtual director of the Royal Gardens at Kew, he sent out many others in search of plants and scientific knowledge. The first was Francis Masson, a Scottish gardener at Kew, who sailed out to the Cape of Good Hope in 1772. Over the next three years he sometimes traveled with the Swedish botanist Carl Peter Thunberg — another protégé of Linnaeus — who was in South Africa partly to learn Dutch, in preparation for traveling with the Dutch East India Company to Japan to collect plants for subsequent study in Holland.

Masson made trips to the Azores and the Canary Islands before a further visit to the Cape where, at Banks's suggestion, he established a garden for his finds until they could be sent back to Britain. Among the introductions from South Africa for which he was responsible are pelargoniums, mesembryanthemums, lobelias, proteas and the winter-flowering heathers *Erica nivalis* and *E. hyemalis*, which get their modern names from being widely grown in the Northern Hemisphere as pot plants for flowering at Christmas.

David Nelson was sent out with Cook's last voyage and later sailed with Captain Bligh to take care of breadfruit on the *Bounty* (see Botanical Gardens). At that time, carrying plants by sea was difficult as salt water "burns" leaves and has to be washed off immediately with clean water. These pampered guests of the *Bounty* caused resentment among the crew and contributed to the sailors' rebellion. Nelson spent eleven weeks at sea in an open boat with Bligh after the mutiny, but died at Coupang on the way to Batavia (Jakarta) in the Dutch East Indies. William Brown, the gardener whose daily duty was the care of the breadfruit, chose to go with the mutineers and eventually arrived on Pitcairn Island.

In 1776 Tobias Furneaux brought back seeds from Australia, including *Eucalyptus obliqua*.

In 1803 William Kerr was sent out by Banks to China. Kew paid his salary of a hundred

Above *Breadfruit was collected in the Society Islands to be taken to the West Indies where it was thought it would provide cheap food for slaves. It makes a decorative plant for tropical gardens as well as being a useful food resource. The fruit grows to a considerable size.*

Left *Sir Joseph Banks.*

Below *Tiger Lily (Lilium tigrinum) found by William Kerr, one of Banks's collectors sent out from Kew.*

How plants were transported

Drawings and dried specimens extended the knowledge of plants, but did not make them available for growing. Seeds were easy to transport once they were collected but germinating and raising them took time and there were many failures.

Many different methods of transporting living plants were tried.

John Bartram used to enclose the roots of a newly-collected plant in an ox bladder, carry it back to Philadelphia in his saddlebag, and then plant specimens in wooden boxes for transport to Europe. Often, plants were carried on deck in slatted boxes where they did get some light but were exposed to wind, salt spray and big changes in temperature. Below decks they might have even less chance of survival, with little light and poor ventilation. On the ill-fated *Bounty*, many breadfruit were placed in wooden boxes covered with a wire frame.

A solution came in 1829 when a London doctor, Nathaniel Ward, discovered that plants could be successfully grown in an enclosed environment. Dr. Ward lived in a smoky part of London and had tried, without success, to grow ferns and mosses in a rock garden. His accidental discovery that plants could live in enclosed glass bottles resulted from observing the chrysalis of a sphinx moth which he put, together with moist earth, into a wide-mouthed glass bottle sealed with a lid. He wished to study how the moth emerged from its chrysalis. While watching the bottle he noticed that moisture, which during the warmth of the day arose from the soil, condensed at night on the inside of the bottle and returned to the earth, keeping it moist. About a week before the adult moth was due to emerge, a seedling fern and grass made their appearance. They immediately captured his attention because of his earlier unsuccessful attempts to grow ferns. He left the fern in the bottle for nearly four years, where it flourished. It was from this chance observation that growing plants in enclosed containers began.

News of Dr. Ward's discovery spread and many people began growing plants in Wardian Cases as a hobby. Some of these cases became highly ornate, while others were simple glass domes. Some were designed for placing on window ledges, others had ornate frames and legs and became part of the furniture in a room. Additionally, they enabled plants to be transported over vast distances through hostile climates.

However, success when introducing plants also depended on the skill of the propagator and his judgment about suitable temperatures and sowing times, or the best way to take and root cuttings. Indeed, part of the success of any collector relied on the skills of nurserymen, most of whom remain forgotten.

The Wardian Case, as developed for transporting plants.

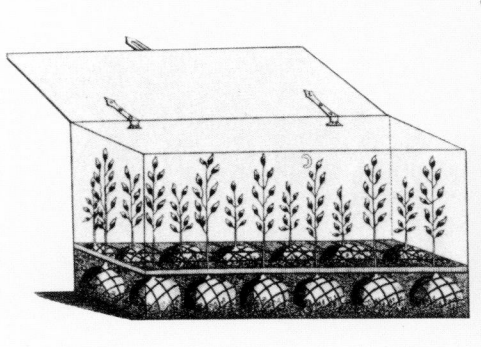

Boxes for conveying plants by sea. The one on the left has slots at front and sides for ventilation, beneath is shown the plants inside, roots wrapped in a ball of earth and moss tied with "packthread," between a crisscross of laths or thick thread to keep them steady. The barrel-like cask is for raising seeds on the voyage. The partitioned box was also for sowing seeds into earth and moss.

pounds a year, while the East India Company paid expenses, although Kerr had to buy his own equipment. He stayed in China for eight years and was the first resident and professional collector in that area, although he did not get any further than Macao and Canton. The popular garden shrub Jew's Mallow (*Kerria japonica*), also known as the Japanese Rose, was named after him, although it was collected by de Candolle in 1816. In recognition of his plant hunting Banks appointed him Superintendent of the Botanic Garden which was to be established in Ceylon (Sri Lanka). Unfortunately, there was a delay of two years before he could take up the appointment, and even after he arrived he could not immediately assume responsibility. He did, however, introduce several superb garden plants, including the Tiger Lily (*Lilium tigrinum*) and *L. japonicum*.

Most plants from Australia are not hardy enough to stand up to the rigors of the winters of northwest Europe or the east coast states of North America, but they flourish in California, where many were taken. However, this did not deter the London nursery of Lee and Kennedy from offering Australian plants in 1788.

In 1814 Banks sent James Bowie and Allan Cunningham to Brazil, from where Bowie went on to South Africa, and Cunningham first to New South Wales, and then up to what is now Queensland where he collected around Moreton Bay, site of modern Brisbane.

Nineteenth-century plant collectors

The introduction in 1816 of a piped hot-water system to heat greenhouses, with the stove on the outside so that its fumes would not damage the plants, and the development of bigger and better structures of glass, made it easier to rear plants from warmer countries. Then, from 1833, the introduction of the Wardian Case, initially used for growing plants and later for their transportation, increased the survival rate of living plants as they crossed the oceans. Instead of losing nineteen out of twenty plants, with a Wardian Case it became unusual to lose one. These developments, coupled with the expansion of the European empires and the opening up of the American West, led to more and more new plants being made available for the garden and hothouse.

Exploring the Americas

In 1799 a superb German scientist, Friedrich Wilhelm Heinrich Alexander von Humboldt, whose interests embraced meteorology, terrestrial magnetism and topography as well as zoology and botany, accompanied by Frenchman Aimé Jacques Alexander Bonpland began surveying and collecting plants in Central and South America. Humboldt claimed they found 40 new species which included dahlias and lobelias, *Lobelia fulgens* and *Fuchsia splendens*.

Pampas Grass (Cortaderia selloana), originally from South America, has found a place in many gardens.

It was not until the second decade of the nineteenth century that Brazil and other parts of the Amazon were opened up to collectors. Allan Cunningham and James Bowie arrived in Rio de Janeiro about 1814, staying less than two years.

Most plants harvested from the Amazon are not garden plants in temperate lands, but are frequently seen as such eye-catching house plants as Gloxinia (*Sinningia speciosa*), also commonly known as the Violet Slipper or Brazilian Gloxinia. However, one of their findings, *Jacaranda ovalifolia*, now better known as *J. mimosifolia*, is widely grown as a flowering street tree in Mediterranean countries.

In 1817 Bonpland returned to take up a post as Professor of Natural History at Buenos Aires, in a newly independent Argentina, still in the throes of revolution. He soon resigned and embarked on a search for plants, directing his attention mainly to Paraguay Tea, which had been monopolized by the Jesuits for many years.

A few years later, James Tweedie from the Edinburgh Botanic Garden arrived, initially working as a landscape gardener. He made several explorations, the best-known plant he found being the Pampas Grass (*Cortaderia selloana*), a member of the grass family with plume-like flower heads at the tops of long, stiff stems. He also found the Spring Starflower (*Ipheion uniflorum*), verbenas and a petunia (*Petunia violacea*).

In 1825 an Irishman, Thomas Coulter, was in Central America, staying longer and surveying a much larger area than Humboldt and Bonpland had done. His travels included Mexico and eventually he collected some 50,000 plant specimens. It is ironic that while he managed to get all of these from Mexico to London, a box containing his journals was lost between London and Dublin.

Plant hunting in the western states of North America began much later than in the east.

Darwin's Berberis (Berberis darwinii) was one of William Lobb's South American discoveries.

However, he progressed to being a well-respected veteran American botanist, introducing many plants and remembered in one of his findings, the Mountain Dogwood (*Cornus nuttallii*). In 1836, after many expeditions, he was appointed Curator of Harvard University's Botanic Garden.

In 1823 the Horticultural Society was looking for a plant collector for North America. A contemporary of Nuttall who had worked in the Glasgow Botanic Garden, David Douglas, a Scot from Perthshire, was recommended. He arrived in New York in early August, visited Nuttall and the gardens established by John Bartram, and a year later set sail for the west coast where for three years he made his base at Fort Vancouver. In 1830 he returned to North America, reaching California two years later. He went on to Hawaii where, in 1834, he fell into a bear-trap and was trampled and gored to death by a wild bull already captured. It was a sad end for such a respected and great collector.

German collectors also visited the western states. Theodor Hartweg's introductions include well-known plants, such as two Californian Lilacs (*Ceanothus rigidus* and *C. dentatus*), Monterey Cypress (*Cupressus macrocarpa*), Californian Fuchsia (*Zauschneria californica*), and the Five Spot (*Nemophila maculata*).

John Jeffrey, previously employed at the Botanic Garden in Edinburgh, arrived in America in 1850 and crossed to what is now British Columbia. His finds were mainly trees and shrubs but also included herbaceous types, for which he was not always given due credit.

Although some areas, especially in Alaska, had been explored by Russians and plants taken to the Botanic Garden at St. Petersburg it was not until 1804 that Captains Merriweather Lewis and William Clark began the first crossing of the continent and approaches from the east were opened up.

Clark was already a botanist and Merriweather was given natural history and botanical instruction in Philadelphia. They set off from St. Louis and crossed the continent, reaching the Columbia River, on the borders of what are now the states of Washington and Oregon, passing down to the Pacific coast in October 1805 and wintering to the south of the Columbia estuary in a fort they constructed. On their journey westward they sent back plants from Dakota and on their return journey collected seeds of the Oregon Grape (*Mahonia aquifolium*) with its wealth of richly fragrant, yellow flowers in early spring, and the Snowberry (*Symphoricarpos racemosus*), now correctly known as *S. albus* and famed for clusters of glistening-white berries from autumn to spring. Their botanical training also helped in the discovery of the bright-faced and herbaceous Blanket Flower (*Gaillardia aristata*), Mariposa Lily (*Calochortus elegans*), Avalanche Lily (*Erythronium grandiflorum*) and the deciduous shrub Creambush (*Holodiscus discolor*) with creamy-white flowers borne in arching sprays in midsummer.

Many plant hunters traveled west in the following years. Thomas Nuttall, a printer from Liverpool, arrived in Philadelphia in 1808, and was initially acclaimed a botanist on the strength of finding a flower he could not name.

These include the Camass (*Camassia leichtlinii*), *Delphinium nudicaule*, Sierra Shooting Star (*Dodecatheon jeffreyi*), Scarlet Fritillaria (*Fritillaria recurva*), Washington Lily (*Lilium washingtonianum*), moisture-loving Umbrella Plant (*Peltiphyllum peltatum*), Mountain Pride (*Penstemon newberryi*), and one of the Campions (*Silene hookeri*).

The next important plant collector, William Lobb (1809–63), was sent out to South America in 1840 by the Veitch Nursery of Exeter, in the west of England, arriving in Rio and traveling across the continent to Chile. Returning home in 1844, he soon sailed again for South America on a new commission from the nursery. The range of plants he found this time was immense, and include many widely grown today, such as the Roble Beech (*Nothofagus obliqua*), Darwin's Berberis (*Berberis darwinii*), the stunningly attractive Chilean Fire Bush (*Embothrium coccineum*), *Escallonia macrantha*, *Tricuspidaria hookerianum* (later to become *Crinodendron hookerianum*), Flame Creeper (*Tropaeolum speciosum*), Chilean Bellflower (*Lapageria rosea*, also known as Copihue and Chile Bells), and the Marmalade Bush (*Streptosolen jamesonii*) which has several other common names including Yellow Heliotrope, Firebush and Orange Browallia.

In 1849 he was sent to California, arriving in San Francisco in the middle of the Gold Rush, when the town was burgeoning with the transit activities of the "Forty-niners." He first went south, later veering north to Oregon and then up the Columbia River. He returned to California in 1853, settling there and sending plants back to the Veitch Nursery until his death in 1863. His introductions are extensive and from North America include the Golden Eardrops (*Dicentra chrysantha*), Californian Lilacs (*Ceanothus dentatus floribundus*, *C. lobbianus* and *C. veitchianus*), *Rhododendron occidentale* and the Western Red Cedar (*Thuja plicata*).

Although it was Lobb who introduced the Fremontia or Flannel Bush (*Fremontia californica*, but later *Fremontodendron californicum*) into cultivation, it was John Charles Fremont who first saw this plant, as well as the eye-catching Tree Anemone (*Carpenteria californica*). He was also one of the first Europeans to describe the magnificent Joshua Tree (*Yucca brevifolia*). Forests of this yucca grew in the Mohave Desert, with stems up to 12 in (30 cm) in diameter and often more than 40 ft (12 m) high.

Plant hunting in Africa

Though plants from northern and southern Africa had already been collected, equatorial Africa presented greater problems. The malaria-carrying mosquito gravely endangered the health of Europeans and although this was not a freak area in that respect — much of the land in the Louisiana Purchase as well as settlements in the Dutch East Indies was riddled with this pestilence — it certainly reduced plant-hunting activities. It was not until the early 1900s that the association of mosquitos and malaria was understood, although as early as 1633 in South America a tree with properties to alleviate the

Below left *The Chilean Fire Bush* (Embothrium coccineum) *makes a dazzling display of color.*

Below *The Fremontia or Flannel Bush* (Fremontodendron californicum) *is a native of California.*

*Busy Lizzie (*Impatiens walleriana*) is an East African form of this popular garden plant which has now been bred in a very wide range of types and colors.*

Below *Ernest Henry Wilson, plant hunter for the Veitch Nursery of London and then for the Arnold Arboretum in Boston, and later its Director. He became known as "Chinese" Wilson because of his experience in the area.*

"fever and ague" was known to missionaries, the natives having used it for centuries.

Mungo Park, the Scottish explorer of Africa, sent specimens and drawings to Banks in 1795 while waiting to explore the Gambia, but like many early explorers his prime purpose was geographical rather than botanical. The Norwegian botanist Dr. Christian Smith, together with David Lockhart, a gardener from Kew, set out on an ill-fated expedition in 1816, while even a blessing from Queen Victoria and Prince Albert did not save Captain Trotter's 1841 expedition to the Niger. Dr. John Kirk, who at one time accompanied Livingstone, was a physician and naturalist who became Consul-General at Zanzibar and sent back a rich range of East African plants including the richly-colored and popular Busy Lizzie (*Impatiens sultani*) but now known as *I. walleriana* and also commonly as Zanzibar Balsam, Patient Lucy, Patience Plant and Sultana.

Discoveries in the East

At the end of the Opium Wars of 1840–42, Hong Kong was ceded to the British, and other entry ports opened up. Robert Fortune was sent out by the Horticultural Society (later Royal), leaving in the late winter of 1843. He took a few Wardian Cases, which assisted him in returning with "live" plants. Most of his plants were gained from the more northerly regions. He returned to Britain in 1846 and again sailed for China two years later, making a further trip in 1853 and his last in 1860. Besides the 190 species or varieties of plants he introduced into cultivation, he is mainly responsible for introducing the tea plant to India, so breaking the Chinese monopoly.

Augustine Henry, a Customs and Medical Officer in the Chinese Customs Service in the latter half of the nineteenth century, sent many plants to Kew and became an authority on Chinese plants.

In 1899 Ernest Henry Wilson was sent out to China by the world-famous Veitch Nursery, where he was instructed to find Augustine Henry and to seek the Davidia, now commonly known as the Handkerchief Tree. He ran into problems during the Boxer rebellion, but eventually found Henry and was given a map of the area in which a davidia had been seen about 12 years earlier. The place was found, but sadly the tree had been cut down to make way for a house.

He revisited China, particularly Sichuan and the border of Xizang (Tibet), in 1903, bringing back a vast array of plants. In 1907 and in 1910 he went back to China again, but this time on behalf of the famous Arnold Arboretum, part of Harvard University. He was more than just a "China" man, and also visited Korea, Formosa (Taiwan) and Japan. Gardeners throughout the world owe much to this collector, who introduced more shrubs and trees than anyone else. These include the now widely-grown Paperbark Tree (*Acer griseum*). He also introduced superb climbers, such as the Chinese Gooseberry (*Actinidia chinensis*), *Clematis armandii* and *C. montana* var. *rubens*.

George Forrest, a Scot, had already emigrated to Australia, and returned by way of South Africa, before he applied for a post at the Edinburgh Botanic Garden at about the age of twenty-nine. At that time, Arthur Kelpin Bulley, the founder of the subsequently world-renowned seed company Bees, was looking for a collector of plants for his new garden on the Wirral Peninsula, near Liverpool. Forrest was recommended and in 1904 arrived in Yunnan, a province in southwest China, which was to become a base for his travels. Unfortunately, his arrival was too late in the year to do much

collecting, so he reconnoitered, visiting the French missionary station at Tsekou on the Mekong and determining to return there the following year. It was a fateful decision, because a rising in Tibet of Batang lamas threatened his party, killing most of them. By chance he fell and plunged downhill, and only after extensive marches and difficulties reached safety.

After twenty-eight years of seeking plants in China Forrest collapsed and died in January 1932. His introductions are many and include rhododendrons, primulas, camellias, meconopsis, *Gentiana sino-ornata*, *Pieris formosa forrestii*, *Jasminum polyanthum* and *Mahonia lomariifolia*. His introductions have enriched the gardening world but many of those from northwest Yunnan were originally discovered by the Abbé Delavay. He and several other French missionaries were also active plant hunters.

Frank Kingdon-Ward was another inveterate collector of plants, who right up to his death in 1958 was planning further expeditions. Three of his journeys were in China, the others in Burma, Tibet and Upper Assam. As well as being a plant collector of considerable stature, he was a skilled explorer and geographer. He wrote a number of very readable books and received many medals from the Royal Geo-

Clematis armandii, just one of the many species from Asia which E. H. Wilson introduced to European and American gardens.

Above center *The Handkerchief Tree (Davidia involucrata), the object of E. H. Wilson's first expedition to China.*

Clematis macropetala. *William Purdom introduced this pendant clematis.*

On one occasion they chanced to meet a Dutch man, Frank Meyer, who had been trained in the Amsterdam Botanic Garden and subsequently traveled to Washington where he worked for the American Department of Agriculture. The Department sent him to China to collect "economic" plants that had hardy or disease-resistant characteristics. During his three expeditions, each lasting about three years, he collected many timber-trees, cereals and fruits, as well as the popular conifer *Juniperus squamata* "Meyeri," the Chinese Horse Chestnut (*Aesculus chinensis*) and the even better known *Rosa xanthina*. He is also remembered as the first foreigner to see the Maidenhair Tree (*Ginkgo biloba*) growing in the wild.

Joseph Rock, an Austrian, was also sent out to China by the Office of Seed and Plant Introductions of the American Department of Agriculture. He was primarily sent to Siam, Burma and Indo-China, to collect seeds of the Chaulmoogra Tree (*Hydnocarpus anthelminticus*) which was then used in the treatment of leprosy. Subsequently he went to China, where he remained, on and off, for 27 years. His journeys were numerous, and, apart from ornithological studies, he collected many seeds, including nearly 500 species of rhododendrons. Perhaps he is most remembered in gardens by the stunningly attractive *Paeonia suffruticosa* "Rock's Variety," also sometimes called "Joseph Rock." It appears that in the mid-1920s he sent seeds of this tree peony to the Arnold Arboretum, North America. The seeds came from peonies growing in the courtyards of the lamasery of Choi-ni.

Without a doubt, there is a vast treasury of plants still to be found in China.

Tibet, Burma and India were explored for plants by several botanists who also managed to enter China, including Frank Kingdon-Ward and Reginald Farrer. Dr. Joseph Dalton Hooker (1817–1911) — later knighted and Director of Kew Gardens — was commissioned by Kew to collect plants in India and arrived in Calcutta in 1848. His travels were many and extensive. He was undeterred by any difficulty and his most important plant hunting was in the Himalayas during the late 1840s. His rhododendron introductions are impressive, but many of his other finds are equally garden-worthy, such as primulas, meconopsis, astilbes, bergeneas, the Himalayan Birch (*Betula utilis*) and several sorbuses. Thomas Lobb, Jonas Thomas Booth, Henry John Elwes, Roland Edgar Cooper, Euan H. M. Cox, Frank Ludlow, Major George Sherrif and Sir George Taylor also searched for plants between 1847 and 1933.

Perhaps one of the most beautiful plants to come from tropical Asia, and especially China, is *Hibiscus rosa-sinensis*, variously known as the Rose of China, Hawaiian Hibiscus, China Rose, Chinese Hibiscus, Blacking Plant and Shoe-black Plant. Only hardy in warm countries, it creates a wonderful hedge or border shrub, prolifically covered with deep crimson, trumpet-like flowers up to 5 in (13 cm) wide. It gains the name Blacking Plant from the

graphical Society for his mapping and surveying activities. His finds include many rhododendrons, primulas, gentians and meconopsis.

Among other collectors in China was William Purdom. He had worked for two London nurseries, H. J. Veitch and Co, and Low and Sons, as well as Kew, and in the early 1900s collected in Inner Mongolia and China. He introduced some now well-known plants, including *Paeonia suffruticosa spontanea*, several primulas, the eye-catching climbers *Clematis macropetala* and *C. tangutica* and the small lilac *Syringa microphylla*.

Reginald Farrer (1880–1920) collaborated with Purdom on several expeditions. Indeed, without Purdom's experience it is doubtful whether their expedition to Tibet would have been possible. Together they found the magnificent winter-flowering *Viburnum farreri*, but often known as *V. fragrans*. It is one of the best winter-flowering shrubs, with sweetly-scented white flowers.

Above and right Paeonia suffruticosa "Rock's Variety" reached the west as seeds from peonies in the courtyards of a lamasery in Tibet and is named for Joseph Rock who collected them.

Meconopsis, *the blue poppy, was seen by the French missionary Jean Marie Delavay but not collected until Frank Kingdon-Ward brought seed from Tibet in 1926.*

A modern hibiscus hybrid developed from the Asian form Hibiscus rosa-sinensis.

juice in the flowers that is used by Chinese women to blacken eyebrows and hair, while in Java it is used to black shoes. In northerly countries it is grown as a house plant and in addition to the normal species there are hybrids in yellow, pink and salmon.

Plant collecting in Japan

Japanese plants had been sought by Europeans in the late 1600s when Engelbert Kaempfer (1651–1715), a German botanist and physician, was employed by the Dutch East India Company. After the "intolerance and cruelty" of Spanish and Portuguese missionaries in the sixteenth century the Japanese had closed all ports and entry to Europeans. The only nations with whom they would trade were the Chinese and the Dutch, who sent no missionaries and who traded only from Deshima. As well as Kaempfer, the Swede Carl Peter Thunberg (1743–1828) held the post of surgeon to the Dutch East India Company, eventually succeeding Linnaeus as Professor of Botany at Uppsala,

Star Magnolia (Magnolia stellata) was collected by John Gould Veitch for the Veitch Nursery.

Sweden. In his *Flora Japonica*, published in 1784, he describes over three hundred previously unknown Japanese plants.

The doors to Japan began to be opened in 1854, toward the end of Philipp Franz von Siebold's (1796–1866) involvement, initially with the Dutch East India Company and later as consultant to the Japanese Privy Council, in part to advise on the introduction of European sciences. Many of his introductions were through the nursery Siebold and Co. at Leiden in the Netherlands, and his introductions include azaleas, lilies, camellias and hydrangeas, as well as bamboos.

The Veitch nursery rapidly sent out John Gould Veitch (1839–70), the great-grandson of the founder, who returned with a wealth of superb garden plants that have enriched gardens throughout the world, and include the striking Star Magnolia (*Magnolia stellata*), M. *soulangeana* var. *nigra*, *Primula japonica*, and the Boston Ivy (*Parthenocissus tricuspidata*) which in fall creates a dazzling display of crimson and scarlet leaves. John was only thirty-one when he died, but in 1891 his elder son James Harry Veitch (1868–1907) collected in Japan.

Other famed collectors include Robert Fortune (1812–80), best known for collecting bamboos, *Lonicera japonica* "Aureo-reticulata," a beautiful honeysuckle with brightly-variegated leaves, and the male form of the Spotted Laurel (*Aucuba japonica*).

Japanese plants were not only sent back to Holland and Britain; American nurseries and gardens also received plants from American collectors. In 1855 Dr. George Rogers Hall (1820–99) visited Japan; within a few years he had established a nursery in Yokohama and in 1861 sent a batch of plants home, many now well known in gardens. These included the Japanese Wisteria (*Wisteria japonica*) and *Hydrangea paniculata grandiflora*. In about 1870 Japanese plants were sent by Thomas Hogg to a New York nursery started earlier by his father, an English émigré.

Others who collected plants for North America were Professor Charles Sprague Sargent (1841–1927) on behalf of the Arnold Arboretum, and Ernest Wilson (who we have previously seen in China) for the American John S. Ames of Massachusetts. However, these were not his discoveries, but came from a nursery at Hatagaya, Tokyo, and were mainly low and evergreen azaleas.

Charles Maries was sent to Japan to collect plants on behalf of the Veitch nursery, sending back such plants as the Kolomikta vine (*Actinidia kolomikta*) and the gloriously blue-flowered rock garden plant *Platycodon grandiflorum mariesii*.

Carl Maximowicz, a Russian of German extraction who had been appointed Conservator of the Herbarium of the St. Petersburg Botanic Garden, collected in Japan for much longer than any other plant hunter, sending plants back to St. Petersburg. His introductions include the magnificent herbaceous *Ligularia clivorum*, *Enkianthus campanulatus*, *Rodgersia podophylla* and the widely-grown *Elaeagnus pungens variegata*. These are just a few of his findings and he must be considered one of the greatest botanists to search in Japan.

The Antipodes

After the initial coastal exploration of parts of Australia and New Zealand there was an awareness of new plants but the difficulties of distance and transportation presented problems. Many Australian plants are not hardy in northerly climes, and introduced species did better in California, not only because the climate was more to their liking but because a ready acceptance of new plants existed, perhaps more so than in the warm countries of Europe. Australian plants were tried in Britain as early as 1788 but New Zealand has more plants that are hardy in northerly climes and include many Hebes and Veronicas. It also has many unusual plants, including the Vegetable Sheep (*Raoulia eximia*), yellow forget-me-nots and Tree Daisies (*Olearia*) which have found places in many northern gardens.

Banks's appetite for Australian and New Zealand plants, whetted on his visit with Cook in 1770, encouraged him to send plant hunters to both countries. The British nursery of Lee and Kennedy sent David Burton to Australia in 1790, but he died prematurely. In 1800 Banks privately sent George Caley and later, in 1816, Allan Cunningham from Kew, and many nurseries sent out plant hunters, including Low and Mackay of Clapton, Lucombe Pince of Exeter, Robert Veitch, also of Exeter, and Joseph Knight of the Exotic Nurseries at Chelsea, London.

John Gould Veitch, who had already visited Japan, arrived in Sydney in 1864, with several Wardian Cases that enabled him to harvest and take home many foliage plants too tender for growth outside in colder regions, but ideal for decorating warm greenhouses. He also visited islands north of Australia, collecting warmth-loving plants now extensively grown for room and greenhouse decoration: the Veitch Screw Pine (*Pandanus veitchii*) from Samoa, and Jacob's Coat (*Acalypha wilkesiana*) from New Caledonia, also descriptively known as Copper Leaf, Fire-Dragon, Beefsteak Plant and Match-me-if-you-can. There were also dracaenas, cordylines, codiaeums and palms.

Allan Cunningham arrived in New Zealand in 1826, returning several years later and finding the outstandingly attractive Parrot's Bill or Lobster's Claw (*Clianthus puniceus*). This warmth-loving shrub with curious claw-like, brilliant-red flowers had been seen earlier by Banks.

Plant-hunting today

Many plants were introduced from eastern Mediterranean countries. In 1960 Rear-Admiral Furse embarked on a two-month plant-collecting expedition to Turkey and Iran, collecting a wide range of bulbs including irises, cyclamen, fritillaria, tulips and lilies, returning there in 1962. A further expedition, two years later, to Turkey, Iran and Afghanistan gained another harvest of bulbous plants.

The work of studying, collecting and recording new plant species still goes on through botanical gardens which send out expeditions to many parts of the world. It is especially important when so many plants are under threat, because preservation through cultivation in botanical collections is one means of survival. Decorative species raised in cultivation continue to find their way into the horticultural trade where they can be purchased and admired by all.

A number of people have made a name for themselves as modern plant hunters, carefully gathering seeds of interesting plants from the wild and making photographic and scientific records. They include such botanists as Chris Brickell, Roy Lancaster, Tony Schilling, Chris Grey-Wilson, Phillip Cribb, Ron McBeath, Keith Rushforth, Peter Cox and Brian Mathew from Britain; Harry van der Laar from the Netherlands; Skip Marsh, John Creech and Bill McNamara from the United States, Geoff Nichols from South Africa and Toshia Ando from Japan. Such people collect with a great deal of concern for the environment, gathering seeds or plants only when it is deemed that it will not harm wild populations and with due care and consideration for the laws of the countries in which they are working.

Unfortunately, there are others not of this breed, and the illegal commercial exploitation of wild plants continues, despite international laws aimed at curbing such practices. In recent years there have been countless examples of species brought near to extinction in the wild by the exploits of those indiscriminate collectors who care nothing for the natural world and whose only aim is to make money from wild plants. Orchids, cacti and bulbs are the most prominent groups of plants at risk from their depredations. When buying plants and seeds, and bulbs especially, make sure they come from suppliers who guarantee that they have been produced in cultivation and not collected in the wild.　　　D. S.

A lunch stop for the 1989 Himalayan expedition from the Royal Botanic Gardens, Kew.

Tulip mania

In Persia, the tulip was a wild flower and a symbol of love and inspiration for painters and poets. At about the end of the fifteenth century, Zahir ud-din Mohammed, also known as Babur or Babar (meaning tiger) and the first Great Mogul of India, counted as many as 33 different kinds of tulips near Kabul, the capital of Afghanistan. During the sixteenth century, tulips were grown in gardens in Turkey. In 1554 Emperor Ferdinand I, Holy Roman Emperor, sent Augerius de Busbecq as Ambassador to the court of Suleiman the Magnificent in Constantinople. It was the first time he had seen tulips, and he brought back seeds — and perhaps bulbs — to Vienna, where they were planted in the Imperial Gardens by L'Ecluse. In 1559 tulips were seen by the German botanist Konrad von Gesner, in the garden of the honorable councilor Herwarth in Augsburg, Bavaria. Von Gesner described them, and then in 1561 published the first known illustrations of the species. This tulip, a central ancestor of today's plants, and later confirmed as a hybrid, was named *Tulipa gesneriana*.

Rich Viennese began to commission Venetian merchants to bring back tulip bulbs from Turkey. Tulips reached England about 1578, probably from Vienna, but they were grown in Holland slightly earlier, in Antwerp in 1562, and later in Leiden in 1590. They reached France in 1608 but did not become popular there until much later in the seventeenth century. In the Netherlands, however, people became passionate about them. Tulips became a mania, as fanciers outbid each other for bulbs. Fortunes were made and lost, with prices of single bulbs soaring. Legislation was finally introduced to limit the price. Speculation reached fever pitch in the three years before the market collapsed in 1637: single bulbs were sold for twelve sheep, eight pigs, four fat bullocks or thirty-six bags of corn. A miller is said to have exchanged his mill for a bulb, a brewer gave up his brewery, and a young Frenchman received his wife's dowry in the form of a rare bulb. Large transactions were celebrated by feasts and no portrait painted at that time

Opposite above *Vertuco — a black tulip, hybridized under the control of Geert Hageman from "Queen of the Night" and "Wienerwald" in 1979 and presented in flower for the first time six years later at the Westfriese Flora flower show in the Netherlands in 1986.*

Right *The modern Dutch bulb industry produces both bulbs and cut flowers for export all over the world, and attracts thousands of visitors in springtime to see sights such as these huge fields of color.*

was complete without including numbers of tulips.

Delivery dates of bulbs sold on contract were frequently missed and indemnity clauses inflicted stiff penalties that often exceeded the seller's financial resources. People slowly lost confidence and on April 27, 1637, a law was passed compelling transactions to be completed like those in any other business. Bulb fever was over and hundreds of people had been financially ruined. Nevertheless, the desire to grow tulips had not been diminished, as the main speculators were neither gardeners nor tulip breeders, and as late as 1836 individual bulbs were being sold for six hundred and fifty pounds.

Early in the eighteenth century tulip mania burst upon the Turks. Tulip fêtes became popular in the court of Ahmed III, where the palace grounds were planted with more than half a million bulbs and more than 1,300 different kinds were available. If bulbs were "blind" and did not produce flowers, they were soon replaced by others that had been individually grown in bottles. The tulips were often highlighted by colored glass lamps, and on one

occasion the Grand Vizier used live tortoises as lamp bearers.

In the nineteenth century, there was a revival of interest in tulips in England, their potential as cut flowers for the florist trade becoming evident, but Holland still remains the Mecca of the bulb world, yearly exporting many millions of bulbs.

D. S.

THE NURSERY TRADE

The growth of interest in gardening, the import of new plant materials and the extension of ornamental gardening beyond the nobility and the very wealthy is reflected in the development of the nursery trade.

Its early strength is demonstrated by the "tulip mania" which swept the Netherlands in the 1630s, and which had no sooner driven men bankrupt than a new vogue for hyacinths began.

In London, the Hoxton area, just north of the City, became the home of a number of nurseries. In 1665, George Ricketts was said by John Rae, a nurseryman-gardener who published a *Flora* that year, to be "the best and most faithful florist now about in London." He sold a wide range of fruit trees — pears, cherries, nectarines, peaches and figs — as well as popular flowers of the time, including gillyflowers, violets and auriculas. Other local nurserymen included Mr. Darby, who stocked "curious greens" and was known for budding hollies and raising mistletoe from seed.

Pearson, established by the end of the century, specialized in anemones, which he sold "only to gentlemen." The nursery of Thomas Fairchild was close to that of George Whitmore, said to be the first English nurseryman to experiment with hybridization; before 1717 he had artificially pollinated carnations.

London nurseries continued to flourish, although pollution appears to have driven them to the west of the city where, in 1681 George London, an English garden designer known for his formalist style, founded the Brompton Park Nursery with three associates: Roger Looker, the Queen's gardener, John Field and Moses Cook. Later, after the others had retired or died, London entered into partnership with Henry Wise, master gardener to Queen Anne. Their nursery became famous, supplying the general public with plants as well as providing material for the many gardens they each designed.

In 1730 the Society of Gardeners published *Catalogus Plantarum*, a catalog of plants available from about twenty nurserymen. It was successful but never progressed beyond its first part, which dealt with trees and shrubs. The year before, however, Robert Furber had published a dozen color plates showing the wide range of plants available to British gardeners for each month of the year from his nursery at Kensington Gore.

By 1771 one of the great European nurseries, Vilmorin-Andrieux, successor to Le Febvre, had produced a catalog of over one hundred pages, containing a stunning variety of trees, shrubs, fruits, grasses and bulbs for sale. They maintained a reputation for the variety of plants they made available by introducing many new species to Europe after the first plant-collecting expeditions to China. The company still has its eighteenth-century shop on the Quai de la Mégisserie.

American nurseries

At first American settlers had to rely on seeds from Europe and indigenous plants. Some grew trees for windbreaks and offered them in exchange for fruit trees; others, like George Fenwick of Connecticut, sold the cherry and peach trees they grew.

One of the first commercial American nurseries was founded in 1737 by William Prince at Flushing Landing on Long Island. He became a major importer of plants and exported American plants to the gardens of the Old World. His nursery remained in business until 1865, by then known as the Linnean Botanic Garden.

John Bartram, the plant collector, also established a nursery which numbered George Washington and Thomas Jefferson among its clients.

Below *Illustration facing the title page of the Society of Gardeners'* Catalogus Plantarum *1739.*

The growing trade

The latter part of the eighteenth century saw a revival of herbaceous gardening in England with nurserymen supplying large numbers of inexpensive and hardy flowering plants. At the same time exotics brought from abroad were eagerly sought after by the well-to-do. John Veitch, whose nursery business began in Devon in 1808, became as involved in sending out plant collectors as the botanists at Kew.

The development of fully-glazed greenhouses and conservatories created a market for exotics from warmer countries and Loddiges, a London nursery founded by a German immigrant in 1790, became specialists in orchids and palms.

Soon nurseries were developing their own strains from both new exotics and established garden plants. An essential marketing device became the "showhouse," a grand conservatory where their glasshouse stock could be put on display.

Flower shows gave growers another opportunity to promote their plants, competing with both amateurs and rival nurserymen and taking space to display their stocks.

Several countries had now established a reputation for the quality and variety of species they produced and as suppliers of particular types of flowers: camellias and bulbs from the Netherlands, lilies, roses and hydrangeas from France and azaleas from Belgium.

In America, although most early nurseries in New England had concentrated on indigenous plants or those imported from Europe, the warmer climates of Florida and California encouraged the introduction of plants from South Africa and Australia. In Florida, a nursery founded in 1882 by the Reasoner brothers grew tropical and subtropical plants, while another in California specialized in fruit and plants from the Antipodes.

The showhouse of E. G. Henderson's nursery in the Edgware Road, London, known as the "Pie-Apple Nursery." Using a glasshouse displaying exotics at the entrance was found to be an effective way of attracting customers.

Below *Robert Furber's plate of the flowers of July.*

Left *Catalog of plants issued by William Prince, son of Robert Prince, in 1790. George Washington bought from them that year but was generally disappointed with their stock. Although satisfied with their young fruit trees, he described the shrubs as "trifling" and found the flowers "not numerous."*

Catalogs of the Park Seed Company in the United States developed into magazines full of useful gardening advice.

In the twentieth century the Yokohama Nurseries in Japan rose to prominence as exporters of a variety of Japanese plant species, bonsai, bamboo canes and statuary to Europe, India, New Zealand, Australia and Russia.

In Australia too, it did not take long for nurseries to flourish. In the 1860s only three-quarters of a century after the First Fleet landed, there were already twenty well established nurseries around Sydney. In Canada settlers established large nurseries growing fruit varieties from Britain and France and also imported shelter trees from the USSR and the United States.

Although all nurserymen collected seed, the gardener's seed merchant seems to have appeared as a natural sideline for a supplier of agricultural seed. In the early years of the twentieth century most backyard gardeners relied largely upon rearing from seeds, which were sold in many shops as well as by mail order. Each year there would also be a regular supply of bedding plants to be bought by the boxful or counted out singly and carried home in a roll of newspaper. And with the spread of suburbia and the increasing popularity of gardening as a hobby, the trade in garden tools and equipment also grew.

Twentieth-century developments

Although the gardener with a small backyard might wish to grow as big a variety of fruit, flowers and vegetables as those with much more land, he or she did not have the space. This was one reason for the increasing use of dwarfing rootstock in the 1930s. It was not a new idea — the Romans had used it for olive trees — but it made available a number of both fruit and ornamental trees which had until then only been suitable for large gardens. Since then nurseries have developed even more compact forms such as the Ballerina which now makes an apple tree a possibility even for a balcony garden!

Much more noticeable, however, has been the change to container-grown plants. In the past bedding plants were raised in boxes, but

The Passion for hyacinths

After tulip mania the Dutch enthusiasm transferred to the hyacinth (*Hyacinthus orientalis*), a native of Greece, Asia Minor and the Balkans. It was known in English gardens before 1597 and grown in Holland earlier than 1576. In 1597 there were only four varieties, but by 1725 this had expanded to more than 2,000.

By the 1630s hyacinths were widely grown in Britain, but it was in the Netherlands that enthusiasm for growing them took off, with the double-flowered forms in most demand. Strangely, a Dutch grower, Pieter Voerhelm, had for many years discarded double forms, but when illness interrupted his vigilance one of them remained. Subsequently it took his attention and he propagated from it, forming the base of his success. The hyacinth business spread in Holland, taking up more and more space, but eventually with a decrease in the number of varieties which by 1911 had shrunk to 300.

In 1685 hyacinths were taken to Germany, in particular Berlin which became a center of cultivation. This mainly relied on the gardening skills of Huguenots, and the cultivation of this flower reached a peak about 1830.

D. S.

perennials, shrubs and trees were lifted directly from the earth where they had been raised. The plant trade, therefore, tended to be very seasonal, with the sale of bedding plants in the spring and others at the times when growth was slow or the plant dormant so that disturbance was minimized when replanted. Raising a plant in a container, where it remains until sold, instead of directly in the ground, makes it possible to transport it easily, even over long distances, and to plant it in the garden at any time when the soil is not frozen and the weather not too wet or too dry.

Container-grown plants not only made it possible to introduce plants and create instant gardens at most times of the year, encouraging an increasing awareness of plants and gardening, but meant that retail outlets could stock plants without having to have large areas of growing beds, bringing plants in from the nurseries as required. Garden centers with container stocks were already known in North America in the 1930s, especially in California, but it was not until the late 1950s that this style of selling reached Britain. It was slow to gain acceptance by traditional gardeners but by the late 1960s was firmly established. Rising property values caused many old-style city nurseries to be redeveloped and new garden centers requiring less space were opened. Around big cities many large centers have been established as non-growing retail outlets where anything from privet hedges to dried flowers and swimming pools are sold. They have often added playgrounds for children and other attractions, and have become popular for family outings. Such competition has made specialization necessary for many traditional nurseries, which offer plants that large conglomerates find unprofitable. Other growers have become wholesale suppliers of plants to retail outlets on an enormous scale. Concentration on large quantities of a small range of plants tends to produce larger profits and this often restricts the variety available to the public. It is fortunate that the specialists are there to provide a wider diversity of plants.

Large refrigerated sheds may now house many thousands of plants to control their growth patterns and flowering periods or to "prepare" bulbs to bloom when the market demand is highest. Light control and chemicals can also be used to induce or retard development. The trade in indoor plants has always made use of such controls. Such procedures sometimes have detrimental effects if the plant is wanted for later planting out but provides instant blossom for those who merely want it as a temporary decoration. At the same time the high cost of heating fuel and the relative decreasing cost of rapid transport have encouraged many warm countries, such as Israel, to grow and export house plants to Europe. Bolivia has become a major exporter of cut

Following pages *Geraniums for sale in the flower and plant market in The Hague, Netherlands.*

Auriculas

Auriculas captured attention and were continuously bred and cultivated for nearly four centuries. They are a type of primula, probably derived from a natural hybrid between *Primula auricula* and *P. hirsuta*, known as *P. x pubescens* and called *Auricula ursi* by L'Ecluse in the late 1500s; also known as Bear's Ears, which referred to the shape of the leaves. Other old names include Vanner's Aprons, Recklesses and Baziers.

P. auricula is a flower from the Swiss Alps and was known to the Romans, but seldom grown in gardens.

L'Ecluse sent a root of the hybrid to a friend in Belgium, Van de Delft, and Huguenot refugees introduced it to England during the late 1600s. By 1693 there were many named forms, striped types being highly prized and fetching twenty pounds each. Interest continued during the 1700s, with the introduction of "edged" varieties, but it was in the 1800s that the biggest upsurge of interest occurred when the cultivation of auriculas was taken up by miners and silk-weavers in several northern counties in England. Auricula societies were formed and exhibitions held, with the peak of interest about 1850.

D. S.

flowers to North America and further afield, and other countries, such as Zimbabwe with proteas, are exporting flowers to earn currency from the more developed nations.

Micropropagation

Since the early 1970s there has been greater use of the technique of micropropagation in the nursery trade, though mainly by large specialist companies. The technique consists of taking a minute section of plant material, treating it with hormones and growing it in a nutrient jelly in a test tube or container. When each growing section has produced sufficient root it can be transferred to a pot and grown like any other plant. The advantage of the technique is that many plants can be produced from a single parent. It forms a useful method of propagating plants which do not usually respond well to traditional techniques, or when large numbers of new plants are needed rapidly. Whereas, in the past, a new cultivar or a disease-resistant strain would at first be available only in small numbers, it is now possible to raise much greater quantities if micropropagation is used.

M. B.

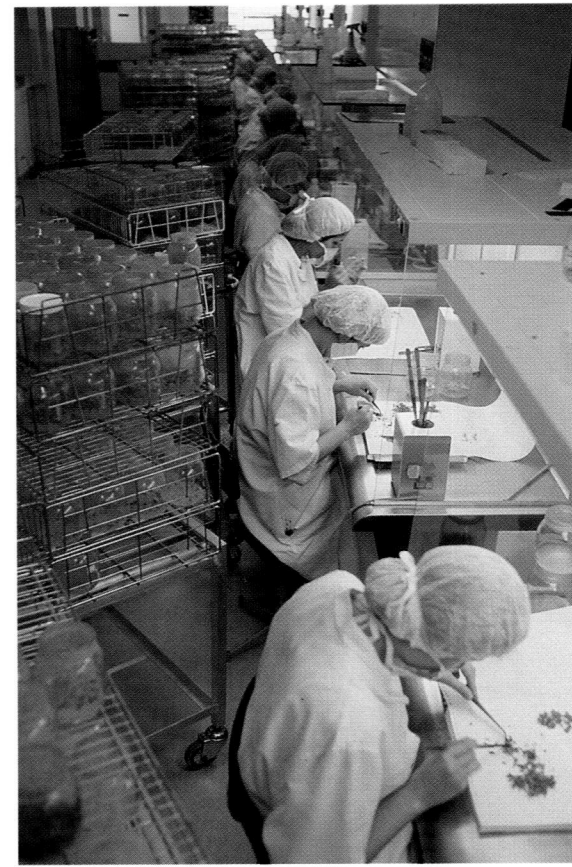

Left *Plant tissues being divided for use in micropropagation, a technique which replicates large numbers of plants normally difficult to raise from seed.*

The cold house where plants can be given conditions which duplicate those in their natural habitats, or be a means of regulating their development and flowering to suit seasonal demand.

Right *With container-grown plants today's gardeners can add instant foliage and color, but establishing a full border takes growing time. Techniques for encouraging germination and coating seeds to protect them from disease add to success with annuals too.*

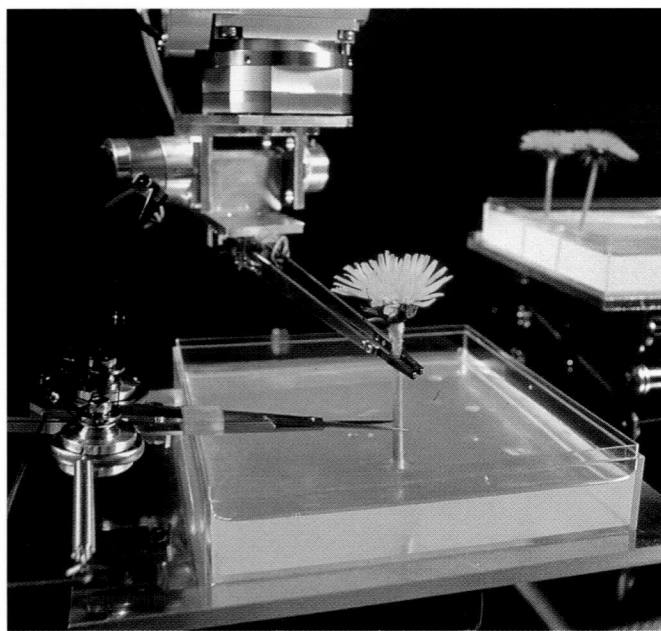

Left *Removing seeds from capsules in which they have been sent into space to see what effect this could have on them. Research on plant development is now extremely sophisticated.*

Far left *A robot which handles delicate plant tissues gently and at great speed has been devleoped by Toshiba.*

BOTANICAL GARDENS

otanic gardens, or botanical gardens — the adjective may be either form (Kew in Britain uses the former) but botanical is in more general use — are very much part of the ancient tradition of plant collection and utilization. Their direct origins, however, lie in the intellectual maelstrom of the European Renaissance when the reassessment and re-examination of classical writings led to a new recognition of the importance of plants.

A botanical garden can be defined as an ordered and cataloged collection of plants assembled primarily for scientific and educational purposes; yet within this necessarily vague definition many types of institution will

Above and right *Inside Adelaide Botanic Gardens Bicentennial Conservatory, built to celebrate the 200th anniversary of the arrival of the First Fleet bringing convicts — and the future first colonists — to* *Australia. The vegetation it displays in its landscape collection is the subject of contemporary concern — the plants of the Australian and Indo-Malaysian rain forests.*

be included, ranging from a science research station to a public park! Botanical gardens are accordingly maintained by a variety of bodies. In the past they were usually under the aegis of universities or attached to governmental or quasi-governmental organizations; today a significant number are run as independent charitable and educational institutions. With such a range of patrons, function and emphasis will vary widely.

Traditionally, botanic gardens have been encyclopedic in their scope, attempting to reflect known plant diversity. Contemporary botanical gardens face the challenges not only of acting as an essential resource for botanical and horticultural research, but also of playing a fundamental role in plant conservation and public education.

The first botanical gardens

The ancient Greek philosopher Theophrastus is sometimes credited with creating the first botanical gardens, and later much botanical knowledge was passed on through the monasteries. Both monastic and domestic gardens raised a variety of useful medicinal herbs and the study of medicine plants was at the heart of the new botanical gardens born of the Renaissance. The first two modern botanical gardens, Pisa and Padua in Italy, were effectively teaching establishments for pharmacology students.

There is some dispute as to whether Pisa or Padua was established first. Pisa is usually acknowledged the earliest, founded in 1543 by Luca Ghini, a leading botanist who had previously taught medicine and botany at Bologna University, where he formed a reference collection of pressed and dried plants mounted on paper — a herbarium. One of Ghini's pupils became the first curator at Padua, which dates from 1545, and Ghini himself was also involved in establishing another botanical garden in Florence in 1550.

The Botanic Garden at Leiden, Netherlands, from a print of 1633. It was founded by Charles l'Ecluse (Clusius) in 1587, though not fully planted until some seven years later. The original enclosure still forms part of the modern Botanic Garden.

The Renaissance botanical garden, although perpetuating elements of the hidden monastic garden (the *hortus conclusus*), was framed by the glory of the Renaissance and, as such, carried themes from the villa-garden. The ordered scientific function led to an ordered design, dictated by utility and ease of reference.

The botanical garden at Florence was divided into eight squares, distinguished from each other by the letters of the alphabet; within these the different plants were indicated by sequential numbering, the corresponding name of the plant being found by consulting a "booklet" similarly codified.

These early gardens were reference collections with plants laid out in ordered formal beds. The garden was often square and subdivided, each section further divided into separate beds or parterres. They could be in ornate geometrical patterns or in a simple straight bed known as a *pulvillus*.

To these botanical gardens, with their ordered plantings, came new plants for study and assessment which had been brought back to Europe by the pioneering fifteenth- and sixteenth-century navigators. The same navigators had, contrary to the hopes of Europe, failed to locate the lost Garden of Eden, long thought to have miraculously survived the Flood, in either the East or the West Indies. Instead, the scattered pieces of creation were to be gathered in the botanical garden. In assembling them the scholar could contemplate the works of God to the benefit of his soul while satisfying his academic curiosity and economic interests. The botanical garden was a microcosm of the known world where, as Edmund Spenser wrote in *The Faerie Queene*, "every sort is in the sundry bed, set by itself and ranked in a comely row."

The sixteenth and seventeenth centuries saw botanical gardens established throughout Europe: Leipzig in 1580, Leiden Botanical Garden in the Netherlands in 1587, and Heidelberg in 1593. In England, Oxford University Botanic Garden was founded in 1621; in France Louis XIII authorized the construction of the Jardin des Plantes in Paris in 1626; Uppsala, Sweden, began in 1665; Edinburgh, Scotland, in 1670; the Physic Garden, London, was started by the Society of Apothecaries in 1673; and the Amsterdam Botanic Garden in 1682.

Commercial exploitation

As the economic power of Europe developed, so botanic gardens grew from being institutions where the lost learning of the classical civilization could be reassessed to become centers for studying the economic worth of plants from new lands. The increased exploration and economic charting of the world led to the discovery of new plants that did not conform with the accepted ideas on botany, what was thought to be a well-documented and cataloged world was shown to be dwarfed by the bizarre and exotic discoveries from the tropics.

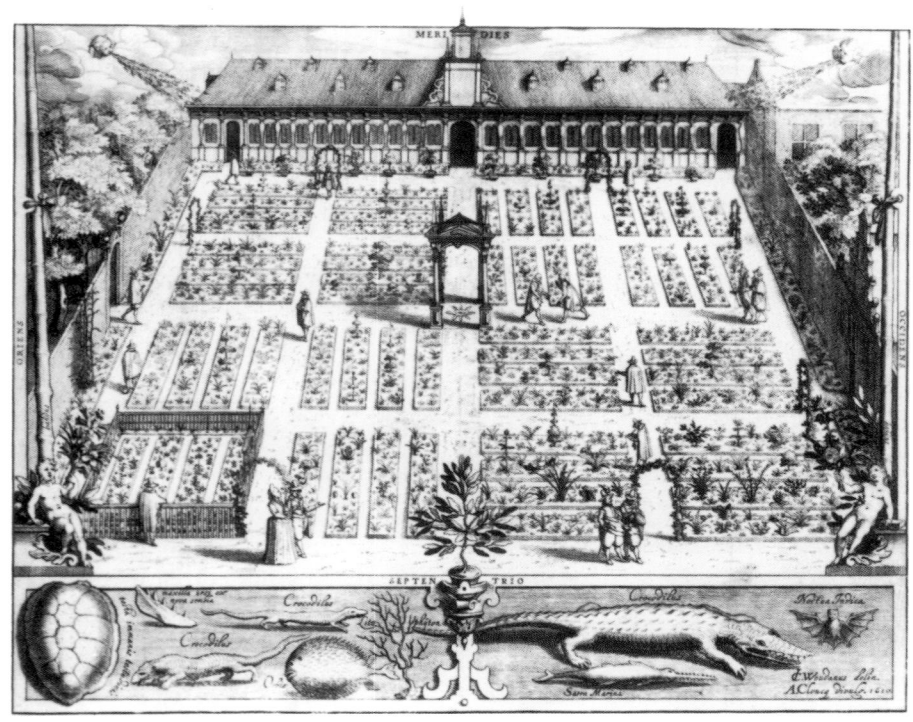

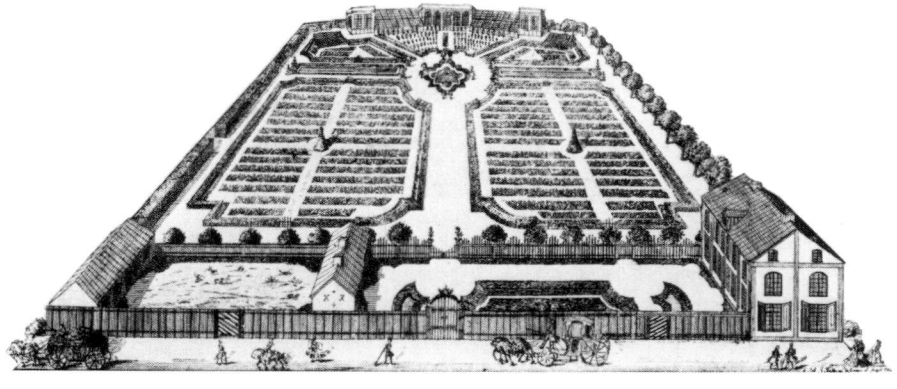

New plants flooded into Europe, brought back for intellectual study, aesthetic appreciation and, importantly, for economic assessment. The race was on, navigators and explorers were searching "the Indies for their balm and spice" and the activities of those early botanic gardens still have a profound influence. For instance, coffee, *Coffea arabica*, now worth billions of dollars as exports from South and Central America, was originally grown in the Ethiopian massif and Middle East and was taken by the Dutch from the Yemen in 1690 to Java, with a further introduction in 1699. A plant from Java was taken to the Amsterdam Botanic Garden in 1706 where it flowered and set fruit. Material from Amsterdam was sent to Suriname in 1718, from where the French obtained it for Cayenne in 1722; in 1727 it was taken from Cayenne to Brazil. Progeny of a plant presented to Louis XIV were sent to Martinique in 1720, with plants taken to Jamaica in 1730, where the famous cultivar "Blue Mountain" arose. As a result, the basis for the lucrative coffee trade was established, its origins largely traceable to one plant in the Amsterdam Botanic Garden.

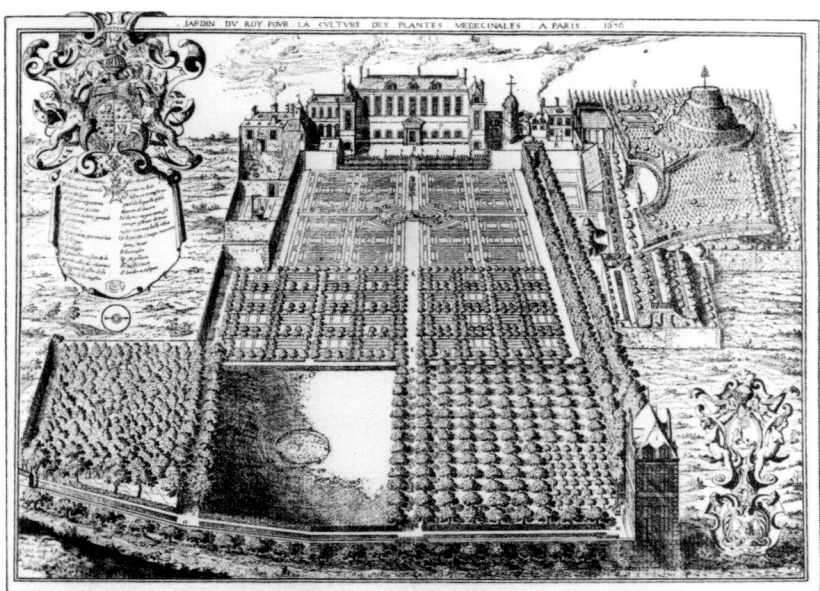

The trade and colonial powers saw botanical gardens as centers of commerce, not merely as ornamental or educational institutes. Colonel Kyd, an East India Company officer described the founding of Calcutta Botanic Gardens in 1787 as

"not for the purpose of collecting plants as things of curiosity or furnishing things of luxury, but for establishing a stock for disseminating such articles as may prove beneficial to the inhabitants as well as natives of Great Britain, and which ultimately may tend to the extension of the national commerce and riches."

Calcutta was one of a number of eighteenth-century botanical gardens set up by trade and colonial authorities to further economic utilization of plant resources.

The first tropical botanical garden was founded in 1737 by the French East India Company on the Indian Ocean island of Mauritius. Particularly associated with this garden is the remarkable Pierre Poivre, administrator, agriculturist, pioneer conservationist and adventurer, a man truly of those turbulent times. In a planned attempt to break the Dutch East India Company's lucrative monopoly on

Top *The Uppsala Botanic Garden, shown as reorganized by Linnaeus in the middle of the eighteenth century. The house in which he lived as Professor of Botany at the University is on the right. The collection was moved to a new site in 1786 but both house and garden have now been carefully restored.*

Center *The Jardin des Plantes in Paris, then the Jardin du Roi, from a print of 1656. Note the enclosed garden with a mount on the right which was created in 1640 and still survives.*

Right *The Chelsea Physic Garden, London, founded in 1673, from an eighteenth-century print.*

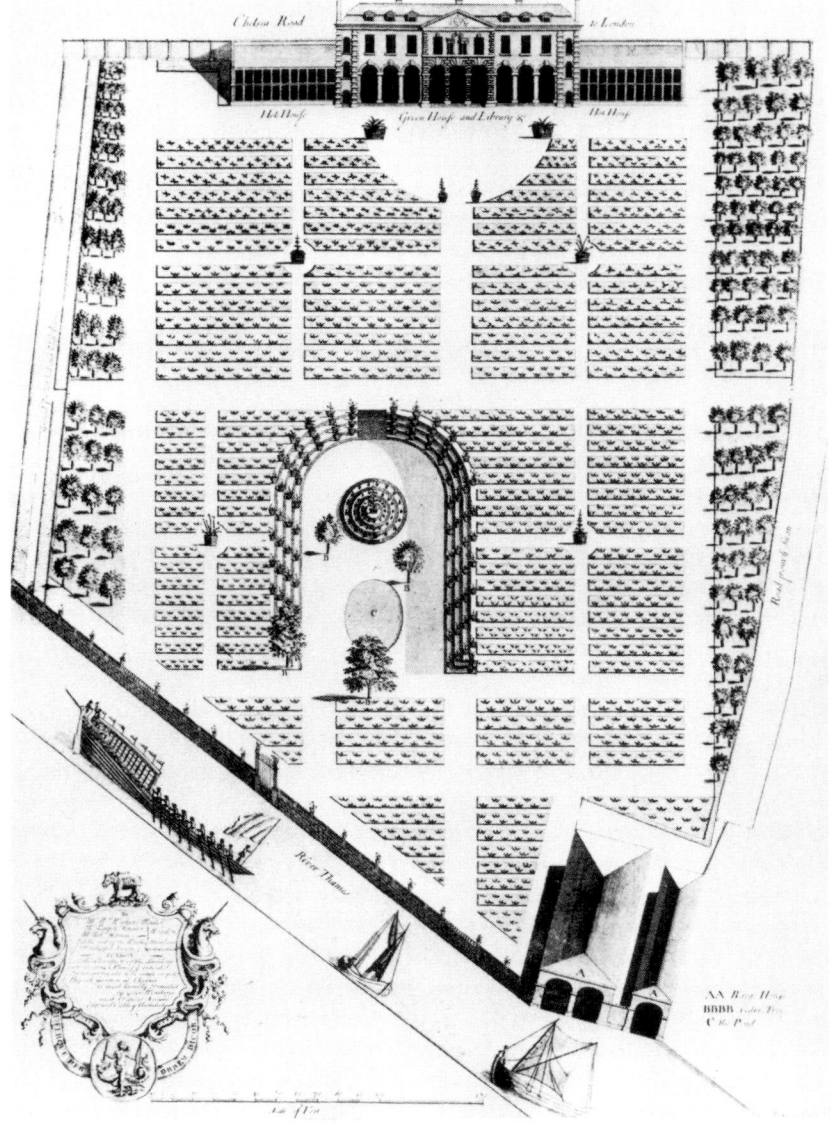

Captain Bligh, Kew botanist David Nelson and others being forced off HMS Bounty by the mutineers. The breadfruit collected in Tahiti were then jettisoned.

Royal Palms in the Royal Botanic Garden Peradeniya (Kandy) Sri Lanka, c. 1903.

" . . . this will give you an opportunity of collecting plants which could by no other means be obtained and of enriching the Royal Botanic Gardens at Kew with plants which otherwise will have been added to the Royal Gardens at Paris and have tended to render their collection superior to ours."

Banks was also reputed, probably unfairly, to bake the seeds of rare plants before replying to a request from a rival botanic garden! The best-known collecting operation involved Banks initiating the introduction of breadfruit from the Pacific to the Botanic Garden of St. Vincent, West Indies. In May 1787 Lord Sydney, a Principal Secretary of State, wrote on behalf of King George III to the Admiralty:

"It is proposed that the Vessel . . . should proceed round Cape Horn and after she shall have arrived at the Society Islands and as many Trees and plants have been taken on board as may be thought necessary, to proceed from thence . . . to pass on the East side of Java, to some port on the North side of that island, where any Breadfruit Trees which may have been injured or have died may be replaced by Mangosteens, Duriens, Jacks, Nancas, Lansas, and in short all the fine fruits of that Quarter, as well as the Rice Plant which grows upon dry land . . . and deposit one half her cargo at His Majesty's Botanical Garden at St. Vincent for the Benefit of the Windward Islands, and from thence to carry the other half down to Jamaica."

The ship chosen was HMS *Bounty* under the command of Captain Bligh and the voyage was terminated by the infamous mutiny and the breadfruit plants thrown overboard. However, a few years later breadfruit was successfully introduced to St. Vincent by two other Kew men, Christopher Smith and James Wiles.

During the nineteenth century the great botanical gardens of Europe consolidated their economic role and entered the time of their greatest influence. The Dutch established the botanical garden at Bogor, Indonesia, in 1817. Under the energetic lead of Melchior Treub this garden was to play a fundamental role in Indonesia's development — especially through its involvement in the introduction of oil palm.

Britain established a network of botanical gardens with Kew as the mother garden. These gardens were scattered through Asia, Australasia, Africa and the Caribbean. They were still predominantly regarded as economic resources; for instance, from chinchona (quinine) plants originally gathered in South America by Kew collectors, the Royal Botanic Garden, Peradeniya, in Ceylon (now Sri Lanka) and its associated gardens, raised and distributed 5.5 million plants to estates which grew them to supply the London quinine market.

During the nineteenth century the Royal Botanic Gardens, Kew, were to send specimens of economic plants throughout the world. Among the more important of these was the rubber plant *Hevea brasiliensis*. Joseph Hooker, then director at Kew, drew up plans to introduce *Hevea* into India. The first attempt failed

the spice trade he was to develop the Jardin de Pamplemousse as a center for economic plants. He obtained spice plants from Timor by legal means, but he and his colleagues also indulged in less reputable activities, such as breaking Dutch blockades and making a night sortie in a camouflaged old skiff to remove nutmeg seedlings under the cover of darkness.

During the eighteenth century, the Royal Botanic Gardens, Kew, probably the world's best-known botanic garden, was established as a result of royal interest. It rapidly attained international importance under the influence of its unofficial director, Sir Joseph Banks.

Sir Joseph set up a network of contacts and collectors that were to enmesh the world and in doing so created a botanical garden with no parallels. He selected and trained collectors who operated on the very edge of the known world; Francis Masson in Southern Africa, William Kerr in China, James Bowie in Brazil, Allan Cunningham and George Caley in Australia among others. Banks was a man inspired primarily by academic curiosity, yet rivalry was not unknown. The rivalry between the Royal collection and the Jardin des Plantes, Paris, prompted the following instructions from Banks to his collector Cunningham

The marsh garden in Singapore Botanic Garden.

Following pages *The Frangipani collection in Singapore Botanic Garden.*

— the 2,000 seeds collected resulted in only a dozen seedlings and these subsequently failed to grow in trials in Sikkim. The next attempt was made by Henry Wickham; he collected 70,000 seeds and these, contrary to popular legend, were cleared by Brazilian customs and not smuggled out as often suggested. They were quickly exported from Brazil to Britain by steamer in order to maintain their viability. On arrival in June 1876 the seeds were taken by special freight train from Liverpool to Kew where glasshouses were waiting. Germination was rapid and by August 1876 rubber seedlings were on their way to Ceylon. Consignments also reached Singapore Botanic Gardens where, in 1888, Henry Ridley devised an efficient method for tapping the trees. As a result, rubber is now a major crop in the Malaysian region.

Botanical gardens in North America

In North America botanical gardens are not developed as the primary agents of economic plant introduction; instead, specialist agricultural centers undertook this vital role. In further contrast to the Old World botanical gardens, North American institutes have placed a greater emphasis on public education and the relevance of a botanic garden to its local community.

The first botanical garden in North America was founded by John Bartram, an eighteenth-century Quaker settler with a natural fanaticism for plant hunting. Under the patronage of wealthy British collectors, Bartram scoured the eastern states of America for botanical gems while, in return, plants arrived at his five-acre

(2 ha) botanical garden by the Schuylkill River near Philadelphia.

This process of exchange was to carry on under the official sanction of Thomas Jefferson. Following a visit in 1785 to the Jardin des Plantes, Paris, and the presentation of some seeds from America, it was agreed that a French botanist should prospect the then primeval forests of America. André Michaux was selected, accompanied by his fifteen-year-old son, François-André. His mission was not only to collect for France but also to introduce European plants into America. Michaux soon established a nursery, first in New Jersey and later at a 100-acre (40 ha) nursery and testing ground in South Carolina. During his stay in America, Michaux is reputed to have sent some 60,000 plants back to France.

These early starts were not to persist and the modern American botanical garden owes its origins to the economic boom of the nineteenth century. The first was the Missouri Botanic Garden created by the wealthy merchant Henry Shaw and inspired by the great botanical gardens of Europe. Opened to the public in June 1859, it was followed by the Arnold Arboretum in 1872 and the New York Botanical Garden in 1895. Adopting some of the roles of an Old World botanical garden, the United States' Department of Agriculture initiated a plant introduction scheme, known as the Office of Foreign Seed and Plant Introduction. This organization employed some of the most remarkable of modern plant collectors. One was Frank Meyer, who collected in China, Russia and Tibet; he was responsible for some 2,500 plant introductions to the US, many of these having played an important role in American agriculture. Two other notable collectors were David Fairchild, remembered for his mango and alfalfa introductions; the other,

Wilson Popenoe, combed Central America for edible fruits and was responsible to a large extent for the establishment of avocado as a crop in California and Florida.

New challenges

The middle years of the twentieth century can now be recognized as the low point of botanical garden history. The gardens' traditional role in the introduction and development of economic crops had been taken over by specialist agricultural centers, leaving many tropical botanical gardens as primarily ornamental gardens. Subsequently, they were often abandoned or left under-supported during time of economic stress as the newly-emergent nations found more important demands on their resources. Temperate botanical gardens, their colonial networks eroded by political changes, underwent a similar decline before the needs of public education and conservation led to an upsurge of activity and the adoption of new roles.

Above *The phenomenal floral wealth of South Africa is well served by a network of local botanical gardens growing only native plants. At Karoo Botanic Garden, eldest offspring of Kirstenbosch, the parent garden, the collection specializes in plants for arid conditions including mesembryanthemums, aloes, haworthias, lithopses and stapelias.*

Above right *Botanical gardens have traditionally exhibited plants as museum specimens, but they can also be displayed as part of a coherent landscape, as here in St. Louis Botanical Garden.*

Below right *Kirstenbosch at Cape Town, on the slopes of Table Mountain, is the first among South Africa's botanical gardens.*

Left *The Burdett Erica collection at Witunga Botanic Garden, once a private garden and now an outstation of Adelaide Botanic Garden. The development of outstations allows botanical gardens to utilize different sites to expand their plant collections. Adelaide has several other satellite gardens.*

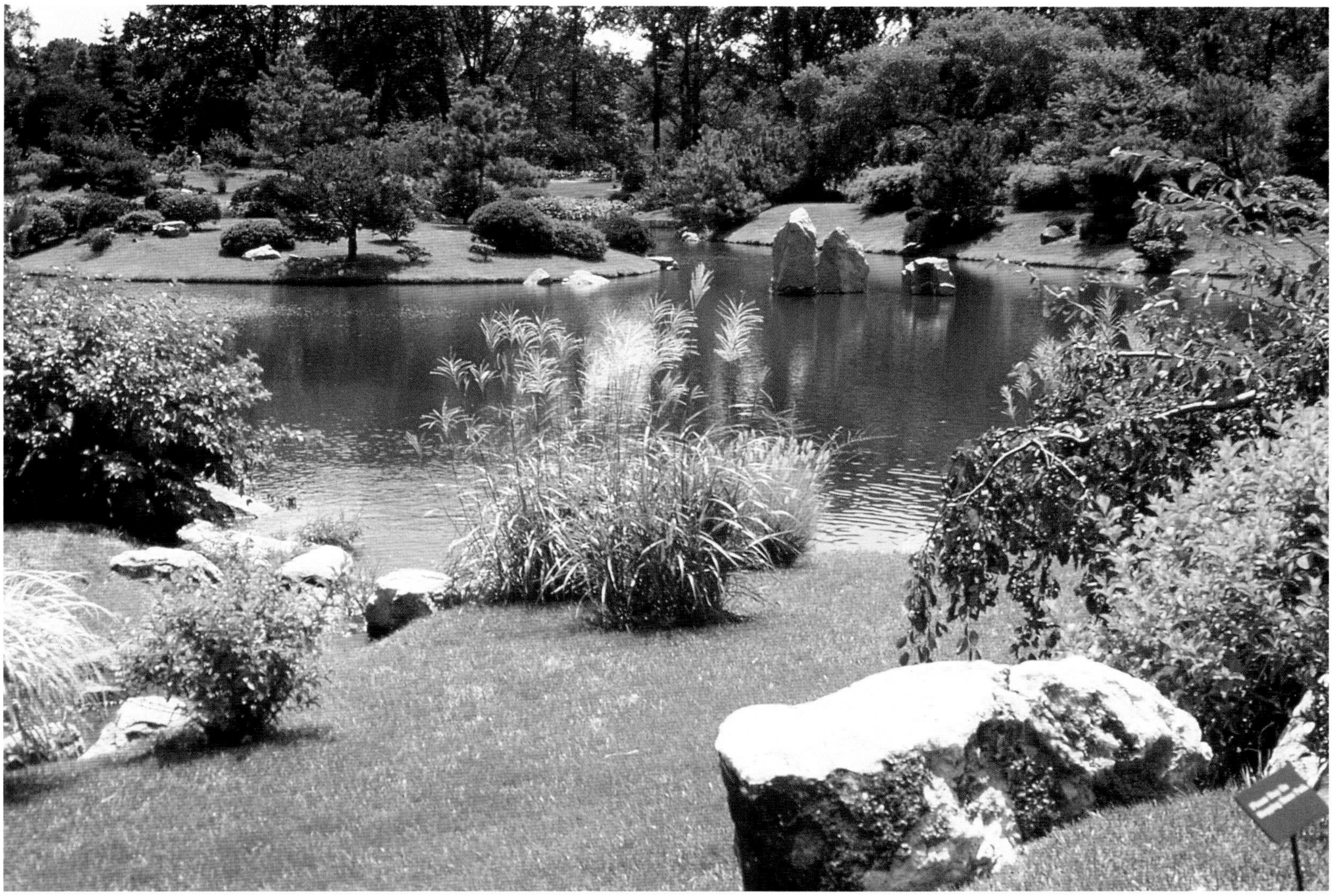

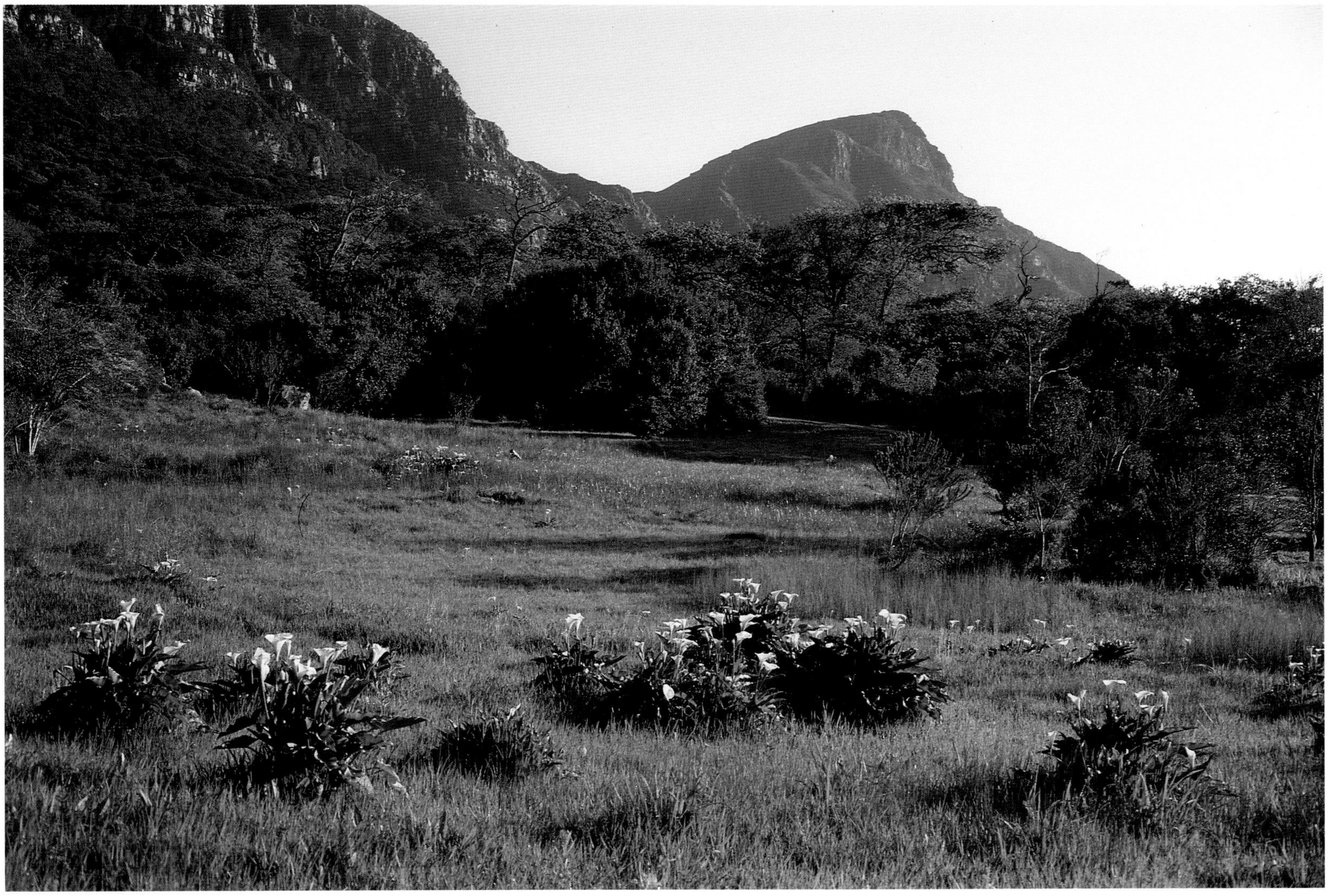

The seed bank at Wakehurst Place, Kew's sister garden. At subzero temperatures and with very low humidity some kinds of seed can be stored for very long periods and in some cases indefinitely. Wakehurst seed bank specializes in the threatened flora of the world's arid zone and researches techniques for storing such valuable seed collections.

Contemporary botanical gardens have had an increasingly heavy mantle of responsibility thrust upon them. On scientific grounds it is no longer justifiable merely to grow a miscellaneous collection of often undocumented plants. The responsibility now should be to maintain and salvage botanical diversity from a global trend of environmental degradation. Botanical gardens can achieve this through botanical research, cultivation and distribution of rare plants and, importantly, through public education.

Botanical gardens have always collected "rarities." There was a strong tradition of growing them as curiosities. They were perceived as representing a small number of individual and esoteric situations but, among them, unrecognized, were the first victims of the now hastening environmental crisis. These plants were the extinction-prone endemics, restricted to specific localities. One such plant was the mysterious *Franklinia alatamaha*, last seen in the wild in Southern Georgia in 1803. It now only exists in cultivation.

In adopting a conscious conservation function botanical gardens are attempting to ensure that plants survive but, away from their natural habitat, this is *ex situ* conservation. The holding of plants in artificial conditions (cultivation) can never be a substitute for retaining the species in a natural habitat (*in situ* conservation). When a wild plant is maintained in its natural habitat, the functioning ecosystem is retained and plant diversity maintained by natural selection, but an increasing number of plants are becoming extinct in the wild; if they can be found in botanical gardens they are not lost entirely.

As facilities for *ex situ* conservation, botanical gardens would appear to be puny agents in the face of such overwhelming statistics. There are approximately 1,600 botanical gardens throughout the world, most of them sited in the relatively plant-poor northern latitudes. These gardens collectively hold between 35,000 and 45,000 species of plants — less than 20 percent of the earth's plant diversity — but the modern botanical garden is, nevertheless, well equipped to take on the enormous contemporary challenge of plant conservation. New techniques, such as micropropagation, combined with the long-established horticultural skills, are allowing botanical gardens to cultivate and distribute endangered plants. Seed or portions of plant tissue are grown under sterile laboratory conditions. It is an extremely valuable procedure for salvaging diseased material, raising large quantities of plants or propagating species difficult to raise by conventional techniques. Because the plants are raised in near-sterile laboratory conditions and distributed in sealed containers, there are fewer problems with the increasingly Byzantine international plant health regulations. A great many botanical gardens are using micropropagation techniques, including Kings Park and Botanic Garden, West Perth, Western Australia; Royal Botanic Gardens, Kew; University of Copenhagen Botanical Garden, Denmark, Vierra y

Clavijo Botanical Gardens, Gran Canaria and many others.

Conservation involves not only wild plants, though they must always be the first priority; it can also involve domesticated plants. The Queen's Garden at Kew grows within its seventeenth-century garden a unique collection of old garden plant cultivars, while the Bogor Botanic Garden in Indonesia and its satellite, Cibinong, are propagating and distributing local cultivars of mango, durian, avocado, rambutan, guava and mangosteen — all locally valued fruit trees. The Tucson Botanical Garden is collecting and distributing indigenous crop cultivars and, in some cases, re-introducing them to Indian communities.

The Cassandras are gloomily predicting patterns of extinction unparalleled in geological time since the mass extinctions at the close of the Cretaceous Period. It seems likely that more than 60,000 species of plant, approximately one-quarter of the world's flora, are at risk of extinction during the present and next generations. This means that over the next 30 years 2,000 plant species may become extinct each year. The diversity of organisms is not evenly distributed across the globe; within the tropical latitudes there are areas exhibiting phenomenally high biological diversity and a high vulnerability to mass extinction. These extinction "hot spots" are, with very few exceptions, sadly devoid of active, conservation-orientated botanic gardens.

Plant collections

To the visiting public the botanical garden is often a garden strangely, but not always obviously, different from the normal. Some of the plants are distinctly dowdy (though no doubt scientifically interesting) and they are labeled with a meaningless Latin binomial complemented by a numerical code. The obvious face of a botanical garden is its plant collection but this forms only one of a botanical garden's unique resources.

The plants form the living collection of a botanical garden, part of a series of resources used for plant sciences. The major botanical gardens such as Paris, Kew, Missouri or Berlin are multidisciplinary institutes where laboratory or herbarium studies utilize the living collections for research. Hidden from the public eye are laboratories, herbaria, seed banks and libraries cataloging and researching the world's plant diversity. The herbaria hold dried plant specimens, a *hortus siccus*; these collections, often containing millions of specimens, are the centers for taxonomic botany. The dried specimens are the ultimate reference point for the science of botanical nomenclature and, without this reference, the natural sciences would tumble into chaos.

Using the specimens, taxonomic botanists can name plants, chart distribution, compile their evolutionary lineages and assess their potential economic roles. The herbaria of today are huge reference libraries containing many millions of specimens. The accumulation has taken centuries. Since the eighteenth century, plant specimens have poured into the great botanical gardens; Baudin's epic voyage to Australia and the Pacific on the *Naturaliste* returned to France in 1804 with 40,000 plant specimens, and a second consignment on the *Geographie* carried 70 crates with seed of 600 species, all destined for the Jardin des Plantes in Paris. In the same year Humboldt and Bonpland returned from five years in tropical South America with 60,000 plant specimens. To the botanists of Europe this was an incredible revelation of the tropics' diversity.

The task of cataloging the world's plants is by no means over; perhaps 30,000 species of plants await discovery, naming and describing, and a large proportion of these will have become extinct before they are "discovered," remaining only as statistics and not known as species! Many well-explored regions require documentation of their botanical resources. Nations as diverse as Somalia or Spain have no single national authoritative guide to their plants. Many herbaria are actively involved in rainforest conservation and are documenting the areas' phenomenal diversity and some, such as the New York Botanical Garden's Institute of Economic Botany, are looking for sustainable crops and viable economical alternatives to clearance of the rain forest.

Native flora

Many botanical gardens are now especially concerned with the vegetation of their own region. The network of botanical gardens in South Africa, as exemplified by Kirstenbosch at the Cape, concentrates on the incredibly diverse and beautiful flora of South Africa. Their work

has saved a number of species from extinction, among them the spectacular Golden Gladiolus *Homoglossum aureum*.

In the US, to cope with the differing climatic regimes and vegetation belts, a number of botanical gardens are working together to protect the native flora. With the Center for Plant Conservation, based at Missouri Botanical Garden, as the central body, the cooperating botanical gardens cover all of the United States, including Hawaii. One of the gardens, Bok Tower Gardens in Lake Wales, Florida, illustrates the modern approach to plant conservation within botanical gardens. Working together with conservation organizations, propagation material is collected from vulnerable populations to establish protected populations in cultivation; eventually these populations may be returned to safe sites in the wild. In addition, Bok Tower Gardens, in common with many other botanical gardens, manages an area of natural habitat; in this case, the highly endangered sand scrub habitat now threatened by rampant real estate development. Another garden with endangered wild species growing naturally within its boundaries is the Royal Botanic Gardens, Peradeniya, Sri Lanka, which contains 72 endemic species of trees, of which 22 have not been found elsewhere on the island.

The modern botanical garden

A multidisciplinary institute such as the Royal Botanic Gardens, Kew, is a reference point for all who work in the natural sciences. Within its walls researchers compile data bases on arid land crops, legume taxonomy, plant poisons and plant conservation, among other subjects; they are also professional educators training

In the Herbarium of the Royal Botanic Gardens, Kew, flowers are removed from a mounted dried specimen, collected in Guatemala in 1975, in order to extract pollen for study. Pollen is a valuable taxonomic tool with important economic implications. It allows the identification of allergy-causing plants and those important in honey production, for instance, and can even be used in tracing the origin of drug consignments.

Auckland's Regional Botanic Gardens show a country concerned with its own vegetation. Pictured here are the New Zealand rock lily or rengarenga (foreground), tree fern, whau, coprosma, koromiko and ti or cabbage tree.

KEW GARDENS. THE PAGODA

1

2

3

teachers and students; biochemists researching new medicines and the storage of seed; anatomists analyzing wood structure or identifying botanical specimens from drug consignments; and geneticists looking at breeding systems and chromosome structure. Beyond the laboratory window, the public sees only a garden!

The last few decades have seen botanical gardens move from being isolated academic retreats to being increasingly fundamental research facilities with a vital public service. As the window into the plant world they carry a heavy responsibility toward public education. The public has always been attracted to botanical gardens and the exotic plants and spectacular glasshouses have caught the imagination of many generations. It is no accident that the exuberant "jungle" landscapes of Douanier Rousseau were inspired by the exotic collections at the Jardin des Plantes in Paris. The now-restored great conservatories of the nineteenth century, architectural statements celebrating colonial power and civic wealth, are a glimpse into the vegetation of the tropical latitudes. The restored Palm House at Kew and the Enid Haupt Conservatories at New York Botanical Garden are glimpses of foreign environments, not random juxtapositions of the exotic. New displays, such as those at the Missouri Botanical Garden Climatron or the Bicentennial Conservatory at Adelaide Botanic Garden, are specifically designed to illustrate the floral wealth and ecology of the rain forest. To create these artificial environments, new technologies are being developed and within a decade the microcomputer has become a commonplace tool for the botanical garden horticulturist.

Botanical gardens have emerged from a period of stagnation into a renaissance in an age where the talents resident within a botanical garden are urgently needed. Today, botanical

1 *An early twentieth-century postcard showing Kew's famous pagoda, designed by Sir William Chambers for the original royal garden in 1761. With an entrance fee of one penny until well after World War II, a visit to Kew Gardens was a popular outing.*

2 *To the spectacle-hungry crowds of Victorian England the conservatories and grounds of the Royal Botanic Gardens at Kew were a glimpse into hardly known foreign territories. The burgeoning wealth from the new colonies was to depend heavily on the botanical and horticultural talents resident at Kew. The Palm House, built to designs by Decimus Burton and Richard Turner in 1844–48 stands behind the glasshouse erected to house the giant water lily (Victoria amazonica). The Palm House was totally renovated and restored between 1984 and 1989. Tropical houses and giant water lilies proved to be public draws in many botanical gardens.*

3 *The Cherry Esplanade at Brooklyn Botanic Garden attracts many picnickers at blossom time.*

4 *The Children's Garden at Brooklyn Botanic Garden has been established since 1914 with a program of educational work which includes practical gardening. Planning, planting and cultivation produces tangible results in the thousands of vegetables, squashes, etc., which the participants take home each year — one and a half tons of tomatoes alone!*

4

gardens are increasingly part of a global network. Traditionally, they have always exchanged plant material; for instance, André Thouin of the eighteenth-century Jardin des Plantes would distribute 80,000 packets of seed annually. Today, botanical gardens carefully exchange documented specimens in an attempt to save endangered species. In addition, through the coordination of the Botanic Gardens Conservation Secretariat, gardens now compare lists of their collections, enabling them to carefully plan their conservation activities. The informal networks of exchange and correspondence, dating from before the eighteenth century, are turning into an electronic matrix reinstating botanical gardens as centers serving the needs of modern society.

Botanical gardens as centers of plant introduction hold a phenomenal wealth of plants. This wealth has not only served scientific research, but has also contributed to the development of gardens and commercial horticulture. Plants have always filtered out of botanical gardens' collections, either as economic introductions to the plantation or nursery trade or unofficially through professional and personal links. Some botanical gardens, such as those at the University of British Columbia, have a plant selection program whereby outstanding ornamental plants are released to the horticultural trade.

As visitor attractions, botanical gardens have a tremendous role to play in public education; this can take several forms involving traditional interpretation, demonstrations and outreach. Apart from educational labels, the visitor may see demonstrations of horticultural interest, such as the Center for Home Gardening at Missouri or the demonstration of mixed coffee-agroforestry at the Francis Xavier Clavijeso Botanic Garden at Xalapa, Mexico.

Education provision can be aimed at all ages and educational levels and many botanical gardens have education programs aimed at specific groups. In addition to formal teaching, botanical gardens are often heavily involved in the improvement of the local community; an example is New York Botanical Garden's involvement with the Bronx Green-Up Campaign.

Currently, approximately 150 million people a year visit the world's botanical gardens; the majority go to enjoy spectacular plant displays or restful landscapes. Yet, increasingly, botanical gardens will be the windows onto a besieged resource, the plant kingdom. A strange mixture of public park, research institute, teaching facility and refuge for endangered plants, botanical gardens have served us well and will continue to do so.

The great glasshouses

For many people the feature which distinguishes the botanical garden from a public park is the

Tropical botanical gardens: a new beginning

Not so long ago it appeared that tropical botanical gardens would persist only as awkward relics of colonial occupation. Despite these fears, a number of tropical botanical gardens are rediscovering new roles and making a valuable contribution to the conservation and sustainable utilization of local natural resources.

The Limbe Botanic Garden in Cameroon, West Africa, illustrates the turbulent history of many tropical gardens. It was founded in 1892 during German colonial occupation, when it achieved a high international reputation followed by a decline from the onset of World War I. From the 1920s onward it was under British administration and entered the colonial network of gardens with Kew as the mother institute. There then followed a period of extensive and prolonged decline. In a combined Cameroon Government, British Overseas Development Agency (ODA) and Royal Botanic Gardens, Kew, project, the garden is being restored as a horticultural and botanical center of excellence for West Africa. The gardens are part of an integrated rainforest program with two extensive forest reserves managed by the gardens.

In contrast to Limbe, the Tropical Botanic Garden and Research Institute, Trivandrum, India, is a new botanical garden. Under enthusiastic management the garden has developed rapidly since its foundation in 1984. Apart from its extensive plant collections and forest areas (which have to survive the incursion of wild elephant during the dry season), the Institute can also boast a micropropagation laboratory, a herbarium and a biotechnology laboratory. It has accumulated specific collections of medicinal plants and local rarities for propagation and distribution.

The island of Réunion, situated in the Indian Ocean some 435 miles (700 km) east of Madagascar, has one of the world's most threatened floras. The new Conservatoire et Jardin Botanique de Mascarin, Réunion, is actively involved in propagating the island's threatened species. Using conventional and micropropagation techniques, plants are being propagated for reintroduction into natural reserves and for the restoration of degraded vegetation.

glasshouse creating an artificial environment in which plants from other climatic zones are grown. These tropical palm and arid houses have their origin in the first orangeries built to protect citrus and other "evergreens."

The first botanical glasshouses were recorded in the 1680s at the Amsterdam Hortus Medicus, Leiden and the Chelsea Physic Garden; they were built with a south-facing glazed front and masonry sides and back. The "lean-to" construction with a back wall was to be the dominant structure until the nineteenth century.

The earliest botanical garden glasshouses were very small because not only was glass very expensive but it was only produced in the form of bull's-eyes and small diamond-shaped panes. In 1688 Louis Lucas de Nehou invented the pouring and rolling process and, as a result, sheetglass could be utilized. This increased and the cheaper supply of glass resulted in a proliferation of orangery construction.

It was not until the 1830s, with industrialized mass production and the introduction of rolled iron I and U section bars and early space frames, that the spectacular glasshouses of the Victorian age could be created. With improved heating systems, the flexibility of ridge and furrow glazing and mass-produced panes of glass, botanical glasshouses were no longer crowded horticultural warehouses but could give spectacle-hungry audiences an insight to the "rich disorder of the primeval forest."

Wood had been replaced by cast iron as the main building material as it was relatively simple to manufacture, flexible, strong and, importantly, resilient to rot. The Palm House of the Royal Botanical Garden, Potsdammer Strasse, Berlin, now the Berlin Dahlen Botanic Garden and Museum, (a huge wooden construction erected in 1821) was replaced after only nine years due to deterioration of the wooden structure.

Situated at the epicenter of French research into botany and zoology, the conservatories of the Jardin des Plantes, Paris, were among the

Top *Old glasshouses in Valencia Botanic Garden, Spain, a garden established in the eighteenth century to receive plants from the South American colonies under the direction of Gomez Ortega of the Royal Botanic Garden of Madrid. A new botanical garden is now being built in Valencia in addition to this small formal garden.*

Center *The interior planting of the Missouri Climatron illustrates the vegetation of tropical rain forest and aspects of its ecology. That of the bromeliads, of the pineapple family, is presented in this display. The spectacular hanging bromeliad is Spanish Moss (Tillandsia usneoides), the original stuffing for the upholstery of the Model T Ford motorcar.*

Right *The Climatron in Missouri Botanical Garden was constructed in 1960, the first geodesic dome to be used as a glasshouse. The sculptures in the foreground are works of the Swede Carl Miller.*

1

2

3

4

5

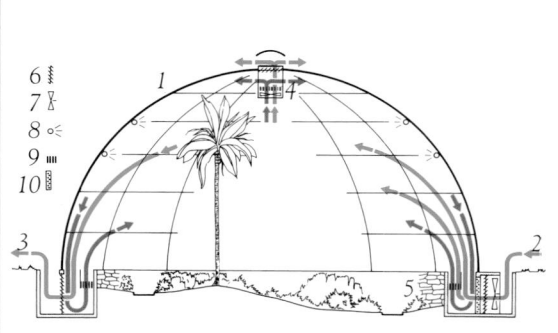

Key 1 *Dome,* **2** *Air intake,* **3** *Air outlet,* **4** *Roof ventilator for extracting and circulating air,* **5** *Wall of tufa for insulation,* **6** *Air baffle,* **7** *Ventilator fan,* **8** *Water sprinkler,* **9** *Convector heater,* **10** *Air cooler.*

6

largest of their time. Dramatically raised above the gardens, with a combination of curvilinear roof and cubic form, they were designed by Charles Rohault de Fleury and built in 1833. With later additions, they housed a magnificent collection of tropical plants for research and public display, and importantly transported the citizens of Paris:

"The River Seine, seen from afar, is framed by these palms, these coconut trees, this banana plantation, . . . and it is difficult not to start dreaming about the Nile or the Ganges."

As the century progressed, so designs became more ambitious and grandiose, among the most spectacular being the Royal Glasshouses at Laeken, Belgium. A huge complex of 36 separate glasshouses connected by glazed walkways, this was Leopold II's "recompense for the demands of reality." Paid for with revenue from Leopold's colonial activities in the Congo Free State (later the Belgian Congo and now Zaire) the glasshouses remain a bizarre monument to the brutal exploitation of a central African colony.

Beyond the botanical gardens of Europe, glasshouses started to grace the landscapes of botanical gardens in America and Australasia. The Enid Haupt Conservatory of the New York Botanical Garden is one such example. Modeled on European examples, it was finished in 1902. This range of glasshouses illustrates the scale of the problems facing contemporary botanic gardens who are financially responsible for the maintenance of architectural conservatories. The Royal Botanic Gardens at Kew have undertaken a renovation program for their historic conservatories; first the Temperate House designed by Decimus Burton and then the famous Palm House designed by Turner and engineered by Turner. Although retaining their architectural authenticity, they have been modified for the contemporary requirements of education with phytogeographical planting, and modern horticultural demands through improved environmental control. In the basement of the Palm House, boiler rooms have been

replaced with an innovative display of marine algae.

New botanical garden glasshouses continue to be built. Lacking the exuberance of their Victorian predecessors, they are increasingly complex analogs of natural environments. An early example of providing a specific artificial environment was the Copenhagen University Botanic Garden Arctic Greenhouse. Built in 1960 to house a research collection of arctic and alpine plants, it provides a model of the Greenland climate with air conditioning, cooling systems and artificial illumination.

In 1960 the Missouri Botanical Garden built the "Climatron," one of the most dramatic of twentieth-century glasshouses. This spectacular geodesic dome, the first to be used as a glasshouse, originally housed a series of different tropical vegetation types, but the system devised to maintain these differences within a single space was not entirely successful and they have now been replaced by a landscaped representation of the tropical rain forest. The Climatron, like many contemporary glasshouses, has moved away from Victorian ornateness and represents a building of its time.

An example of particularly dramatic design are the new glasshouses of the San Antonio Botanical Society, Texas. With glazed pavilions emerging from sheltering banks and corridors, the architect Emilio Ambasz has created a place of both drama and refuge, a contemporary echo of the *hortus conclusus*.

The Missouri Climatron originally contained a series of differing vegetation types within one volume; the later Princess of Wales Conservatory built at the Royal Botanic Gardens, Kew, has divided the conservatory into a series of self-contained units each with its own computer-controlled environmental parameters. Within this modernistic steel construction there are ten distinct environments, allowing the cultivation of a wide variety of often difficult plant groups, such as plants from the cloud forests of South America or deserts of southwest Africa.

M. M.

GARDEN DESIGN

Planning a garden

The designer of a garden must begin by getting to know as much as possible about the site and its surroundings. It is essential to understand the existing features and to assess the potential of the location. The best way of doing this is through a process of survey and analysis.

An accurate scale drawing of the site is a prerequisite. If the site is small it may be a simple matter to measure and record the details but large or complicated locations may require the assistance of a land surveyor to ensure an accurate scale representation.

Above and right *Creative use of papyrus, tussock, agapanthus and various shrubs, all tolerant to salt air, complements the existing shoreline trees of this cliffside garden. The* *maritime setting is emphasized by the use of rocks and bleached railroad ties in constructing the path, resulting in a harmonious blend of all features.*

If changes in ground levels or contours are contemplated, or any construction which requires deep or extensive excavation, the position of any underground obstruction or hazard will be vitally important. The diversion of any service to meet new levels will almost certainly cause additional expense and delay, which will have to be allowed for, and damage to an existing land drain can cause water-logging or even flooding to the detriment of soil and property.

A photographic survey of the site will be a useful source of reference during analysis and design, as well as providing an interesting record of "before" and "after." Photograph individual items and make an all-encompassing view of the site by swinging the camera around, taking a series of overlapping shots so that a panoramic impression can be made by linking adjacent prints. Aerial photographs are useful for larger properties and are usually obtainable from aerial survey companies.

The drawn survey of the property will confine itself to the facts within the site; the photographs, except in totally enclosed courtyards, will extend to details beyond the boundaries and begin to address the question of the garden's relationship with its surroundings, a vital relationship which must not be ignored. Each and every garden is part of a larger landscape or townscape and must be designed with reference to its setting. A map of the district is essential to discover more about the locality and it may be useful to turn to old maps and surveys for historical details which may be relevant to the design; even climatic and geological maps may furnish useful information.

Once the survey is complete, copies of the drawing can be used to record information that is not normally the concern of surveyors or mapmakers but is essential to the garden designer. Plotting existing vegetation comes first. This is an excellent indicator of soil and climatic conditions in the region and on the site. Simple kits are also available from garden centers to test the pH of the soil. The success or otherwise of existing plants is a useful pointer to the choice of future garden plants. A surveyor may well mark trees and even hazard a guess at their species, but smaller plants or groups of plants will be ignored, even though to the gardener these may be of greater significance and potentially of value in the new garden.

It may require the skills of an ecologist to realize the significance of the wild plants and of a horticulturalist or a botanist to accurately identify all the species and recognize that they include a rare old cultivar or an endangered wild species, but anyone can make a start. Unfortunately, because of the seasonal nature of herbaceous plants and bulbs, their presence may be missed in a survey of property acquired when they are not visible, but in an established or neglected garden where change is contemplated and the owner still in residence, first-hand knowledge can provide details of plants which may not be noticeable at the time of survey but which are valuable enough to be retained in the new design, either in their original position or lifted before work commences and replanted in a new position.

Record existing soil conditions. On larger properties there may be great variation of soil type and even in small gardens differences in soil quality can be experienced within a few feet, caused perhaps by the activities of hungry, invasive plant roots, intense cultivation, manuring or having lain fallow.

If an extensive soil survey is required, a series of trial holes made in a grid pattern will enable soil to be examined and depth of topsoil, subsoil and underlying rock strata to be determined. In wet soil such excavations may become partially filled with water, indicating the depth of the water table and the need for drainage. Samples of topsoil from different locations, clearly labeled, can be sent for analysis of soil acidity and available nutrients or

Making a survey

The survey drawing should be to scale and show site boundaries — *what* as well as *where* they are — and all important features: buildings, paths, drives and other surface materials, existing vegetation, changes of level and contours (preferably related to the nearest bench mark), exposed rock or water sources, and all underground services such as gas, electricity, telecommunication cables and drainage runs, if possible. Supply companies can usually provide drawings showing the locations of their services or by lifting a few manhole covers the direction of the runs can be assessed. Both manhole covers and the line of the underground service should be on the survey.

A survey drawing for a garden in north London. Existing features have been noted. The garden is on a hill and slight changes of level are indicated along the paths.

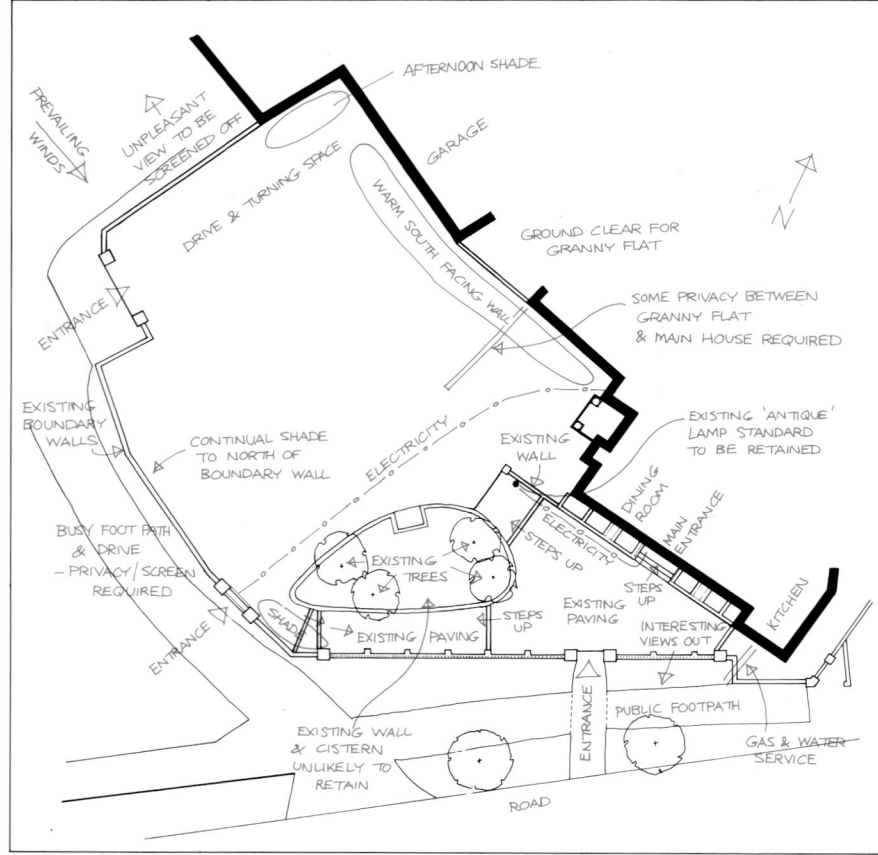

Below *This enclosed backyard garden in Philadelphia offers an environment where the surrounding buildings and divisions between properties will give some protection from wind and from frost. Cities produce heat and their roads, bricks and concrete retain the heat of the day, giving temperatures higher than the surrounding countryside. Buildings, however, may throw shadows for much of the day, reducing the amount of sun available to plants and affecting growth.*

Brick can be persuaded to follow curves by accepting angles in the joints and cutting bricks to fill the larger gaps with these eye-catching results.

perhaps the unfortunate presence of pollutants, all three of which will affect the type of plants that can be selected.

In general, it is best not to fight the soil conditions that exist, but accept that on alkaline soil lime-tolerant species should be used and on acid soil to design with calcifuges. It is expensive to import "alien" soil and to maintain it in its required pH value. Invariably those plants for which the changed soil conditions have been made will also look alien when compared to surrounding vegetation.

If there is no existing soil, in a rocky location perhaps, or if extensive soil importation is necessary to replace polluted material or to cover a roof garden for example, then a new soil type is more acceptable. However, a change in the character of vegetation should be carefully con-

sidered in the design. It is probably preferable that this new ecology — for that is what it will be — is distinctly separated from its surroundings rather than attempting to merge one with the other.

Microclimate considerations

Climatic — or rather *microclimatic* conditions can also be included on the survey. They are important factors in design and plant selection. Aspect and orientation of the site in relation to the daily course of the sun is fundamental in its effect on plant growth. In colder Northern Hemisphere climates a well-aligned south-facing slope is warmer and will produce earlier than a nearby north-facing slope of the same

soil type; the gentler microclimate is also more acceptable to people as well as to plants. This rule will, of course, be reversed in the Southern Hemisphere. In a warmer latitude the same orientation may scorch both plants and people and a shadier position with the opposite aspect may be better.

The orientation of the site to prevailing winds should also be considered. Any ill effects could override the advantages of a sunny area if strong winds (either hot or cold) are experienced, or where salt spray is carried inland from the sea.

The extent and pattern of rainfall should also be studied and run-off and drainage requirements noted. Water in trial pits can vary in level from day to day, particularly in rainy weather. Provided that the level remains 2 ft

(60 cm) below the surface there is no need for concern. Water which constantly stays closer to surface level, particularly in winter, will be detrimental to plant growth (except for those that enjoy wet conditions) and if such areas are extensive an improved drainage plan should be considered. In some cases it may be sufficient to clean out ditches,. an operation which may result in the discovery of outlets from an existing drainage system that, once unblocked, may operate satisfactorily. In other places a new system may be required and unless a simple network of open ditches is enough to effect improvement the advice of a drainage expert may be necessary.

The presence of water close to the surface may suggest the development of a pool or lake in the new layout. Introducing a water feature provides many benefits: a change of habitat, a source of movement, of reflections, or the pleasant sound of running water. In climates where sudden heavy rainfall causes excessive surface run-off, a storm drainage system that collects, conducts and disposes of surface water will be necessary to prevent soil erosion and periodic flooding. An increase in paved areas will add to this problem and large areas of hard surface will need accompanying drainage, either subsurface or open, the latter, of course, being cheaper. The need for and means of drainage will affect design layout, and open systems could become a feature.

Once microclimate details have been noted, thought can be given to modifying the local climate by creating sheltered or shaded locations in the new design. When a new building is to be constructed, its placing may be determined by the microclimate, taking advantage of shelter, sun or shade as preferred, but its presence will also provide an opportunity to create new conditions. It may give shelter and the warm sun-facing walls of centrally-heated houses can provide a further lift in temperature that will enable more tender plants to be grown in colder climates. Groups of dwellings or outhouses can give further protection. The presence of urban "heat islands" is well known and often allows the successful cultivation of species which would not survive in the surrounding

The sound of water can disguise traffic noise from busy roads.

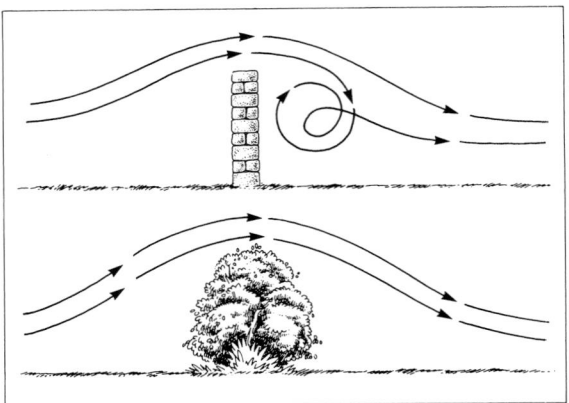

Below *A belt of trees or a hedge will give good wind protection but walls can produce a damaging eddy effect.*

countryside. Courtyards totally enclosed by well-heated buildings may remain untouched by frosts outside.

Less dramatic modifications of climate can be obtained by the creation of shelter belts, particularly of large-scale plantings near the sea where shelter in the lee of more wind-tolerant species will allow the growth of subjects otherwise too sensitive to blasts of salty air. Even a humble hedge can act as a useful barrier to wind damage. Walls are less effective, because they produce an eddying effect behind them, although the increase in temperature on sun-facing walls, caused by absorption of heat by the brick during exposure to the sun, produces a warmer microclimate which will help tender plants.

Contours can also affect wind patterns. There is a particular danger that gullies running in the same direction as prevailing winds will act as wind channels. Extensive change in contours to prevent wind damage may be prohibitively expensive for small sites though perhaps possible in some public projects.

Visual analysis

Views within and outside the garden should be evaluated so that interesting features can be emphasized or highlighted and ugly or unpleasant sights eliminated or screened in the new design. Views of the garden from its surroundings should also be considered. It will be necessary to assess potential vantage points so that screens of new planting or more solid barriers, fences or walls, can give privacy where required. On the other hand, an attractive garden can

Top left *Mounds of planting in this bed at Sam Bibler Garden, in Montana, echo the landscape form of the surrounding hills.*

Left *A sheltered garden in Mexico. Even with the gate closed the attractive courtyard is still visible from outside.*

Below *At Polesden Lacey, Surrey, a wall aperture frames a fine sundial surrounded by irises which contrast in both color and texture with the hedge behind. From inside a garden such apertures can frame a view, from outside offer a moment of delight for the passerby.*

make a positive contribution to a neighborhood. Enticing views into the plot through the entrance gate or "windows" in a surrounding wall or screen, can be exciting additions to the street scene as well as welcoming vistas for the visitor.

Sources of unwelcome noise and activity close to the property should be noted. Although little can be done to diminish noise from streets or highways, unless very thick screens of vegetation can be planted, hiding the source from view can have the psychological effect of diminishing the nuisance.

Establishing garden use

The next stage in designing a garden is to decide what is required and for whom. Demands on a modern garden are often more complex than in the past, with a large number of activities taking place within a comparatively small area. Carefully planning the location of each activity and its relationship to others is of paramount importance.

Gardening is the primary activity in most cases, and will require a number of garden elements to satisfy particular horticultural endeavor: specimen trees, shrub beds, lawns, herbaceous borders, rockeries, ponds and streams, greenhouses and frames, and other practical features such as compost heaps. Vegetable and fruit growing will make their own demands and most gardener-cooks will want to make space for a patch of herbs.

However, not all who enjoy a garden want to devote a great deal of time to gardening. For them the priorities may be to achieve an attrac-

Top right *The solution to disguising the dominant garage wall in this garden was to feature a large mosaic designed by Marc Chagall and cover the rest with creeper.*

Right *Foliage provides privacy and even in winter the bare branches of these young trees will break up the view of the flat blank wall which dominates the sky. The balustrade provides a strong horizontal which helps keep the eye level down and the enclosure of the paved sitting area makes this small garden seem larger.*

Left By raising pools or flowerbeds, protection can be given to plants from people, particularly children, and small children can be protected from water. Raised beds are also easier for the elderly or the handicapped to tend, either from a wheelchair or to save bending.

1 When it is clothed with climbing plants this pergola below the entrance gate to an Australian garden will form an enticing punctuation on the path, partly concealing what lies beyond.

2 Garden and walls here combine to draw the visitor up the steps to the entrance courtyard and the welcoming if weeping tree.

3 Stone treads seem to fly upwards in this original stairway, giving "a flight of steps" real meaning, its smooth slabs contrasting with the surrounding foliage.

4 A tennis court is often placed at the far end of the garden and then separated from the rest by trees or a high hedge, but it would require a very high barrier to hide it in this Australian garden. Instead, it has been left totally exposed and open behind so that the eye carries on to the fields beyond. Yellow lines instead of white make the court grid less obtrusive and with a parallel line of stone at either side emphasize the outward view. When the court is in use play is easily visible from the shade of the upper lawn and the veranda.

tive ambience with the minimum amount of maintenance, and while a careful choice of plants can help in this, part of the solution may be to limit the planted areas and make a greater use of paving and other surfaces.

The garden will be used for many things other than growing plants. Some people find the garden an ideal setting for their work — not garden maintenance but office or manual work. A potter's studio or a writer's study might be in an attractive summerhouse that could be a prominent feature of the garden, but so too could any office, providing a restful outlook for the worker, and worth considering now that electronics make it possible for more people to work at home. Sheds for manual work are usually best treated in the same way as those for garden maintenance and stores, hidden away with the compost heap and perhaps given an overcoat of climbing plants to further disguise their presence. Garages and carports may also require this treatment.

In most gardens play space has a higher priority than a place to work. For children this may simply mean an expanse of grass, or a covered area of pavement to allow for outdoor play during summer showers, or a place for more elaborate equipment such as swings and slides.

Adults may find an expanse of grass sufficient for an impromptu ball game but the more serious sportsman will be more exacting. Tennis, badminton, croquet and swimming pools require precisely leveled areas and take up a large proportion of a small garden. Fencing around such areas for safety or to contain balls will require screening if it is not to dominate the garden visually. The danger of deep water to small children requires that it should be placed within view for easy supervision, if the pool is not enclosed within a lockable enclosure. In some places secure fencing is required by law.

Small gardens do not have space for sports, and gathering points will be for more social activities such as talking and eating. These areas can be given a permanent foundation with fixed tables and benches upon a hard surface, perhaps with a built-in barbecue, either covered by a weatherproof structure or a simply defined space or enclosure which can be used temporarily on fine days or special occasions.

Play areas for children

The traditional swing of rope and wood slung from the branches of an old tree is far more pleasant than its modern steel-framed, plastic-seated equivalent, just as a primitive self-built tree house is more attractive than a store-bought house. In the smaller garden without a mature tree there is little choice.

Moving and potentially dangerous play equipment is best sited where visible from inside the house so that a degree of supervision is possible. Softer ground surfaces are preferable, sand or grass being more suitable than pavement despite the unsightly areas of worn grass that may result.

Sandpits should be designed so that they can be easily covered to avoid waterlogging in heavy rains, and to protect them from soiling by pet animals. A sunken pit can be designed in such a way that it can be easily converted to a pool when children are older.

1

2

3

4

World-famous author, Victoria Holt, relaxes beneath a magnificent bougainvillea arch in David Bateman's Auckland garden, perhaps contemplating her next book.

In both cases it is necessary to estimate the numbers likely to be involved and assign a space that is appropriate.

Perhaps the most frequent use of a garden is for quiet contemplation. A comfortable seat in a sheltered place with a good view, either within the garden or beyond it, is often the only feature required — and for even the most outgoing and sports-loving garden owner a place for calm relaxation is a necessary balance to the activity areas.

A garden must also fulfill a further function: to provide a circulation pattern that will link its individual areas sensibly and practically. Drives and paths must be wide enough to carry the intended traffic and as direct for practical purposes as the levels on the site allow. Where aesthetic rather than practical considerations are dominant they may be deliberately indirect to provide a change of vista and to add interest to the way in which the garden is revealed when moving through it.

Remember that the garden's functions may change as time goes by. The owners' interests may alter, their sports become less active, and their children will grow up. A design must have flexibility to allow for this; the tennis court may become a croquet lawn, the sandpit a garden pool, the carport a garage. Wherever possible, change should be anticipated and the design made suitably adaptable.

Some garden users may have special requirements because of age or handicap. Gardens without steps or steep inclines are important for the blind and those in wheelchairs. Textured paving or handrails can act as a guide and make progress through the garden safer. Raised beds can make practical gardening easier for the elderly or disabled.

The amount of work and the cost of maintenance will be important considerations for any gardener. Sweeping a paved surface will probably require less effort than maintaining planted areas. Shrubs and perennials with suitable ground cover will be less labor-intensive, and watering systems can now be installed to provide water effortlessly when and where it is needed.

Making bubble diagrams

Use tracing paper over the survey plan to plot the basic lines of the site. Then freely mark in an approximate location for each activity without bothering too much about the exact shape and size you draw.

Add dotted lines to indicate the circulation pattern that will link each area. This may follow existing paths if these are appropriate but new routes may be necessary.

Refer to the levels and contours of the survey. Activities that require level ground must be positioned where the ground is already flat or where minimum recontouring is necessary to make it so.

Take all the other survey notes into account. Consider locations for screening, views and vistas to emphasize, existing vegetation to highlight, microclimates to take into account and noise sources to be softened. Include these in your diagram.

A succession of diagrams will probably be needed before you reach a solution that meets most requirements and some compromises may be necessary.

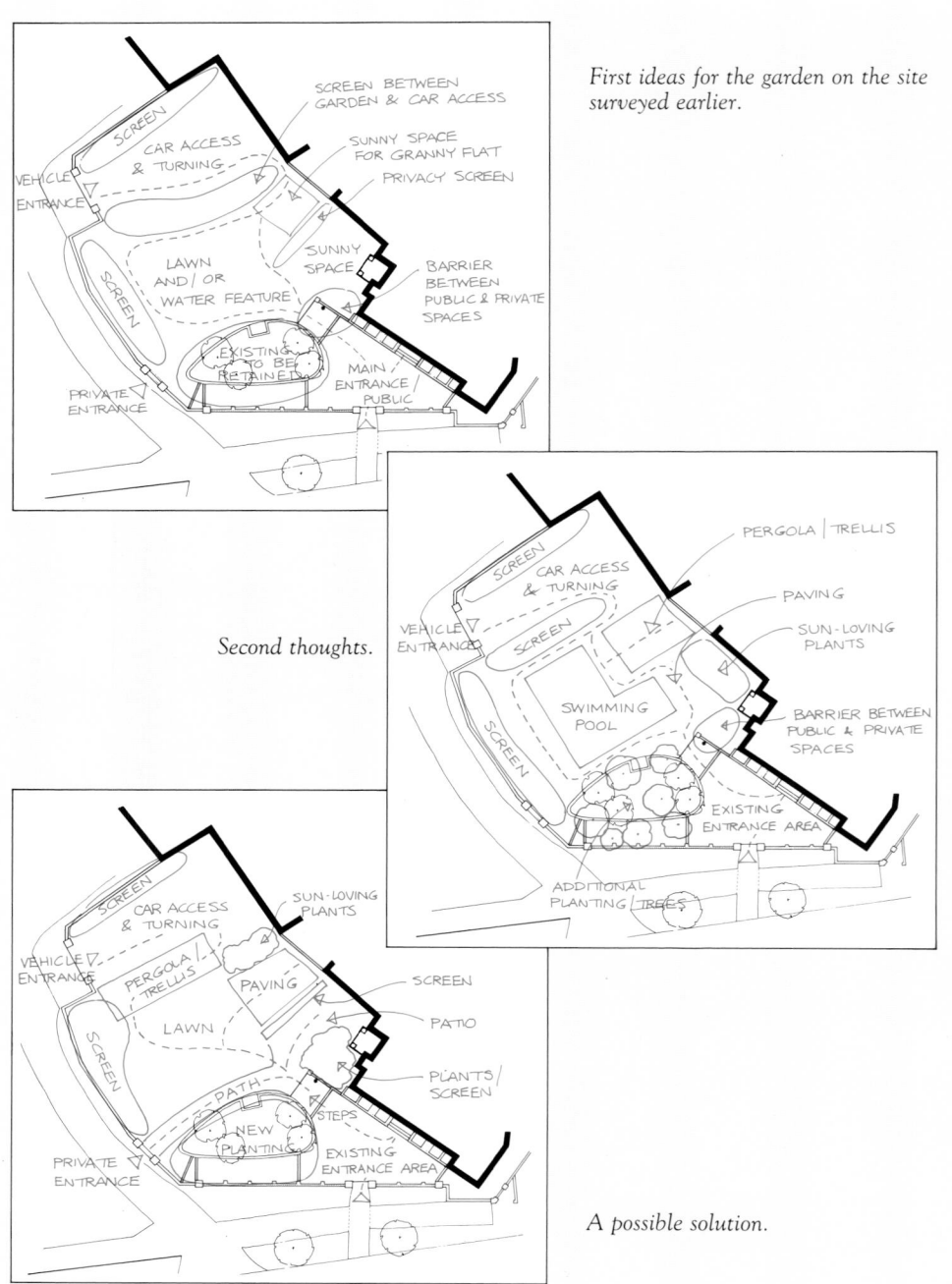

First ideas for the garden on the site surveyed earlier.

Second thoughts.

A possible solution.

Assigning areas

Finding a satisfactory arrangement of different garden areas that will be both practical and produce a pleasing relationship between each other and with the house can be aided by making a "bubble" diagram — sketching a group of bubbles to represent the various use areas. Experiment with several different diagrams trying out different arrangements.

The aim is a diagram that answers all the needs of the user, but this may not be possible. Comparison between what is there, as shown on the original survey, and what is required, as expressed in the diagram, will reveal what can or cannot be achieved.

Choosing a garden style

When bubble diagrams have produced an acceptable arrangement the question of garden style arises. The most obvious differentiation is between the formal and the informal garden but a garden need not exclusively be either. Symmetry and natural freedom can be blended without difficulty, provided that the boundary between each idiom is carefully handled, and within the two broad divisions of style a variety

of treatments are possible according to the tastes of the individual.

Particular national styles are frequently adopted by gardeners in other countries to give a flavor of the country of origin. French, English, Spanish, Islamic, Japanese or Chinese styles have been recreated throughout the gardening world, sometimes with success and authenticity, although national styles do not always travel well, even when the climate is suitable. Within overall national styles there are many subdivisions of historical origin or related to the function or location of the garden.

Garden history shows many distinctly different approaches, and location in town or country, on a roof, by water or in woodland, may predetermine some elements. Style can also be derived from the plant content. Rose gardens, herb gardens and heath gardens are obvious examples but other plant groups have also been the core concept for a design.

Some garden designers have developed a personal style which gives their work a recognizable signature; others who attempt to emulate that style are seldom successful.

It is generally best to avoid a very precise style for, unless it is entirely appropriate to the situation, it can severely restrict the designer's

The rear garden at Hall's Croft, the house where Shakespeare's daughter and her doctor husband lived in Stratford-upon-Avon. A sundial acts as a focal point at the end of the stone path and, although the choice of plants is not entirely accurate as a representation of early seventeenth-century planting, it makes a fitting accompaniment to the timber-framed house.

imagination. If you are fortunate enough to live in a medieval manor house, then a garden of that period may be the answer, but others should seek something more relevant to their times and needs. The best expression of garden design is an honest, practical attempt to solve the problems of the site and meet the needs of the users without imposing a pre-selected style. It may, however, be possible to adopt a theme that is well suited to a garden's location, or the feelings of the owner, which can be expressed in part of the garden or as a recurring mood which is reflected throughout.

Scale and proportion

Gardens should relate to human scale in all their elements. Materials, plants, ornaments and enclosures should be in proportion both to each other and to the human figure. What constitutes proper scale and proportion will depend upon purpose and use. If the intention is to provide a setting for vast concourses of people or to dwarf the individual to induce awe and respect, then the vast spaces of a Versailles may be the correct scale. For most people, however, such space is neither available nor desirable and the aim will be to achieve comfortable spaces in which to feel at ease; enclosure sizes may then be much more closely related to room size in dwellings.

Time

Time is a more important factor in the design of the garden than in other art forms. All art objects are susceptible to destruction and decay but gardens are especially fragile. A year or two of neglect is enough to produce changes that may be irreversible. Time has, however, an

even greater relevance because as a garden grows to maturity it undergoes major changes. And the changes must continue. The herbaceous border must be divided and replanted and more drastically, though essential, a decaying avenue must be felled and replaced with new saplings, or a shrub border gutted and replanted.

Time also plays its part within the year and the seasons bring changes to individual plants as they wake from dormancy to a peak of inflorescence and then decline as the year turns. In some the annual change can be remarkable and barely visible buds produce a bulk of summer growth of amazing volume.

The designer must try to foresee the effect of time, allowing for the growth of small cuttings and insignificant saplings into noble trees, for seasonal change which brings leaf and shade as well as blossom, affecting the growth of other plants.

Gardens with a strong architectural form and a high proportion of hard materials in their make-up may survive better than others, as may those which follow local nature and are close to the ecological climax vegetation. Durability in built elements and sound ecological planting will offer the best chance of achieving permanence.

Structure and space

The form of a garden is hewn (an appropriate word, for garden form is much like sculpture) from the space it occupies by an underlying structure composed of trees, shrubs, hedges and walls. These elements are the nearest that a garden can achieve to mass, the solid space that the architect or sculptor manipulates, and as with their media of stone, brick or timber, it is the juxtaposition of mass and void that is fundamental to garden design. Just as empty rooms can be satisfying spaces when devoid of furniture, because of their pleasing form and proportion, so should each garden space be satisfying even when lacking the furnishing of plants and ornament.

Structure in architecture opposes the force of gravity and thus defines the building it supports. Structure in garden design opposes the pull of diffusion, defining the form of the place and the spaces within, segregating it from the "chaos" around and, in the best gardens, creating a powerful presence that can communicate with the human spirit through the emotions, not only responding to the function of its spaces but satisfying and delighting those who use them.

Space may be compared to a liquid, invisible yet tangible, channelled by the masses of the garden structure so that it may appear at rest, as a reservoir of space, or moving and diverted to flow in desired directions. When garden elements rise above eye level the contrast between enclosure and openness becomes more powerful; people and their activities become directed, segregated and contained like the space itself. The screens created not only provide shelter,

A white bridge, doubly emphasized by its own reflection in a still pond, provides a powerful focal point and draws the eye down from the distant horizon while the lush garden contrasts with the dry New South Wales landscape beyond.

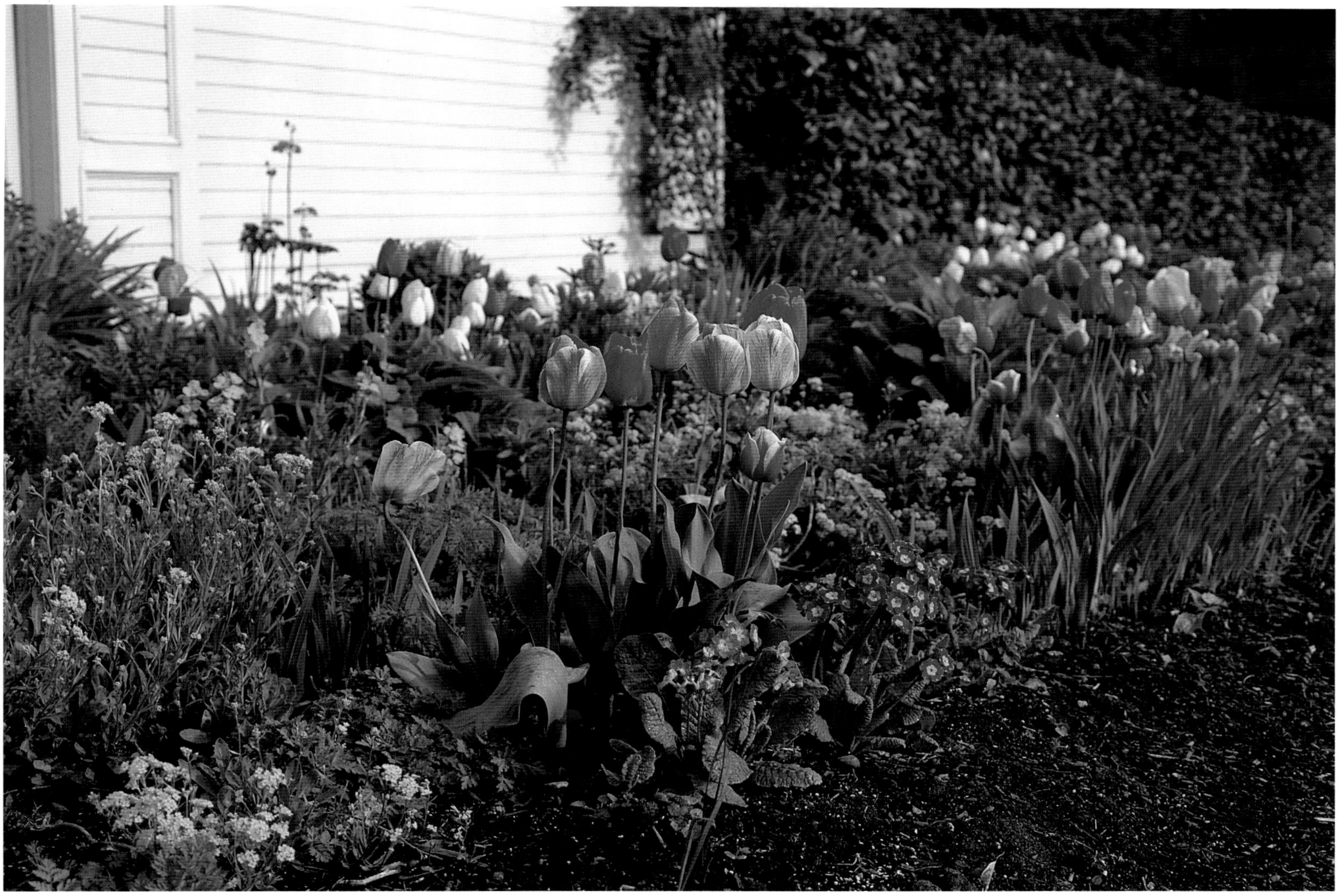

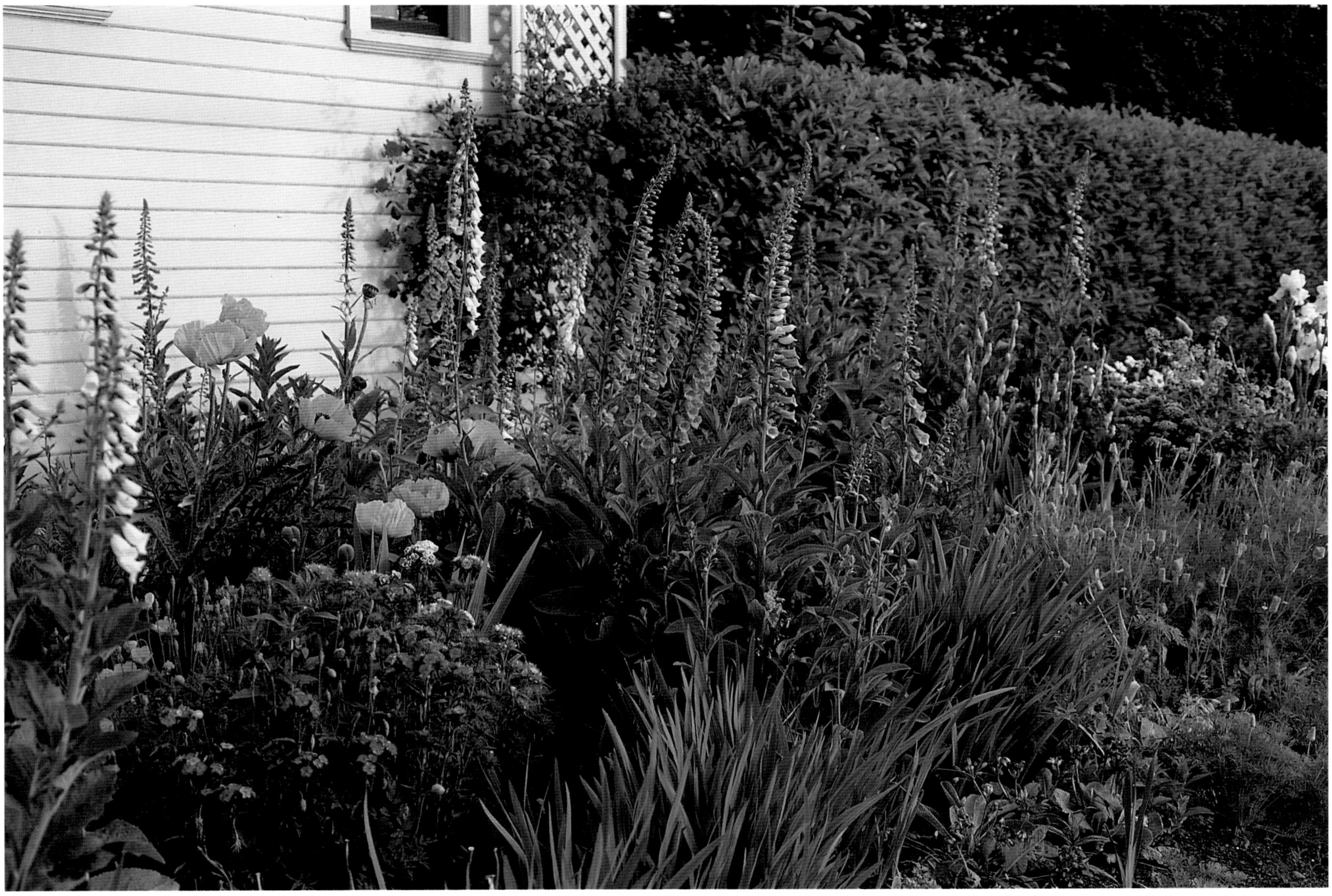

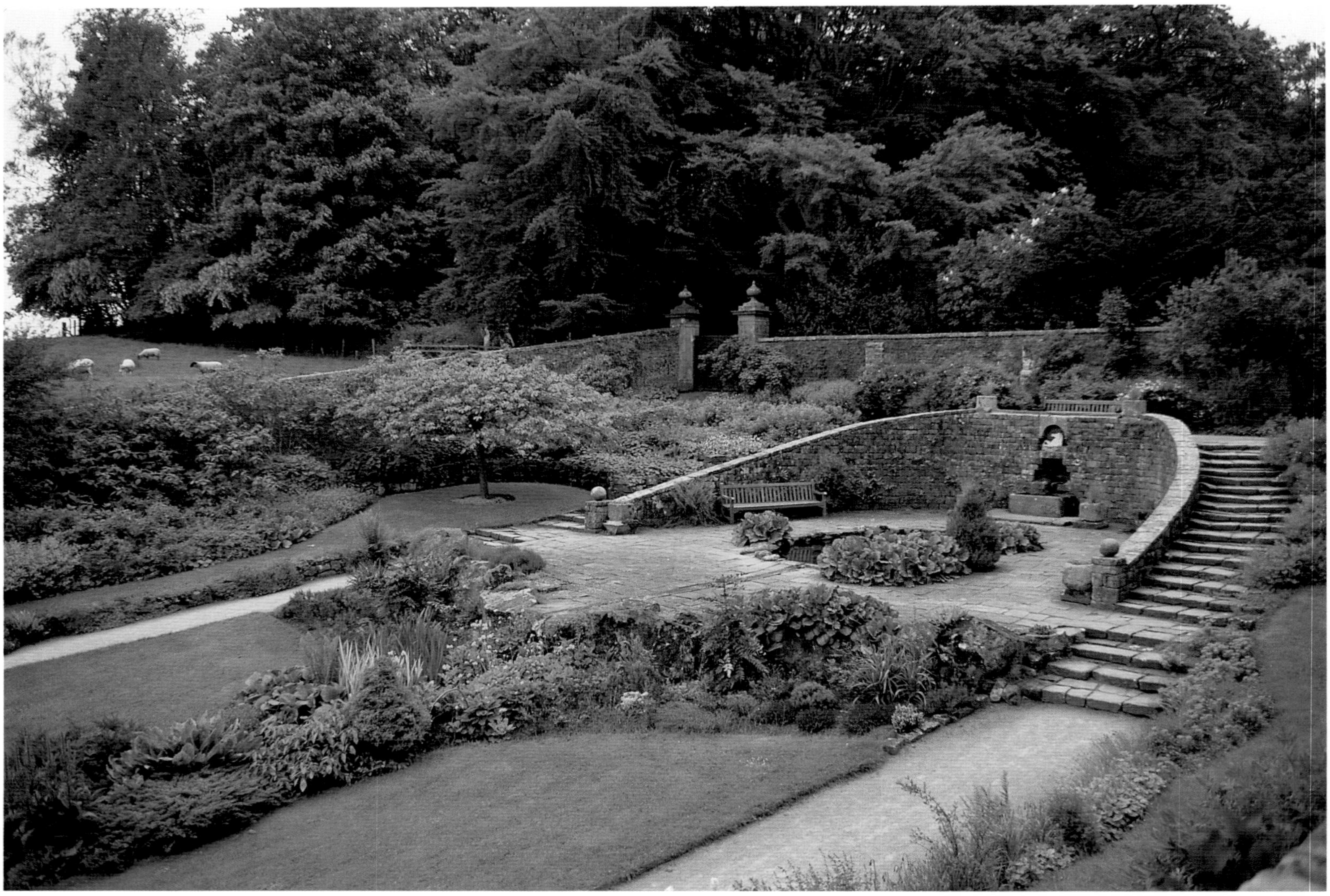

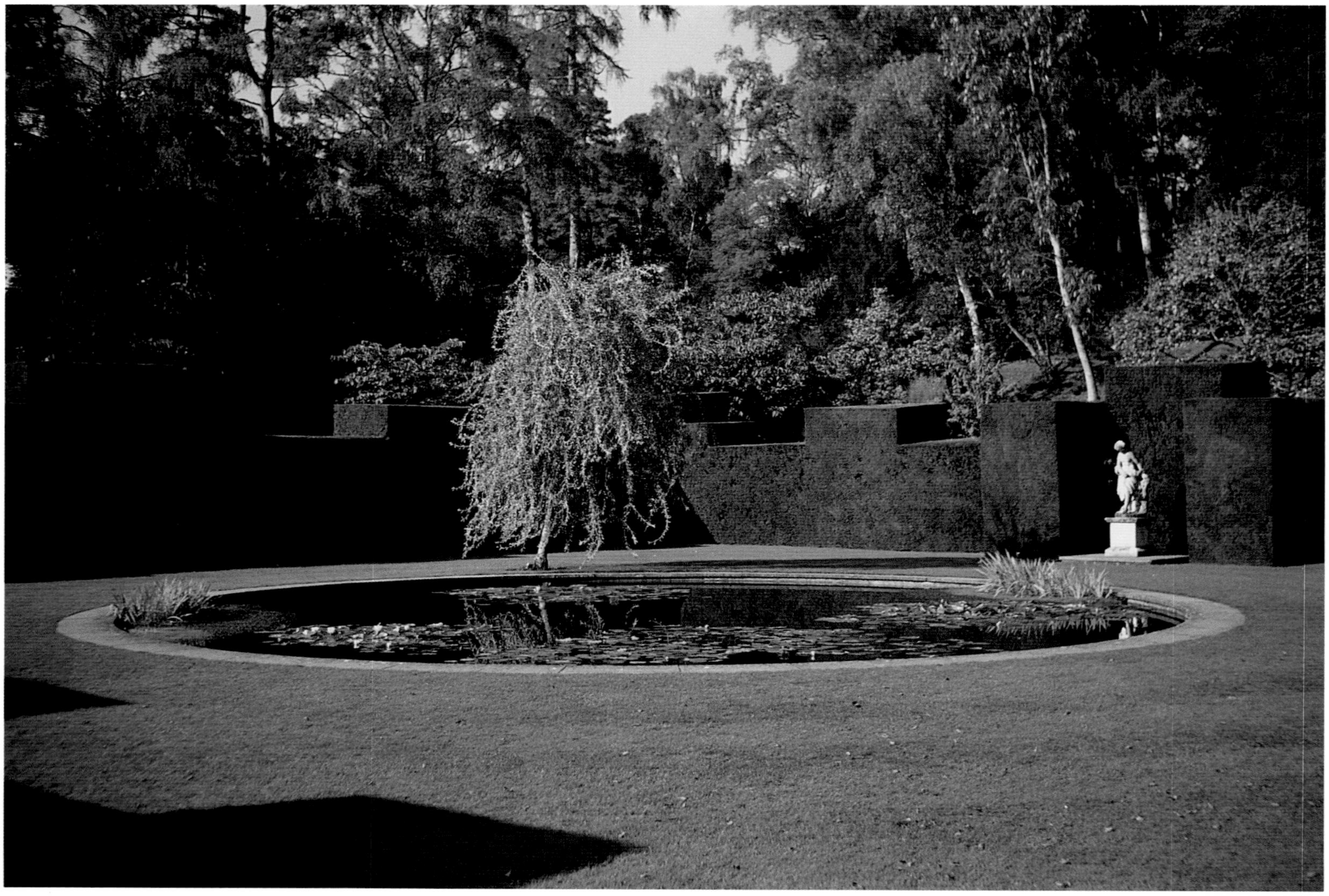

modifying the microclimate, but can be used to emphasize features and can create surprise by concealment and revelation, privacy and repose through a sense of refuge resulting from containment and drama through the effects of darkness and light.

Less than the architect, but more than the sculptor, the garden designer is bound by utility. He or she not only has to please the eye but also pamper the body and provide warm shelters or cool shady retreats for leisure, or bracing exposed elevations from which to survey the surroundings, challenge the elements and dominate the environment.

Defining the structure

The first step is to create the garden in fantasy, then make it more real on paper before it can be realized in fact. Even for those with no skill in drawing, sketching their ideas will help to test them out.

Making a design

The basic composition of a design can be seen as a structure of lines. In architecture these are usually hard and straight, marking the elevations; in a garden, as in a painting, they may be less apparent, blurred by softer forms and wandering vegetation. However, just as a painter's original sketch will probably show the compositional structure more precisely drawn, the garden designer should first draw in the linear composition which defines the construction of the garden. As with the bubble diagram a number of experiments will probably be necessary.

The lines in a drawing reproduce the lines in the potential garden and represent three characteristics:

The outline of objects and the junction between materials
Changes in level
Pattern or texture

Lines representing hard materials can usually be drawn with precision. Their positions can be accurately determined and once built will remain. Lines representing soft materials can only be approximations, for, although the exact positions of plants or the extent of a bed containing them can be determined, their free growth will spread and blur their edge. Lines defining the junction between materials, such as grass, brick and shrubs, will also outline the path, lawn or shrubbery as well but in making a drawing the nature of the defined object should be reflected in the strength of the line used. The greater the visual

Purpose will be the first consideration. A tennis court must be level and conform to the regulation size, but if grass is intended only as a child's play area its shape and level can be varied. If hard pavement is to bear vehicles the width of turning circles and need for parking will dictate the space required. If an area is for human relaxation, an elderly couple will probably require less room than a younger family. Some people may wish to entertain large numbers; other places may be for solitary use. Widths of paths or sitting spaces must be practical sizes. Planted areas will either be defined by the growth rates of plants chosen or vice versa.

The nature of a material will affect its form. Materials cannot be twisted into shapes beyond their flexibility, either because using the material in whole units dictates the extent of a curve or because the expense of working a material may preclude its forming a more adventurous shape. Square-cut paving units dictate a square pattern into which they will fit.

impact in reality, the thicker the line upon the paper. The line dividing the brick wall of the house from the brick line of a path should be stronger than that which divides path from grass. Lines which show pattern or texture within a material should be finer than those which define junctions. The change of level at a step or retaining wall should be stronger than the junction between two ground surfaces.

Opposite above *The water source is given emphasis and importance by the horseshoe steps and the formal symmetry provides a contrast with the fields and wood beyond.*

Opposite below *A single specimen of* Pyrus salicifolia, *the Willow Leafed Pear, stands out against the clipped yew hedge which defines the space, competing with the statue for attention beside a simple circular pool; an effective composition at Knightshayes Court, Devon.*

A working plan based on the preceding bubble diagrams.

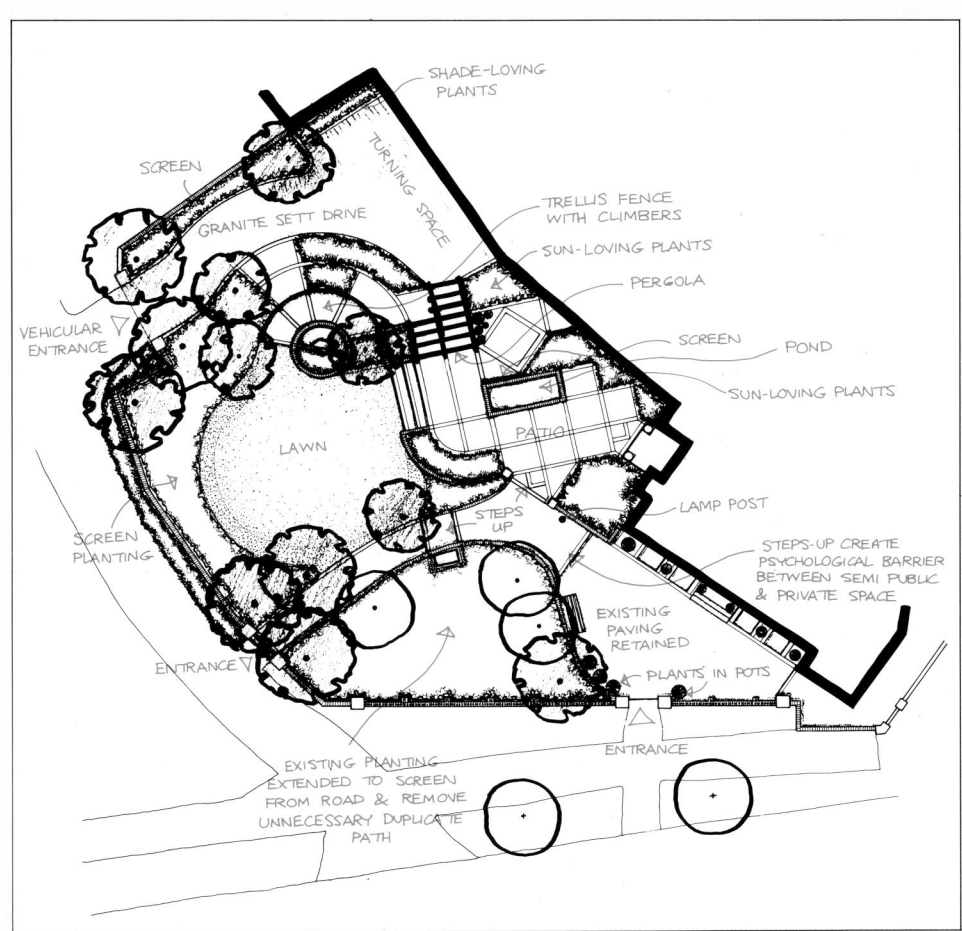

Left *The angularity of the wooden pergola, garden seat, stone walls and paving contrasts with the soft outlines of shrubs, climbers and sprawling plants to produce a moderately formal but inviting effect. In contrast, the plantings (**below**) have been aimed at producing informality and ease of maintenance with shrubs, ferns, perennials and bamboo, whose outlines are blurred so they seem to merge together.*

Gravel or grass, on the other hand, can "flow" into freer shapes. The trim or curb that limits these elements can be of more flexible materials such as timber or metal.

Unless the design is for a totally enclosed space, the visualization should always include the broader landscape beyond the garden and there should be continual cross-reference between plan and eye level views.

Only when a line has been provisionally located on the plan or in a sketch in response to function and material is the designer free to introduce his or her own feelings into the concept, though without the essential ingredients of imagination and artistry the result will be unsightly and sterile.

Unity in design

Unity is the first principle of garden design, a oneness which results from singleness of thought and singleness of purpose. Clarity of concept is the basis of unity and results in truth of expression. "Design with beauty and build with truth" is the motto of the Architectural Association in London and what applies to architecture and the other arts applies equally to the garden. There are, however, factors in the quest for garden unity which do not apply to other arts.

To some extent all natural landscapes possess unity. It is imposed by the ecological determinants of climate, soil and animal activities which evolve natural communities of plants, sculpt the landform and, if uninterrupted, result in a climax vegetation such as the northern temperate forests. A garden, strongly influenced by soil and climate conditions which limit its plant content, may also achieve a sense of unity and the closer to the natural landscape

Rosemary Verey's laburnum walk at Barnsley House, Gloucestershire, England.

There is a natural unity in nature created by limited plant material and a restricted range of colors as in this natural glade of ferns and foxgloves.

the design the more easily unity is achieved. However, few gardeners are content to allow nature to control their activities and the moment we begin to tamper with the natural scene we must adopt design methods to achieve unity.

The establishment of a dominant is one way to impose unity. In most gardens the house is the dominant feature which ties the composition together, though this is not necessarily the case. At Stourhead, for example, it is the broad sheet of water of the lake that dominates and ties together the other elements; at the Villa d'Este it is the ever-present water itself. In the smaller modern garden, where the house may not be surrounded by land but is only a vantage point from which the garden is viewed, there is a need for a dominant element within the plot. In the various compartments of the larger garden there is also the need for sub-dominants for each smaller enclosure within it.

Dominants may be ornaments, sculpture, pots, structures such as small buildings or shelters, natural features, rocks, water sources, trees or plants that make a larger impact than

their fellows either through form or color. However, a dominant alone might prove inadequate if other principles for achieving unity are ignored.

The manipulation of the landform is itself a tool for achieving unity. In the formal garden it is essential that the land is not just regularly and symmetrically divided but that these divisions are level planes that demonstrate a conscious intention to regulate nature and impose a geometric discipline. Similarly, if the landform is of sweeping natural contours, precisely engineered interruptions in the ground plane may destroy unity by their incongruity — as demonstrated by many a badly planned tennis court on sloping ground.

The use of geometry, particularly of right angles and plan rectangles at right angles to each other, has long been a way of achieving unity in both architecture and gardens. This may be made more powerful by the adoption of a module, a series of standard measures which relate each space or element to another, each becoming part of a grid which impresses a strong logic on the design.

Above *An evergreen-covered pergola at the Rookery, Streatham, in a London park, creates year-round shade in contrast to the open space beyond. On sunny days the movement from any shady path into a brightly lit area adds interest and variety, and moving from light into shaded cover provides an element of mystery and adventure.*

Top *After the shade of the bosquet paths the open space around the Bassin de Bacchus at Versailles seems dazzlingly bright. Such contrasts can be created on a large or small scale by dense planting.*

Left *The tower is the dominant feature over all the gardens at Sissinghurst, created by Vita Sackville-West. Their geometry relates to its presence and it is visible from each separate enclosure.*

Far left *A sense of scale is essential in a garden. A statue in a glade at Champs is well attuned to the size of the space that contains it and the path that approaches the glade.*

Left *The pool and its fountain dominate the white garden at Kiftsgate. In a centralized design a raised element at the axis will inevitably catch the eye. When there is a large paved or turfed central area the single plane itself becomes the dominant.*

Opposite *The trunk of a clipped evergreen forms the focal point of a path between herbaceous borders whose plants are stepped back in height to allow all to be seen without the taller subjects masking their smaller companions.*

The repetition of particular features will also create unity. If the repetition is also at regular distances it will also add rhythm to the garden. The simplest and most frequent example of rhythm in the garden is the avenue but it is also apparent in fencing, balustrades and ground patterns.

Unity is often achieved by simplification, either in the total form of the garden or in the limitation of materials. One paving material throughout, or even the same material used for paving, walls and ornament immediately links all parts of the garden. This limitation can also be applied to plants, a garden devoted to roses or to rhododendrons, for instance, can use the simple restriction of species to achieve the desired effect.

Above *At Lytes Cary, Somerset, topiary shaped to echo the roof beyond add to the unity created by a formal avenue.*

Center left *In this garden in Hampshire, England, not only gates and gateposts but obelisks and the trimming of the box trees all carry the upward forms of the house gables, windows and gable panels, a continuation of a motif which inexorably links house and garden.*

Left *The repetition of the same plant, here a pink astilbe, at different distances creates continuity, as does the repetition of the white treillage arches.*

1

2

3

4

5

1 *The symmetry of a formal pool in Filoli Garden, California, is repeated by the planting and paving that surrounds it.*

2 *A precise geometric handling of the ground plan creates strong lines and angles at Dartington Hall, Devon, broken by the irregularity of the tree and its shadow in striking contrast to the man-made order.*

3 *Land forms that slope away from the eye can strengthen a vista but a slope across the view is disturbing, as here in the formal gardens at Sceaux, where the balance is broken by the uneven cross slopes.*

4 *Used deliberately, as in the crazy tilting of the ground around the Fontana di Pegaso at Bomarzo, unbalanced planes can be exciting and disturbing, suggesting a volcanic upheaval or some divine intervention in this extraordinary fantasy garden.*

5 *In the Japanese designer Noguchi's garden at UNESCO's Paris headquarters the line that defines the granite setts provides an interesting shape in both plan and elevation.*

Above right *Brazilian Burle Marx's garden at UNESCO in Paris uses a composition of carefully drawn curves, emphasized by different colors and textures. The vertical emphasis of the sculpture contrasts with the recumbent tracery of the foreground tree.*

Below right *Red makes objects appear closer and defines shapes very clearly in the landscape, whether in planting or structural features. The painting of the bridge in the Japanese garden at Fanhams Hall, Ware, draws it to the attention and adds a dash of color to the tranquil landscape.*

Following pages *At Nooroo Nursery, Mount Wilson, Australia, the balancing masses of fall color are accentuated by the dark green underplanting and the white pavilion beyond.*

Ground modeling

A design cannot simply be imposed on existing contours. It must evolve from the landforms that are present, or changes made to the land itself. Ground modeling will be limited by resources of manpower or machine and by the kind of material being worked: each soil type has a natural angle of repose beyond which slopes cannot be contemplated. It may follow architectural lines, with level planes, slopes and geometric forms, producing clearly man-made terraces and banks which are often only achievable by building retaining walls. Alternatively it may use flowing contours and curving slopes to blend in with the original contours and produce a natural look.

Altering the shape of the land is a form of sculpture and will sometimes be considered for aesthetic purposes — manipulating levels to create special effects, channel water or produce exciting landshapes — but reasons for earth moving are usually more mundane: the need to create a level plane to set a building on, accommodate a pool or playing area, to create paths or drives level enough for comfortable passage.

Earth moving is expensive and can be harmful, interrupting or damaging drainage patterns and underground services, causing loss of topsoil, affecting vegetation and wildlife, with the possibility of an unsightly result. On the other hand, even minor changes of level, particularly in a small garden, can produce exciting effects. Shrubs which otherwise might be below eye level, if planted upon a low bank will be capable of screening, allowing an otherwise impossible containment of space. Small-scale terracing or sunken areas can add considerable interest and divide areas without erecting visual barriers.

Color

In many famous gardens the architectural organization of space or the modulation of planes and textures command more attention than color, the addition of which would be intrusive, but color can often make an important contribution. Blossoms provide the brightest and most striking hues but are transitory and unreliable. They are not the only medium for color. The built elements of the garden have more muted colors but provide the background against which the more showy flowers will be set and have to be lived with throughout the garden's life span.

Generally it is wise to choose paving which contains an earthy base color that will complement rather than contrast with plant colors but, in climates where a limited plant palette is available and where the plants are themselves muted by strong sunlight, paved surfaces can become a major source of color with elaborate patterns in brick or tiles. Vertical surfaces are more prominent than those beneath the feet and can often be treated as an ornamental element within the garden. If not decorated with the representational colors of a mural they can be given a strong color, pattern or texture to transform a functional barrier into a decorative feature. Greater harmony can be achieved if the same material is used for both ground surface and vertical planes, so that both retaining and free-standing walls seem to grow out of paving rather than constitute a separate element.

When, as in many gardens, plants are grown upon walls, fences and barriers the vertical surface should make an unobtrusive background against which flowers and foliage can be seen at their best. Most gardeners inherit walls, rather than specify them, and the process is reversed: plants must then be chosen to harmonize with the brick or stone. In such a case even the dullest-seeming wall should be carefully assessed as a background, for what appears to be a muted yellow or red may stand out with unfortunate vigor against an ill-chosen plant, and the difference in color when either wet and dry should also be observed and taken into account.

Gates and other apertures in walls or fences are suitable subjects for strong color, emphasizing their presence and function. Color in garden furniture and ornament can also be used to give them emphasis but their color relationship within the whole composition, particularly to plant colors, must not be treated lightly.

Some of the horizontal and vertical planes formed by plants themselves, especially lawns and hedges, are a softer alternative to paving and walls, with less control over their color. Green is so universal that many gardeners scarcely consider the background of lawns and hedges to have a color, but effective compositions can be made in green alone, particularly by the use of hedges of different species. In them, the color is in the foliage and will be affected by clipping and the resulting texture.

All plants have foliage color, usually more permanent than the blossom and sometimes as striking and memorable, with a continuity to be relied upon throughout a large part of the year. The "artificiality" of leaf color in some species makes them difficult to handle in garden design. The knowledge that many leaf variegations are the result of viral infection leads to the feeling that the plant is sick, making the original plain green form a preferable choice, but the choice of a variegated sage would be much less controversial than that of a large variegated acer, whose distinctive coloration might extend into a wider land-

Warm colors advance and cool colors recede as in this planting of grape hyacinths, tulips and narcissus in a formal arrangement within a natural woodland setting at Keukenhof in the Netherlands.

Often plants of closely related species, such as these blue and white hydrangeas, will associate well in form and color.

scape where its presence would be alien and unwelcome.

Plant color is ephemeral. Certain base colors are always present in hard materials, varied only by climatic conditions, but the colors in all parts of a plant alter from season to season, from day to day and even from hour to hour as conditions change and a plant grows and ages. What may seem a satisfactory association at one season may become an unfortunate combination at another and, as flowering times can also vary from year to year, even a planned color association may fail to occur if the plants do not produce their flowers together.

There are so many potential colors, even within a single plant or part of a plant; mixing them would seem a task for an expert with a knowledge of color theory — and remember that it is not only colors but forms and textures which must be related to each other. Most people are aware of an emotional response to colors: reds and yellows seem warm and cheering, soft blues cool and mauves soothing, orange exciting, white peaceful yet lively and green quiet and relaxing.

The appreciation and therefore the use of color is very individual, subject to all kinds of prejudices both personal and social, affected by

Some basic points on color

* Reds and yellows, associated in the mind with fire and sunlight, are warm colors. Blues and white, associated with water and moonlight, are cool colors.
* Warm colors appear closer than cool colors, which recede from the eye. Depth can be given to color compositions by gradation from warmth to coolness.
* Warm colors will seem to be warmer and brighter if surrounded by cool colors and vice versa.
* Colors have different intensity according to the light. In strong sunlight, especially in hot climates, colors are bleached and only appear at their best at dawn or dusk. Paler colors, even in cloudy atmospheres, are best in shade and can seem to shine with a light of their own.
* In daylight the intensity of pure colors may also seem to increase or decrease according to their distance from the observer.

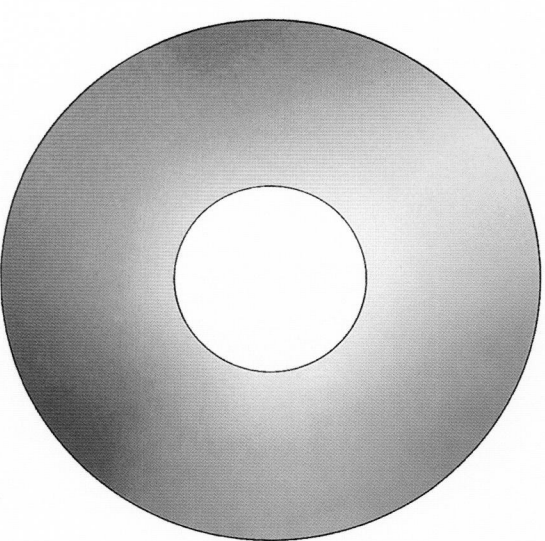

It helps to be acquainted with the layout of the color wheel. Harmony results from adjacent colors in the wheel's sequence and contrast from color on the opposite rim.

* Plant color is transmitted through the form and texture of the plant and unlike the painter, the gardener cannot change its form.

Left *In a delightfully subtle planting in the Sissinghurst herb garden the flush of blue in the petals of the Opium Poppy (*Papaver sommiferum*) links with the color of the Borage (*Borage officinalis*) which is planted behind it.*

changing fashion and taste even in the garden and one's views may change with time. In garden design, detailed observation of plants and their relationship to one another is of greater value than any color theory.

Study the color effects of plant association in other gardens. Note the striking and previously unconsidered relationships between quite common and ordinary plants which can often be seen in small suburban or country gardens which are not found in grander, more publicized places. Written notes at the time help increase awareness. Photographs can be helpful too, but should be treated with caution for the camera often fails to record the true colors of the garden. Even pick samples of foliage or flowers (with permission of course) and carry

them home to consider their possible inclusion within your own garden.

Color arrangements involving only one or two colors are the easiest to plan and can be very successful. The simplest, and often the most effective approach, is to highlight a single color against a dark background, allowing less chance of an unfortunate color contrast.

Using only one color in a border, or even a whole garden, demands more forethought because of the variation in hues, but few gardeners are content to so limit their horticultural palette and a riot of color is more often the aim. To be effective this needs careful planning. Learn from one year's flowering and reorganize the plants for a better display the next.

1 *Red* Crocosmia *and blue* Aconitum *shows an extreme contrast between warm and cool colors, each emphasizing the opposite quality of the other.*

2 *Blue agapanthus and white galtonia together create an icy coolness.*

3 *Blue and gray planting matches the stone of William Robinson's Gravetye Manor.*

4 *Some gardeners prefer a riot of strong color.*

5 *A white theme is strengthened through plants and furniture to give a strong sense of unity. Single color gardens can be very effective.*

6 *A similarity in form between the flowers of* Anemone japonica *and the florets of* Hydrangea petiolaris *aid the association already established by their colors.*

Left *Spikes of* Verbascum *make vivid strokes of yellow against the pink red background of* Alstroemeria ligtu *hybrids.*

1

4

5

2

3

6

Left *Bold masses of primary colors in distinct plantings of equal strength show a very positive way of handling color in the long border at Great Dixter.*

Opposite *The use of one plant in an uncompromisingly "natural" dominance can be a bold design decision but the effect can be breathtaking. Above is* Scilla messenaica *and below* Narcissus bulbocodium.

Left *The warm color of* Kochia scoparia *is intensified by the cool silver-gray of the Senecio at its base.*

Linking the colors of one plant with those of another makes for harmony, whether the color is present in two sets of flowers or matched between flowers in one and foliage or stems in another.

Plants with similar habits allow an easy gradation of color. Those with different forms give greater contrast. Color relationships in beds and herbaceous borders are usually carefully considered but those between widely differing plant forms are often overlooked. They may be just as rewarding, however. A carpet of blue Forget-me-not (*Myosotis*) beneath the opening foliage of a copper beech matches ankle-high plants to a tree far above them but can be as satisfying as any border arrangement.

Such color effects may last only a few weeks and it is best to have a distinct time break between color periods before another grouping comes into its own. Ideally, they should be arranged to give a season by season color succession.

If a garden view opens to include its surroundings, landscape or townscape, the effect of colors beyond it must be borne in mind and the impact of the garden in relation to it considered. Unnatural colors within a natural landscape may be interesting and effective but detrimental to the wider scene.

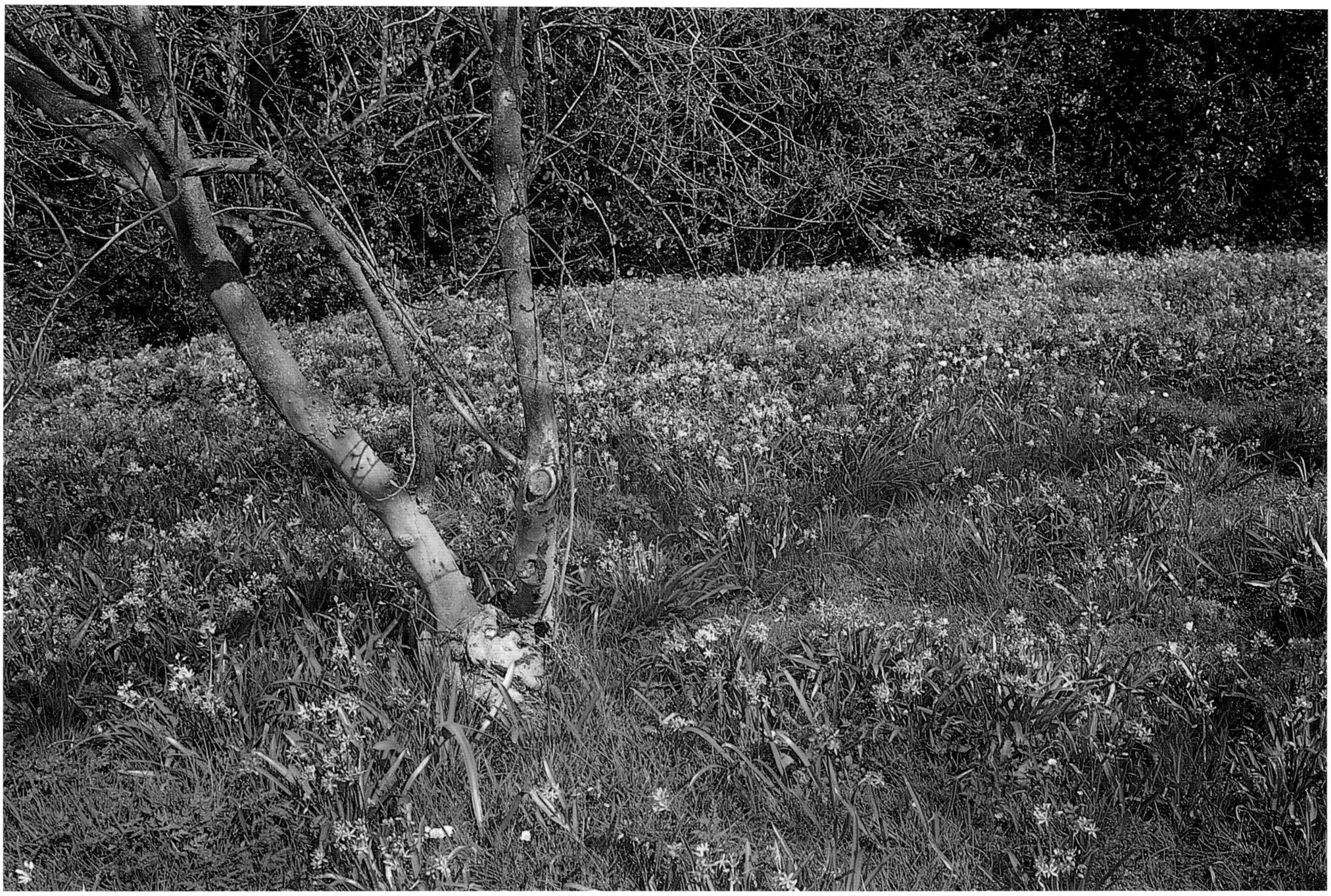

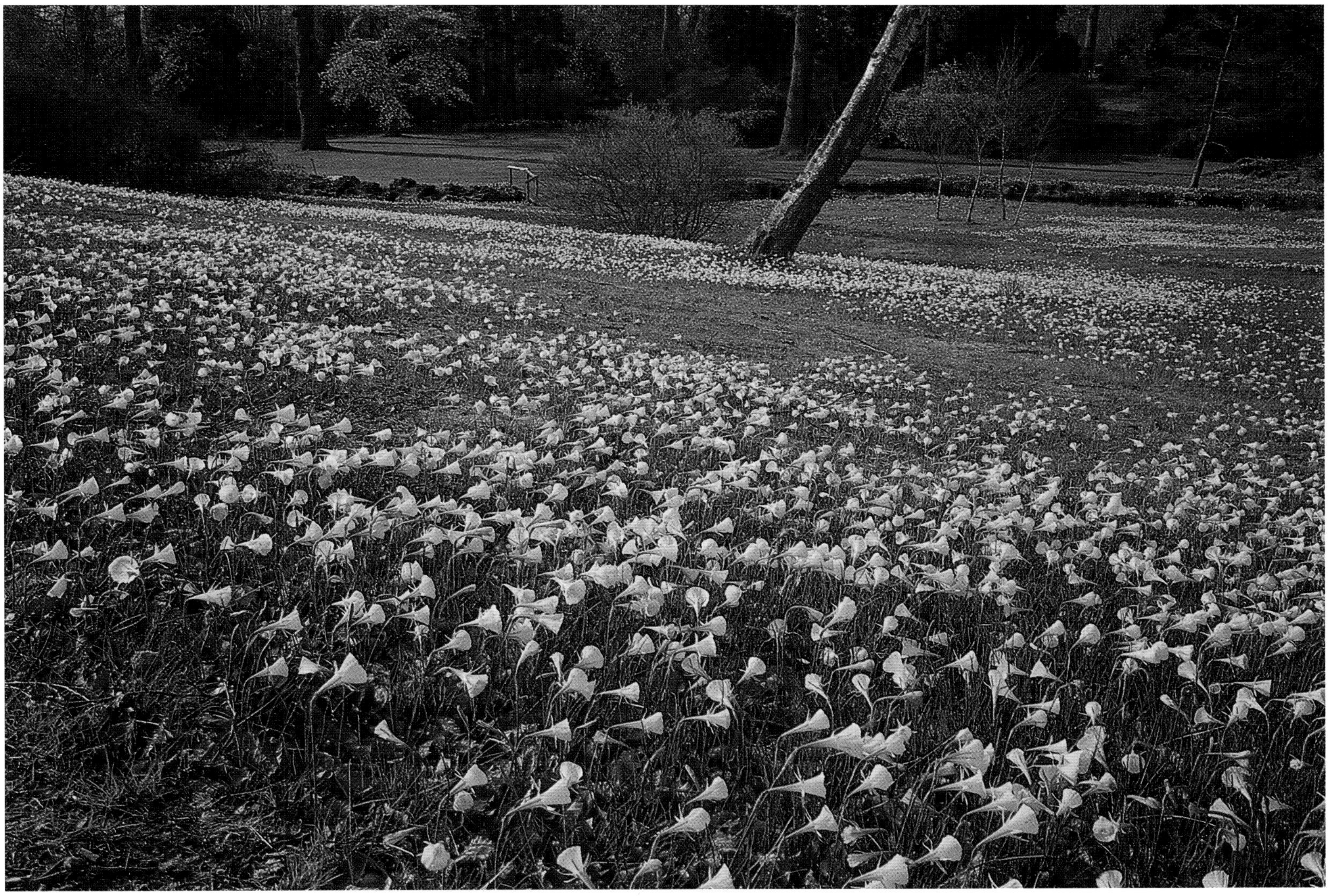

1

2　　　　　　　　　　　　　　　　　　　3

Texture

All surfaces have texture and identical materials can be given totally different characteristics by their surface treatment. Concrete, in particular, lends itself to the introduction of texture to the finish.

Ideally, it is not only a matter of touch, for it can also be seen, the eye interpreting not merely a patterning on the surface but its "feel," as in the surface of a clipped hedge, a gnarled trunk or a mossy clump. The sensing of texture through the soles of the feet can be useful. Coarse, uncomfortable textures can be used to deter access, directing pedestrians to finer-textured walking surfaces, a springy lawn being the most pleasant experience of all.

Visual experience of texture is heightened by contrast, by the juxtaposition of coarse and fine, both in plants and hard surfaces.

Texture in plants is not just a matter of leaf form and surface and bark; the arrangements of the inflorescence and all parts of the plant have textural significance.

Pattern in plants

Plant color and texture can both be used to create pattern in bedding, topiary and elaborate parterre, but the replanting of annuals, trimming or dividing of growth or replacement of casualties, requires a considerable amount of work.

1 *Three plants of different color and type still achieve harmony through similarity of texture:* Erinacea anthyllis *(left),* Alyssum saxatile *(right) and a* Hebe *cultivar (rear).*

2 *A broad-leaved hosta makes a textural contrast with the delicate serrated foliage of ferns.*

3 *The green foliage of* Santolina *harmonizes with the similarly fine texture of the buds of the* Sedum spectabile.

Three surfaces at Het Loo offer a gradation of texture: soft green grass and two sizes of setts which provide a clear distinction between a footpath and a carriageway.

Right *In this contemporary form of broderie the pattern is created from low-growing plants of similar form and texture winding over gravel:* Teucrium chamaedrys, Berberis thunbergii *"Crimson Pygmy" and* Santolina chamaecyparissus *"nana."*

Form

For a garden, as with all the arts, it is the comprehension of its total form which gives a true understanding of the creator's intentions, but so completely can the beauty of individual plants (and especially flowers) beguile the senses that its main themes may often be completely ignored. Important though flowers are, their presence in design or appreciation of a garden should never override the entirety or the garden is in danger of becoming merely a collection of plants.

The totality of a garden is, perhaps, harder to comprehend than any other art form. Its size and complex layout often baffle visitors. Even though the main vista, the major theme, is usually apparent from some vantage point, a garden is gradually revealed as the visitor wanders from one part to another. In some large gardens, even after several visits and studying a plan, visitors may still be deceived and lose their way and, in part, this deception contributes to their delight. Smaller gardens may also practice this deceit, for concealment and surprise have ever been essential ingredients in successful garden design.

Above *A simple arrangement of stone, wood, ceramic, gravel and plant textures is very effective and ideal for a roof garden where there is no depth of soil.*

Left *Palm fronds at first conceal, then on approach reveal a small pool with a carved stone lotus.*

Right *In this small Dutch garden a clipped low table of box creates an interesting plane of green texture.*

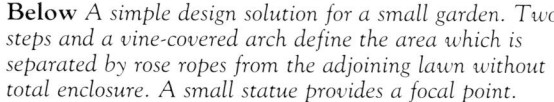

Below *A simple design solution for a small garden. Two steps and a vine-covered arch define the area which is separated by rose ropes from the adjoining lawn without total enclosure. A small statue provides a focal point.*

Choosing plants

Choosing plants for the garden must begin with discovering which plants will grow successfully in the conditions imposed by the site. Suitable species should not only tolerate but positively thrive in their intended position, so their reactions to soil and microclimate must be foreseen. Potential growth and spread must match the scale required; although many species can be trimmed back if they get too large, it is difficult to speed up growth.

The original survey will have defined the conditions and most good books on plants will list their needs. Many nursery catalogs also helpfully provide lists of plants which will prosper in adverse conditions. From those which suit each location the selection can then move on to choose, according to a plant's ability to form a clipped hedge, climb, develop dense ground cover, make a colorful accent point or whatever function will be required of it. Plants must match the character of the space where they are used. Those with bold, exotic forms, such as *Fatsia japonica*, may lend a subtropical air to gardens in temperate climates but will be out of place in a garden aiming to have a wholly "English" or "French" ambience. Bamboos will suggest an oriental flavor and may seem unsuitable in a garden of otherwise western character. Hybrids and varieties resulting from human intervention seldom look right in a "natural" garden and should be restricted to a more contrived garden closer to the house.

The character suggested by a plant does not only apply to its appearance. Its country of origin, date of introduction or the way it has been used in the past may all influence its suitability, not only when planning a garden in a particular period style but because such associations color the response of people who know about them.

When these criteria have been met the designer can indulge in personal taste, which is formed partly by past

Above left *Simple steps of roughly laid stone allow a variety of colorful plants to soften their treads while the bold form of a* Euphorbia *catches the eye above.*

Left *In hot dry climates the exciting forms of cacti and succulents give bold architectural emphasis to borders. Potted flowers define the landing on the steps.*

experience of plants and memories of other gardens, but will mainly be a reaction to shape, texture and color. Then, in placing one plant against another, the effects of differing textures and colors must be foreseen and harmonies and contrasts explored.

Relationships of scale, the creation of an accent or a focal point, the repetition of a plant or group of plants to create a link between parts of the garden and to lead the eye from one point in the garden to another are all to be considered.

A section of the planting plan for the borders of a serpentine path in the Lanning Roper Memorial Garden in London, and the borders as planted. The view is from the path at the right edge of the plan. The designer's precise instructions were not always followed, as some plants were unavailable.

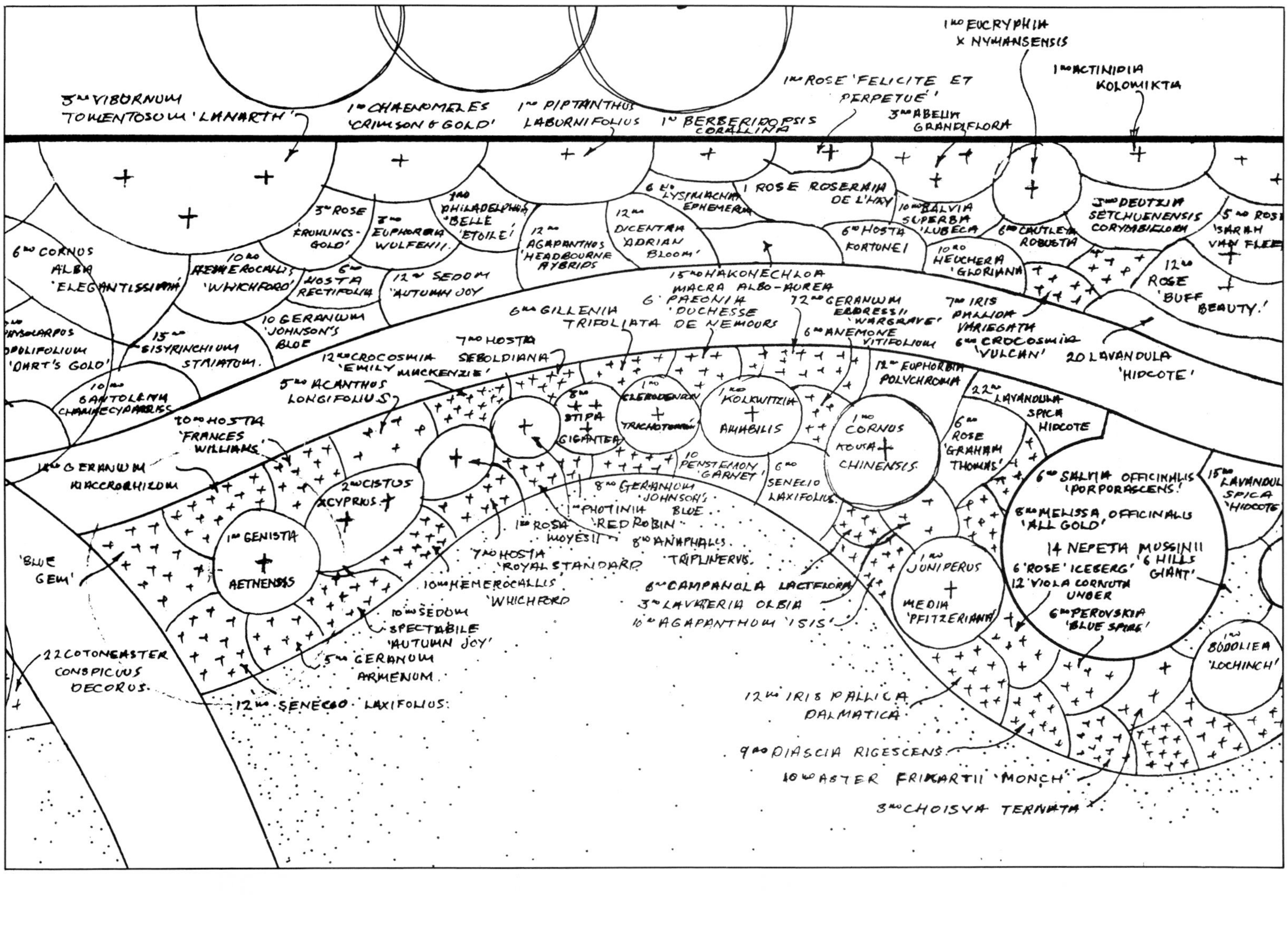

Water features

Water can be used in the garden, as an activity area, as a reflective surface or in fountains, cascades and other moving elements as an aural addition to the atmosphere and a cooling element in warm climates.

Pools and fountains do not have to be large to be effective. A miniature pond in a barrel or ceramic bowl, or a tiny pool in a hollow among rocks beside a path, will capture reflections and the sparkle of sunshine, adding interest and mystery.

If you use a half barrel as a pond it will lose water until the timber has swollen enough to make it watertight, so will need topping up at first. Buried in the ground, it will last quite a few years. Today there are also ready-made shapes in fiberglass and thick plastics which can be used both as single ponds and small ponds as stages for a cascade. These are usually comparatively shallow. A pond can also be made with a sheet of heavy-duty plastic laid in a pre-dug hollow, or in a cavity between built walls. A lining of sand will provide a soft support. The edges of the plastic are dropped over the wall or over rocks around the pond edge and then weighted down with rocks or a layer of paving stones and soil around the outer edge. This effectively keeps it in position and hides the artificial edge of the pond. Plastic will stand up to normal wear and tear for many years but will not survive puncture with sharp instruments, although patches can be repaired.

In areas of heavy clay, the traditional method of pond-making is simply to scoop out the hollow and then to "puddle" the surface of the damp clay to form a polished-looking outer layer which is relatively impervious. This is the most natural of all ponds and allows the best build up of wildlife, although it will be the most difficult kind of pond to clean out should it prove necessary. Puddling clay with straw under pressure until the mixture becomes watertight can be a messy business. A modern alternative is a coating of bentonite clay — natural sodium bentonite, an inert, nontoxic volcanic clay from Wyoming which expands on contact with water to seal leaks.

An alternative is to line the hole with hardcore and pour in a surface of concrete which must then be compacted and smoothed into position.

If it is possible to drain off the pond to a lower level then it is wise to put in a drain and fit it with a suitable plug which can be removed when the pond needs cleaning. A low-lying pond will usually be easier to empty with a pump when necessary. Larger ponds and lakes develop a better ecological balance and stay fresh, though if they attract a heavy deposit of leaves and other debris, dredging may be advisable every few years.

Installing a pump to operate a cascade or a fountain and circulate the water will aerate it and keep it fresh. Filters may also be needed and care should be taken not to import blanket weed and other organisms which could clog the pump.

Swimming pools

Swimming pools may be made of concrete, tiled or plastic-lined. They will require filtration and in temperate climates will often be heated to extend their use into the cooler months. Today sophisticated devices are available to make construction and maintenance easier. Fiberglass pools can be lowered into place, vinyl liners can be supported on frames, and concrete can also be used, often sprayed over metal reinforcement. If the water is heated — and especially if you use a small pool as a spa — make provision for a pool cover to retain that heat. Even without heating they can keep the water warmer and extend the swimming season.

While an ornamental pond can be constructed by the amateur, it is wiser to engage professionals to install a swimming pool. Pool shape and size must be matched to use. If you want a pool for exercise and lap-swimming you must have sufficient depth for end turns and a length that allows for a reasonable stroke rhythm to be developed. For a multi-purpose pool a size of at least 12 x 32 ft (3.5 x 7 m) is recommended.

A pool approaching this size will be a very dominant feature in a small garden. Before deciding on a shape, mark out the outline with a garden hose and see how it looks from the house and other parts of the garden. The simpler its shape and the more closely it reflects the surrounding forms the less overpowering it will be. Careful planning of the decking, paving and planting areas can make it a natural element rather than an intrusion.

Under British skies a blue-painted pool can look cold and alien on dull days. Black-painted concrete will give a more natural look and greater reflective quality, and make it a year-round feature.

Siting pools and ponds

Aesthetic considerations are not the only aspects of siting a pool. In a very large garden it is possible to place it at a distance with its own pool house, but it will generally be convenient to allow for easy access changing rooms while ensuring that when pumps and other equipment are in operation they are not disruptive. A position in the sun, aligned to face its path and absorb as much heat as possible, will reduce both fuel costs and algal growth. Try to keep pools away from trees; leaf removal can be a nuisance, although surrounding walls or hedges will improve the microclimate by providing shelter from winds.

Formal ornamental pools in which you want the water to be clear should also be sited in sun and away from trees, but if you do not mind a naturally dark and muddy pond, then leaf fall

Making a pool

Concrete is the best material with which to construct a long-lasting pool of a size and depth to suit the design and location, rather than accepting a predetermined plastic pool shape.

At least 6 in (15 cm) is recommended for base and walls in 1:2:3 mix concrete. Reinforcing wire can be used in the concrete if the stability of the ground is in question. Once the hole has been excavated for the pool, a timber framework must be constructed to hold the walls while the concrete is setting. The depth within the pool should vary to suit the growing requirements of different types of aquatic plants.

New concrete has a toxic alkalinity which can affect many plants and will kill animal life, particularly fish. This problem can be overcome by allowing the water to stand for several months, and then emptying and refilling the pond before stocking it. Concrete may also be painted to isolate the alkalinity, or acid or permanganate of potash can be used to neutralize it. Black bituminous paint is an effective barrier, and produces a natural color effect.

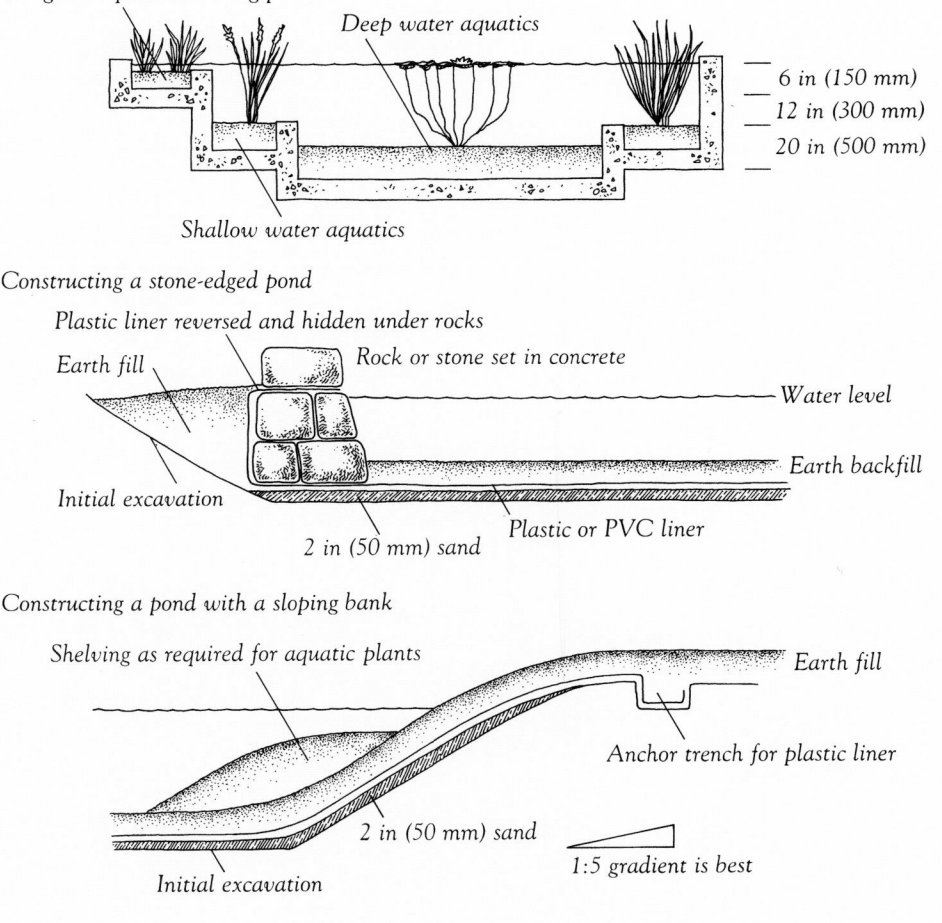

Marginal aquatics and bog plants

Deep water aquatics

6 in (150 mm)
12 in (300 mm)
20 in (500 mm)

Shallow water aquatics

Constructing a stone-edged pond

Plastic liner reversed and hidden under rocks

Earth fill

Rock or stone set in concrete

Water level

Earth backfill

Initial excavation

2 in (50 mm) sand

Plastic or PVC liner

Constructing a pond with a sloping bank

Shelving as required for aquatic plants

Earth fill

Anchor trench for plastic liner

2 in (50 mm) sand

Initial excavation

1:5 gradient is best

A formal pool which dominates the space around it but is balanced by the scale of the tree beyond.

Far left The angled paving around this pool in Florence, Italy, inset with turf and plantings, links the pool area with the surrounding gardens.

Below left The smooth waters of this inviting swimming pool with its stone edging contrasts with the spiky sculptural forms of the adjoining cactus planting.

will be unimportant — provided you do not intend to introduce fish. Fish need a well-oxygenated pond and decaying leaves on the bottom can produce toxic gases, particularly dangerous in winter when the surface may be sealed by ice. They can also smell if the bottom is disturbed, but this will not usually persist and is a small cost for a natural environment which will attract wildlife.

Planting a pond

The edges of formal ponds are best left clear and plants limited to lilies and other species which can be placed in baskets in the pond and removed when it is cleaned. An informal pond, however, will look more natural if plants come up to and overhang its edge. Building a shelf in the pool itself, or placing planters on bricks, will make it possible to raise plants which need to be kept slightly above the water level. Different species like different levels for their roots and supports can be placed to match their needs. Oxygenating plants can be planted on the bottom of the pond.

J. M.

GARDEN ORNAMENT AND FURNITURE

Decorative material and colors

rnament should not be mere decoration but should support and reinforce the design of a garden or it will detract from, rather than add to, the overall effect. Forms and materials should be carefully chosen in relation to the other elements of the garden.

What seems the most natural of ornamental materials? Wood was used in pergolas by the ancient Egyptians. The Chinese loved rock, representing *yang*, the masculine element, and built false mountains (*jai shan*) or used a sculpture-like individual piece (*shi feng*) probably just as long ago. The Chinese have the oldest continuous tradition of gardening and the element of water (the feminine *yin* to balance *yang*) is perhaps one of the earliest features, though the Chinese have a quite

Above and right *A row of lidded urns at Wakehurst Place, the country arm of the Kew Royal Botanic Gardens.*

A rose arbor and statuary at Waddesdon Manor.

different concept of decoration from that of western tradition. As new materials were made — brick, and metals such as cast iron and lead — these too came, through continued usage, to seem "natural" in the garden.

Ornament was applied to these "natural" materials, such as carving on the upright pillars of the pergola, and the classic borders on the stone columns of the Greeks. Aging would be a development originally rejected, but later accepted as the gardener began to prefer his ornament to look old, to be antique. Now we have "antiquing," the application of chemicals to speed up the aging process. Many modern bricks, for example, look raw and crude in a garden, so specially-fired types will be sought after or genuinely old bricks re-used to give the desired effect of age. Painting the bricks is an alternative, not so much for protection as to hide their over-smooth texture or crass coloring. Where there is pollution, the aging of bricks can be accelerated by painting them with sour milk or yoghurt.

Taste in color schemes varies. For centuries white was used everywhere, but is now sometimes replaced by shades of green, blue and brown, which perhaps better match the brown, green and orange lichen which give the patina of age to an ordinary stone.

Today, to some extent, "natural" materials are being replaced by plastic because the best wood for furniture comes from the Far East and is in increasingly short supply: its high cost dictates the substitution of cheaper, less durable and rather unsatisfactory softwoods or by plastics of various kinds which can be used to simulate material ranging from wood to bronze. Today many sculptors work in resin-based materials which can be indistinguishable from the bronze, stone, terracotta and other materials they represent. Their sculptures, if expertly made, appear to have a long life and to age like "natural" materials, although experience with them is still limited. Museums are gradually changing to resin-based reproductions because,

"Pope's Urn." This swirling-fluted design was created by William Kent.

Coade stone

In 1769 George and Eleanor Coade bought a London factory which made terracotta-based artificial stone. Although George died within a year Eleanor and her daughter added other ingredients to the mix and created an unmatched weatherproof material, less easily eroded than natural stone. Using only the best artists to model their figures and decorations they established a very successful business. The daughter died in 1821 and the factory closed in 1840, the secret recipe unrevealed and lost. Coade stone was used on many famous buildings as well as for garden ornaments.

A Coade stone pedestal.

although more expensive than the traditional plaster, they will withstand weather, which plaster will not.

Amateurs can now buy the materials needed to make flexible molds in which resin-based models can be cast, and metal or plaster can be introduced into a hollow cast to give it the weight which resin-based sculpture lacks. Such molds can also be used to cast sculpture in concrete and similar materials, although they will not have the precision and delicacy of resin and may not be frostproof.

Earlier "fake" materials have acquired respectability — and brick, cast iron or artificial stone are basically just as fake as plastic. Take for example the glamor which is now attached to Coade stone, once a cheap form of reproduction but now a collector's item. The Coade-ware firm was closed in 1840 and its secret formula lost but there have been many other artificial stones, including Ransome's Siliceous Stone and Pulhamite, used to make fake rocks, piled into "natural" outcrops.

Containers

Pots and other containers are often the most convenient way of planting for roof gardens, patios and some small urban areas. In arid climates they can make it much easier to ensure the survival of plants that need frequent watering, and they fulfilled a special need when plants imported from warmer lands had to be moved from the open garden and placed under cover in winter. Pots have been used for propagation as well as ornament since ancient Greek times.

For centuries the most popular material was terracotta. The oldest plant containers may have been the two-handled amphorae used to carry wine and oil; they may also have been used to ship rose plants from Egypt to rose-loving Rome, which could not have enough of their petals for the sensuous pleasures of its ruling classes. It would be easy to convert amphorae into containers for free-growing plants or even small trees such as the oleander. Ancient amphorae look magnificent on a low pedestal, especially when plantless. The reproductions available commercially today are fat with wide necks and openings. Those exported from Crete are fired in a furnace fueled by grape seeds which perhaps gives them their attractive chalky bloom. When used locally they are painted white or green and decorated with spots, stripes and zigzags, but customers in northern Europe prefer the subtle natural pink covered with the speckles which come from the salts in the clay from which they are made.

Even earlier than pots in gardens may have been the urn used to hold the ashes of a loved one, but now universally adopted, with or without its lid, for planting. An urn is usually distinguished from a vase by the narrow waist below the container. Some of the finest have low, loop handles, originally designed for carrying the container from the funeral pyre to a place of rest. The grandest urns feature deep reliefs which make them almost sculptural.

Urns are sometimes available today in a plastic version of bronze but stone is the traditional material, or lead, popular in the seventeenth century and still in production.

The lidded urn, in whatever material, has a certain gravitas which indicates a "serious" area of the garden.

As with all such ornaments, an urn or vase can be out of scale; the usual mistake is to choose one which is too large for its site. Mistakes can be expensive so check for appropriate size by first erecting a pile of bricks or other substitute *in situ* and scaling up or down until a satisfactory proportion is reached. Use the same method to experiment with the height for plinths when mounting decorative objects. A plinth should be plain if the object is highly decorated and vice versa. Avoid too much decoration. Beauty often lies in simplicity.

A classical frieze decorates this mid-nineteenth century urn illustrated in C. McIntosh's Book of the Garden *(1853). He instructed his readers never to place what he calls vases, or other ornaments, so that they appeared to rise immediately from the ground. He preferred to see them unplanted, or at worst used with acanthus, agave, euphorbia and other plants with architectural associations.*

Left *A bowl-shaped container decorated with flutes and an egg and dart border, in the gardens of Stourton House, Wiltshire.*

An urn or vase can add distinction in many places. It may look well at the top and bottom of stone steps, against a green hedge, standing alone in front of a fine view of surrounding countryside or as a finial at each end of a wall or flanking steps. The traditional finial, placed at the tip of a gable and other elevated positions, is a stone ball on a plinth, an obelisk or an extended diamond shape.

An urn on a plinth can be a focal point in a garden. Placed at the corner of a wall it can clearly mark the end of the garden or of a garden "room."

Ancient Greek and Egyptian civilizations both used terracotta pots for growing plants. Some bowl-shaped examples were excavated beside the Temple of Hephaistos in Athens, though these were possibly only used for propagation. Large Roman pots found at Pompeii had a hole in the bottom and three low on the sides, perhaps to allow roots to push through — Pliny describes pots with "breathing holes" for

roots being used for importing lemon trees — but pots were used in roof gardens and on window ledges as well as for ornamental plant containers in gardens. Both earthenware and metal pots were used in the Middle Ages and a great variety of shapes and sizes can be seen in medieval paintings and illuminations.

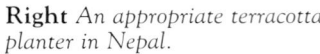

Right *An appropriate terracotta planter in Nepal.*

Below *Gilded urns, statuary and basins at Petrodvorets, Peter the Great's summer palace near Leningrad.*

Bottom *A huge terracotta pot ornaments the gardens of what was once the Queen of Romania's seaside summer residence at Balchik, Bulgaria (in an area once part of Romania).*

Wooden containers and even wattle baskets were also planted. Renaissance pots were often highly decorated but simple wooden tubs, ringed with metal like a barrel, also came into use, followed by the classic cube-shape of the Versailles tub.

In the nineteenth century terracotta and metal pots were mass-produced in a variety of designs but the familiar shapes of today became most popular. These have been copied, often very successfully, in plastic. Modern Italian and British terracotta suppliers cling to classic shapes, although individual potters have done their best to dramatize the container and have produced some elegant designs. A triangular fired-clay container displayed at the Chelsea Show a decade ago allowed individual units to be built up into a wall from which plants could trail naturally; an interesting idea but one which did not become popular. However, the past decades have seen many simple shapes for planters, sometimes self-watering, fed from an

A jardiniere with a scrolled design attributed to Gertrude Jekyll.

Below *A mixture of clay and plastic pots house a colorful display of plants inside a nunnery at Mistra, Greece.*

internal reservoir, and often designed to group together.

Probably the most successful new idea has been a plastic version of the wire hanging basket of Victorian origin. Despite their watering problems, these moss-lined containers in various shapes and sizes have found their way into private and public gardens all over the world.

Chinese gardens often featured beautiful glazed pots, frequently placed on plinths or stands, and the traditional design of the dragon pot has been widely exported in recent years, though glazed ware is not suitable for outdoor use in places with extremes of climate. In temperate regions jade green Chinese and Balinese pots are popular and in Australia containers cut from volcanic larva are considered especially effective for planting alpines, houseleeks and small bulbs.

Although simple shapes in concrete and plastic have added a new range of larger planter forms for gardens in the latter half of the twentieth century, there has been a continuing tendency to turn to the past for inspiration. Ancient artifacts, from lead water cisterns to antique stone baths and sarcophagi, have been adapted and reproduced as plant containers. Although sarcophagi are frequently already well decorated and planting may seem an added fussiness, they can look magnificent set on a low platform. Few gardeners seem to find inspiration in anything more modern than an unused wheelbarrow, firegrate, trough sink, chimney pot or haybox, and although they can be purchased new, their use has generally been a nostalgic attempt to indicate that a garden has roots in the past.

Brewery barrels sawn in half join terracotta and plastic pots as the most common and economical planters, but all kinds of containers have been pressed into use. Gasoline cans and metal boxes, brightly labeled or freshly painted,

can sometimes make a remarkably effective display, and there is virtually no garden where a container of some sort would not add charm to its design.

Seating and tables

If living in the garden is as important as gardening in it, then convenient and practical furniture is as important today as it was for Pliny the Younger, with his benches of white marble, or the Renaissance prelates with their water-cooled dining tables. But furniture can play a further role. The Countess of Rosse, one of the most talented of today's garden designers, uses seats as features which "beckon from afar." She considers it an "obvious rule that a seat should never be set anywhere that does not offer an interesting view" and, logically, seats that beckon from afar must still do so when we reach them. In placing seats to enjoy and contemplate a garden, focal points are not the only consideration. Sun or shade can be equally important and when arranging seating in a small garden, or placing a dining table, the immediate ambience may be the key.

Stone seats are most durable and the long horizontal of a stone bench draws the eye. Antique styles may have arms or backs with elaborate carving to attract attention and can be offset against a dark green hedge.

Simpler seats can be made by placing a long slab on stone balusters or brick supports. Twentieth-century architects turned from stone to concrete which, despite its failure to weather to an attractive color, was a cheaper and more durable material than wood, especially in public places for which many examples of a simple design could be mass-produced. Concrete can be softened by timber seating and in an appropriate setting such benches and matching tables can provide satisfactory dining areas.

When marble became too expensive substitute materials were used with considerable success. Wooden furniture had been almost entirely utilitarian until the eighteenth century when Thomas Chippendale designed splendid wooden pieces in the Chinese style, reproductions of which, generously wide in their seating

Left *A lead water cistern, dated 1701. Such decorative features make fine ornaments on their own even when not planted.*

1 *A stone bench set between formal topiary at Knightshayes Court, Devon.*

2 *A simple planter and a wooden bench to a German design.*

3, 4 and below *In gardens in the United States, Australia and England, respectively, all these seats show the influence of Chippendale's chinoiserie designs.*

5 *Simple blocks of stone form this arbor seat in the garden of the Spencers at York Gate.*

1

2

3

4

5

Right *Simple park, or boulevard chairs, which fold up easily, set on the paved and turfed outdoor dining room of designer Jack Lenor Larsen.*

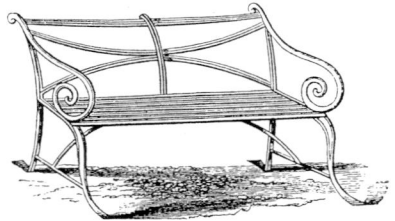

A wrought-iron bench of the mid-nineteenth century which was recommended as being lighter than cast-iron seats of similar size and easier to move about the garden.

A wrought-iron circular seat designed to take advantage of shade beneath a tree. Such seats were sometimes divided into compartments by scrolled arms.

Right *Modern seating and an arch in welded metal echo Regency and early Victorian gothic designs.*

(for they were originally intended to accommodate the fashionable hooped skirts of the eighteenth-century ladies) are still being made.

Some of Chippendale's designs simulated bamboo and these designs were later copied in metal, but real bamboo does not stand up well to either sun or rain and is liable to collapse. Even the heavier cane, although it looks attractive, does not last well. Wicker, made of any pliant wood, but usually willow, is the best of these types of furniture because, if well made, it can be comparatively strong and durable in most climates.

The best wooden furniture is made of teak which is slow to season and so continues to mature and harden as its surface weathers. It develops a pleasing light gray color which can be kept free of lichen by occasional scrubbing with a weak bleach (unlike lichen on stone seats which should be lovingly maintained). Teak comes from a single species *Tectona grandis*, a tree indigenous to south-east Asia. Though now plantation-grown to avoid robbing the natural forest, increasing demand makes it scarcer and more expensive every year.

Elegant folding seats are available, some based on the slatted seats used on the decks of ocean liners, but the simplest form of folding seat is the slatted chair of iron and wood often known from its French origins as the "boulevard," or, in English, the "park" seat. Many of the plastic seats produced today are collapsible for storage like the park seat or molded in stackable form.

Wrought iron, used for centuries as a decorative material, became a firm favorite in the nineteenth century. Blacksmiths could obtain ready-decorated strips of iron alloy and would work it into suitable shapes. The result was sometimes still short on comfort, even though allegedly shaped to the curvature of the human spine.

A variation, cast iron, also came into its own in the nineteenth century with the rustic movement. Rustic work, constructed directly from natural branches, but frequently simulated with the same forms cast in metal, became universally popular, decorating inns and public houses, railway platforms and parks as well as gardens. Its origins go back at least to 1750 when the first books were written about rustic buildings. Early in the nineteenth century it was commonplace and the style was even applied to stone. A roofed, rusticated specimen can be seen at Cirencester House; it is known as Pope's seat because the poet used to collaborate on garden planning with the estate's owner Lord Bathurst.

Iron originals are scarce but because of the elegance of their "Gothick" tracery of ferns, leaves and grapes, they have been much-copied. Alas, in the process much of this fine detail is lost.

The deck chair, originally designed for passenger liners, enjoyed a period of popularity from the 1920s to the 1950s, but since then its supremacy has been eroded by the so-called director's chair — indispensable on movie sets — and by the arrival of plastic. The deck chair

Left *Painted cast-iron furniture in a garden in South Carolina. Cast iron can carry elaborate ornamentation. Unfortunately, modern aluminum and plastic copies rarely have the strength or the fine details of the originals.*

was often complemented in the garden by a swinging seat with an awning, presumably developed from the garden swing. It has continued in popularity, although the garish colors of its cushions and awning rarely add charm to overall garden style. A recent design of teak bench, matching a teak suite, has opened up new possibilities for the swinging seat.

Plastic is also becoming a universal furniture material. It is light and, at least when of good quality, weatherproof and durable in temperate climates, though it may deteriorate badly if continually exposed to strong sun in hotter lands. The best molded furniture is equally at home indoors or out and particularly useful for balconies and roof terraces, but too few manufacturers employ designers with any flair and they are rarely imaginative with color. Over a century ago, Gertrude Jekyll pointed out that

"the common habit of painting garden seats a dead white is certainly open to criticism. The seat should not be made too conspicuous. Like all other painted things about a garden . . . the painting should suit the environment; it should in no case be so glaring as to draw almost exclusive attention to itself."

Her words have been ignored by most manufacturers, particularly those using resins, which could just as easily be produced in greens or browns. Those who produce cushions for garden use and fabrics for deck chairs and softer seating have also a great deal to answer for in the matter of garish coloring.

There is a tendency to economize on garden furniture and move it from place to place in pursuit of sun or shade. In the larger garden it is better to have a number of less expensive pieces which can be left permanently in place, particularly in temperate zones where weather is uncertain. Shelter will then almost certainly be a consideration. It can range from seating

inside the little trellis pavilions which William Kent built at Rousham to a "room" inside a dense hedge.

Another alternative is to build seating into the structure of the garden using the same materials as for retaining walls and paths. A simple bench of brick will offer a convenient perch, especially with a cushion added for comfort, but will merge into the background when not in use. Those who want to indulge nostalgia for the archaic can recreate the favorite of the medieval nobility, the turf- or chamomile-covered bench along a wall. There is a modern example in the Queen's garden at Kew, and Vita Sackville-West built a herb-covered version at Sissinghurst, although whether she ever sat on it in the damp Kent climate is not recorded.

Above *A white wooden chair to a design used by Sir Edwin Lutyens and Gertrude Jekyll in some of their garden schemes.*

Left *A hammock is perhaps the most comfortable of all ways of relaxing in the garden.*

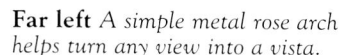

Far left *A simple metal rose arch helps turn any view into a vista.*

Left *Pillars of open laths make a strongly architectural pergola.*

Right *A simple timber pergola is given enclosure by trellis at each end.*

Below far left *Trelliswork in two different densities forms fencing and is carried over onto the gates in Deepwood Gardens, Oregon.*

Below left *Stonework piers and concrete pillars carry this wisteria-draped pergola.*

Arches, arbors and pergolas

The Italian word, *pergola*, means "a close walk of boughs," usually vines, and as the centuries have passed it has come to mean a covered walk which goes somewhere, unlike an arbor, which doesn't. Used by ancient Egyptians to support vines and allow grapes to ripen, as well as shading people working below, it was not long before its inventors were carving and painting the pillars to make them decorative. The structure itself, however, was never highly ornamental for the plants that it supported would smother it, particularly across the horizontals. Strength and stability are the design criteria.

A simple pergola is ornamental by virtue of its plantings, but designers have developed intricacies of their own, such as the trellis or treillage which the great American designer Frederick Olmsted inserted between the pillars of a pergola for his clients the Vanderbilts. Gertrude Jekyll and Lutyens were enamored of the pergola, for which they often specified pillars of local stone and beams of oak, though brick piers were also a feature of the English Edwardian garden. In her book *Garden Ornament* Gertrude Jekyll described exactly how a pergola should best be built, specifying, for example, that the beams across the piers should be slightly cambered because "the upward curve, if even quite slight, gives a satisfying look of strength."

While the pergola ought to lead somewhere, or at least lead the eye, it can be used to define an area of a garden, being cheaper to build than a wall and quicker to reach fruition than a hedge. It gives the impression of enclosure but, when we reach it, we find it is not enclosed at all, since it leads to a door or opening and another walking area. It can add an element of surprise.

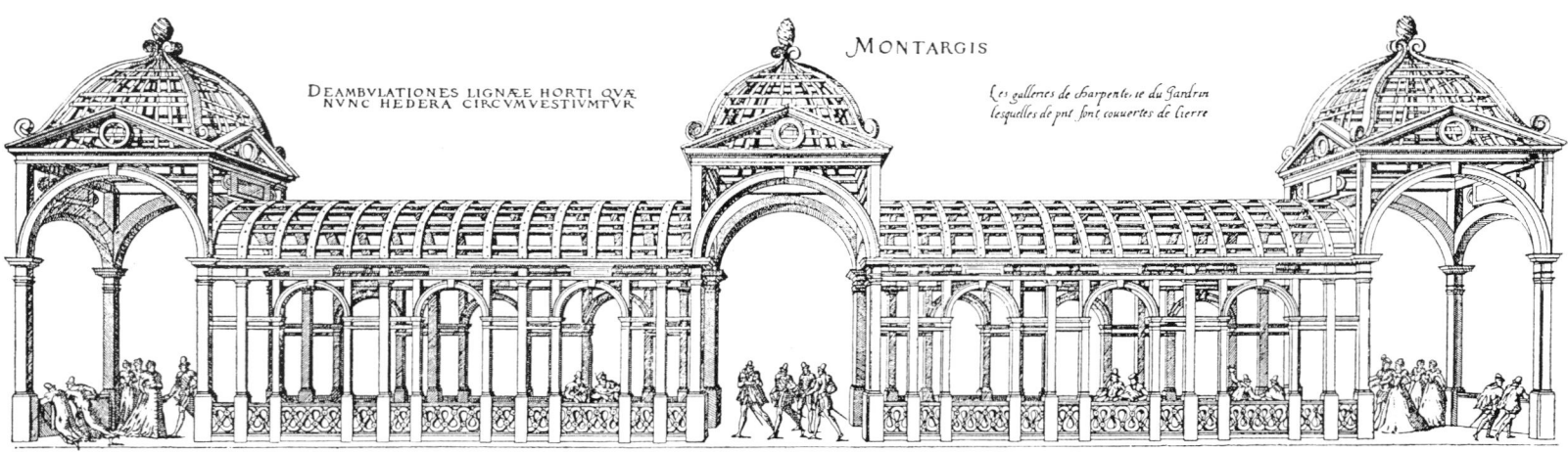

DEAMBVLATIONES LIGNÆE HORTI QVÆ
NVNC HEDERA CIRCVMVESTIVNTVR

Les galleries de charpenterie du Jardin
lesquelles de pnt sont couvertes de lierre

The "carpenter's work" designed by Jacques Androuet du Cerceau for Montargis was strongly architectural in form.

A gazebo and a tunnel in Deepwood Gardens, Oregon.

Vita Sackville-West did not much like pergolas, on the grounds that "they drip." This can hardly be helped, in climates like that of Britain, if the crossbeams are covered with foliage, and the walker may be in danger of getting a caterpillar as well as a raindrop down the neck. One solution is to create the effect of a pergola by a series of arches at intervals, rather than a continuous tunnel, if the purpose is visual rather than to provide shade and shelter. Ready-made metal arches are convenient for this and should be firmly based in concrete. The logical extension is the walk, which looks like, and is sometimes called, a tunnel.

A laburnum walk, like the one at Barnsley House, matures surprisingly quickly. At Birr Castle, in Ireland, Lady Rosse has a fine hornbeam tunnel and other imaginative gardeners have done great things with apple and other fruit trees.

The shortest form of tunnel is a simple arch. The most basic is trees joined overhead, although some kind of wooden or metal structure is usually required to give form and maintain inherent strength. Also very basic is a metal arch, like an inverted U, often seen in cottage gardens, though more stylish gothic shapes are now commercially available. In wood, arches are usually rectangular or form an inverted V.

An arch stops the roving eye, which then looks through it to see what is beyond, so the structure must "take" the viewer somewhere. Its most obvious site is at the entrance to a garden or to a garden "room" where, like the foyer of a theater, it sets the mood for what is to come. Grand arches are strictly for grand gardens and should not be used when what is beyond is simple or unpretentious, although they have sometimes been used effectively when in fact they lead nowhere.

An arch which leads nowhere can give the illusion that the garden is bigger than it is, though to pass beyond it only to find the com-

post heap and tool shed can be an anticlimax. Placing a mirror on the far side of the arch to reflect the garden is one solution.

If the arch is a scene-setter, so is the arbor. The word comes from the old French *herbier*, meaning "a place covered with grass or herbs." As early as 1418 this was being reinforced with lattice structure to make a "privie playing place." The simplest form of arbor is the shelter of a tree. Add a seat, perhaps a semicircular wooden one, and the arbor is complete. A more complex structure can be made by planting a ring of hornbeams with a curved seat at its center and in ten years the tops can be trained in to make a natural dome. Another type is made by creating a topiary arch, with a hedge behind and a seat fitted into the recess, or by cutting a gap in a yew or box hedge, with a wall or fence behind, and placing a seat in the gap. In the latter case there should also be a roof, easily constructed by placing posts outside the four corners of the seat, fitting runners across the top, and covering these with climbers such as ivy, virginia creeper, evergreen honeysuckle, clematis or roses. More complicated versions require carpentry or the use of one of the many kit sets now available which include lightweight metal sections. "Tented" arbors look particularly attractive in the center of crossing paths.

Give careful consideration to the choice of color for the structure of arbors, arches, pergolas and the like, and of the climbers which will cover the man-made bower and create a feeling of intimacy, even secrecy. Jasmine and other sweet-smelling plants will add romantic atmosphere. On the other hand, to draw attention to the structure by emphasizing the design of the canopy and its supports, a less flam-

boyant climber will be effective, and paving the area for a yard or two in front will give the arbor a "presence."

In the evening such structures can be lit internally if an electricity supply is available, or lanterns with night lights can be hung from the roof or pillar supports.

Trellis or treillage

Trellis goes back to Roman times, but it was then strictly utilitarian and its elaboration does not seem to have developed much before 1300, when it was recommended for tunnels, tents and houses as well as a plant support. The trained plant was one of the great hobbies of the gardener in the Middle Ages.

In the late sixteenth and early seventeenth centuries the French took "carpenter's work," as treillage was often known, and added inspiration. Pierre le Nôtre, grandfather of the

Treillage trompe l'oeil in the courtyard of the Savile Club, London.

Treillage obelisks and a rotunda on the Ile d'Amour at Chantilly, France.

famous André, submitted elaborate treillage designs of willow and nut poles to those judging his suitability to become a master gardener of the Paris Gardeners' Guild, and old engravings show how complex lattice structures had become and how widely they were used. At Chantilly there was a complex *Temple d'Amour*, but like most such structures of such a frail nature it has not survived, though copies of them exist, such as the simple arbors at Villandry which follow a seventeenth-century design. By the seventeenth century trellis was usually made of Spanish chestnut and painted. Early in the eighteenth century iron trellis was introduced.

Today protective finishes can give treillage a longer life. Whole sections can be bought ready-made and stained brown, green, or painted white. The subtleties of the French work can best be achieved by hand for its perspective effects are gained by cutting each of the receding lines in ever-narrowing section. French practice was to mount such trompe l'oeil effects on a wall to suggest that further vistas lay beyond. This is another occasion to use a mirror, placed behind the trellis work to reflect the garden and increase the illusion of greenery to come, a technique particularly effective in small gardens or to hide obtrusive buildings whose utility is not matched by charm.

Since the French elevated treillage to an art form many designers have followed their path, creating not only trompe l'oeil effects on walls and small buildings but also pillars and obelisks up which plants may climb.

Tents and temporary buildings

A miniature, now in the British Museum, which illustrates the work of a sixteenth-century Mogul poet, shows a prince sitting in his garden on a gilded throne surveying a circular pool. Above his head a carpet elevated on painted poles provides protection from the sun. There are not many carpets in gardens today, but much more use should be made of ornamental tents or temporary cloth arbors. An elegant decoration could be devised by running a canvas arcade from one part of a garden to another — an impermanent version of the arcades which are found in the gardens and mosques of Islam which the Muslims introduced to Spain.

The vast rectangular umbrella, originally made in Italy and now available worldwide, is a close relative of the tent and somewhat easier to erect. In pale fawn canvas it is gaining wide and well-deserved popularity. Canvas may also be used to make a canopy either in the form of a sun blind which slides down from a permanent wall-mounting into which it rolls for storage, or a temporary version which can be fastened to a wall by hooks through holes in

Above *A canopy which can be rapidly erected consists of a piece of canvas or other fabric set with metal "eyes" which can be slipped over hooks on a wall and then over poles with a ridge to stop them slipping. They look very stylish with the poles at an angle and the fabric fringed.*

Right *Chairs with a tented canopy.*

Below *A garden house of stretched reflective fabric in Jack Lenor Larsen's garden. Its Mogul shape is matched by a central water channel in the garden which is flanked by double rows of London planes.*

the canvas and then lifted by poles staked in the earth which fit into similar holes along the canvas front.

In medieval times a small canvas pavilion, providing shade from which to view a garden, was sometimes known as a *glorietta*, anglicized as gloriet. The word seems to be Spanish in origin, the literal translation of the Arabic *aziz*, meaning glorious. It was commonly used for a vine-covered arch or bower placed at the crossing of a path and later for the brightly-tiled pavilions which replaced them. Applied to any kind of pavilion, it seemed appropriate for the decorated tent. Indeed it seems an eminently suitable name to apply to the newest of garden developments — the garden as office. Modern man or woman will need a structure in which to install the electronic communications system when the home becomes the workplace as is already happening in some professions.

An alternative to the fabric tent could be a structure of trellis, glass or plastic as a decorative temporary shelter to suit a particular season or a temporary need. It only requires imagination in design and then a name. Gazebo, perhaps, which is dog Latin for "I will gaze" and historically a raised structure at some vantage point, but frequently misused today for any small shelter; or *kiosk*, an Islamic term used originally for an elevated building; or the more mundane summer house.

Grottos

In ancient times caves were often cult centers or the site of religious mysteries, and Plato in his *Republic* compared the passage of life to sojourn in a cave, but it was not until the Renaissance that patrons of gardening felt the need to have their own grottos in which to contemplate the mysteries of the universe. Two main forms evolved, the rustic imitation of a cave and the grander and obviously man-made architectural nymphaeum, the latter usually ornamented with sculpture and with fountains and water effects in honor of the nymphs and muses to whom it was dedicated.

Fine grottos were created in Italian gardens like the Villa d'Este and the Villa Lante, and the Boboli Gardens where the grotto was on two levels and consisted of three interconnecting "caves" with sculpture by Michelangelo. The French became enthusiastic for such constructions and at Versailles there was a grotto, now dismantled, dedicated to Thetis (the Nereid mother of Achilles). Its interior was encrusted with mirrors, mother-of-pearl, sparkling gems and coral, while hydraulic machines set crystal globes revolving and operated controlled dripping water and other effects.

It was not until the eighteenth century that the British really took up the fashion, but when they did the results were splendid. One of the best known was Alexander Pope's grotto at Twickenham, where the poet constructed an underground passage to connect his garden with a lower lawn on the banks of the Thames. He described how, when lit up, it could be seen to be embellished with shells, glass, mirrors and luminous stones which he described as "Marbles, Spars, Gems, Ores, and Minerals" in the title of the Ode he wrote in its honor. Samuel Johnson was rather critical of Pope's effort, complaining in his gruff way that he "extracted an ornament from an inconvenience, and vanity produced a grotto where necessity enforced a passage."

However, Pope's enthusiasm won the day and over 200 years later his grotto is being

Designs for grottos from William Wright's Grotesque Architecture or Rural Ornament, *1790.*

restored. Grottos never went entirely out of fashion although they were altered in form. Stourhead has a circular domed space with an ornamental floor, which is lit from above through a hole in the roof. A statue of a river god presides over this eighteenth-century underworld where the source of the River Stour flows from an urn and a nymph sleeps nearby. Some grottos were built indoors in European palaces, sometimes serving as a link between palace and garden, others became tea houses or even theaters. Antonio Gaudi, the Spanish architect, created a crypt-like grotto at the Parq Guëll around 1900 and an American designer, Keisler, produced plans for a Grotto of Meditation for New Harmony in Indiana in the 1960s. In Wiltshire, England, garden designer Julian Bannerman still devotes a lot of time developing this curious ornamental feature for twentieth-century clients.

One of the features of grottos designed by the sixteenth-century potter Bernard Palissy for aristocratic French gardens was an upper story peopled by life-size models of human figures. This may have influenced those later Frenchmen who had a passion for hermitages. At first they peopled them with real people, probably all in holy orders; later hermitages were staffed with dummies. When real hermits were hard to come by some were made of wax, others were clockwork or stuffed. A craze for such curious décor swept England in the eighteenth century.

Dovecotes and other "practical" ornaments

Dovecotes, either separate structures or as part of other buildings, were originally for entirely practical use. They housed pigeons being fattened for the table and their droppings provided excellent manure. Some sheltered as many as a thousand birds but as other sources of winter meat became available the dovecote shrank in size and the birds became largely decorative. English poet, painter and composer Lord Berners used to dye those in his Oxford-shire garden in delicate pinks and blues. While some may welcome doves as an ornament in themselves and find their cooing an appealing mood enhancer others may find it irritating.

Sometimes a dovecote can be built as a kind of "lantern" on the top of a pavilion or gazebo, or incorporated in the eaves of a building, but it must be possible for those who tend the birds to get in to clean the roosts. Small wooden dovecotes, pole-mounted or wall-hanging, are more suitable for smaller gardens. Thatched or tiled roofs above decorative arched entries can be a charming addition to a cottage-style garden.

Aviaries were a feature of classical gardens and some very attractive and elaborate structures have been created over the centuries.

Birdbaths to attract free-flying birds became a garden feature from the late 1850s. They are rarely beautiful, usually just a flattish dish on a pedestal, but this is a field which modern potters and designers might enter with more

color and imagination, though shallow fountains will offer birds much the same benefits. For centuries gardeners were more interested in scaring birds away, but with the growing interest in nature, many have become bird-watchers, and baths and bird tables are more popular.

The typical sundial of early twentieth-century gardens somewhat resembles the birdbath in shape. Today it can have little practical purpose, especially when inaccurately aligned in relation to the movement of the sun, but may fit some nostalgic idea of an "old" garden and can sometimes serve as a useful focal point for a garden design. Wall-mounted dials can give interest to a blank wall.

Ornamental boundaries

Roman paintings show latticed fences and Virgil writes of woven barriers to keep out animals, and through the Middle Ages right up to our own day many methods of enclosure have been used: brick, stone and earth walls, wooden fences and palings, metal and railings, a variety of constructions and patterns being employed. Hedges have been used at all times, often with thorny plants to keep out animals.

"Fence" suggests a certain flimsiness, although some wooden designs can be more durable than stone. Much depends on whether a wall is intended to mask what lies behind or be a barrier against animals and people, or whether it is mainly decorative and can reveal the view beyond.

A planted wall may seem less expensive than a permanent structure but this is not necessarily so. Plants die, are eaten by rabbits and

Designs for rustic fencing sold in ready-made panels early in the twentieth century. They were available either with or without bark covering.

Center right *Woven fencing as an alternative to wattle.*

Right *Wall decoration in heavy relief matches the cactus garden outside a condominium in Rio de Janeiro.*

sheep, are blown away in gales, or suffer from what insurance companies defensively describe as Acts of God. They take time to develop and, although a hedge can be reasonably looked on as an architectural feature once it has attained its full height, it then requires the costly maintenance of regular clipping.

One of the most attractive hedges is beech, brown in winter when its leaves cling on and green in summer. A compromise, such as a wire or timber fence, overgrown with roses, honeysuckle or other climbers, is attractive but still requires careful maintenance, particularly if the supporting structure proves fragile.

Magnificent stone walls, decorated with finials, urns and statues cost too much for most people to build today, even when appropriate stone is obtainable, though imitation stone is widely sold for walling, often in pierced forms that sadly lack the beauty of Eastern and Renaissance pierced styles. Dry stone walls (without mortar), traditional in Britain in the Cotswolds and the North, are viable if local craftsmen still have the skills to build them. Brick, however, is the most usual choice in Britain and Europe. Once it weathers, it has an affinity with the plant life growing at its base or up it.

Brick and grass make congenial partners. Both brick and breeze blocks can be rendered with cement and painted, and can be effective in sunny, hot climates. They can also look well bonded with cement if the bricks themselves are of two or more colors, introducing a patterned effect. To be strong, brick walls need thickness, but this can be achieved by using buttresses, in themselves ornamental. They can create recesses which in the past were sometimes used to site fires to heat fruit trees espaliered on the other side of the wall. In the eighteenth century serpentine walls were fashionable, the graceful curves adding to their strength and offering more protection in their curves. The actor David Garrick described an

estate as "none of your straight lines here — but all taste — zigzag — crinkum-crankum — in and out — right and left — to and again — twisting and turning like a worm." Tastes today are usually more orderly.

Doors and gates can be decorative in themselves and their borders may be patterned. The grand gates of the past, which reflected their owners' status, were sometimes so heavily decorated that they offered a fanfare of trumpets in stone as the visitor passed through. Even today some gateways echo this grandeur, using sculpture, obelisks, etc., to give presence. Similar ornamentation can be applied to the wall itself, using fragments of stone, including sculptured pieces, but the simplest method of decorating walls is to use plants. Short pieces of drainpipe can be cemented into a wall horizontally for planting, so that the vegetation can trail down, or plants can grow at its base — ivy,

virginia creeper, roses and similar climbers. Growth can be encouraged by placing a metal or wooden trellis a short distance in front of the wall. Ornamental trellis can also be used to heighten a solid wall that is too low; it can turn a rather dull enclosure into a pleasantly decorated frame.

Trelliswork and other forms of wood have mainly replaced ironwork for the more open forms of enclosure, and wooden panels, usually larch, set between posts are the most common form of fencing. A cross-braced fence of rustic poles, of the type used in pergolas, can be attractive, although unless plant-covered it does not provide full concealment.

If blocking out neighbors (and the shared view of each other) is required, then a wattle fence, with its rough, interlocking fingers, is visually more interesting. Diagonal slats can make an interesting alternative and carpenters have made other variations on the picket fence — fretting the tops, decorating the horizontals or using half-round posts or verticals with square and rectangular sections.

In the East split bamboo is widely used and has been adopted for small gardens in both Europe and the United States. Attractively simple, it has a pleasant natural color, but is not durable. The Japanese have devised an interesting variation using vertical lengths of rough cut boards 5 in (10 cm) wide and set 12 in (5 cm) apart and supported on horizontal rails. The gap between the boards is filled by two vertical thin bamboos, spaced equidistant from each other and from the adjacent boards.

Exits and entrances

Psychologist Ian Appleton has a theory that contemplation of landscape produces a sign-stimulus indicative of environmental conditions favorable to human survival millennia ago and still in our genes. These stimuli are evoked by the sight of a quarry or a predator without being seen (providing prospect) or when able to hide from a prospective enemy while still being able to see around us (refuge). The theory is offered to explain the excitement with which we approach a door or opening.

The desire for privacy dictates the siting of apertures, but the twentieth-century fondness for garden "rooms" is also relevant, because the way in which a visitor enters the "room" may influence the effects of the plants inside.

Designers have often chosen not a simple door or arch but a colonnade or pergola which allows intermittent views beyond and alternate

Top *Wrought-iron gates, flanked by urn-topped brick pillars make an elegant gateway in Old Westbury Gardens, New York State.*

Center *A cast-iron gate in a shady Australian garden.*

Right *Added height gives simple emphasis to this well-proportioned gateway in Tryon Palace Gardens, North Carolina, but the flanking stone seats spoil the design. They would be attractive in an arc but their curves are unsuitable against a straight wall.*

framing which will turn the most basic of gates and doors into fine entrances.

The Romans edged their flower beds with stone. Later, horizontal timber planks were used to retain the soil of each plot, or they were fenced in with pointed-topped palings, or low latticework in wood and metal, and in English palace gardens under the Tudor monarchs by low rails painted with diagonal stripes or chevrons. Later, metal hoops and bobble-topped tiles edged many Victorian paths. Simple brick edging is frequently used today if beds are edged at all, while in more formal gardens the beds may be retained behind low walls of only three or four courses of bricks.

Sculpture

The bold pool decoration is very different in style from the relief of the Annunciation set on the wall, but both are matched by the rounded forms of plants and trees in this garden in Canberra, Australia.

Comic dwarfs and characters from the Commedia dell'Arte are among the many statues that line the terraces of the Villa Buonaccorsi in Tuscany.

shelter and shade for the visitor. A gate or half door does not block out the view; it simply limits access, while suggesting that something interesting lies ahead. Great skill has been applied to the ornamentation of gates to strengthen the sense of occasion on arrival, but a door or gate should always be made in a material which suits the surrounding enclosure. Many French country hotels have a large iron hoop from one side of the entrance drive to the other, often decorated with rambling plants and perhaps sporting a central lantern or sign.

Simple wooden picket gates appear "natural," more sophisticated versions with openwork lattice can give a distinct feeling that the garden inside has great elegance. Yew, climbing roses and other natural materials can provide a

Francis Bacon, that prolific writer about gardens, was critical of the use of sculpture, observing that it "added state and magnificence, but nothing to the true pleasure of a garden." When he wrote this in the seventeenth century statuary had lost the religious element of its use in classical groves and, although it was used symbolically by the Mannerists in some great gardens, in most cases gardens were being treated as outdoor museums, like the Belvedere Court in the Vatican. Unhappily, the vast majority of garden designers since have followed the sixteenth-century popes in using gardens to show off sculpture, believing that carved figures added tone, provided that they were either genuinely of sufficient antiquity or had been antiqued. By the eighteenth century originals had acquired such rarity that fakes were being manufactured to meet the demands of collectors.

There is nothing wrong with antique statues, even fakes or copies, except that they are too often displayed merely with the object of giving status to the owner, rather than as an integral part of the garden. How different the work of the contemporary Scots sculptor and poet Ian Hamilton-Finlay, who believes that gardens should appeal to all the senses and that, as well as inspiring calmness or animation, they should be capable of provoking thought, both serious and trivial. Thus, the plants and objects in his own garden are pleasurable in their own right and (the objects particularly) also have significant meaning, but not as status symbols.

His lake, for example, is the setting for a marble model of a paper boat, symbolizing the innocence of childhood adventure. Beyond is the beautifully functional shape of the conning tower of an atomic submarine which is also reminiscent of the sinister fin of a killer shark. Instead of conventional birdbaths there are miniature stone replicas of American and Russian aircraft carriers whose helicopter landing pads are perfectly scaled to serve as perches for sparrows to drink and bathe.

Hamilton-Finlay's love of the written word is frustrated by the fact that "people find it unacceptable unless it is inscribed upon a sundial or something resembling a memorial tablet," although in fact his work, however dissimilar artistically, continues a garden tradition of verse and texts engraved on stone which found its peak in William Shenstone's Leasowes.

Conventional garden sculpture usually plays a more mundane part in our gardens, providing a focal point or adding interest to a terrace or fountain. Representational sculpture gives human scale to a garden and nowadays there is a vogue for animals like sheep or dogs which, while clearly not real, give the viewer the impression that the garden owner may intend them to be real. Like other trompe l'oeils, such as fake bridges, they titillate the senses. True or false, such sculpture leads the body and the mind around the garden, although the effect should not be overpowering. The material used by the sculptor adds or detracts from the illusion; stone and wood is natural in most gardens, while a smooth-surfaced material like marble may appear alien to its surroundings

Above *An unusual statue in carved brick in the garden of Charleston Manor, which was the home of painters Duncan Grant and Vanessa Bell.*

Above left *Fanciful classicism among the spring bulbs makes an arresting exhibit.*

Below left *Careful siting can ensure that natural and sculptural forms complement each other.*

Below *An unusual earth sculpture, designed by Conrad Hamerman as part of this Pennsylvania garden, is a simple pyramid of clay which stays continually damp to support its covering of moss and liverworts.*

unless it is close to water. Bronze or other metals are clearly "unnatural" because introduced into the garden and for that reason they have a formality which is a special attraction.

Modern sculpture differs from almost all other garden ornament in that it is making a clear statement about itself which includes the idea "this is a work of art." Antique statuary and the copies which prevailed from the Renaissance onward did not make that kind of impression — the concept would have been meaningless until well after the Romantic movement gave the artist a special status.

Whatever one's reaction to abstract sculpture, there can be no doubt that it is often more acceptable outdoors than inside the house. A modest piece of abstract work will usually retain the interest and the eye for much

The garden gnome

In contrast to the classical figures and architectural forms which decorate so many formal gardens, the most popular figures found in gardens are a quite different species — the garden gnome. Enthusiasts all around the globe have filled their gardens with these little fellows in every conceivable posture. At the Gnome Reserve, in north Devon in the west of England, more than a thousand gnomes, claimed to be the world's largest gnome population, "inhabit" woodland glades and flowery paths, attracting a regular flow of visitors who are offered pointed gnome's caps to wear as they go around "so the gnomes think you are one of them."

The original gnomes were a kind of earth spirit. The name was used by Paracelsus for a group that was responsible for animating the elements, an idea taken up by the Rosicrucians. Ann Atkin, who created the Gnome Reserve and founded a Gnome Society, believes her pottery gnomes attract real gnomes, characters from Celtic tradition whose presence she claims to feel. It has also been suggested that gnomes are the same kind of spirit as the mischievous Robin Goodfellow (Shakespeare's Puck), who could both bring good luck and play prankish jokes, or the house goblin of eastern European tradition.

In 1791 Erasmus Darwin, uncle of the evolutionist, included them in his poem *Botanic Garden* as "guards and guides of Nature's chemic toil" responsible for volcanic action and rock formation.

The now ubiquitous garden gnome bears a striking resemblance to the miners shown in woodcuts which illustrate a sixteenth-century book on metallurgy, figures echoed in Walt Disney's treatment of the seven miner dwarfs in his *Snow White*, but it may have had its origin in the satirical drawings of dwarfs which became popular in Germany early in the eighteenth century. The Viennese Imperial Pottery made porcelain dwarfs, the peak period being 1744–50, and thirty years later the Derby pottery in Britain produced a set. Goethe gives an example of a colored dwarf figure used as a garden ornament in his poem *Hermann und Dorothea* (1797) and though they went out of fashion, and were replaced by cherubs and classical figures, there seems to have been a nostalgic revival the following century.

Loudon advocated the use of miniature figures in the garden in his *Encyclopedia of Gardening* (1850) and when Sir Charles Isham began to make the first English collection of bonsai trees, choosing slow-growing miniature specimens to plant in an elaborate rock garden in holes made in the rock, he decided to people the display with little people. He got his gnomes from Nurnberg, where they must still have been in production or at least still in stock, arranging them naturally, including a group of striking miners complete with slogan placards! Isham's gnomes are said to have been the first in Britain and were celebrated in garden journals. Another famous group was arranged around an underground cave in the rock garden at Sir Frank Crisp's Prior Park, where the rockery, known as "the Henley Matterhorn" was said by Robinson to be "the best natural stone rock garden I have ever seen."

At first gnomes were an upper-class fashion which spread rapidly during the Edwardian period so that now they may be seen in countries all around the world, sometimes in local variations, such as an Australian version with a swaggie's hat and holding a sheep.

At the Gnome Reserve.

Gnomes have been created in all shapes and sizes.

longer than one of those Italianate figures in stone or lead which P. G. Wodehouse referred to as "a young boy with a bit of a tummy on him."

Obelisks and their modern derivatives are abstract shapes for those who do not want to take the plunge into contemporary non-representational sculpture. An alternative for the faint-hearted is to use a natural form such as an interesting rock or large tree trunk and give it a formal position either by clearing the area around it or by using planting to focus the eye on it. At night it might be spot-lit. Effective garden sculpture of an abstract kind can also be designed with sizable stones or large pebbles arranged in patterns on a terrace or some other flat surface or low plinth.

Fountains

Much garden sculpture and statuary has been used as fountain decoration or to actually issue water. Figures with an obvious water association, from Neptune and personifications of rivers to fishes, have always been popular, water sometimes pouring from jugs, urns and other naturalistic containers or like springs from rocks, but often issuing from a variety of orifices, human and animal. One of the simplest and most effective fountains is a spout issuing from a wall — a simple pipe or the mouth of a stone satyr or lion. Lions have had a long association with fountains, originating in ancient Persian gardens — in pre-Muslim Persia lions were linked with the spirit of life itself and hence with water, and the same word means both lion and waterspout — and from there, through Moorish Spain to the rest of Europe. Something more original was conceived by gardening writer Graham Rose who

Right *The Neptune fountain in the Boboli Gardens.*

Below *An animal fountain at Versailles.*

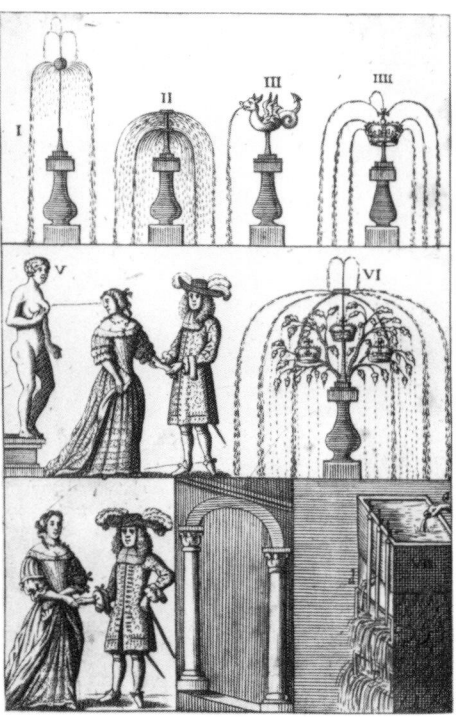

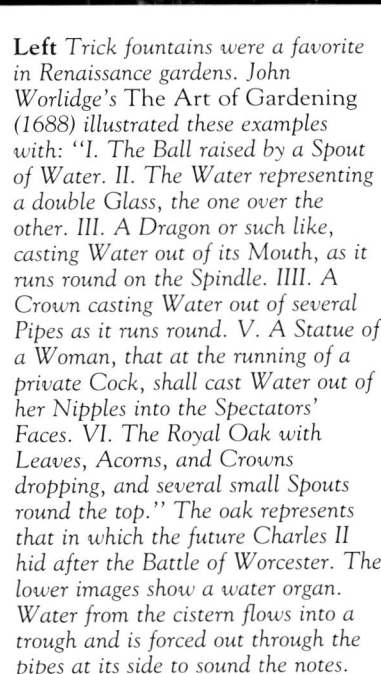

Left *Trick fountains were a favorite in Renaissance gardens. John Worlidge's* The Art of Gardening *(1688) illustrated these examples with: "I. The Ball raised by a Spout of Water. II. The Water representing a double Glass, the one over the other. III. A Dragon or such like, casting Water out of its Mouth, as it runs round on the Spindle. IIII. A Crown casting Water out of several Pipes as it runs round. V. A Statue of a Woman, that at the running of a private Cock, shall cast Water out of her Nipples into the Spectators' Faces. VI. The Royal Oak with Leaves, Acorns, and Crowns dropping, and several small Spouts round the top." The oak represents that in which the future Charles II hid after the Battle of Worcester. The lower images show a water organ. Water from the cistern flows into a trough and is forced out through the pipes at its side to sound the notes.*

has built a wild boar plunging through the wall of his house, mouthing water into a basin below. Imaginative concepts of this kind are within the reach of anyone who has the necessary do-it-yourself skills.

Fountains do not need carved figures, however, for the water is a form of sculpture in itself, jetting and arcing into the air, or falling through abstract forms, perhaps setting in action a variety of spacial rearrangements.

The fountain reached breathtaking complexities in the great gardens of Renaissance and Baroque France and Italy but became more prosaic in the Victorian period and afterwards, usually centered in a pool and, because of faults in its pumping equipment, often failing to deliver the required spout. Modern electric pumps have eliminated most such inefficiencies and water can be flung from a plain pipe beneath the surface in a variety of pleasing patterns or made to flow over or through features with ease. The simplicity of modern fountain work has not meant the loss of originality in water engineering. Rather the opposite. Sculptor Naum Gabo made a wonderful work of turning spouting metal which can be seen in action in the gardens of St. Thomas's Hospital, London, on the south bank of the Thames.

Fine modern water sculpture can be seen in the open-air collections or sculpture parks which are now found in many countries around the world. Examples are the Energy Fountain by Isamu Noguchi at the California Scenario at South Coast Plaza, Costa Mesa; the Fattoria di Celle's Themes and Variations by Fausto Melotti in Tuscany, Italy; and Miro's Labyrinth at the Maeght Foundation on the French Riviera. One of the most imaginative marriages between modern sculpture and water was designed by Sir Geoffrey Jellicoe at Sutton Place in England. Unfortunately, this garden is no longer open to the public.

Bottom *A fountain at Charleston.*

Below *A ceramic fountain in Guadalacajara, Mexico.*

Large garden structures

Garden buildings and structures range from the banqueting house to the tool shed. They can be made unobtrusive by being hidden beneath climbing plants or by treating surfaces with trellis as a continuation of other garden features, or they can be used as focal points. A utilitarian building can be dressed in other clothes and project a romantic or fanciful image as a grotto, temple, or a gothic ruin. A solid structure will make a major statement and so will act as much more than a focal point, affecting the whole atmosphere of the garden.

Left *The pagoda at Chanteloup, designed by Louis Denis Le Camus who laid out the park with classic vistas of which it formed the focal point. Inspired by Chambers's Kew pagoda, it was dedicated to friendship.*

Below *A modern American gazebo and bridge.*

A tree summer house at Pitchford Hall (photographed in 1901).

The profile presented, whether the actual structure or a facade, can be used to strengthen the garden composition in just the same way as an obelisk or any other decorative feature.

A bridge may not be strictly necessary except to reach an island or cross a stream but can be a useful way of spanning levels without using steps. Placed at one end of a pond it can give the impression of a much bigger water feature, as well as providing a useful platform from which to feed the fish or ducks. Bridges add charm and character to a vista. On a short span plain timber planking can support the floor and rustic poles can provide a railing. A zigzag bridge can be made by driving posts into shallow water and mounting boards across them. The minimalist bridge may be simple timber or stone slabs resting on a rock, or even reduced to a line of stepping stones to invite closer contact with the water, perhaps linked with a similar pathway crossing turf. Bridge ornament is usually applied to the sides and entrances but bridges can also be roofed in thatch or tile or tented. Stone bridges can feature finials, urns and statues; iron arches and handrails can be fitted to timber bridges. Ready-made bridges are available in wood or metal, usually painted and priced according to their span. If only the visual effect is required, there is no need to build or buy a complete bridge. Use a facade placed to enhance the vista — one side only with no road or footway — and perhaps provide a talking as well as a focal point. There are plenty of precedents in historic gardens, and not just of bridges — at Compton Wynates there is even a false windmill.

P.K.

Lighting

Lighting can be an important decorative tool, both to illuminate the garden view by night and extend garden use after daylight has faded. Lighting has long been used to create a gentle romantic setting or give an atmosphere of festival with torches, flares and lanterns of all kinds, but electricity now enables a very sophisticated degree of control of both intensity and direction. Lighting can also be important in illuminating pathways to the house and providing security, although these requirements may not coincide with ideal decorative treatments.

Lighting fixtures may be inconspicuous or be made decorative features in themselves. In an area used for dining or entertaining out of doors a visible light source in traditional lantern form, or even strings of colored bulbs to provide a holiday atmosphere, may be preferable and will probably be temporary fittings. Their purpose will be largely to provide illumination for social activities. Lights to illuminate pathways may be built into walls or steps, or simple fixtures which are inconspicuous by day and throw light downwards may be placed along path edges. To paint the garden itself with light, fittings can be hidden in trees, among the planting and in water.

Some lights are permanent fixtures but those designed to be easily relocatable can be extremely useful in establishing the best placings for a lighting pattern. One type is mounted on a spike and can be inserted in the soil for uplighting or angled for a lower beam. Others can be mounted on holders screwed into a wall or other surface and a third type has a clamp by which it can be fastened to a branch or part of a garden structure.

It should be remembered that incandescent tungsten bulbs disperse a warm light while tungsten halogen bulbs give out a more concentrated, colder beam. For warmer glows there are colored bulbs and filters. Downlighting is the most natural form, imitating sun or moonlight. Uplighting is more dramatic, casting long shadows. Backlighting is more subtle and, combined with the other two, soft-washes a wall or fence so that the lighted feature is seen against a background and is not unnaturally stark.

Spotlights are effective for a single feature like an urn or piece of sculpture. A single spot can appear boring —

borrow a trick or two from the theater and use more sources to create depth and interest. Put the emphasis on the principal player; light up any area of scenery that plays a key role in the action. When the curtain goes up the audience should gasp with delight.

Large specimen trees should be uplighted, not only when in leaf but when their skeletal structure can make a graphic statement. Extraordinary effects can be achieved by lighting when there is snow on the ground. Lighting on the far side of water can produce magical reflections.

Garden lighting can be run directly from the household mains or subsidiary circuits at garage or pool, and at normal voltages can be dangerous — indeed lethal — if mishandled or if cable is damaged. This kind of lighting is best installed by an expert, especially if water is involved. However, a much safer and very convenient alternative which allows designers great freedom is low-voltage lighting. A transformer reduces the mains current to a 12-volt supply which will not hurt or harm. It is claimed to be totally safe and will not short even in water. Cables do not have to be buried or protected and

some types of fitting can be clipped onto the cable at any point without requiring fixed outlet sockets. Lamps can be placed unobtrusively exactly where they are needed and their smaller bulbs usually produce less glare, allowing for very precise and subtle effects.

For those who wish to be at the cutting edge of lighting technology there is another choice — fiber-optic lighting cables, which transfer light, not electricity, to the desired point.

Lighting tips

* Fit a dimmer on the outside circuit. When looking at the garden from inside the house the reflection on the glass requires lights to be full on. Upon going outside lighting can be turned down.
* Small gardens often require more lights than large ones, which may need only one or two floods under larger trees and highlighting of one simple feature to give a hint of scale. In smaller gardens the aim will be more to create the idea of an outdoor room, an extension of the indoor space rather than a separate night world.

Discreetly hidden floodlighting among the trees, and poolside striplighting, paints the trees and pool without any direct glare. Electronic dimmers give maximum control and achieve a sense of depth and dimension.

GARDENS WORLDWIDE

Gardens around the world exist in an almost infinite diversity, limited only by the equally widely differing tastes and interests of gardeners. In creating gardens to complement their home, their location or their life style, or designing them to suit some public purpose, they may follow a traditional style or create inspired originals.

Some gardening skills are pitted against local conditions — trying to create a perfect English lawn under a tropical sun or growing calcifuge plants where both land and water are full of chalk. Rumors tell of a Texas gardener who dynamited holes in subsurface limestone and filled them with peaty acid soil to grow azaleas, and there are bog gardeners who bury shower curtains to create pockets of saturated soil.

Above and right *Pink and red pelargoniums brighten up the flower beds by the veranda of Monet's* *farmhouse at Giverny, in France, an echo of the green woodwork and pink-washed plaster of the building.*

Equally determined is a Maryland gardener who regularly ices his cool-climate bunchberries *Cornus canadensis* to help them survive the steamy summer so many degrees south of their home latitude, or the New Hampshire gardener who grows his tender bamboo in a pit and buries it each winter. There is the gardener from Atlanta, Georgia, where hot and humid summers deal disease to cool climate perennials. He starts anew each year, buying delphiniums in January, growing them in the greenhouse, then transplanting them into the garden in early spring to achieve his "English garden" look by May and June, though by late summer, despite regular sprays of fungicide, the battle has been lost and they are replaced with annuals. These are all American examples but their like exist in every nation, though increasingly there is interest in exploiting native plants in natural styles, in creating habitat for wild life and in conserving threatened species and old varieties.

There is room for all, but the pages that follow are not concerned with the eccentricities so much as with the pleasures of the garden and to show something of the great variety of gardens around the world.

H. L.

Above *Set against green vines, geraniums, petunias, lobelias, nasturtiums and nepetas cascade from window boxes and hanging baskets to make a wall of color on this house in Butchart Gardens, Victoria, British Colombia.*

Top *A colorful display of old-fashioned flowers leads through to an inviting pool, combining the delights of the flower garden and a place for recreation.*

Center *On this allotment at Lubin, Poland, the vegetables have had to make way for flowers.*

Right *A mixed border of traditional country flowers at Stancombe Park, Gloucester, England.*

Left *Spring bulbs in a formal setting at Greenwich, Connecticut.*

COTTAGE GARDENS

Unlike other styles of gardening, which reflect the architectural tastes and fashions of their age, cottage gardens were from the outset practical and utilitarian. Land was not set aside for leisure activities nor was space wasted on plants which were decorative but had little practical application. The land worked for the inhabitants and over the years they developed the skills necessary to make their land productive. In the process a style of gardening developed which, over the centuries, has influenced many of the horticulturists and designers who have worked in the great gardens of the leisured classes.

It is likely that the first cottage gardens were reserved entirely for livestock. Bees, fowl and a few milk-giving animals were kept beside the cottage for the sustenance of the inhabitants, and as time passed, cottagers began to grow the herbs and vegetables needed by the household and their animals. At this early stage the garden probably had little orderly plan, although one can assume that there was some sort of path leading to the door. Livestock were probably contained within wattle hurdles, which could be moved with the seasons, allowing for a natural rotation of crops and animals. Sometimes the household privy was mobile too and made a valuable contribution to the fertility of

the land. Even the bee skeps or hives were moved with the seasons, depending on the availability of pollen and the need for shelter.

Thomas Tusser, who wrote for ordinary people and whose first book was published in 1557, recommended dozens of plants for the kitchen. His list of edible plants included parsley, parsnip, endive, pumpkin, carrots and peas. A considerable number, including lavender and tansy, were also commended as deterrents for fleas and lice. Hops were included for brewing, mandrake and rhubarb for physic, and many which today we think of as purely ornamental, such as primroses and violets, were included in his list of useful plants.

While most of the species which were grown had a culinary or medicinal application, it is

Above left *The cottage garden style as exported to Australia, with foxgloves, roses, alyssum, godetia, lavender and pansies growing beside the path from front gate to front door.*

Left *A typical English cottage garden. Honeysuckle tumbles over the porch while iris, poppies, geraniums and rubus grow either side of the neat brick path.*

likely that others were cultivated close to the dwelling for their magical, religious, sentimental or mystical significance. Scented plants were thought to ward off infection and to be health-giving and, when planted next to the path, cottagers would have been able to enjoy their benefits as they went about their daily business.

In many parts of southern Europe the cottage garden remained a purely productive unit. These southern European gardens have hardly changed over the years and today look much as they probably did two or three hundred years ago. The land, which is intensely cultivated, is devoted almost entirely to the production of vegetables and animals. The only open space is ground left fallow for a season in order to rest the soil and enhance its fertility. Well-pruned vines may be used for shade and to provide the family with fruit and wine. Salad and root vegetables are cultivated in neat rows. The smaller herbs are nurtured in pots placed close to the kitchen door and the odd fruit tree may occupy a corner of the plot. Little if any space is devoted to ornamental plants but occasionally a few pelargoniums are cultivated in containers, or a single rose bush may be trained against a wall.

The difference between these gardens and the well-known British model is the absence of frothing flowery borders along the edges of the path and under the windows. Whereas the Mediterranean gardens have been fairly static in their design, contents and objectives, British cottage gardens developed in a different way and have inspired gardeners all over the world with a fanciful vision of a flowery paradise.

Many plants which in the first place may have earned their place in a British cottage garden for their utilitarian or mystical associations, were retained for their decorative attributes long after the early significance had been forgotten. But it would seem that from the earliest time, some modest British gardens contained a few plants grown solely for their beauty. These were often nurtured in pots.

Thomas Tusser lists columbines (*Aquilegia*), carnations, roses, snapdragons (*Antirrhinum*), sweet williams (*Dianthus barbatus*), marigolds, lilies, peonies, love-in-a-mist (*Nigella damascena*) and hollyhocks as flowers for the garden, and makes it plain that he is not just speaking of the gentleman gardener.

In time the abundant colorful style of floral display achieved in the cottage garden attracted the imagination of the rich and from the eighteenth century on, when there was a fashion for building *cottage ornée* surrounded by the appropriate flowery cottage garden, garden designers have repeatedly turned to it for inspiration.

While the cottage garden remained a mixture of heights and colors and the joy was in the uncontrived abundance of flower, fruit and vegetable, refined and formalized systems were developed in the herbaceous borders of the rich. The vegetables retreated to the confines of the walled kitchen garden and the fruit trees were grown in the orchard — where those who enjoyed a naturalistic style of gardening copied the cottage gardener and planted bulbs beneath the trees.

Just as the garden designers of the wealthy found inspiration in cottage gardens, so the cottage gardeners, over the years, adopted plants and borrowed ideas back. It was probably they who tended the gardens of the rich and attended to the propagation of both rare and ordinary plants. It seems likely that many plants which they thought to be of value found their way into the cottage gardens. While the owner of a great garden might indulge himself in vast, nonproductive parterre gardens decorated with elaborate topiary, the cottager might decorate the top of his hedge, which served the purely utilitarian purpose of keeping the animals out of the garden, with a few fanciful topiary creatures. Occasionally one sees topiary chessmen or cake-stands of considerable antiquity in front of a cottage but the cottage garden was and remains, by its very nature, a productive unit.

S.G.

Left *Waterside plants and alpines grow beside a stream running through a Gloucestershire cottage garden, instead of the old-fashioned traditional plants, but the mixture of planting and its informality are well within the cottage gardening tradition.*

Opposite *The garden of the cottage where poet and novelist Thomas Hardy lived in Dorset, England, has a seemingly riotous but actually carefully controlled mixture of lupins, roses and popular garden flowers, while a trimmed sphere of privet adds a slightly formal touch near to the house.*

Below left *Globeflower, goatsbeard and iris thrive in the damp around the trough outside this English cottage while beyond the wall the blues and pinks of delphiniums, lupins and the wall shrub* Actinidia kolomikta *make a pastel background.*

GIVERNY:
Monet's Garden

In 1883, the year he first rented what is now the Musée Claude Monet near the Seine at Giverny in Normandy, the French Impressionist painter told his dealer that he wanted to live in the country because he loved it so much and believed he could paint masterpieces there. Giverny proved a perfect location for him to practice his art, interpreting the constantly changing patterns of light on leaves, water, hills and the surrounding countryside.

Monet found a property with a flowering orchard and a stream. He purchased it in 1890, and turned the orchard into a flower garden with trellised arches and rambling roses, though he saw it as a farmhouse garden, not as a formal garden. He did not want to see bare earth and insisted that his gardener plant very densely with one display of flowers replacing another.

When he acquired an extra stretch of land on the other side of the road he diverted water from the River Epte to create a pear-shaped lily

pond which became the subject of many paintings from 1892. It is reached from the *Clos Normand*, the old part of the garden, via a tunnel under the road.

The pink and white farmhouse is now a museum and the garden, carefully restored much as Monet knew it, is open to the public.

M. B.

Left *Claude Monet's* The Water Lily Pond, *one of the many pictures he painted of the garden at Giverny.*

Below left *Monet was an admirer of Japanese art and had a collection of Japanese woodblock prints which provided some of the inspiration for his water garden, especially for the bridges, though he did not paint them the traditional Japanese red. If he had, some of the best known of Impressionist images would have looked very different.*

Above right *In summer nasturtiums* Tropaeolum majus *spill over the gravel of the main path turning it into a meandering walkway of vivid color. Roses and dahlias provide flanking splashes of red, yellow and pink.*

Below right *The lily pond, with its clumps of pink and white* Nymphaea *floating on the surface and overhanging willows is easily recognizable as the inspiration for Monet's sequences of lily paintings. In this part of the garden grassy paths meander through day lilies bordering the stream that feeds the pond.*

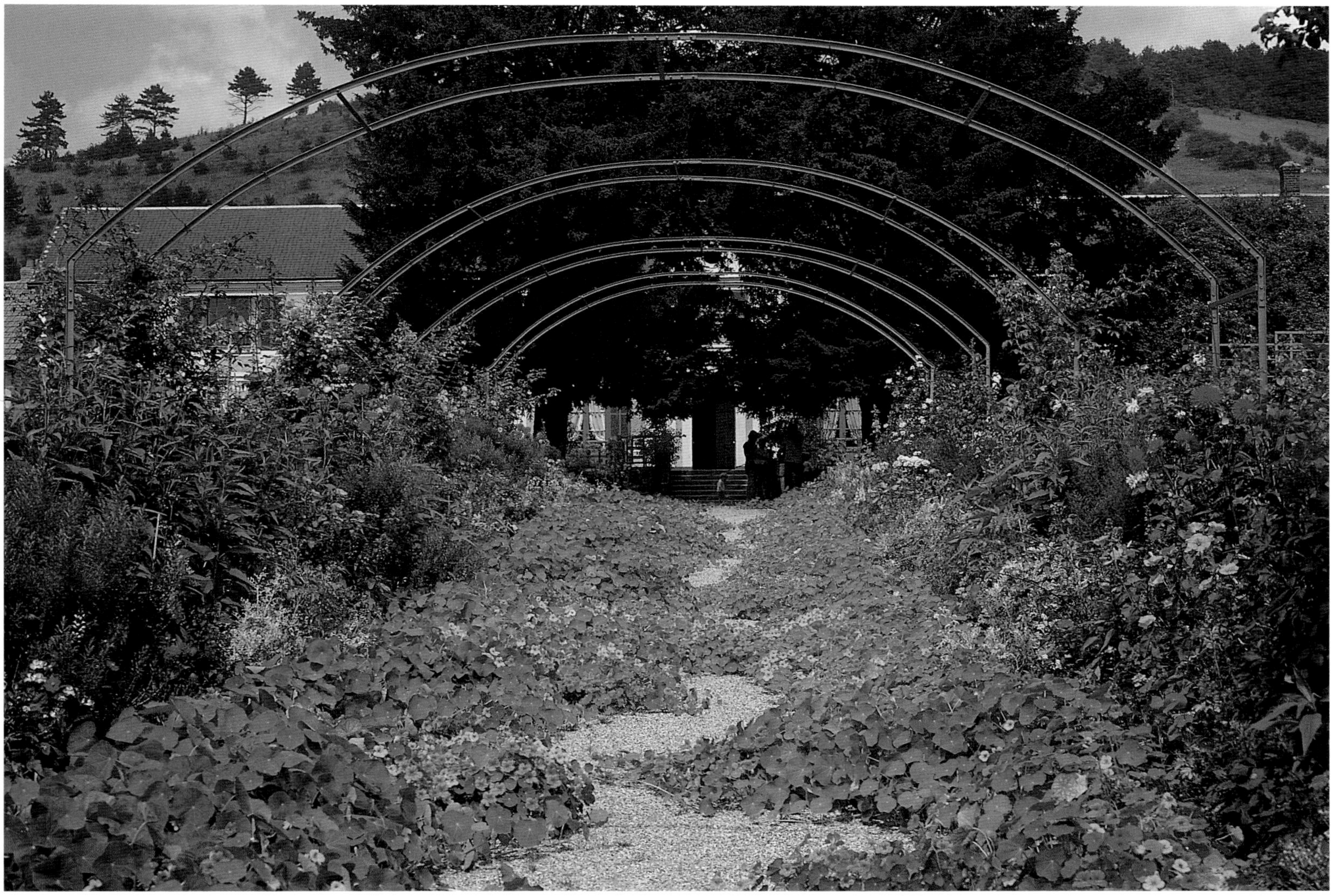

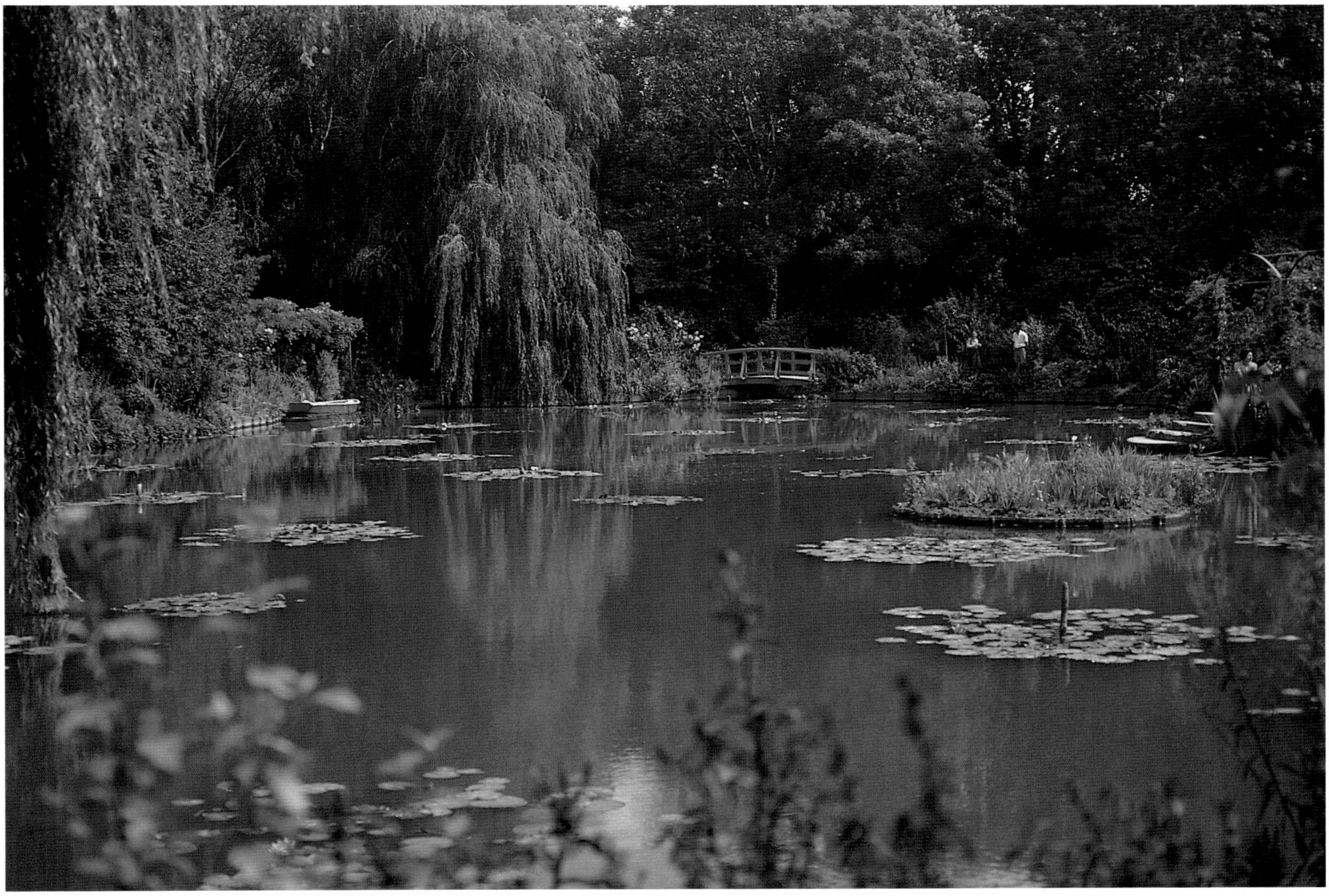

VEGETABLE GARDENS

The inclusion of edible plants in garden design has been cyclical. Sometimes they have been much in favor, like a beloved persimmon in a Chinese emperor's palace garden or orange trees in the Orangerie at Versailles; at other times banished from view totally, as in the landscape styles of eighteenth-century England or in today's American foundation-style front yard.

Varying acceptance of edible landscapes is founded on both the whim of style and a few practical considerations. For instance, the growing of edible plants is associated with helping the budget, and falls out of fashion in a society obsessed with status since it could be taken to indicate need. Sometimes growing them becomes a national duty, as in the Victory Gardens of the United States and the English "Dig-for-Victory" campaign during World War II. Occasionally, edible plants are not practical because fruits require harvesting at inconvenient times, or fruit or nuts might drop where they could be a nuisance.

Many edible plants are inherently beautiful and this, together with a desire for pesticide-free, truly ripe, fresh foods has made them an important part of the contemporary landscape.

Gardeners today, in any climate, whether they favor formal or informal gardens, can look for inspiration in living gardens that preserve

Above *Cabbages and bay make a formal composition with lobelia, calendula and violas.*

Above left *The Garden of Eden, begun by Adam Purple in the Loisaida section of Manhattan in the 1970s on a vacant lot. After eleven years it was a flourishing oasis of vegetables, fruit and nut trees, raspberry patches and flowers in the heart of one of New York's worst slums — until bulldozed for a housing project.*

Right *Parterre gardens, such as these classic gardens at Villandry, are typical of Renaissance formal style, geometrically laid out and with plant growth strictly controlled. Edible plants such as chard, artichokes, endive and ornamental cabbage form the decorative focus of the beds, not flowers, unusual for this style of gardening. They are contained by tiny clipped box hedges with standard roses placed at intervals.*

Left *The vegetable garden at Tryon Palace, North Carolina uses a very formal planting of its leeks, beetroot, peas, lettuce and cabbages. Such close planting can produce very high yields.*

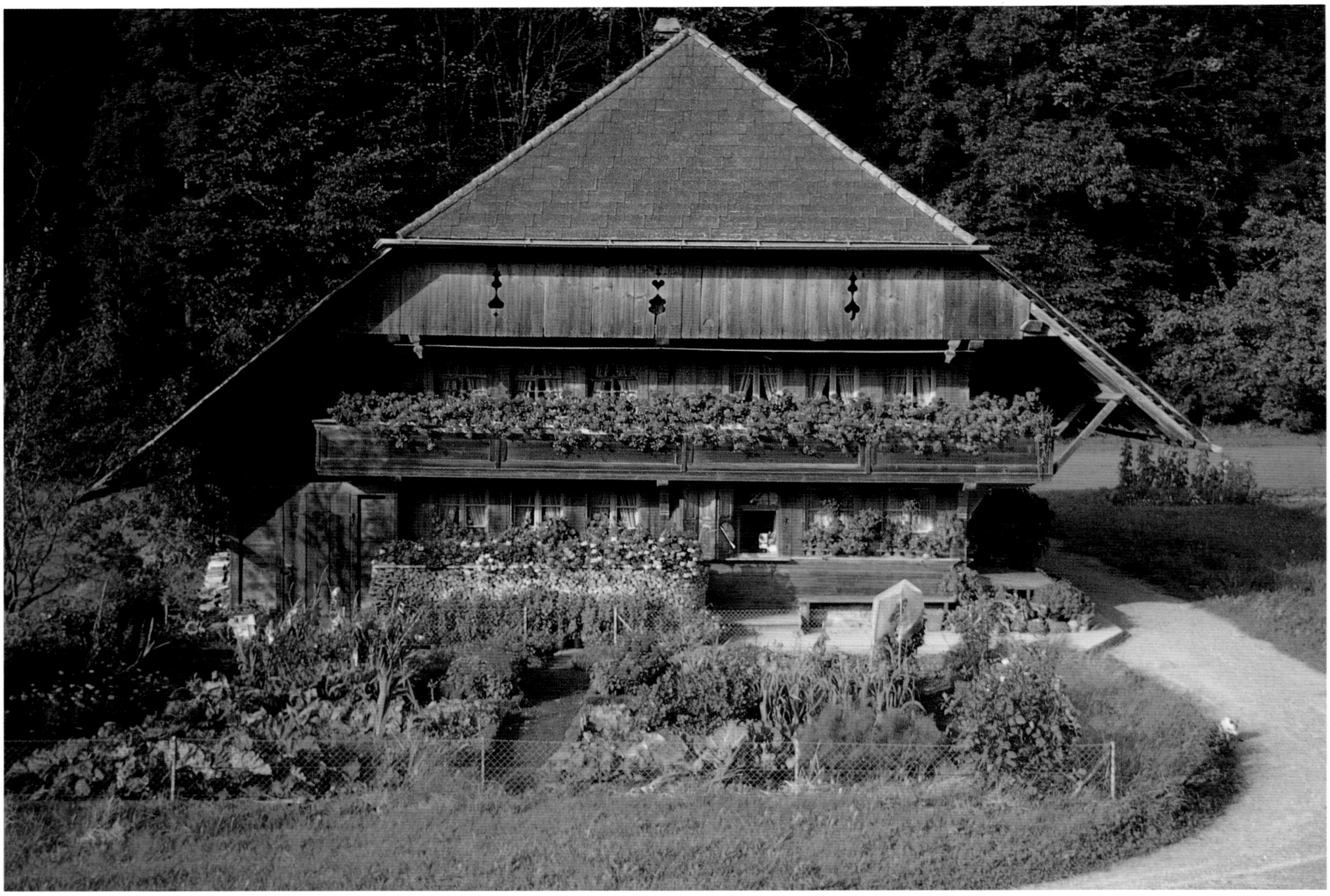

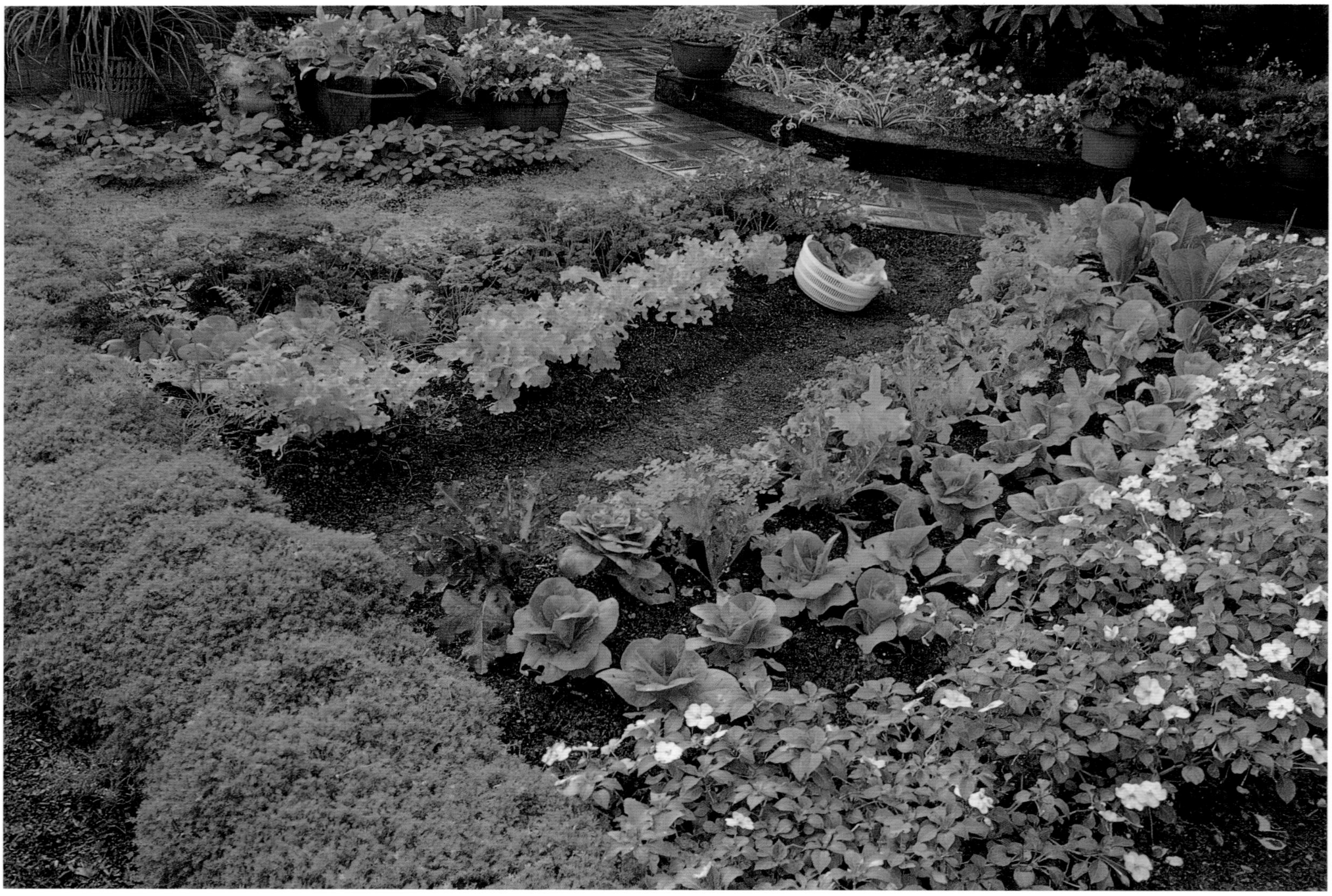

Left *The balconies of this chalet in Switzerland are burgeoning with flowers, which have also invaded the vegetable patch.*

Right *The kitchen garden at Barnsley House, Gloucestershire, England, shows how, with a little imagination, vegetable growing can be both practical, ornamental and fun.*

Below left *Kitchen gardens are most useful when they are close to the kitchen and filled with the vegetables and herbs which the cook uses most. Here a spring salad garden is filled with lettuces, chervil, carrots, strawberries and flowers.*

Right *Ornamental cabbages in the vegetable garden at Villandry.*

Below right *The children's community garden at Brooklyn Botanic Garden attracts many enthusiastic young practical gardeners.*

Far right *Allotment gardens at Stoke-on-Trent in the English Midlands. Sometimes known as community gardens, or Victory Gardens in the United States during World War II, these small plots rented by enthusiasts or allocated by a city or organization to people without garden space have been thriving for many years. The separate strips recall the strip farming of village fields in the Middle Ages before the wealthy landowners enclosed the countryside. Often the center of thriving gardening clubs, they provide a place for city gardeners to grow their own vegetables and flowers and an opportunity to share information and experience with other gardeners.*

historic garden styles. Classic gardens, such as the recreated monastic kitchen garden in the courtyard at the Cloisters in New York City, the French parterre gardens at Villandry in the Loire Valley, and the formal royal gardens in Peking, all showcase edible plants in widely contrasting styles. And home landscapes in as varying circumstances as a California front garden, a tropical fruit garden in the Pacific Islands, and a kitchen garden in Germany, all illustrate the versatility of edible plants.

R. C.

HERB GARDENS

The herb garden was a feature of ancient kitchen gardens and its cultivation an essential part of monastic life. Here were grown the flavorings for food and the ingredients of medicines and perfumes. They encompassed a much wider range than those which most people think of as culinary herbs today, and included many decorative flowers such as nasturtiums, violets, columbines, roses, sweet peas, iris and even hollyhock.

Most herbs are herbaceous plants, perennials that die back to the ground each winter, but some are woody shrubs so that a herb garden, even in the limited form which is common today, can have a solid structure of permanent planting. Herbs such as rosemary and thyme, which are native to arid Mediterranean hillsides, require very good drainage and flourish in full sun. Annuals, such as sweet marjoram

Above right *Washington Cathedral herb garden, Washington D.C. To the right of the path, planting includes the tall purple-tinged* Salvia sclarea *"Clary,"* origanum, *and pale-foliaged* Stachys byzantina. *The bed on the left has a traditional border of box.*

Right *An informal bed in the England Herb Garden, set among meadows at Honeybrook, Pennsylvania, mixes* Achillea filipendulina *"Moonshine,"* Lavandula augustifolia *"Hidcote,"* Alchemilla glaucescens, Santolina, Allium gigantaeum *and Stork's Bill* Erodium.

Far right *The Henry Price Garden at Wakehurst Place in southern England. This "modern cottage garden" was designed using many herbs to a careful scheme using only the hard colors of the spectrum. Silver-gray foliage predominates with pinks, lilacs, mauves, maroons, soft blue and purple — not hot colors such as scarlet, yellow or orange. Everything is mellow, blurring and flowing together in easy visual harmony. Herbs in the foreground include the pink Obedient Plant* (Physostegia virginiana), *gray-foliaged Wormwood* (Artemisia *sp.*), *and gray and mauve Lavender* (Lavandula augustifolia) *with Catmint* Nepeta *"Six Hills Giant" in the right middle distance. Other plants common in cottage gardens include the Sweet Pea "Burgundy" and the blackish-red-flowered* Cosmos atrosanguinea *silhouetted against the gravel, while the feather plumes top left are an oriental grass* Miscanthus sinensis *and the round lilac flowerheads of Globe Thistles* (Echinops ritro *and* E. banaticus).

also like sun and warmth, but need richer soil and watering; parsley needs both moisture and shade. Mint — of which there are nearly 40 varieties — is the only one of the herbaceous plants generally classed as herbs that likes a lavish supply of water and it too likes some shade.

In the old physic gardens plants were carefully grouped together and planted in separate beds so that they could be easily identified, and avoid any danger of confusion — important when they were used medically. Some guide to the many species used is given by their scientific names. Whenever the specific name is the Latin *officinalis* you can be sure that it originally had a place in the pharmacopeia — though other plants were used in healing too.

Today the herb garden may be just a patch of culinary herbs close to the kitchen door or even on the kitchen windowsill, but there are still many that have been laid out in the manner of the herb gardens of old, sometimes once

Rosemary, thyme, savory, lemon grass and other herbs all grow well in the herb garden of Melbourne's Botanical Gardens, benefiting from the mild climate of Victoria, Australia.

again including the lettuces and other "sallet" plants and the flowers which were previously included, or using the soft grayish-greens of herbs with lavender and other plants to form a gentle background to the flowers of a restrained and aromatic garden.   H. L.

SCENTED GARDENS

A garden which provides fragrance as well as delighting the eye gives an extra dimension of pleasure, and one which the ancient Persian gardeners understood well. Roses were — and are — appreciated as much for their perfume as their beauty, but there are many other beautifully scented flowers. Leaves too, on many plants are aromatic when bruised beneath the feet, rubbed between the fingers or sometimes when merely brushed against.

A surrounding hedge or wall, or a sheltered situation will ensure that breezes will not reduce the strength of a garden's fragrance. Planting by a door or window allows the scent to waft into the house and to be enjoyed when going in and out. Plants with aromatic foliage, such as lavender, origanum and rosemary, will be more fragrant on a sunny border (south-facing in the Northern Hemisphere) and are ideal beside paths, where they are brushed against in passing. This can be taken one stage further by making chamomile seats or lawns. When the leaves are crushed the fragrance is magnificent, especially the non-flowering variety *Anthemis nobilis* "Treneague" which has been developed for such places and requires little mowing. Creeping thyme is also excellent underfoot, planted in the fissures of paths.

If a garden is to offer a variety of fragrances different plants should not be too crowded together, or the scents will become overpowering and difficult to distinguish. A better plan is to use non-scented species to separate the fragrant plants so that each scent can be appreciated for itself.

There are scented plants for almost every circumstance and climate. They range from scented trees and shrubs such as lilac, honeysuckle, the Mexican orange tree *Choisia ternata* (though beware — despite its sweet-scented flower its crushed leaves smell of tom cat!), and sharper-scented eucalyptuses and the aromatic myrtles (especially *Myrtus communis*), to stephanotis, hoyas — *Hoya carnosa* from Queensland is ideal in tropical areas, jasmines, lilies, lily of the valley and hyacinths. Two species, *Cosmos atrosanguinea* and *Osteomeles schwerniae*, have the intriguing smell of white chocolate. Some plants — the tobacco plants (*Nicototiana*) for instance and the strongly-scented but insignificant-looking Night Scented Stock (*Hesperis*) — give off most perfume at night.

The water garden can add its fragrance with beautifully scented water lilies. Tropical species have the finest scents, especially the lotuses,

In this scented garden a high wall prevents the breeze from blowing away the fragrance of its roses. White flowers of Astrantia major *and pale blue* Polemonium caeruleum *complement the more dominant and abundant pinks.*

Left *Sweet Peas* Lathyrus odoratus, *as their Latin name suggests, make a valuable contribution to a fragrant garden. Their pastel colors blend well with those of the* Borago officinalis *planted below it.*

Above right *Formal and informal ideas combine to good effect in this scented garden, making full use of foliage texture to add to interest.*

Right *The gardens of Mottisfont Abbey, in Hampshire, England, are renowned for their roses. Herbs in the borders add to the variety of fragrances which tantalize the visitor during the summer months.*

some of which are also night-scented forms. Other perfumed water plants include the Water Hawthorn (*Aponogeton*), and bog garden plants like Lizard's Tail (*Saururus cernuus*) and for warmer climates Spider Lily and Bog Lily (*Crinum americanum*).

M. B.

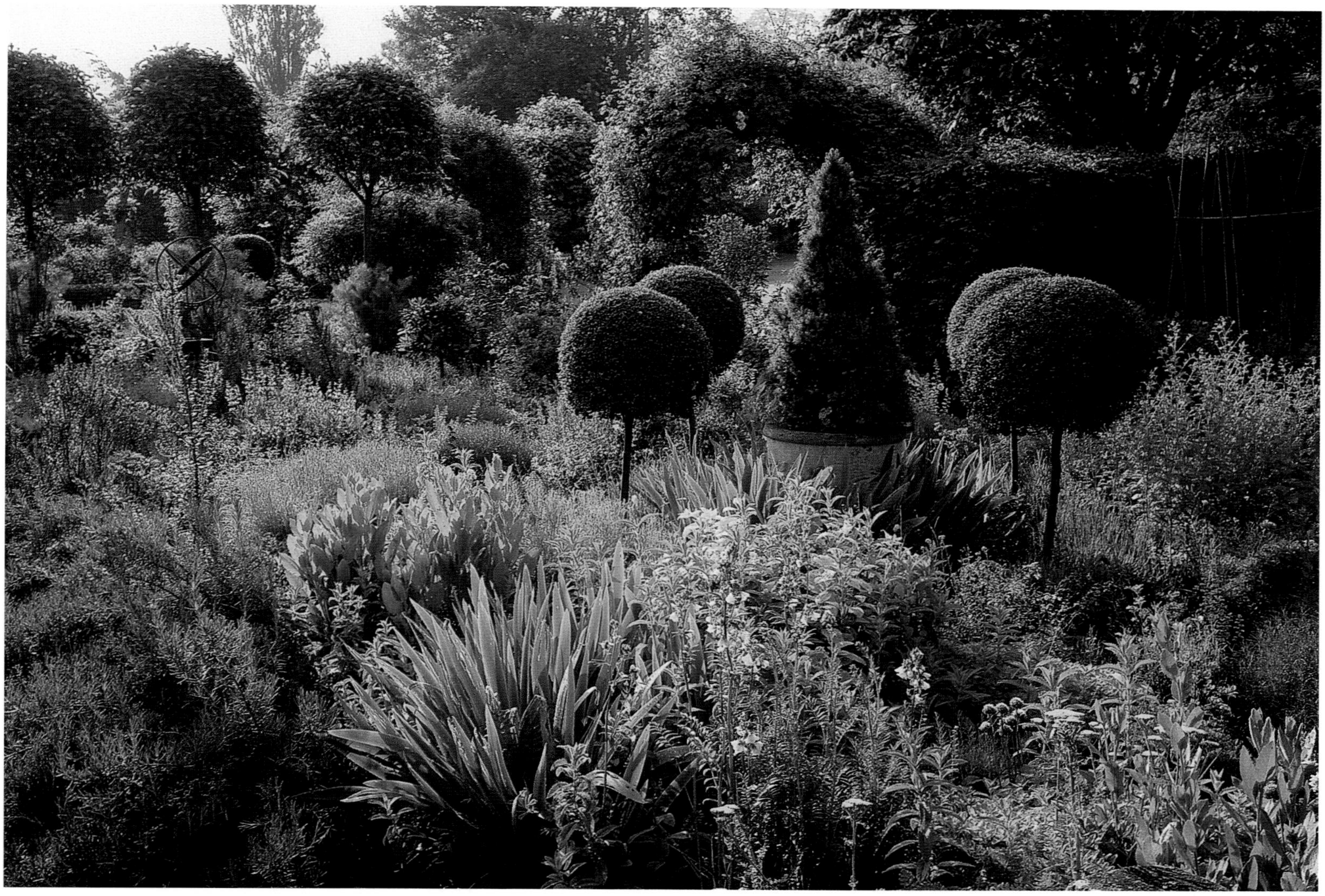

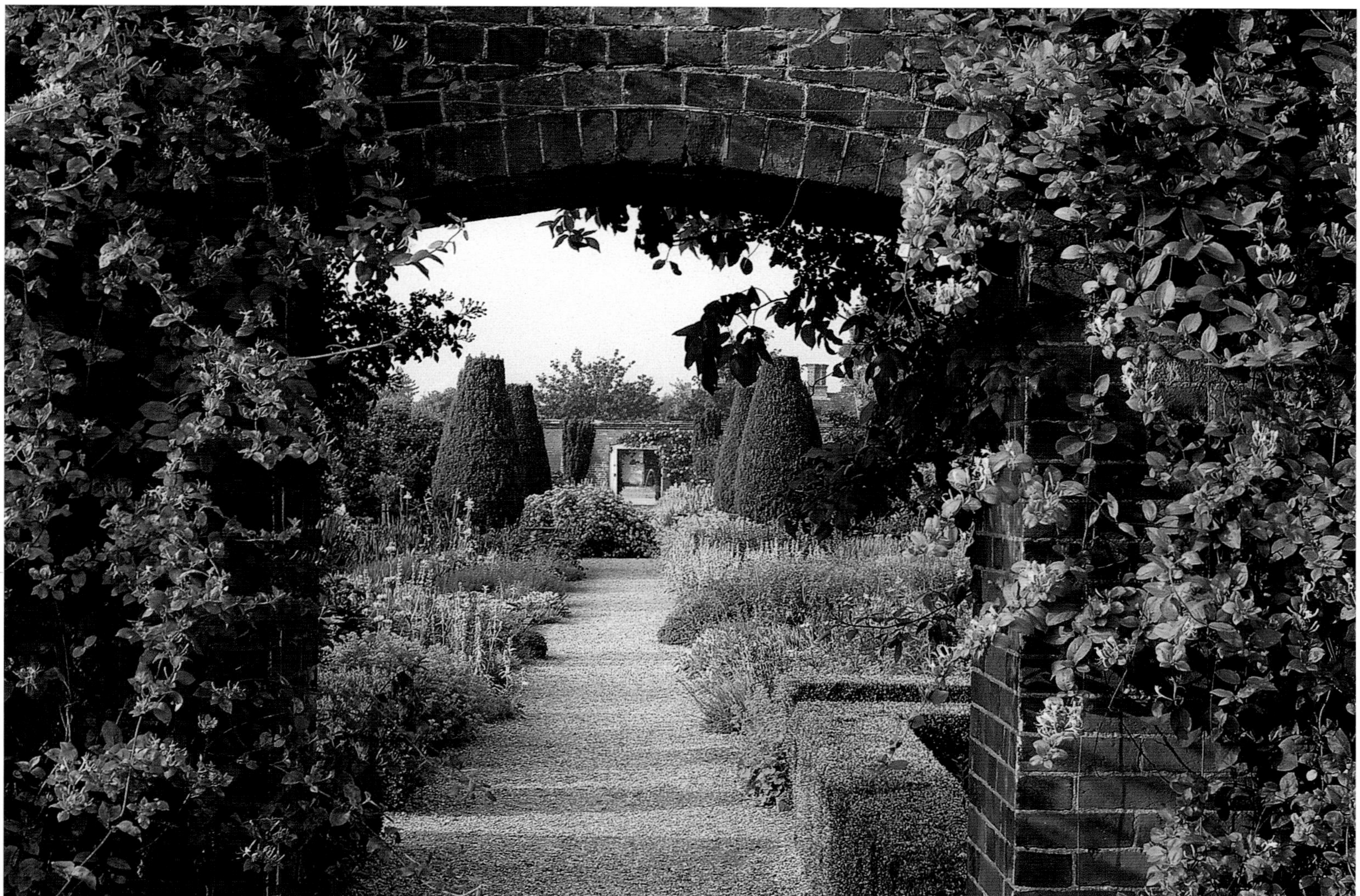

ROSES

There are some 120 different wild roses, each sufficiently distinct for botanists to agree upon its status as individual species. For almost every habitat a rose has been able to adapt successfully. There are roses from the prairies of North America and the steppes of Central Asia, roses from the seashores of Scotland and Japan, roses in the steamy sub-Himalayan jungles and in English hedgerows, roses from the mountains of southern India and Mexico. None, however, cross into the Southern Hemisphere without human help.

In form and habit they are amazingly diverse; some climb aggressively, others make humble little twiggy bushes. The Chinese *Rosa gigantea* throws great swags from tree to tree, putting on 50–60 ft (15–18 m) in a single season; the burnet or Scotch rose runs in and out of the tussocks of grass within the sound of the sea, hiding from the salt gales. Few wild roses fail to protect themselves from browsing animals, having developed a fine armory of thorns, but even these respond to habitat. Roses of open ground have straight spines, while those of species that have taken to using other plants for support possess downward pointing hooks; once growths have pushed up through a host bush, nothing short of a tempest will bring them down.

It is floral structure, not vegetative characters, that make a genus hold together botanically. In this roses are wonderfully constant, although the five- or seven-part pinnate rose-leaf pattern is also usual and distinctive. In botanical terms rose flowers are pentamerous; five sepals, five petals with a mass of stamens and stigmas in the center. This is the simple single rose of heraldry — in fifteenth-century England the red rose of the House of York, the white rose of Lancaster — and the rose of gentle beauty that

Opposite *The parc of the Chateau de Bagatelle, in the Bois de Boulogne, has an outstanding rose garden where trials are held and past winners of medals grown. The "Chinese pagoda" dates from the end of the eighteenth century when the park was first laid out.*

Left *"Blue Nile" won a gold medal at Bagatelle for the French breeder Delbard in 1981 for its perfect hybrid tea shape combined with a superb perfume and, of course, for being on the way to blue. It is unlikely that a true-blue rose will ever appear, but that does not stop breeders trying, nor trying to convince gardeners that they have succeeded by naming a new introduction "Blue . . . .". Descriptions, however, have to be more exact: lavender, lilac, lilac purple or mauve are closer to the truth.*

the Christian church throughout the Middle Ages identified with the Virgin Mary. It appears in illuminated manuscripts painted by devout monks in religious houses around Europe, the buildings themselves using the rose motif to make great rose windows, to decorate ceiling bosses and choir-stall misericords, and in stained glass to add symbolism to devoutness.

The use of roses of all the types then available as sources for artistic endeavor can be traced from early times in both East and West, from Chinese scrolls to Dutch flower-pieces. They reflect the roses grown and the type of roses currently admired. Typically, sprays of wild or near-wild roses flow elegantly in oriental art, whereas seventeenth-century Europe concentrated on intensely double-flowered forms. Such art emphasizes the place that roses were accorded not only on rice paper or canvas but in the garden.

The cut-flower rose trade today employs the most modern techniques of computer-controlled environments in enormous glasshouses, but commercial rose cultivation is by no means new. The thousands of roses used to decorate palace halls for the legendary excesses of Roman emperors were imported out of season from Egypt. (Eliogabalus was said to have smothered guests to death in roses as huge quantities were thrown down from the ceiling.) These were probably the precursors of Damask roses. A millennium later, a rose industry developed and flourished until the nineteenth century, around the town of Provins south of Paris, to cater to the demands of medicine. The Rose of Provins (not to be confused with the Rose of Provence) was — and is — a wonderfully perfumed semidouble form of *Rosa gallica*, known today as the Apothecaries' Rose.

Its striped form *Rosa mundi* appeared in the sixteenth century and has been cherished in gardens ever since.

Gallicas, damasks, albas and centifolias, with the few dog-rose forms, were the only roses available to European gardeners until the turn of the eighteenth century. Then, feeding upon each other, two things occurred to promote roses beyond anything that had happened before; fashion and availability. At the Chateau de la Malmaison, Josephine de la Pagerie, wife of Napoleon Bonaparte, assembled between 1803 and her sadly premature death in 1814 by far the greatest collection of roses hitherto known. In those same years roses from China became widely known and with the recent understanding of the techniques of plant breeding the time was ripe for an explosion of garden roses in which the Empress Josephine was a major influence.

Until this time the season of roses was a short one; June was a blaze of glory, a compendium of soft colors and of scents. Like other flowering shrubs, most roses had a single flowering; only the Musk Rose, the rather erratic *Rose à Quatre Saisons* or Autumn Damask offered a later show. This remains a major drawback with old-fashioned roses.

The China roses introduced from the Chinese treaty ports brought one extraordinary gift: that of remontancy or repeat-flowering. The first, "Slater's Crimson China," was initially called *Rosa semperflorens*, and "Parson's Pink China," which arrived in 1793, was equally floriferous. A blush-colored and a yellow one, strangely tea-scented, soon followed and were eagerly sought-after for rose-breeding programs using different combinations of old and new roses. As the nineteenth century progressed,

1

2

3

4

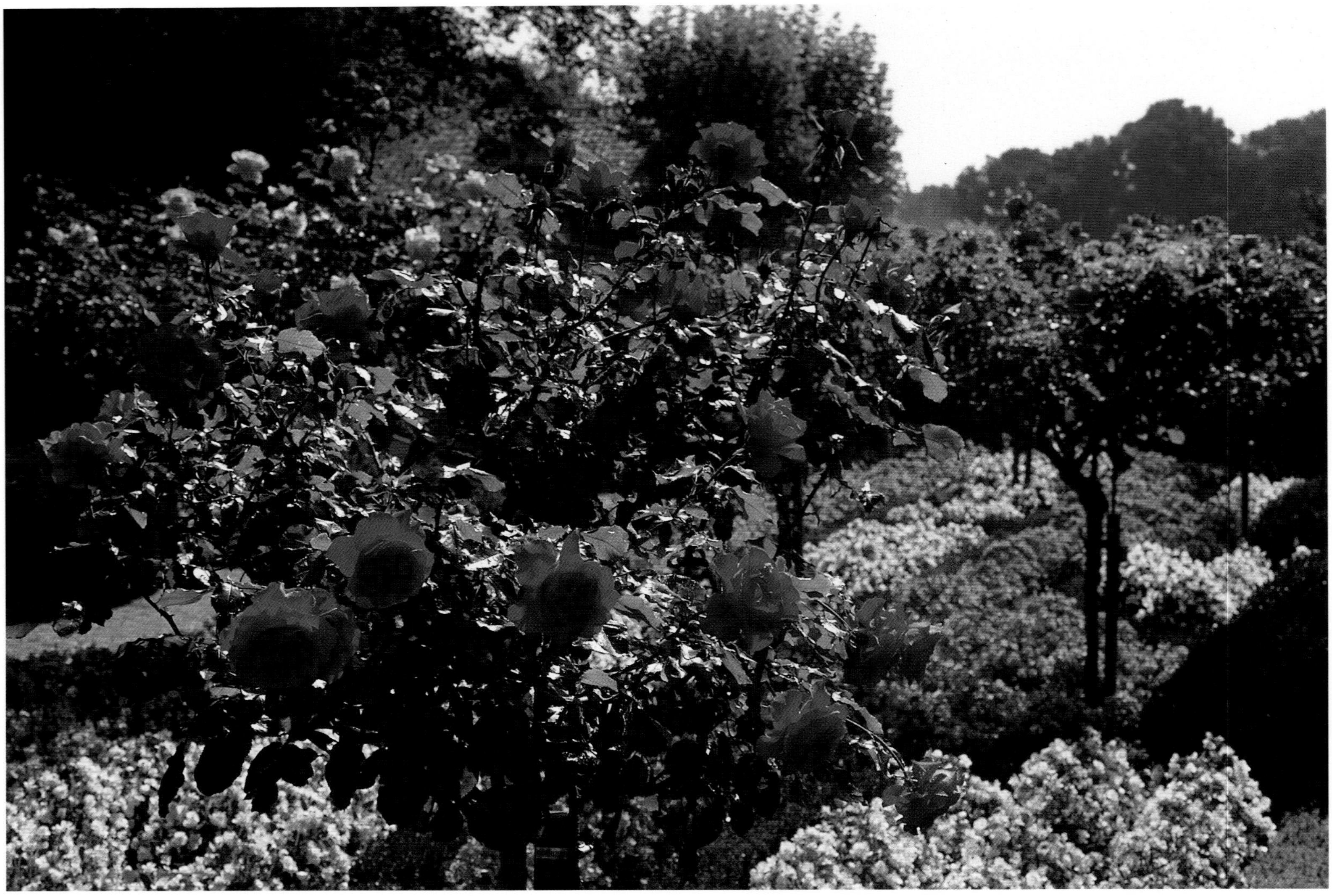

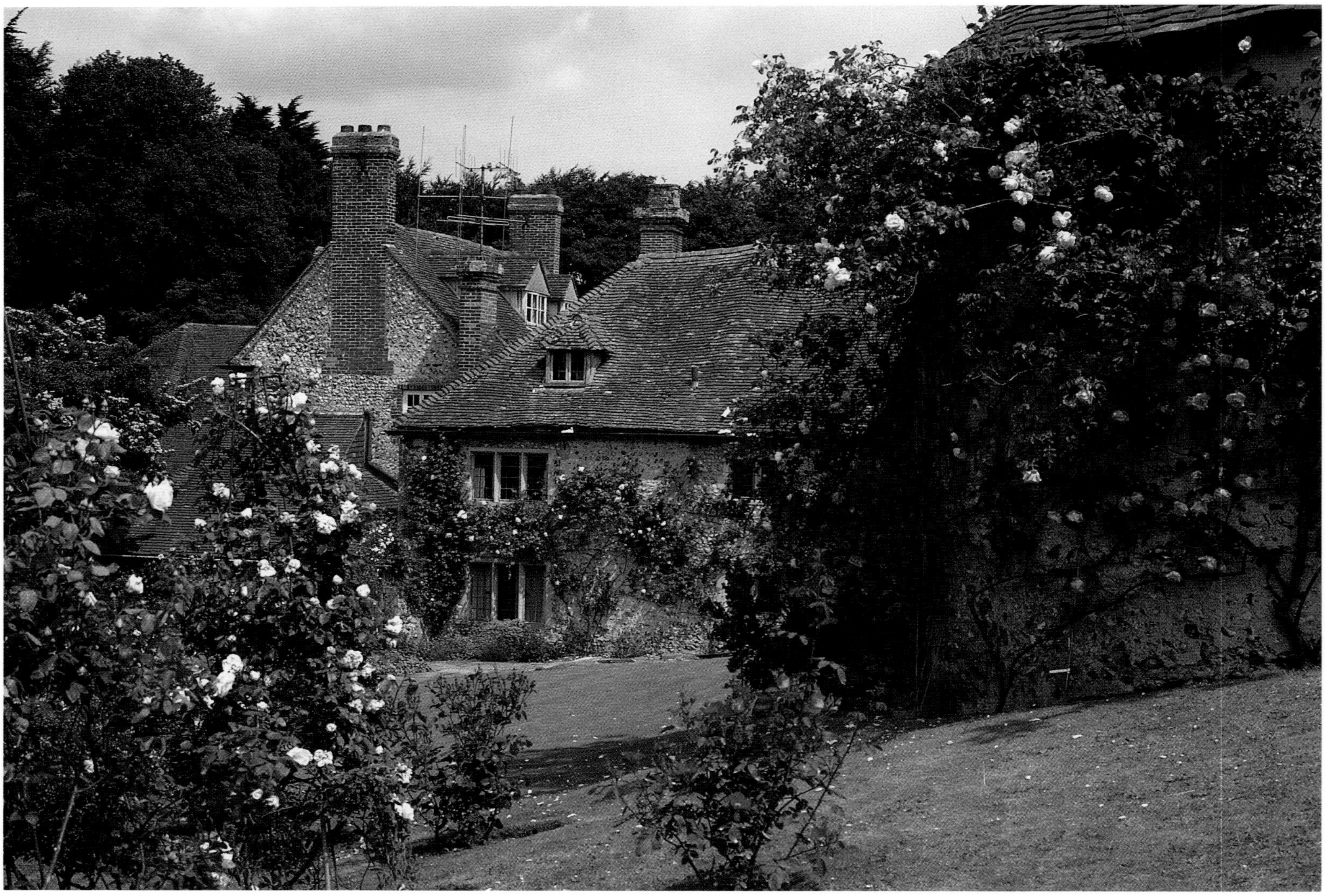

Left *At the Filoli estate, at Woodside south of San Francisco, one of the most spectacular areas is the Chartres Window Garden. It repeats the kaleidoscope of colors seen in the stained glass of the French cathedral. In spring, specially grown Pacific Giant Polyanthus, and in summer Wax Begonias, act as ground cover to the standard hybrid tea roses. Immediate dead-heading and lavish watering and feeding ensure a succession of blooms for many months.*

Right *On rose arches in Longwood Gardens, Pennsylvania, "American Pillar" makes a fine display. It was introduced by Dr. W. van Fleet in 1902 by combining Rosa wichuriana from East Asia, with the Prairie Rose (R. setigera) and an unnamed red Hybrid Perpetual. He aimed to produce roses that would maintain their wood through the severe New England winters. It is a classic rambler, each season producing fiercely armed growths up to 20 ft (6 m) long which the next year carry huge heads of flowers in a short but spectacular show. The whole flowering shoot is then pruned out and the current season's growth trained in its place.*

Below left *At Charleston Manor, on the chalk downs of Sussex, roses are important in a traditionally simple garden. Climbers and ramblers clothe the walls and cascade from a circular dovecot (right), others are supported on tripods while modern cluster-flowered bush roses stand singly in the lawn. Even in the erratic English climate a careful choice of roses can be expected to provide flowers from May to Christmas every year.*

Right *The Royal National Rose Society's headquarters at St. Albans, Hertfordshire, where the gardens are the home of new roses on trial. There are up to 450 cultivars at any one time, the best of which will enter the trade, and permanent collections of about 900 rose species and cultivars. Among the hybrid tea and floribunda roses seen here beside the main walk leading to the house is the orange-red floribunda "Matangi," bred and introduced by Sam McGredy in 1974. It won a gold medal here, at the R.N.R.S., and at trials in Rome and Belfast.*

Hybrid Chinas, Portlands, Bourbons, Tea Roses, Noisettes, Hybrid Perpetuals and Hybrid Teas cascaded into gardens as if from the inexhaustible cornucopia held by the Goddess Flora herself.

Only clear strong yellow and brilliant flame-orange roses were lacking until eventually in our own century genes from the Austrian Yellow and Austrian Copper provided these; thus the full range of modern rose colors were available in further hybrid teas, floribundas and now even miniatures. For such diversity, however, a price has to be paid. The subtropical China roses brought frost-tenderness, and the Austrian Copper a dire susceptibility to black spot disease.

Rose breeding continues today, just as no doubt it will into the twenty-first century, and as long as gardeners grow this, the Queen of Flowers. It is no longer concentrated in Western Europe; the famous Northern Ireland firm of McGredy moved to New Zealand in the 1960s, an even gentler climate. At the other end of the scale, Buck in Ohio and Svejda in Ottawa have concentrated upon one very necessary factor for rose-growers in extreme continental climates — frost-hardiness. Where winter temperatures plunge to -13°F (-25°C) and below (Zones 6, 5 and so on in North America), conventional rose bushes are killed to the ground and, even with winter protection (committed rosarians in the northern prairie states lift and store their roses over winter), growth is slow in spring and seasons are short. Roses to withstand these conditions are not easily produced; that the work continues is proof of the love of roses across the world.

While we see roses in small private gardens everywhere — a few bushes lining the path to a suburban front door, perhaps, or a climber trained over a cottage porch — it is in the big collections that the diversity and indeed prodigality can best be seen. Sadly, though the Chateau de la Malmaison is still well cared for

by the French State and looks much as it might have in the time of the First Empire, the famous rose garden did not long survive its maker.

Suitably, however, the present rose garden there does include "Souvenir de la Malmaison," a lovely Bourbon rose, but one which, dating from the 1840s, the Empress could not have known.

One has to look elsewhere for roses in or near Paris — to L'Hay les Roses and to La Bagatelle in the Bois de Boulogne. At the latter, established roses are displayed and new roses grown under trial. Further south in France, in Lyon, the Parc de la Tête d'Or is noteworthy with up to 100,000 roses.

Germany's interest in roses is stimulated by famous breeders such as Tantau (who produced the famous "Blue Moon" in 1964) and Kordes in Sparrieshoop and fine collections at Dortmund, in the Palmgarten at Frankfurt, on the almost subtropical island of Mainau in Lake Constance, and Sangerhausen near Dresden, which maintains many historic roses which had been lost to Western gardens.

Every country in Continental Europe has rose gardens to match national pride, from Norway's Molde (known as the Rose City), to the Rosaleda del Parque de Oeste in Madrid; from Brno in Czechoslovakia to Belfast in Northern Ireland. North America is similarly studded from the Royal Botanical Gardens in Ontario to Balboa Park in San Diego, California; probably no state in the US is without at least one. But, as roses are plants of temperate climates and need something of an annual resting period, they do not succeed in the tropics, nor where the seasons are not marked, though to some extend a higher altitude can substitute for lack of latitude. The enviable climates (so long as irrigation is available) permit fine roses to bloom in parts of South America, South Africa, Australia and especially New Zealand. Roses are universal.

A. P.

HIDCOTE

Hidcote Manor, in Gloucestershire, England, broke with nineteenth-century concepts of garden design and established a style which has been much copied, not least in the planning of the gardens at Sissinghurst Castle by Vita Sackville-West who called Hidcote "a jungle of beauty; a jungle controlled by a single mind." That mind belonged to an American expatriate, Lawrence Johnston, who bought Hidcote in 1907. Perhaps it was the cold site, high on the Cotswolds Hills which led him to plan his garden as a series of linked compartments, hedged in to give both shelter and seclusion.

Major Johnston abandoned the concept of rigidly separate herbaceous borders and shrubberies which were popular when he arrived. He planned his garden on a rising path which forms the axis for a series of "garden rooms" each very different in mood and treatment. Here there is an alley of pleached hornbeams — the "Stilt" Garden; there a pool with water lilies and goldfish; beside a stream, very natural plantings with ferns and comfrey give a wild look. Some enclosures are designed around a single group of plants — fuchsias, roses, or devoted to a single color. All is not closed in, the largest "room" is a smooth lawn sweeping up to ilexes and birch trees and a view out beyond the garden, while gates from several "rooms" open directly onto the countryside.

The enclosed spaces at Hidcote hark back to the paradise gardens of the Islamic world and the *gardino segreto*, and the formal hedges which divide them have clear links with classical Renaissance gardens, but Johnston was also influenced by the many new plant introductions of the nineteenth century. He was a keen plantsman and there are a number of varieties — most well known perhaps being the famous lavender — which now carry the name "Hidcote."

H. L.

Top *The White Garden at Hidcote is walled with trimmed yew, the beds edged with box, four topiary doves marking the intersection of the paths. Silver-leaved plants and pale flowers predominate, phlox and tobacco plants here succeeding the earlier season's primroses, tulips and daisies. The bright red of Tropaeolum speciosum climbing on the hedges breaks the color scheme, and through the arch a bust of Major Johnston can be seen. This garden is overlooked by a large cedar whose branches tip into the picture.*

Center *The "Pillar Garden" consists of formally trimmed yews, at the base of which are low-growing shrubs and bulbs with contrasting lighter foliage.*

Right *Approaching the "Swimming Pool Garden" a soft-colored brick path leads the eye past beds of blue scillas to the fountain and the garden seat in the further garden with promises of ever more secret places to discover. At Hidcote the garden continually presents a further promise to lure the visitor on.*

Left *The red flowers of dahlias and salvias and the leaves of a Phormium are prominent in the "Red Border" at Hidcote — actually two borders lining a turf path leading to these two gazebos and the "Stilt Garden" of pleached hornbeams beyond. The gazebo with its open french doors on the left is in fact an archway leading to yet another green allée.*

GRASS GARDENS

Grasses have been called "the hair of the earth" and the 7,000 genera of the grass family (Gramineae) grow everywhere on our planet except in the sea and on the Antarctic continent. The ubiquity of grasses makes them friendly and familiar additions to gardens. Their great diversity ensures handsome and sturdy plants for every kind of climate and situation.

Grasses have been grown for millennia, as food and fodder plants. History is full of references to them but no one knows exactly when they jumped the fence from field to ornamental garden.

Not until 1782 does one find a reference to a grass as purely ornamental. The catalog of Englishman John Kingston Galpine, "Nursery and Seedsman at Blandford, Dorset," lists an English native, Feather Grass (*Stipa pennata*) with other flowering plants.

One hundred and one years later, in 1883, when William Robinson published *The English Flower Garden*, grasses were well established as ornamentals. Robinson described *Stipa pennata*: "In May and June . . . the tuft is surmounted by numerous gracefully arching flower-stems, nearly two feet high, and covered with long, twisted, feather spikes." Other grasses recommended for the English flower garden included: Giant Reed (*Arundo*), Pampas Grass (*Gynerium argenteum*, syn. *Cortaderia selloana*), Clump Bamboo (*Arundinaria nitida* syn. *Gargesia nitida*), the Quaking Grasses (*Briza*), Brome Grass (*Bromus*), Drooping Sedge

Above *Grasses, at left a Giant Miscanthus* (Miscanthus floridus) *and, right, Giant Reed* (Arundo donax) *add movement and drama to a long herbaceous border at the North Carolina State Arboretum in Raleigh, North Carolina.*

Right *A dazzling stylized meadow at the Ottesen garden in Maryland is a mixture of Fountain Grass* (Pennisetum alopecuroides) *and Switch Grass* (Panicum virgatum).

Right *The combination of Rudbeckia "Goldsturm" and Fountain Grass (Pennisetum alopecuroides) is long-lasting and ideal for covering the foliage of bulbs after their flowering.*

Opposite above *A great variety of ornamental grasses are available to the gardener who wishes to follow the style pioneered by Oehme Van Sweden to create a garden which is low on maintenance.*

Opposite center *June in the Rosenburg garden on Long Island, New York. A stylized meadow of Sedum (Sedum spectabile) "Autumn Joy" flows around a large Moor Grass (Molinia caerulea ssp. arundinacea) "Windpiel" (center left) and a clump of Sodiopogon (Sodiopogon sibiricus) (center right). The small grass in the left background is Flame Grass (Miscanthus sinensis ssp. purpurascens).*

Opposite below *Golden Reed Grass, Showy Stonecrop (Sedum spectabile) "Autumn Joy" and yucca in a Maryland garden.*

(*Carex pendula*), Lyme Grass (*Elymus*), Millet Grass (*Milium*), Switch Grass (*Panicum*), Fountain Grass (*Pennisetum*), and River Oats (*Uniola* syn. *Chasmanthium*). All were perennials to be planted with other herbaceous flowering plants.

Thirty years later, Gertrude Jekyll added, among others, Eulalia Grass (*Miscanthus sinensis*) and *Luzula sylvatica* to the palette of grasses used in her gardens. She placed the Giant Reed (*Arundo donax*) at pond sides and mixed the English native *Elymus* with other glaucous plants.

In Victorian times, the imposing dramatic forms and exotic plumes of large species peaked in popularity. Large grasses such as Ravenna Grass (*Erianthus ravennae*) or Giant Reed were planted to stand like sentries beside stone entry posts on country estates; Pampas Grass (*Cortaderia selloana*) served as spectacular specimens on lawns.

The fashion for grasses crossed the Atlantic. Large ornamental grasses became a common feature in American zoological and botanical gardens around the turn of the century. In the years between 1890 and 1930 American seed company catalogs typically offered between ten and twenty kinds of ornamental grass seed. In 1930 the Wayside Gardens Company of Mentor, Ohio, offered plants of *Elymus*, *Erianthus*, two kinds of *Eulalia*, *Festuca*, *Pennisetum*, and *Phalaris*, but by 1950 these plants had all but disappeared from the American scene.

One place in the United States where an interest in grasses survived was at the University of Wisconsin. There, in the 1930s, Aldo Leopold began a large-scale prairie restoration. It was to be a scientific investigation of a prairie community, but the result was unexpectedly beautiful. Other Midwestern arboreta followed suit. These restorations exerted a powerful influence on garden design in the American Midwest that continues to the present. Grasses, once the dominant vegetation of the plains, are still the most climatically suitable plants.

Another place where grasses continued to enjoy favorable interest from the 1930s to the present was Bornim, Germany, where Karl Foerster, the legendary German horticulturist and nurseryman, bred ornamental grasses and perennials. His book, *Eintritt der Graeser und Ferne in den Gaerten*, begun during the political upheavals of the 1930s, was not published until 1957. He inspired two generations of German landscape gardeners, some of whom brought Foerster's exuberant, grassy, cottage garden style to the rest of the world.

Today, especially in the United States, grasses are again returning to ornamental gardens, but on refreshing new terms. In addition to their use as handsome isolated specimens or subtly color-balanced components of a perennial border, grasses appear as lyrically beautiful elements in nostalgic stylized meadows. For those living in a highly mechanized society, these gardens suggest the country fields of a simpler, rural past. That they are also easy-care gardens, requiring no chemicals and providing food and habitat for wildlife, adds to their charm.
C. O.

ROCK GARDENS

Rocks as decorative garden features go back a very long time. The Greeks and Romans used them in the construction of the grottos which regained popularity during the Renaissance. In the nineteenth century there was a fashion for the reproduction in miniature of mountains such as the Matterhorn, but this was a short-lived trend, quickly ridiculed by persons of taste. The rock garden style we know today has, to a large extent, evolved from the prolific and forthright writings of Reginald Farrer — sometimes called the father of English rock gardening — who spent his childhood days botanizing in the limestone hills of his native Yorkshire Dales. His keen and critical eye,

sharp wit and his "purple pen" came together to produce those two alpine gardeners' bibles, *The English Rock Garden* and *The Rock Garden*. Within their pages he spelled out the rights and wrongs of rock garden landscapes, casting scorn on the bizarre mountain reproductions and other related monstrosities. Those he especially ridiculed he dubbed "Almond Puddings," "Devil's Lapfulls," "Dogs' Graves," "Drunkard's Dreams," and "Plum Buns." Although botanically dated, *The English Rock Garden* is still a highly respected book turned to by gardeners of today for its cultural advice and for the entertainment of the author's extravagant literary style.

Farrer believed in the use of large stones, firmly set and deeply buried, which would copy nature; not a whole mountain in miniature but

Right *A garden at Toowoomba, Queensland, Australia, effectively uses large boulders as an informal border to a lawn. To match the scale of the rocks the planting includes azaleas and other larger plants as well as ferns, New Zealand Flax (Phormium), orchids and Cedrus deodara "Pendula" below. Dense mixed foliage forms an effective background.*

Above center *A scree garden with deep blue* Gentiana acaulis, *stonecrop, yellow* Alyssum saxatile, *miniature daffodils and pink* Erinus alpinus, *with a magenta Pasque Flower (*Pulsatilla vulgaris*) and the arching stems of* Genista lydia *behind.*

Below center *Troughs with plenty of sharp drainage make a practical and very effective setting for alpine plants and other miniatures. This is an ideal way of growing plants from a different habitat since specific soil mixtures can be used, enabling acid-loving plants, for example, to be grown in areas of chalk — though care must be taken that watering is with lime-free water. In areas with very hard water rainwater can be captured. Stone troughs are now difficult and expensive to obtain but can be simply fabricated from a mixture of concrete and peat poured between two cardboard boxes, one placed within the other. The base should be set with wooden pegs which will ensure holes for drainage.*

Another technique for the specialized culture of choice alpines is to drill holes in pieces of tufa rock for growing plants such as cushion saxifrages, drabas, raoulias and others which require starving and sharp drainage.

an outcrop or bluff imitating Nature at her best. He advocated the setting of rocks to follow the lines of stratification and the same angles of tilt.

Rocks should never be laid in level horizontal strata; they should lie at an angle to the slope so that crevices are formed between them to allow pockets of soil to accumulate, and provide good opportunities for rooting.

Although rock gardens have often been designed as a setting for alpine plants, they need not necessarily be restricted to them. If alpines are featured, however, the rock garden must try to reproduce the conditions under which they grow. They require good drainage, for wet winters are killers of alpine plants. In nature the winter-dormant plants are covered in snow and therefore protected from both desiccation and an excess of moisture. The spring melt brings them to life and they flower precociously with a short growing season. Alpines grow in harsh environments and have to find what nutrients they can in the rock crevices; they live a life of hard regimen and when cultivated resent rich soils and artificial fertilizers.

In Mediterranean climates such alpine conditions are difficult, if not impossible, to create and succulents become a more suitable subject for a rock garden. Under baking sun and in parched soil the succulent or shrubby euphorbias and the garigue plants of the open hillsides and coastal cliffs, such as dwarf species of *Cistus* and *Helichrysum*, are more suitable.

The alpine purist may wish to match species to the type of rock, but few rock gardens are formally organized as ecological creations,

A stepped path through a conventional rock garden in Oregon, planted with alpines. Magenta Aubrieta deltoides and yellow Alyssum montanum "Mountain Gold" form mounds at the top. Sedum spathulifolium spreads along the rock crevices just as it does in nature along the bluffs of the Columbia River Gorge, which borders the State. The rocks used for the steps, though set horizontally, are all different shapes and some have beveled upper surfaces which vary the geometry in a very natural and visually acceptable way. The moss and lichen growing on them reinforces the natural look and shows how well established this garden is.

Left *A lava garden in Mexico City, planted with cacti and succulents. The dark color of the rock makes an interesting contrast to the cacti and succulents.*

Right *The rock garden in Kirstenbosch Botanical Garden, Cape Town, South Africa. Mesembryanthemums, sedums, aloes and Lampranthus amoenus suit the climate here, on the slopes of Table Mountain. The rocks are not arranged in any clear stratification but this is acceptable; such erratic rock arrangements do sometimes occur in nature.*

Below right *An informal rock garden at the Tavola Karaca Arboretum, a private garden and collection created by a Turkish botanical enthusiast near Istanbul. The rocks are arranged somewhat haphazardly and the hard edge to the pool needs further growth to soften its line. Plants include red and yellow potentillas in the foreground with pale violet Aubrieta picea var. glauca "Albertinia conica." The rockery spreads down a hillside and around pools, merging with lawns and tree planting in a horticultural complex which includes its own herbarium and is unique in Turkey. The chalet in traditional local style forms the high focal point for the whole garden.*

Left *A corner of one of the finest rock gardens of its kind in the world, at the Edinburgh Botanical Gardens. It is built of hard and unabsorbent rock from the Scottish Highlands and arranged in a very natural way. The path acts as a foil to the rockwork and its serpentine form draws the visitor's eye onward. Rocks and plants give an interesting range of textures. The Polygonum affine, right foreground, is a superb Himalayan alpine plant but somewhat invasive and has to be kept within bounds if it is not to smother neighboring plants. In winter, when the alpine plants are dormant, the dark leaves of the conifers which give substance and extra height in the distance and the silver trunk and branches of the birch will continue to give out of season interest.*

although the Cambridge University Botanic Garden is one notable exception. This is planted both ecologically and in a series of geographical areas and uses water-worn limestone rock to great effect.

It is vitally important to keep a sense of scale between the rocks and the plants chosen to grow between them, as well as between the plants themselves. This may demand considerable maintenance to ensure that one plant does not dominate another as their respective vigor will vary considerably and an artificial balance will need to be contrived.

Two alternative natural styles of rock gardens are moraine and scree gardens. The moraine garden is developed in a linear fashion, mimicking the pattern of the rocks deposited along the edge of a glacier. The scree garden is composed of small loose rocks sited in a fan-like representation at the base of a bluff of rock. Both forms can be blended into the general landscape of the major rock garden and adjacent lawns to form part of a wider landscape.

T. S.

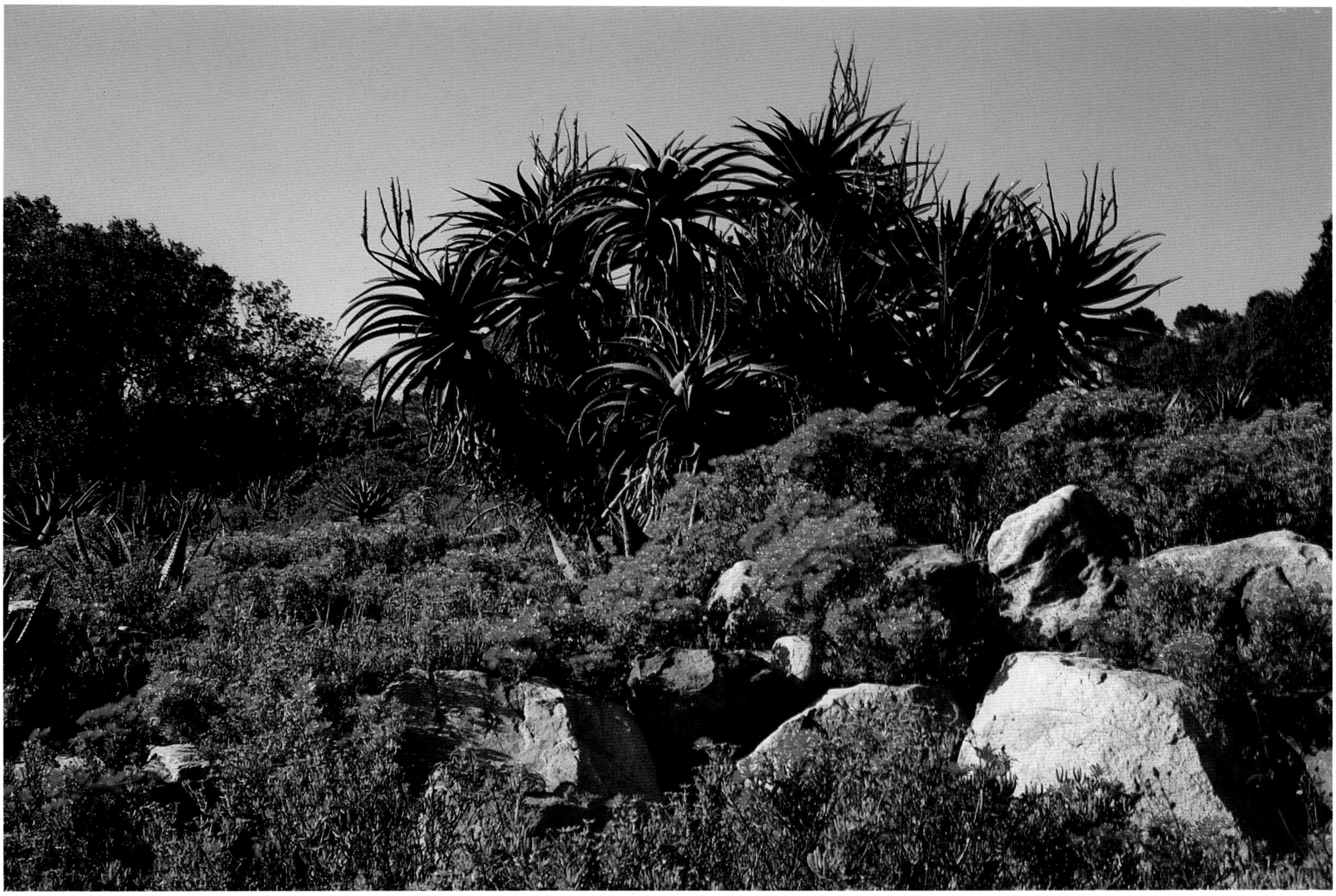

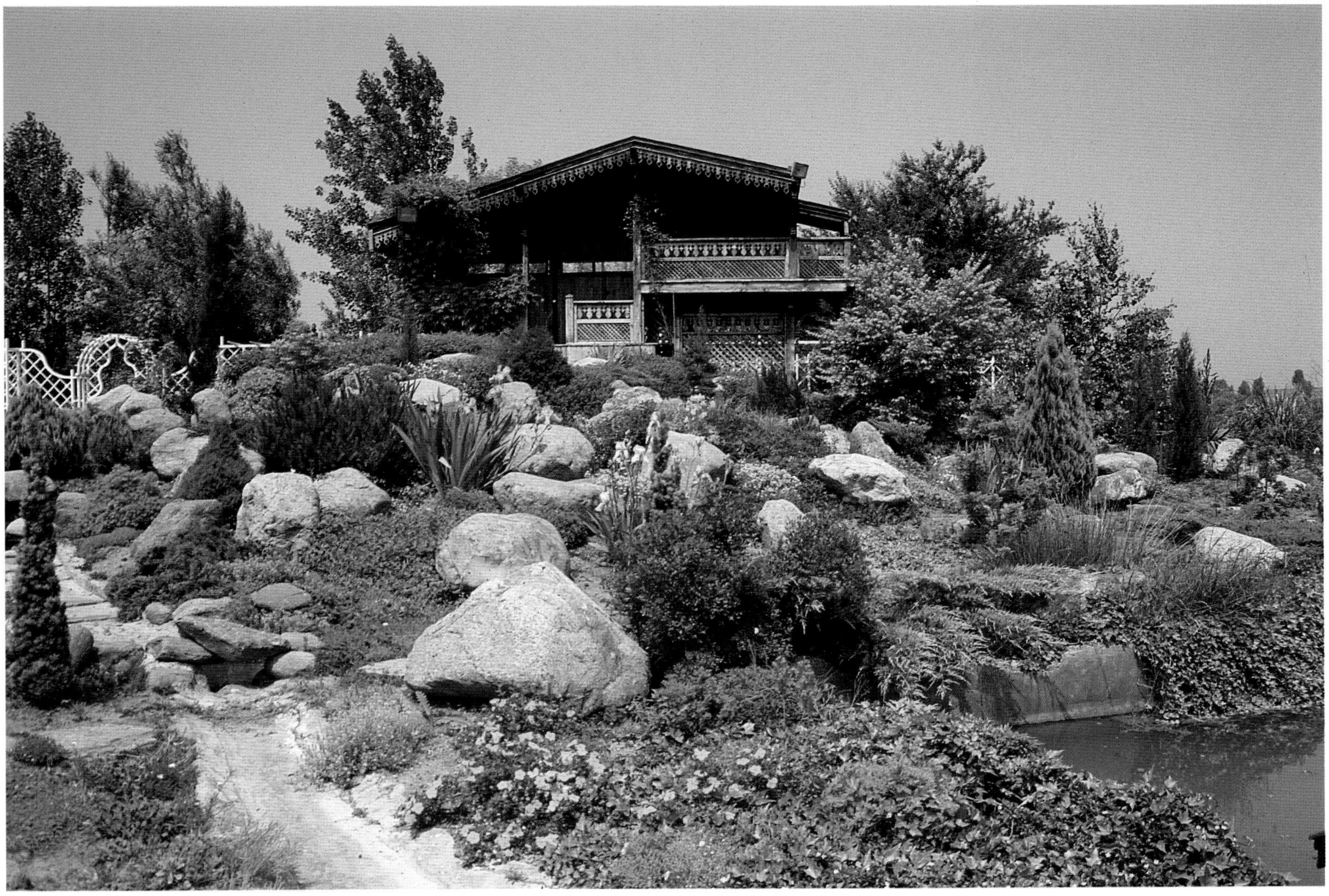

"JAPANESE" GARDENS

The opening of Japan to foreigners and foreign trade in 1868 had a far-reaching influence on other cultures. For some this was a superficial fashion for objects *à la Japonais*, or the use of Japanese settings as in Puccini's *Madame Butterfly*, but many Western artists, including Vincent van Gogh and Paul Gauguin, were influenced by Japanese woodblock prints. Though pictures and descriptions of Japanese gardens awakened some interest and around the end of the nineteenth century some gardens were created in a Japanese style, they seemed artificial to some tastes. Plant-collector Reginald Farrer considered the Japanese butchered plants by their cutting and control.

Josiah Condor's *Landscape Gardening in Japan* (1893) was the first major account to be published — though this presented the ideas of contemporary nineteenth-century Japanese gardens rather than the classic style of the great gardens of Kyoto. Now, however, a wider understanding of Japanese gardening is growing.

The use of water, stone lanterns, maples and azaleas, perhaps with a red-painted bridge or a tea house, is not necessarily going to result in a garden of Japanese style and, although such gardens were created, sometimes by genuine Japanese gardeners, it was not until after World War II — when in Japan itself gardens were being carefully restored — that Westerners began to properly comprehend the ethos of the Japanese style. Individual elements, such as stepping-stones and dry stream forms have been imitated, and with the creation of a number of gardens as gifts from Japan — such as that at Brisbane — originally created for international fairs, examples closer to the genuine article are now more widely found.

The minimalism of the Japanese dry garden is particularly suited to the small town yard, especially when enclosed, and with the renewed fashion for Japanese style which developed in the 1980s, both bonsai and classic garden styles are more often seen.   H. L.

Left *In the Japanese garden at Portland, Oregon, garden stones and clipped azaleas surround a traditional boar scarer. Water from the upper bamboo stem falls into the mouth of the other, filling it until it tips forward, dispensing its water into the bowl. Its weight then makes it pivot back so that the opposite end strikes against a stone, making a sound to scare animals away and raising the mouth to receive more water.*

Below *The Japanese pond garden at the Brooklyn Botanic Garden was designed and constructed by Takeo Shiota in 1914–15. The shape of the lake is derived from a Chinese character for heart or mind. The Torii arch, indicative of a shrine nearby, is modeled on one at Miyajima.*

Left *A garden in Kyoto.*

Right *The Japanese garden at Clingendael, The Hague, Netherlands.*

Below *In another part of the Japanese garden at Portland, Oregon, mossy stones with raked gravel and a path of flat stones both copy Japanese forms. The bamboo fence and the low spreading weeping* Prunus *are individually also Japanese elements but the proximities here do not achieve the balance of the best Japanese style.*

NATIVE PLANTS

Below *Nothing but plants native to California grow in the Grier Garden in Lafayette, California, designed by Ron Lutsko, Jr. Many species of* Ceanothus, Arctostaphylos *and* Baccharis *form the backbone of this garden, which also includes* Artemisia, California Poppies, thrift, Galvezia speciosa, *native irises and many salvias. Low, ground-hugging plants mimic the wild vegetation on the surrounding hills.*

Gardeners have always treasured and coddled rare and exotic plants. For the most part the natives, the common plants of the wayside, were too available and grew too easily to be valued but, from time to time in the great swells of interest in the rare, the exotic, and the greatly improved that sweep over the gardening world, a current of enthusiasm has surfaced for gardening with native plants. Now is such a time: in an age of environmental concern native plant gardening is again gaining new

converts, especially in the United States and Australia.

These countries inherited from England, along with a language, a body of literature that included extensive garden writing and a gardening ethic that strongly influenced garden design. What did not come from the mother country was her climate.

In the United States and Australia, few of the regional climates can support unaided the same range of plants that thrive in a cool, temperate island climate. In hot and humid summers the use of fungicides and insecticides on lawn, roses and many perennials has become the rule in the United States and Canada. In the American Southwest and parts of Australia where rainfall is seasonal, the installation of irrigation systems or daily watering is necessary to keep many exotic plants alive.

In recent years, gardeners in these places have had to reconsider the high cost — in maintenance hours and to the environment — of keeping exotics alive in inhospitable climates. In southern California, Arizona and parts of Colorado, there are restrictions on water use. Everywhere there is growing unease about the use of chemicals for lawns and gardens.

Gardeners are taking a long, hard look at plants of the local wayside and woodland and finding in them subjects better suited to the vagaries of local weather.

In its place of origin, a native plant has had millennia to adapt to the vicissitudes of a particular climate. Once established, it does not require human intervention to keep it alive.

Left *Mt. Cuba in Delaware is dedicated to flora of the Piedmont. At left are a low-growing dog bobble* Leucothoe axillaris *and native* Rhododendron catawbiense. *Blooming at right and in the background is* Fothergilla major.

Far left *In Arizona rainfall is seasonal. The native salvia, yuccas and verbena within the walls of this garden, designed by Steve Martino, would survive without watering. A frugal three to five hours of drip irrigation each week, however, keep them in top form. Outside the walls plants such as the native saguaro cactus fend for themselves.*

Supplemental irrigation and chemical sprays are unnecessary. Better than any other plant, the native is equipped to survive whatever a climate hands out — heat, cold, or drought. And it does so at no cost to the environment.

Instead of using up resources, a native plant pays back dividends, providing habitat and food for wildlife. It also contributes aesthetically. The end result of thousands of years of balancing plant characteristics and site conditions, native plants are triumphs of evolution, looking absolutely right in their places of origin. Native plant communities impart a sense

of appropriateness to a landscape, enhancing "the genius of the place."

There is also another, sad factor contributing to the rising popularity of native plants: in some places, common plants of the wayside are disappearing because the waysides are disappearing. Plants that cannot adapt to new sites become extinct. In June 1990 the US Fish and Wildlife Service issued a list of 200 endangered and threatened plants.

In the United States, a number of arboreta and botanic gardens have responded to this situation by setting aside nature preserves, by

Below left *A meadow in the National Arboretum in Washington, D.C., was created by simply allowing what was there to grow. Exotic species and seedling trees were removed.*

Below *The Tilden Botanic Garden in the hills above Berkeley, California, is devoted to native plants. Here bracken fern and* ceanothus *cover the ground around a western plane tree* Platanus racemosa. *In the background is a large bristle-cone pine.*

Right *At Strybing Arboretum, in San Francisco, Ron Lutsko, Jr. designed this Californian-style meadow covered with wild irises (Iris fernaldii), meadow foam (Limnanthes) and California Poppies. The blue-flowering plants are forms of ceanothus; at left is a native oak.*

Below *A Cumberland Azalea (Rhododendron bakeri) blooms in the Fred Galle Native Azalea Garden at the State Botanical Garden at Athens, Georgia.*

assembling collections of natives, and by installing restorations of native communities. Of the 250 leading arboreta and public gardens, at least 80 have added native plant collections, many in the last three decades. These include Strybing Arboretum in San Francisco, which installed a native plant garden designed by Ron Lutsko, Jr. in 1989, and the Chicago Botanic Garden, which contains prairie restoration, a collection of 110 trees of Illinois, and 15 undisturbed acres.

Seventeen public gardens are devoted exclusively to regional natives. An eighteenth, the Mount Cuba Center, dedicated to flora of the Piedmont, is slated to open soon. Some of these gardens have subgardens featuring special plants. The Fred Galle Native Azalea Garden is part of the State Botanical Garden of Georgia. The Crosby Arboretum in Hattiesburg, Mississippi, boasts a pitcher plant bog. The Local Flora Section at the Brooklyn Botanic Garden grows plants indigenous to the area within a 100-mile (180 km) radius of New York City.

Displays of native plants have a trickle-down effect. The Texas Highway Department has been sowing bluebonnets, Indian paintbrush and daisies along state roads for more than 50 years and has figures to show that the wild-flower plantings both beautify and save taxpayers' money by cutting down on the amount of mowing needed. Forty-five states have followed suit and established some form of native growth program. Amateur gardeners are banding together in native plant societies in 31 of the 50 American states. Canada has a society for wildflowers and another for prairie lilies alone.

This renewed interest in native plants may be the result of environmental awareness and a need for lower-maintenance gardens. It may have come about because it is now easy to obtain formerly rare exotics and, conversely, hard to find disappearing flora that have rarely been marketed. It may be that one associates the words "native plants" with climate-specific plant communities — not weeds.   C. O.

Above and below *The 20 ft- (6 m) high supporting pillars of the Main Conservatory are clothed in* Ficus pumila *and the central floor area carpeted with grass. The flourishing floral display is changed with every season. Foxgloves, daffodils, and hydrangeas border the lawns, while elsewhere more foxglove spires rise from a sea of white lilies* Lilium longiflorum.

LONGWOOD GARDENS

Longwood Gardens, at Kennet Square, Pennsylvania, were begun in the year 1700 when the property was purchased from William Penn by the Quaker Pierce family. At the end of the eighteenth century Joshua and Samuel Pierce started to cultivate an arboretum. In 1906, when the trees were about to be milled for lumber, the property was purchased by Pierre S. du Pont, who became the principal designer of what is now one of America's greatest gardens. They are open to the public and cover about one-third of the entire property of 1,000 acres (400 ha). There are fountain gardens, an open-air theater seating more than 2,000 which was inspired by an Italian *teatro verde*, rose, rock and vegetable gardens, but most memorable perhaps is the huge Main Conservatory and its associated corridors and smaller conservatories, totalling 3.75 acres (1.5 ha) under glass, which are thronged with tropical plants, palms, orchids and year-round displays of flowers which form true indoor gardens. H. L.

Left *The main fountain garden at Longwood, facing the conservatory, covers about 5 acres (2 ha) and is illuminated at night. Some of the jets can rise to 130 ft (39 m).*

Below *Wisteria grown as a standard forms a floral echo of the many Longwood fountains.*

Above *Many of the Greek islands are very dry in summer; some have no water sources whatever but rely on cisterns and shipped-in supplies. But potted plants and small built-up, soil-retaining beds can still produce a bright display.*

Right *Overlooking the harbor of Valetta, Malta, the municipal garden at Merhba tries to defy its climate. Shallow depressions around plants help to retain moisture after watering. The cycads in the center of the bed on the left are more suited to local conditions than the roses which need a greater supply of water.*

MEDITERRANEAN GARDENS

Northerners who travel to Mediterranean lands for summer vacations on beaches in the sun may get a superficial impression of dry and barren lands, but in the springtime even the seemingly barren rocks of Greece are bright with wild flowers. In the Mediterranean-type climate seasonal contrasts are great, with cool wet winters and hot dry summers. There are many spring-flowering summer-dormant plants. Bulbs are typical and herbaceous plants that flower throughout a temperate region summer have often already begun to die down in Mediterranean lands. Most typical perhaps are the highly aromatic plants which are grown everywhere as herbs.

True Mediterranean gardens are often designed more to provide shade than color and the great classical gardens of the past were mainly architectural with much use of water, often brought from a distance. Summer drought makes lavish use of water impossible without irrigation systems, but even the humblest home is usually brightened by pots of colorful plants.

Areas of central and southern California, Namibia, Cape Province, central Chile and of southwest and eastern Australia all share a similar climate. In California the storage of winter water in the dams and reservoirs of the Californian Water Project used to provide plentiful water for summer irrigation; gardens often boasted English-style lawns and lush displays of flowers. In recent years, however, reduced rainfall has left reservoirs low and water in short supply. This looks likely to continue and water conservation is now the rule. Drip-irrigation systems which economize on water are now being encouraged, as well as the growing of Mediterranean plants adapted to long dry summers. California's native plants make up 25 percent of the United States' endemic species and there are many more from the Old World to choose from.

Elsewhere too, interest is growing in xeriscape (Greek *xeros* = dry) and indigenous plant gardening rather than trying to create gardens at variance with the environment. Though dry landscapes may conjure up ideas of only cacti and aloes, typical plants also include winter and spring bulbs, mimosa and flowering almond and glorious summer displays of oleander, bougainvillea and hibiscus.

M.B.

Above *The gardens of Tresco Abbey in the Isles of Scilly, off the southwestern tip of Britain, are warmed by the waters of the Gulf Stream and sheltered from the strong gales which sometimes sweep the islands by a protective belt of evergreen trees and clipped hedges. This makes it possible to grow many Mediterranean and subtropical plants as well as temperate species.*

Left *Pots and cans are pressed into use on the island of Kos.*

Above *Drought-resistant
bougainvillea gives color and shade in
a California yard.*

Right *At the historic Casa del
Herrero (House of the Blacksmith), in
drought-stricken Montecito in
southern California, lawns, pools and
fountains create an impression of
abundant water, but plantings are of
drought-tolerant plants with others in
containers strategically placed to lend
color.*

Far right *Bougainvillea can flourish
even in drought conditions and, when
well watered, will tend to produce
more foliage and fewer flowers.*

A garden at Palm Beach, New South Wales, Australia. The foreground succulents include Houseleeks (Sempervivum) and Fibrous-rooted Begonias — both suit such dry, exposed situations. In the background are bananas and Norfolk Island Pines (Araucaria heterophylla), a tree which survives in sandy soil and resists salt spray.

Left Black boy, bottlebrush and gum trees thrive in this garden at Dalkeith in western Australia.

Far left Lush lawns in a rock star's Californian garden are threatened by the water shortage of the 1990s, but the lemon tree and the succulents are native to such climates and can cope with limited supplies.

Left *An avenue of Royal Palms* Roystonia regia *in Rio de Janiero, Brazil.*

Right *At the Botanic Garden at Adelaide, South Australia, is an avenue of Moreton Bay Figs (*Ficus macrophylla*), an indigenous tree named for the area around Brisbane in Queensland, Australia.*

Below right *Yew and cedars line the ancient avenue at Montacute House, Somerset, England.*

AVENUES

In gardening terms an avenue is an approach to a house which is bordered by trees, usually all of the same species and set at regular intervals on either side of the driveway. Sometimes double rows of trees give an even more impressive effect.

In the past in the gardens of the great mansions of Europe, avenues were intended as an impressive entry. In England it was usual to plant the trees so that, framed by the sculpture of their majestic trunks, the park and surrounding landscape could be seen between them. In France and Germany, where many of the chateaus and castles were situated in deep forest, the formal arrangement of trees indicated the approach to a great establishment.

It takes many years and a lot of space to create such an avenue, but today many of the old northern European and North American avenues of oaks (*Quercus*), beech (*Fagus sylvatica*), elms (*Ulmus*), lindens (*Tilia*) and horse chestnut (*Aesculus hippocastanum*) can be enjoyed as the trees reach the fullness of their maturity. In other parts of the world different trees are used to suit a wider variety of climates. Moreton Bay Fig (*Ficus macrophylla*), Jacaranda (*Jacaranda mimosifolia*), albizias, Royal Poinciana (*Delonix regia*, also known as Flame of the Forest or Peacock Flower) and Tulip Tree (*Liriodendron tulipifera*) are all popular avenue trees.

Most of the trees chosen for avenues have thick trunks and spreading branches, and are well spaced so that the avenue can be appreciated as a whole or the trees enjoyed as individuals. Sometimes narrow trees like poplar, or trees which display long slender trunks such as eucalypts are used, in which case they are planted close together and the beauty derives more from the mass than the single unit.

Smaller trees planted at regular intervals along a garden path are usually described as a "garden walk." Today gardening on the grand scale is rare because of the space and labor required; avenues are seldom planted in private gardens, and garden walks are popular. Pleached lime walks, like those of streets in France, cherry walks and avenues of the smaller dogwoods (*Cornus*) also have appeal.

S.G.

Right *Reflections play an important part in the designer's plan at Courances. The building, known as* La Foulerie *has the romantic aura of one of Marie-Antoinette's fanciful farmsteads but was in fact a genuine working building used for soaking flax.*

Below *Courances is a melding of green grass, water, gray stone and trees which throw a dappled light. Its name comes from the many sparkling springs which feed its calm pools and canals.*

CHATEAU DE COURANCES

André le Nôtre is said to have been involved in the design of the park of this seventeenth-century chateau, south of Paris and about 16 miles (25 km) from Fontainebleau. It is approached by a drive between narrow canals and an avenue of plane trees said to have been planted in 1782 but allowed to grow naturally, not clipped in the formal French style. To the west of the house lies a box *parterres de broderie* beyond which a rectangular pool begins a vista of grass and trees which is crossed by other *allées* where grass, trees and water form a series of formal green spaces. The present appearance of the park is largely due to Achille Dûchene, engaged by the Marquis de Ganay before World War I to restore the park, where a formal French-style *jardin l'anglais* had been created in the nineteenth century. It has since been carefully maintained by the de Ganay family.

H. L.

Above *In one of the wide allées that cross the central axis at Courances a series of shallow-stepped cascades elegantly divides a canal set in a smooth carpet of green. Trimmed hedges border this formal space but above them the free growth of the trees gives a delightful softness, unlike the rigidity of classic seventeenth-century French gardens.*

TOPIARY GARDENS

Topiary, the clipping of trees and shrubs into ornamental shapes, has been popular since Roman times, and perhaps before. Revived in the Middle Ages, it became especially popular in the seventeenth century, was satirized by Alexander Pope and went out of fashion with the development of the landscape garden, came back into fashion in the nineteenth century and now is popular again.

Eastern gardeners carefully trim and train trees and plants to produce more dramatic versions of natural growth patterns in both full size and bonsai forms, but the topiarist trims into geometric or sculptural forms quite unrelated to natural growth. A hedge sheared into a smooth-sided rectangle is the simplest shape, varied by changing levels or the creation of mounds, balls, cones or pyramids.

First cypress, then box was used by the Romans for topiary; John Evelyn claimed credit for encouraging the use of yew in England, where cypress did not fare well; holly, laurel and bay were all used in seventeenth-century France and privet is often used today.

Simpler shapes can be formed as a tree or bush grows — the earlier the start the better — but for more complicated shapes Renaissance gardeners often formed a supporting frame of pliable willow stems. Today, wire can be used, the plant tied to it and trimmed to shape as it grows, a process that can take several years even for simple forms.

Slow-growing plants eventually require much less maintenance but there is longer to wait before their shape is formed. Impatient gardeners can imitate true topiary by covering a wire frame with chicken wire, packing it with sphagnum moss and then growing a small-leaved ivy or other climber over it and trimming off surplus growth.

H. L.

Top left *Geometrical shapes in a cemetery garden at Tulcan, Ecuador, have panels and reliefs clipped into their sides, a technique sometimes used for house names and numbers, while in the foreground a turtle tops a Cypressus amazonica plinth.*

Center left *An elephant herd at Ayutthaya in Thailand. Topiary has been taken up all round the world.*

Opposite *The topiary at Compton Wynates, Warwickshire, in the heart of England, seems to complement the early sixteenth-century house, but it dates from 1895, not from Tudor times. It was designed to replace Victorian parterres which were proving too expensive to maintain, though historical suitability did play a part in this choice. Now it is gone: the cleverly shaped yew and box trees were all dug up in 1983.*

Left *Topiary does not have to be on a large scale as this clever design for a Sydney, Australia, garden shows.*

TROPICAL GARDENS

"Tropical garden" is a term which describes not only gardens between the Tropics of Cancer and Capricorn, but many others where frost, rarely, if ever, occurs, where there is plenty of glorious sunshine and where generous helpings of moisture and warmth are the rule.

Such a garden might seem to be a gardener's paradise, but it has its own set of plant stressors and climatic limitations. Heat, drying winds and, if the garden is very near the sea, salt spray and salt are common problems in most tropical gardens. In addition, there may be little difference between day and night temperatures. Plants that need a significant nighttime drop or, like the tomato, a cooler temperature in which to bloom or set fruit, will not perform well. Some, like the Poinsettia, bloom in response to shortening day length and need that variation.

Many of the world's warm regions experience seasonal rains alternating with dry periods, and plants that originate in such areas respond to the presence or absence of moisture. For example, bougainvillea flowers most profusely during a dry period: withholding water for two weeks prior to blooming will induce flowers on the almost lifeless branches.

Other plants have evolved unique coping mechanisms in response to drought. The Pony Tail Palm (*Beaucarnea recurvata*) stores its own water. The yucca's dense, waxy leaves retain moisture and tolerate salt spray. *Yucca gloriosa*, growing 6 ft (2 m) in height, and *Yucca filamentosa*, more compact, are excellent plants for seaside gardens.

The key to successful gardening in the tropics lies in choosing plants from a climate very similar to one's own. Then there is the greatest chance of success.

Ferns and aglaonemas thrive in humid, shady gardens. The Bird's Nest Fern (*Asplenium nidus*) makes a beautiful specimen, its lime-green leaves forming a perfect rosette. The diversity in leaf shape, size, and variegation found in aglaonemas make them suitable for mass-planting in semi-shaded locations.

Hibiscus does best in full sun. The variety "President" and its variegated leaf sport, "Cooperi" are excellent for hedging. Hibiscus varieties are so numerous that it is probably best to choose what most appeals to you when you see it in bloom at the nursery. Water hibiscus plants thoroughly to encourage deep rooting and to discourage bud-drop.

For color and effect, *Mussaenda* spp. and the Jade Vine (*Strongylodon macrobotrys*) are real winners. The mussaendas are colorful, sun-loving shrubs that can attain 6 ft (2 m) or more in height. Although they bear small yellow flowers, they are mainly prized for the magnificent floral bracts which surround the flowers. *Mussaenda frondosa* bears masses of white bracts; those of *Mussaenda erythrophylla* are bright scarlet. Prune these shrubs after flowering

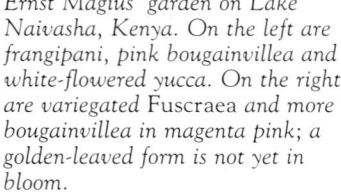

Ernst Magius' garden on Lake Naivasha, Kenya. On the left are frangipani, pink bougainvillea and white-flowered yucca. On the right are variegated Fuscraea *and more bougainvillea in magenta pink; a golden-leaved form is not yet in bloom.*

John Allerton's garden at Kaui in Hawaii after a heavy tropical storm. Some of the palms are said to have been planted at the time of Captain Cook's landing.

is finished to induce new shoots. The Jade Vine requires consistently moist, rich soil and will thrive in a warm, humid garden. A strong trellis will be required to support the 80 ft- (24 m-) long vine which bears masses of blue-green flowers on long pendulous inflorescences. Site this magnificent plant in a sunny location. Place a decorative bench nearby and enjoy!

One thing is certain, plants which respond to sunshine, moisture and warmth will grow quickly in a tropical garden. Nutrients must be regularly supplied. Judicious pruning will be required to control and direct plant growth while good garden hygiene will be needed to keep weeds, plant pests and diseases at bay.

Most important of all, choosing plants carefully with regard to their individual requirements for soil, moisture and light will ensure success in tropical gardening. The right plant in the right place will respond to optimum conditions of light, temperature, moisture, humidity and nutrients by growing to perfection. M. L.

Below left Heliconia psittacorum.

Below *Torch ginger* (Etlingera elatior)

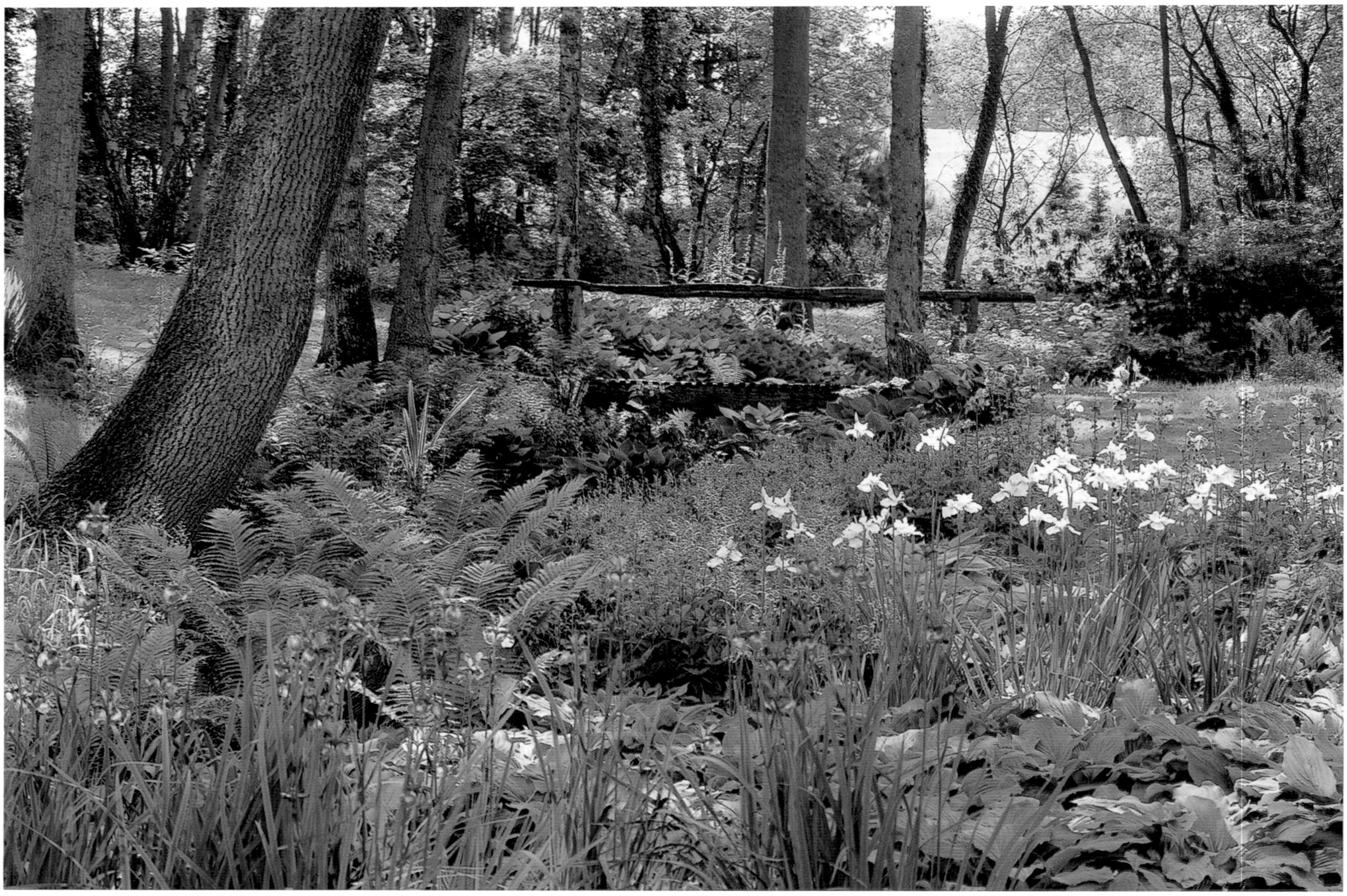

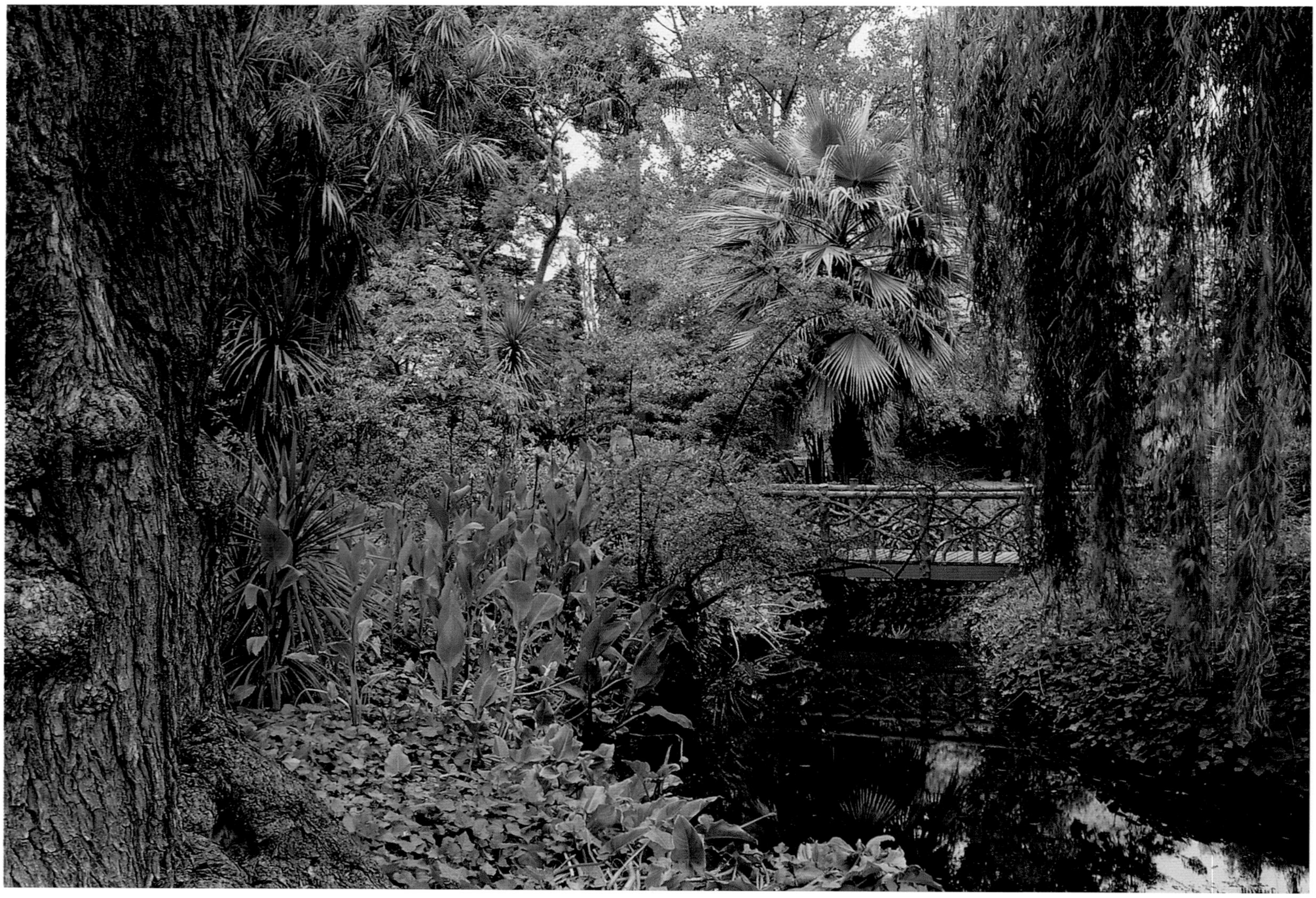

WOODLAND GARDENS

Left *In Sheffield Park, Sussex, drifts of naturalized iris and Canterbury bells, foxgloves and ferns give flower and foliage interest to the lower layer of planting.*

Right *Azaleas and rhododendrons make a dazzling display at Leonardslee, in Sussex.*

Below left *Rippon Lea, Victoria, Australia is a nineteenth-century garden created around a mansion in the suburbs of Melbourne. With plentiful water available it can support a lush growth of dense foliage through which paths wander. A lake is dotted with islands linked by rustic bridges which are of cast iron made to look like wood. A mixture of species from different climates can be grown including here the Cabbage Tree (Cordyline australis), the rain forest Fan Palms (Livistona), Cannas, Arum Lilies (Zantedeschia), Royal Palms (Roystonea) and Weeping Willows (Salix).*

Below right *Fall color at Wakehurst Place, Sussex.*

Woodland has been an important feature of many gardens from Pliny's classical villas to the medieval orchard, the bosky plantations of Versailles and the landscaping of "Capability" Brown, but the idea of the woodland garden is closely linked with the introduction of exotics and the development of plant collections, especially the rhododendrons and azaleas which arrived in Europe in the nineteenth century.

Arboretum collections at first tended to show off individual specimen trees rather than be planned as a pleasing whole, but a more natural arrangement developed later, especially under the influence of William Robinson's concept of the Wild Garden. The rhododendron and other new shrubs suffered from exposure to cold winds and needed shading from strong sun to avoid drying out. A woodland environment, like that in which so many of them grew naturally in the Himalayas and other areas from which they originally came, proved ideal for them.

Robinson espoused the idea of mixing exotic and native plants which liked the same conditions: "the winter aconite flowering under a grove of native trees in February; . . . the Apennine anemone staining an English wood blue before the blooming of our bluebells." He was enthusiastic about the naturalization of daffodils and bluebells in woodland, and advocated planting in "cloud patterns."

The mixture of native and new trees, shrubs and plants, if carefully planned, allows three distinct layers of plant growth: the trees and tall shrubs form a canopy which gives both frost protection and shade to smaller shrubs which in turn protect the ground cover and shade-loving smaller plants. Leaf fall provides useful mulch and helps maintain acid levels as the leaves decay.

Although new planting to provide windbreaks could be developed as woodland gardens, the fast-growing conifers do not create good conditions for growth beneath them. Woodland gardens take a long time to become established and most such gardens have been developed from existing woodland, carefully thinned and with the addition of native or exotic shrubs and herbaceous plants chosen to fit the site and its earlier growth.

Large numbers of trees are not necessary to create the effect of a woodland garden. A small group, or even a single large tree can provide many of the same conditions, although densely-leaved or shallow-rooting trees can keep direct rainfall off the ground immediately below, and may take so much moisture from the soil that only the hardiest plants can grow beneath them.

H. L.

WATER GARDENS

Water will add an extra dimension to any garden, whatever its size. It can offer a variety or even a choice of moods, from the reflective calm of a smooth pond to the turbulent rush of a cascade or the graceful plumes of a fountain jet. In large parkland a lake can become the dominant feature of the landscape but in a small garden, unless it is only one of a succession of spaces within a larger garden, it is best to keep the expanse of water comparatively small. Swimming pools, except in climates like that of California where they may become the focus of activity on which the whole garden centers, are usually best in a separate compartment, screened from the rest to avoid a conflict of style.

To make the most of reflections in the water, at least two-thirds should be kept free of plants,

Below *The bog garden at Wakehurst Place, Kew Garden's "country branch," is bright with swathes of pink polygonum and red and yellow primulas. A bog garden is easily created by extending the edge of a pond to form a separate soil-filled pocket into which water can percolate, or even using a tub or digging a small hollow and lining it with plastic where there is no pool or pond.*

Left *Formal tanks of water at the Alcazar, in Cordoba, Spain, in the direct tradition of the Islamic garden, are planted with lilies.*

Far left *Nymphaea "Pink Sensation" is a hardy lily that produces several flowers at a time over a long season.*

Below *The views at Sheffield Park, Sussex, originally laid out by "Capability" Brown, have been changed by later planting but large expanses of water still mirror the feasts of fall color.*

1 *In the Portal Gardens of the Alhambra, in Granada, Spain, water flows through narrow channels from pool to pool cooling the air and filling it with constant sound.*

2 *Soft grasses, clipped bushes and trees make interesting contrasts in an unusual tidal garden in Tokyo, and the falling tide reveals rock patterns that change the scene.*

3 *The willow fountain at Chatsworth, Derbyshire, England recalls the speciality fountains of Persian and Renaissance gardens.*

4 *A beautiful pool in Shropshire, England. Linked to the surrounding walls and building, the stone edging on the far side looks right, and overhanging vegetation breaks up any harshness to the line. Irises, marsh marigolds and primulas lead the planting inwards to the water lilies, which will make a fine display later in the year, and anemones, foxgloves and geraniums make this a cottage garden by the waterside.*

1

2

3

4

but planting, together with fish and other creatures, prevents a pond from becoming stagnant. Plants should be chosen carefully to avoid excessive growth of algae or one plant taking over the whole pond. A pump used to produce fountains or a cascade will oxygenate the water and keep it fresh.

Siting a pond or pool requires some care. A pond that is intended to appear natural may just look out of place if sited too near the house and will be most effective in a natural-seeming hollow or at the lower end of a garden. A formal pool or fountain basin on the other hand, can be effective on a terrace or on higher levels as well. A formal pool, hard-edged in stone, looks best when the edges are not concealed by planting, but a "natural" pond benefits from edging plants that blur the outline, especially if it is necessary to conceal concrete or a plastic liner. If vegetation is allowed to overhang the water, the water level and any scum line or plastic above the water will be thrown into shadow.

If the pond freezes in winter, a smooth slope, wider at the surface, allows ice to expand easily upwards, minimizing the risk of cracking or other damage.

Ledges around the pool, or containers mounted on bricks allow plants to be grown at the depth they require to flourish. Adding pockets which are filled with earth but kept damp by overflows from the pool will provide the habitat for bog plants.   H. L.

Above left *A quiet pool at Barnsley House, Gloucestershire.*

The Sacred Lotus Nelumbo nucifera *is not hardy in temperate climates and needs frost-free winters to be grown outdoors, but its lovely blossoms raised above the water and the fine scent they produce make them wonderful water-garden flowers.*

Below *Magnolia Gardens, South Carolina.*

ROOF GARDENS

For apartment-dwellers or those living in close-packed city blocks a roof or balcony may provide the only opportunity for a garden. Large apartment buildings and department stores sometimes have shared gardens which are accessible to all residents or customers, and business premises may also exploit their roofs in this way.

Large roof gardens, with a quantity of soil and subsoil and extensive planting, require considerable support and will usually have been purpose built. The weight-bearing capacity of the roof should always be expertly checked before embarking on such a project, and you may need landlord's, neighbors' and even local

government agreement before going ahead. The roof must be watertight and well drained, a layer of asphalt often being laid to ensure this, with tiling or wooden decking over that.

Growing plants in lightweight containers is usually more practical than laying soil. Vermiculite is a lighter growing medium than soil, but contains no nutrients and requires regular feeding with fertilizers, which will be needed in any case to replace nutrients which leach away from soil-filled containers.

Rooftops and high balconies are often exposed to the wind and windbreaks may be needed, which will also help to provide a measure of privacy and to hide unsightly parts of the view. Hardy plants may form a sufficient barrier, but trelliswork and other conventional screening, and plastic or glass sheeting are alternatives according to the protection needed. With plants growing over them they will not be obtrusive, but they must be securely anchored so that they cannot blow away and cause damage or injury below.

On an exposed rooftop containers dry out quickly and frequent watering may be necessary. A water supply on the roof will make watering much easier, and it may be worth installing an irrigation system for a large roof garden, especially if it has to be left untended for days at a stretch. Remember, however, that the use of self-watering containers will add to the weight which a roof or balcony has to carry. If a balcony is vertically aligned with others beneath make sure that you do not give them a soaking when watering!

H. L.

COURTYARDS
AND ATRIA

The atria of Roman houses and the patios of the houses of Moorish Spain set a pattern for courtyard gardens which persists into our own time. No longer merely an enclosed area in a domestic building or a palace, the courtyard may now be the light well or central focus of an office block, and the atria no longer be open to the sky but glassed-in as part of a bank, hotel or shop.

Planting is usually restricted, tiles or paving and plants in containers providing a more easily maintained scheme. Where climbing plants are used, or where balconies and upper floors offer further plant locations, the courtyard garden can extend upward and become a focal point for the whole building.   H. L.

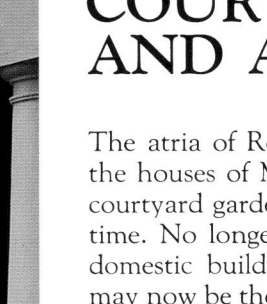

Above *Formal plantings of cypress and box complement the pattern in brick and stone in this central courtyard; a fountain completes a pleasant garden that can also be enjoyed from the surrounding floors of Skyline Place.*

Opposite *In a courtyard in Cordoba rose arches curve in to the central palm, while creepers have been carefully trained to follow the arcading.*

Above left *Geraniums and roses in the courtyard of San Cristobal de las Casas, Mexico.*

Left *The atrium of Marriott's Desert Springs Hotel at Palm Springs exploits a geometric cascade and extensive plantings, on the central terraces and from the balconies of each floor.*

Illustration Credits

The publishers wish to thank the following for permission to reproduce photographs and other illustrations. (a) above; (b) below; (c) center; (t) top; (l) left; (r) right.

A-Z Botanical, 66-67, 204(b).
Adelaide Botanical Garden, 140, 141, 148(b), 156(l), 279(a).
Ashmolean Museum, 112(t).
Matthew Biggs, 101, 105(a), 230(cl).
David Bateman, 168(a), 241(c).
Bistum Archiv Hildesheim, 24(b).
Peter Brandham, 149(b), 165(al), 263(a).
Bridgeman Art Library, 298-299, 76(al); Bib. Nat. Paris, 26,
Bib. Nat. Vienna, 24(a); BM, 90(b); Christies, 71(a).
British Museum, 25(ar), 34(b), 36(a), 45(b), 64.
BTA, 234, 251(l).
Brooklyn Botanic Garden, 152-153(b), 156(4); Calabrese, 100, 265(r); Malave, 153(r).
Geoff Bryant, 116.
Chatsworth Carpenters, 209(r).
Ciba-Geigy, 294(b).
C. Cottrell-Dormer Collection, 70(a).
Country Life, 40(b) 89(a), 226.
Rosalind Creasy, 239, 240, 241(bl)(br), 243(a).
Dalton Pavilions 224-225(b).
Barbara Dobbin, 149(a).
Andrew Driver, 292.
ET Archive, 37, 39(a)(b), 54-55, 58(b), 152-153(t).
Mary Evans, 83(a).
EWA, 62, 63(all), 68, 95(b), 103(bl), 111, 113(a), 114(all), 115(t)(c), 117, 118, 119(b), 122-123, 124(al), 125(r), 126, 127(al), 128(b), 161, 165(b), 167(al), 179, 193, 198, 210(al), 210-211(a), 219(b), 220, 230(b), 232-233, 233(a), 272; 276(a), 277(a), 286(a)(b), 293(t)(c)(b), 294(a); Harpur, 192(b), 199(a), 221(bl); Harpur/Hicks NSW, Aust, 167(ar); Hicks, 282(b); Sir Peter & Lady Finlay, 207(3); Westwater, 218(b), 219(t)(c).
Werner Forman, 27(a), 29(a).
French Govt Tourist Board, 74(l), 225(a).
Futile Press, 94(ar)(c)(b).
Garden Picture Libary, 69, 70(c), 90(a), 230(t); Garden Picture Library/Thomas, 248-249.

Gnome Reserve, 222(a).
Susan Griggs Agency/Yeomans, 204(c).
Gil Hanly, 3, 4, 5, 6, 7, 8, 9, 151, 158, 159, 174, 175, 227.
Harry Haralambou, 194(b), 211(ar), 238(bl), 267, 272-273(a), 273(b).
Historic Annapolis Inc., 79(a).
Historic St Mary's City, Maryland, 61.
Michael Holford, 13(b).
Hunt Institute for Botanical Doc., 124(b).
Hutchison, 92(b), 130-131, 178(c), 274(b), 279(b); Beddow, 47; Berman, 30(b); Collomb, 221(ar), 224(bl), 275(b); Egan, 223(a), 274-5(a); Gerard, 283; Hatt, 56(br), 223(bl), 312(a), 319(b); MacIntyre, 31(b); Martin, 41(a); Motion, 295; Pate, 121; 297(t); Pemberton, 29(b) 42; Regent, 53, 228-229, 236(b), 237(a)(b), 297(bl); Rippon, 202(a); Taylor, 224(al), 282(c); Wright, 282(t).
Margaret Johnson, 89(b), 156(2), 164(b), 172(a), 203(b), 235(a)(b), 262(a)(b), 263(b), 284, 285(t), 285(br), 287(a)(b), 288(bl), 291(t), 296.
Peter King, 213(a).
I. Kirby, 96(b).
Kunst Institut, Frankfurt, 23(a).
Andrew Lawson, 71(b), 72(a), 73(a), 74(r), 82, 156(3), 169, 170, 187(3)(4), 189(a)(b), 206(b), 207(1)(5), 210-211, 222(b), 231, 241(a), 244-245, 246, 247(a)(b), 250, 254(a)(b), 255, 261(al), 290(3)(4).
Marilyn Light, 119(a), 285(bl).
Sam McGredy, 108(all).
Mansell Collection, 14(a)(b), 72(b), 76(b).
Julian Matthews, 112(br), 128(a).
Lewis Matthews, 104(all).
Michael Maunder, 155(all).
John Medhurst, 15, 19(a), 20(l)(r), 21, 23(b), 32-33, 38, 58(a)(c), 59(a), 163, 172(b), 176, 177(all), 178(t), 180(3)(4)(5), 181(a)(b), 184, 185(a), 186(a)(b), 187(1)(2)(6), 188(a)(b), 190(all), 191(l), 192(c), 195(a)(b), 197(a), 213(b), 254(c), 280-281(all), 289(a), 290(l).
Mendel Foundation, 107(r).
Monticello/C. Harrison Conroy 78(b), 79(b), 110(bl).
Tony Morrison/South American Pictures, 97(a), 278.
National Gallery, London, 236(a).
National Library of Australia. 144(a).
John Neubauer, 77, 166(a), 187(5), 196, 209(a), 221(al), 259(t)(b), 297(r).

Old Salem, Inc., 81(a).
Carole Ottesen, 31(a), 50, 78(a), 80, 94(al), 97(b), 110(br), 165(a), 178(b), 207(4), 208(a), 209(b), 217, 221(br), 256-257, 258, 259(c), 266(a), 268(a)(b), 269(all), 270-271, 272(al), 291(b).
Park Seed Co., 134(a), 138(c)(br), 214(c)(b).
A.P. Paterson, 249(r), 251(2)(3)(4), 252(a)(b), 253(b).
Jerry Pavia, 109, 167(ac), 180(al), 191(r), 192(t), 173(a), 218(c), 238(r), 242(b), 261(br), 266(b).
Joanne Pavia, 162, 164(a), 171(a)(b), 210(b), 212(b), 230(r), 242(a), 264-265.
Paul C. Pet, 136-137.
Plimouth Plantation, 60.
Royal Botanical Garden, Kew, 150(a), 151, 290(2).
Royal Horticultural Society, 75(a)(c), 83(b), 133(a).
Scala 35(all), 40(a), 41(b), 44; Scala/Museo dell Terme, 16-17.
A.D. Schilling, 51(a), 180(ar), 200-201, 204(t), 205(b), 206(a), 216, 243(b), 253(a), 275(ar), 288-289(b).
Science Photo Library/Fraser, 324.
Scott Polar Institute, 123(c).
Singapore Botanical Garden, 145, 146-147.
John Smith-Dodsworth, 103(al)(ar).
South African Tourist Board, 148(a).
Spectrum Picture Library, 30(a).
Frank Spooner, 75(b), 131(a); Gamma/Kurita, 138(bl); Gamma Liaison/Terry, 238(al); Gamma/ Vioujard, 138(t).
David Squire, 98-99, 102, 113(a), 115(bl), 122(a), 123(r), 124-125, 127(ar)(b), 139.
Survival Anglia/Price, 105(b); Survival Anglia/ Steelman, 106.
Swiss Tourist Board, 240(a).
Topkapi Museum, 51(b).
Dick Tracy, 276(bl)(br).
Victoria & Albert Museum, 10, 11, 48, 49.
Roger Viollet, 56(a).
Weldon Trannies, 182-183, 260, 277(br).
ZEFA, 59(b), 85(b), 87, 93.
Zurich Botanic Garden, 156(5)(6), 157, 291(c).
Other illustrations come from the publisher's collection. Every effort has been made to trace copyright holders. Any person or persons believing themselves to have legitimate copyright claims should contact the publishers. The passage from *Lark Rise* by Flora Thompson is quoted by permission of Oxford University Press.

INDEX